International Arbitration and Global Governance

International Arbitration and Global Governance

Contending Theories and Evidence

Edited by

Walter Mattli and Thomas Dietz

OXFORD
UNIVERSITY PRESS

OXFORD
UNIVERSITY PRESS

Great Clarendon Street, Oxford, OX2 6DP,
United Kingdom

Oxford University Press is a department of the University of Oxford.
It furthers the University's objective of excellence in research, scholarship,
and education by publishing worldwide. Oxford is a registered trade mark of
Oxford University Press in the UK and in certain other countries

Published in the United States of America by Oxford University Press
198 Madison Avenue, New York, NY 10016, United States of America

British Library Cataloguing in Publication Data
Data available

Library of Congress Control Number: 2014931015

ISBN 978–0–19–871672–3

Preface

Jan Paulsson

The authors of this volume have set out to fill a void they perceive in the literature on international commercial arbitration, due to the circumstance that it is preponderantly written by insiders, and is therefore mostly practice-oriented and imbued with a natural inclination to self-validation. As a result, the expanding function fulfilled by the arbitral process in the international community is not adequately examined, whether conceptually or indeed critically.

There is truth in this premise. As national societies, we must judge our judges, and for that it does not suffice to listen to their pronouncements, or to those of the advocates who make a living appearing before them. The international community has no public judiciary of its own to resolve trans-border commercial disputes, which therefore by default typically fall to be resolved by arbitrators presumed to be neutral and competent. As members of the international community, we should welcome—indeed insist upon—critical examination of a process which provides the legal foundation for the vast flow of economic exchanges that are essential to humanity.

Insiders who are proud to participate in a remarkably successful institution,[1] and secure in their good intentions, may recoil from criticism, and be

---

[1] The backbone of the international commercial arbitral process is the 1958 UN Convention on the Recognition and Enforcement of Foreign Arbitral Awards (conventionally referred to as "the New York Convention"). It was the UN Secretary General Kofi Annan who affirmed in 1998, on the occasion of its 40th anniversary, that "we proudly commemorate the Convention and reaffirm our commitment to its tenets . . ." [Opening address, June 10, 1998, published in *Enforcing Arbitration Awards under the New York Convention—Experience and Prospects* (New York: United Nations Publications, 1999)] and referred to the disadvantages suffered by states who did not participate in the system created by the Convention as follows: ". . . entities investing or doing business in those States lack the legal certainty afforded by the Convention, and businesses cannot be confident that commercial obligations can be enforced. This increases the level of risk, meaning that additional security may be required, that negotiations are likely to be more complex and protracted, and that transaction costs will rise. Such risks can adversely affect international trade" (*Enforcing Arbitration Awards*, 1999). Lord Mustill (as he was to become) declared famously that: "This Convention has been the most successful international instrument in the field of arbitration, and perhaps could lay claim to be the most effective instance of international legislation in the entire history of commercial law" (Michael Lord Mustill, "Arbitration: History and Background," *Journal of International Arbitration* 6, no. 2 (1989): p. 49).

quick to point out factual misunderstandings and lapses of scholarly rigor. And, true enough, a reasonably well-informed promoter of arbitration who reads this volume with the aim of finding fault is likely to find a number of easy targets.

Thus, here and there the myth of an arbitral "cartel" is perpetuated on no other basis than that it has been repeated before. Statements such as "the same actors continue to appear in the majority of large arbitration procedures" are made as mere assertion, bereft of any citation to authority, and seemingly without stopping to seek to account for the fact that the ICC International Court of Arbitration appoints some 1,300 arbitrators every year, that more than 800 of them are different individuals of some 70 different nationalities, and that for all its qualities the ICC's Secretariat simply does not have the means to maintain such a heterogeneous and far-flung cohort as a closed shop. (Indeed, a majority of the appointees are freely identified—"nominated"—by the parties.)

Suggestions are made, here and there, to the effect that arbitrators are creatures of contract, and therefore necessarily the laissez-faire servants of whatever bargain the parties have made, irrespective of its conflict with public policy—seemingly ignoring the fundamental insight, thoroughly explored and assimilated by the arbitral community long ago, that typical arbitration clauses referring to all disputes "arising under *or in connection with* their dispute" are broader than the contract, and therefore not only authorize, but command the arbitrator to deal with claims that it is invalid or illegal.

Another common flaw in the accounts of outsiders stems from their limited ability to separate the wheat from the chaff in the existing literature, and their tendency to repeat without question such statistics as the 90 percent rate of "voluntary" compliance with international awards, which serious insiders, however much they might like it to be true, have long since dismissed as bogus (in the sense of being unverifiable).

One contribution to this collection may even evoke near-faded memories of mid-20th century Marxist rhetoric, advancing the proposition that international commercial arbitration is part of a political project conceived and pursued by a "hegemonic mercatocracy" seeking to secure and advance capitalist class power by imposing legal disciplines on the "policy and legislative autonomy" of states. Insiders are likely to wonder how the arbitral process could be either conceived or operated as a cog in an international capitalist conspiracy, and how this type of speculation could be squared with any number of contradictory observations, such as the fact that no capitalist enterprise has managed to participate in the international commercial arbitral process with greater success over the past half-century than the state-owned oil corporation of Algeria, Sonatrach, whose mastery of the ICC process is notorious, whose former legal director is now a vice-president of the ICC Court, and whose state ideology remains, as it has since independence, socialism.

But such rebuttals miss the larger point. Of course insiders may easily use their red pencils to blot the copybooks of outsiders. It will inevitably be said, by reference to the book's subtitle, that it is long on theories and short on evidence. Yet it would be both ungrateful and self-defeating not to avail one's self of the benefit of probing questions, new ideas, challenges to habit and self-perpetuation. Errors are to be corrected politely, and with gratitude for having the occasion to do so. And the fundamental questions addressed in the pages that follow remain to be answered—all the more so, if they disturb self-validating convictions. In the same vein, the overarching theme of international arbitrators as more or less unwitting instruments of a form of global governance could fail to intrigue only the most obdurately incurious practitioner—and should cause all involved in the process to take stock of their broader function, and the inherent and unavoidable responsibilities it entails.

Arbitrants, arbitrators, and advocates who read the volume in this spirit should derive much benefit. At the outset, they will see that most of these scholarly inquiries are not unsympathetic to the process, and do not deny its value in facilitating commerce and reducing legal risk premiums. The best proof is that the careful reader will soon perceive that the misapprehensions to be found in one contribution or another are not shared by other authors. For example, more than one chapter evidences a perfectly adequate understanding of the fact that arbitrators may, should, and do apply relevant norms of public policy even if they nullify bargains. (Thus: "arbitrators are not exclusively creatures of discrete contracts. . . . [W]ith the "judicialization" of arbitration, tribunals have strengthened their capacity to govern in the name of a larger, transnational community.") Moreover, several authors note that a part of the process is the element of judicial control; awards will not be enforced if doing so would contravene public policy. Still, it is permissible to ask whether that it enough. After all, awards may be effective without being subjected to judicial scrutiny. Parties may prefer to have a reputation for compliance with arbitral decisions. Does that leave us with the fear that the cohorts of arbitrators who emerge in practice have cognitive biases that make them insufficiently sensitive to the public interest and too often immune from judicial scrutiny? It is an open question, not a rhetorical one; it is legitimate, and deserving of our fullest attention.

This volume suggests perspectives over the broader social implications of the process as it has evolved. International arbitration may once have been little more than a way for traders from different countries to resolve their disputes. Today, the vast stakes and the variety of conflicts often involved mean that we are observing the emergence of an institution of the world legal order—such as it is, with all its shortcomings. If its practitioners—particularly, but not solely those who have a decision-making function in it—continue to focus on nothing more than doing a workmanlike job for the particular arbitrants in individual cases, they run the risk of failing to perceive that they are to a greater or lesser extent—depending on the case and the circumstances—custodians of the legitimacy of an institution of great general interest. These essays, in other words, should engender an indispensable *prise de conscience*.

True enough, there is little new under the sun, and one should not exaggerate the novelty of the process being observed. The proposition that arbitral determinations may potentially conflict with the policies of public authorities has been examined in the past. But not all such policies are to be given automatic credence. Come to think of it, why is it that totalitarian regimes abhor arbitration? For decades, Franco's Spain and Salazar's Portugal maintained the Iberian peninsula as a veritable backwater for arbitration, even as Western Europe was moving steadily toward the recognition of arbitral autonomy. After the eclipse of those regimes, arbitral legislation quickly entered the international mainstream and institutions were revitalized, as though they were natural concomitants of democratization. This merits reflection. Those of us who belong to a liberal tradition will not forget that most prosperous countries have developed their successful economies within legal frameworks in which fundamental notions of public policy prominently include that of the freedom of economic actors to enter into binding agreements—including agreements to arbitrate.

Before getting too carried away with abstract speculation about the risks to governance goals of allowing too much leeway to arbitral authority, perhaps we should study actual legal systems such as that of Sweden, where for a very long time the default mechanism for resolving disputes has been that of an arbitral clause, and a favorable judicial disposition toward arbitration is well established in a rich body of case law. Has this led to lawlessness in the land, or to a frustration of public goals? It would seem not. Above all, one must compare the advantages and disadvantages of what would replace it; in a world where the rule of law in so many national systems is sorely lacking, it is only with international arbitration that law has a chance to prevail over politics, influence-peddling, and corruption. The reality is that this planet's population needs to be fed, housed, and given medical care, and that such necessities are unlikely to be assured without international flows of goods, services, innovation, and capital. Such transactions are impeded in direct proportion to the legal risk surcharges which suppliers must extract to survive in environments of high legal incertitude.

Not one of these comments puts in doubt the value of careful consideration of the essays in this volume. Rather, they suggest that we can predict that many of the propositions advanced by these authors will encounter varied fortune as they confront reality; some will resonate in practice, and influence future developments—others not. But make no mistake: attention must be given to the reservations articulated by these authors; ignoring them is not a way to defend the status quo. Indeed, it may be said that the international arbitral process deserves to be known in the plural, as *processes*, depending on the particular organizational frameworks and environments within which it proceeds. Not all of them are easily defended, and quite a few require correction. The status quo, let us say without fear of the paradox, must be dynamic, and must respond to the insights of those, like the authors of these essays, who ask the big questions.

Contents

List of Contributors

Walter Mattli is Professor of International Political Economy and Fellow of St. John's College, University of Oxford.

Thomas Dietz is Assistant Professor in Politics and Law, University of Muenster and Research Fellow at Wolfson College, Faculty of Law, University of Oxford.

Jan Paulsson is Michael Klein Distinguished Scholar Chair, University of Miami, and President of the International Council for Commercial Arbitration.

Alec Stone Sweet is Leitner Professor of Law, Politics, and International Studies at Yale Law School and the Department of Political Science at Yale University.

Florian Grisel is Research Fellow (Chargé de recherche), Centre National de la Recherche Scientifique (CNRS), Centre de Théorie et Analyse du Droit (Université Paris Ouest Nanterre La Défense).

Ralf Michaels is Arthur Larson Professor at Duke Law School.

Joshua Karton is Assistant Professor at Queen's University, Faculty of Law.

Moritz Renner is Lichtenberg Professor for Transnational Economic Law and Theory at the University of Bremen.

A. Claire Cutler is Professor of International Law and International Relations at the Department of Political Science, University of Victoria.

Thomas Hale is Research Fellow at the Blavatnik School of Government, University of Oxford.

Horatia Muir Watt is Director of the Centre for Global Business Law and Governance and Professor at Sciences Politique, Paris.

1

Mapping and Assessing the Rise of International Commercial Arbitration in the Globalization Era: An Introduction

Walter Mattli and Thomas Dietz

Two decades ago, *The Economist* called international commercial arbitration "the Big Idea set to dominate legal-reform agendas into the next century."[1] The scene then called to memory the flourishing era of arbitration practices and institutions associated with the international trade fairs of medieval Europe. The number of arbitration forums had grown from a dozen or so in the 1970s to more than one hundred by the 1990s, and the caseload of major arbitral institutions had more than doubled during the same period. *The Economist*'s prediction proved correct, and the number, diversity, and caseload of arbitration forums have continued to grow at an astounding rate.

Arbitration is a binding, non-judicial, and private means of settling disputes based on an explicit agreement by the parties involved in a transaction. Such an agreement is typically embodied in the terms of a contract between the parties. Unlike judges in public courts, who must follow fixed rules of procedure and apply the laws of the land, arbitrators can dispense with legal formalities. Also, the parties are free to choose whatever procedural rules and substantive laws they consider most suitable to their case.

Arbitration becomes international when the parties to a dispute reside or conduct their main business in different countries. The term "commercial" in international commercial arbitration (ICA) is broadly conceived and covers

---

[1] The Economist, July 18–24, 1992.

activities such as sale of goods, distribution agreements, commercial representation of agency, leasing, consulting, transportation, construction work, joint ventures, and other forms of industrial or business cooperation.

Two broad types of ICA can be distinguished: universal arbitration and specialized arbitration.[2] The former is offered by major arbitration centers such as the International Court of Arbitration of the International Chamber of Commerce (ICC), the London Court of International Arbitration (LCIA), the Arbitration Institute of the Stockholm Chamber of Commerce (SCC), the Singapore International Arbitration Centre (SIAC), and the International Center for Dispute Resolution (ICDR) of the American Arbitration Association (AAA). These centers accept cases from a wide range of companies and industries. Specialized arbitration, by contrast, is conducted in forums established in specific industries by the respective international trade associations, such as the Society of Maritime Arbitration, the Grain and Feed Trade Association, and various stock and commodity exchanges, and is open only to the members of these associations and exchanges.[3]

Figure 1.1 provides an aggregated overview of the caseload of our five examples of universal arbitration houses from 1992 to 2011. Figure 1.2 shows

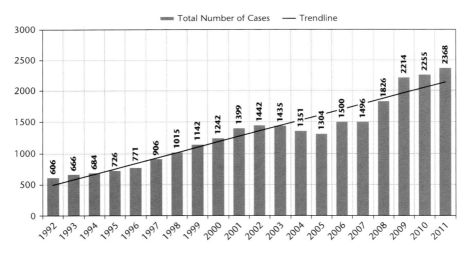

Figure 1.1. Caseload of five major arbitration houses 1992–2012 (AAA/ICDR, ICC, SIAC, LCIA, SCC).

---

[2] Christopher R. Drahozal, "Private Ordering and International Commercial Arbitration," *Penn State Law Review* 113, no. 4 (Spring 2009): pp. 1031–1050.
[3] See, for example, Bruce Harris, Michael Summerskill, and Sara Cockerill, "London Maritime Arbitration," *Arbitration International* 9, no. 3 (1993): pp. 275–302; Derek Kirby Johnson, "Commodity Trade Arbitration," in *Handbook of Arbitration Practice*, edited by Ronald Bernstein and Derek Wood, 2nd ed. (London: Sweet and Maxwell, 1993), pp. 257–285.

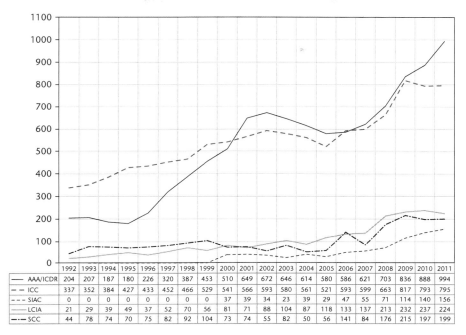

	1992	1993	1994	1995	1996	1997	1998	1999	2000	2001	2002	2003	2004	2005	2006	2007	2008	2009	2010	2011
—— AAA/ICDR	204	207	187	180	226	320	387	453	510	649	672	646	614	580	586	621	703	836	888	994
– – ICC	337	352	384	427	433	452	466	529	541	566	593	580	561	521	593	599	663	817	793	795
– – – SIAC	0	0	0	0	0	0	0	0	37	39	34	23	39	29	47	55	71	114	140	156
—— LCIA	21	29	39	49	37	52	70	56	81	71	88	104	87	118	133	137	213	232	237	224
—·— SCC	44	78	74	70	75	82	92	104	73	74	55	82	50	56	141	84	176	215	197	199

Figure 1.2. Caseload of each of the five major arbitration houses separately 1992–2012 (AAA/ICDR, ICC, SIAC, SCC).

their individual caseloads.[4] Figure 1.3 conveys a sense of the vibrant role played by specialized courts on the global arbitration scene. It presents the recent caseload of the London Maritime Arbitrators Association (LMAA),[5] a major center for maritime arbitration. All trend lines are upward-sloping.

A third type of international arbitration—investor-state arbitration (ISA)—has gained in prominence only in the last decade or so. The main provider of such arbitration is the International Center for the Settlement of Investment Disputes (ICSID). ICSID was created in 1966 by the so-called Washington Convention and is part of the World Bank organization. ICSID's authority is limited to investment disputes where one of the parties is the host state.[6] The growing popularity of ICSID arbitration (see Figure 1.4) is largely due to the explosion of bilateral investment treaties (BITs) in the 1990s (see Figure 1.5).[7]

[4] The data for Figures 1.1 and 1.2 come from the Hong Kong International Arbitration Centre (HKIAC), available at: <http://www.hkiac.org/index.php/en/hkiac/statistics>.
[5] The numbers are published by the London Maritime Arbitration Association (LMAA), available at: <http://www.lmaa.org.uk>.
[6] The ICSID Secretariat, which has a staff of 50, provides institutional support for the initiation and conduct of arbitration and conciliation proceedings.
[7] The numbers for Figures 1.4 and 1.5 are published by the International Centre for Settlement of Investment Disputes (ICSID), available at: <https://icsid.worldbank.org/ICSID/Index.jsp>.

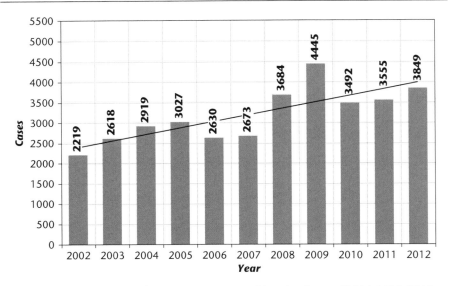

Figure 1.3. Caseload of the major maritime arbitration house LMAA 2002–2012.

The contributions in this book mainly focus on ICA, but several chapters also comment on investment arbitration, especially where the underlying challenges and difficulties are similar from a governance perspective.

Most literature on international arbitration is practice-oriented, technical, and promotional. Michaels explains: "Almost all scholars of international arbitration also practice as arbitrators and are thus interested in its success . . .

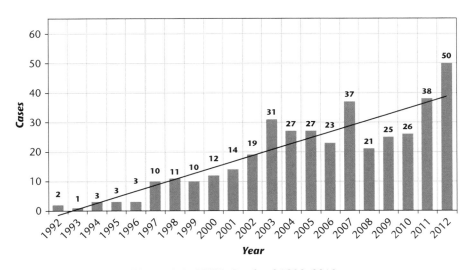

Figure 1.4. ICSID Caseload 1992–2012.

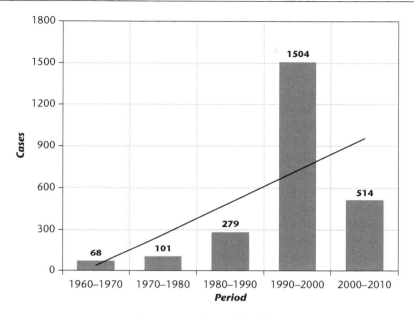

Figure 1.5. BITs 1960–2010.

Scholarship on international arbitration is frequently also expansion of practice and advertisement. Outside analyses by non-participants are still very rare."[8]

This book boldly steps away from this tradition of scholarship to reflect analytically upon ICA as a form of global governance. It thus contributes to a rapidly growing literature that describes the profound economic, legal, and political transformation in which key governance functions are increasingly exercised by a new constellation that includes actors other than national public authorities.

It has been widely noted that the transformation of modern statehood involves partial transfer of authority to international organizations, such as the United Nations, the World Trade Organisation, or the European Union. These organizations are based on international treaties among nation states. Their governance power and legitimacy derive to a large extent from the central role played by representatives of national governments in these inter- and supranational organizations. States are the architects and responsible masters of these institutions. By contrast, arbitration courts do not involve government representatives. The powers exerted by arbitrators are not directly linked to nation states. Unlike international governmental organizations, international commercial arbitration courts present a form of transnational private authority.

---

[8] Ralf Michaels, "Roles and Role Perceptions of International Arbitrators," in this book, ch. 3.

This book brings together leading scholars from law and the social sciences to assess and critically reflect upon the significance and implications of ICA as a new locus of global private authority. The views predictably diverge. Some see the evolution of these private courts positively, as a significant element of an emerging transnational private legal system that gradually evolves according to the needs of market actors without much state interference. Others fear that private courts allow transnational actors to circumvent state regulation and create an illegitimate judicial system that is driven by powerful transnational companies at the expense of collective public interests. Still others accept that these contrasting views serve as useful starting points for an analysis but are too simplistic to adequately understand the enormously complex governance structures developed by contemporary international arbitration courts to date.

In sum, this book offers a wide-ranging and up-to-date analytical overview of arguments in a vigorous interdisciplinary debate about arbitration courts and their exercise of private governance power in the transnational realm. This debate is generating fascinating new insights into such central topics as legitimacy, constitutional order, and justice beyond classical nation-state institutions.

Our introduction is organized into three sections. Section 1 presents four principal models or theoretical understandings of arbitration governance. Most contributions in this book fit within one of these analytical approaches. Section 2 offers a summary of the individual chapters, and Section 3 provides suggestions for further research.

1 Four Main Models of Arbitration Governance

Most scholarly contributions to the international arbitration literature implicitly or explicitly make assumptions and claims that can be captured by four distinct analytical models: the economic-rationalist model, the cultural-sociological model, the power model, and the constitutionalization model. These models serve much like Weberian ideal types; that is, no presumption is made that any of these types corresponds to all characteristics or aspects of any one particular arbitration case or process. Types or models are organizing devices of a complex reality, privileging certain key factors over others. The various models need not be mutually exclusive, but can overlap, interact, or even inform each other. The claim that power matters, for example, need not be inconsistent with a cultural account since power relationships may shape culture and culture may shape power relationships. Similarly, the constitutional model can build on or be molded by elements of power, culture, and economics. The exact nature of the relationship among the different models is largely context-specific and a matter for further research, as we suggest in the concluding section.

1.1 *The Economic-Rationalist Model*

The economic-rationalist model of ICA is based on insights from new institutional economics and the rational institutional design school in political science.[9] These intellectual traditions conceive of governance structures as organizational frameworks within which the integrity of a contractual relationship is decided and maintained. Governance structures emerge and adjust to minimize the costs and risks of transacting in markets. That is, transaction costs are economized by assigning transactions (which differ in their attributes) to governance structures (which differ in their adaptive capacities and associated costs) in a discriminating way. The higher the asset specificity of a transaction, for example, the greater the governance complexity needed to promote efficient exchange.

With globalization, the volume of transactions in international markets has grown exponentially, and so have the potential costs and problems associated with these transactions. In response, states and businesses have designed a wide range of novel transnational governance structures to minimize transaction costs and maximize the net benefits to firms and societies of operating in global markets.

International commercial arbitration is one such governance structure. The surge in its popularity as a method of dispute resolution can be attributed to features or attributes of arbitration that economic agents operating in global markets value, including flexibility, technical expertise, privacy, confidentiality, and speed. From the perspective of the economic-rationalist model, agents use, select, or design particular dispute resolution forums based on their evolving needs and priorities.[10]

An illustration of an arbitral governance structure that appears to fit the economic-rationalist model is the International Court of Arbitration of the International Chamber of Commerce.[11] It seems to have evolved to maximize the efficiency of dispute resolution in a challenging and rapidly changing international economic environment. For example, its rules and institutional apparatus effectively override obstacles that a non-cooperative disposition by

---

[9] Oliver E. Williamson, *Markets and Hierarchies* (New York: Free Press, 1975); Oliver E. Williamson, *The Economic Institutions of Capitalism* (New York: Free Press, 1985); Barbara Koremenos, Charles Lipson, and Duncan Snidal, "The Rational Design of International Institutions," *International Organization* 55, no. 4 (Autumn 2001): pp. 761–799.

[10] Joseph Jupille, Walter Mattli, and Duncan Snidal, *Institutional Choice and Global Commerce* (Cambridge: Cambridge University Press, 2013).

[11] Walter Mattli, "Private Justice in a Global Economy: From Litigation to Arbitration," *International Organization* 55, no. 4 (Autumn 2001): pp. 919–947.

one of the parties to an international commercial dispute may pose. If one of the parties refuses to participate in the arbitral proceedings (despite a contractual obligation to do so), the International Court of Arbitration is entitled to appoint the arbitrator(s) and constitute a tribunal. The notice and summons procedure is performed by the ICC secretariat and is supervised by the court, assuring the arbitrators that the defaulting party had notice of the arbitration.[12] If one party fails to sign the Terms of Reference, the court may approve them and the proceedings continue. After the Terms of Reference are approved, the opportunity for a party to engage in dilatory tactics by presenting additional claims and counterclaims is minimized because such claims can only be heard on the agreement of all parties.

The court closely monitors the arbitral proceedings, ensuring that time limits and due process principles are respected.[13] It replaces arbitrators who do not fulfil their functions or who are behind in their work. At the end of the process, it scrutinizes the award in relation to jurisdiction and applicable law. This monitoring and checking increases the quality of the arbitral award and, in turn, reduces the chance that the losing party will challenge the award in a national court. As noted by an experienced international arbitrator, "most final awards rendered under ICC auspices are carried out voluntarily by the parties, because [of their high] quality . . . A company that fails to carry out an [ICC award] is almost certain to lose subsequently[14] and in addition runs the risk of jeopardizing its reputation in international circles."[15] Indeed, only about 5 percent of awards have been challenged, and of these only one in ten awards rendered under the aegis of the ICC have been set aside by a national court.[16]

This remarkable organizational sophistication and efficiency is not unique to the International Court of Arbitration. According to the economic-rationalist approach, different types of international arbitration respond in different ways to the specific requirements of different sets of economic actors. Thus, the rules and institutional approaches of specialized arbitration as conducted in maritime affairs or offered by various stock and commodity exchanges are different from those designed for users of universal commercial arbitration or investor-state arbitration. In each case, optimal institutional design and organizational efficiency are assumed to emerge

---

[12] Gerald Aksen, "Ad Hoc Versus Institutional Arbitration," *ICC International Court of Arbitration Bulletin* 2, no. 1 (1991): p. 12.

[13] Principles of due process include transparency of the arbitral process; the right of the parties to be called and heard; and equal treatment of the parties in the exchange of pleadings, in evidentiary matters, in resort to expertise proceedings, and in the holding of hearings.

[14] That is, if and when the winning party applies to a national court for recognition and enforcement of the award.

[15] Aksen, "Ad Hoc," p. 22.

[16] See Laurence Craig, William Park, and Jan Paulsson, *International Chamber of Commerce Arbitration*, 2nd ed. (New York: Oceana Publications, 1990), pp. 32–33.

given the backdrop of intense competitive pressure that each forum faces. Forums that do not innovate and adjust in order to address their clients' needs and priorities will lose arbitration business and become obsolete.

Direct state intervention in ICA governance is neither necessary nor desirable as market pressure keeps arbitration centers on their "organizational toes." States may help indirectly by ensuring the functioning of ICA is not hampered by state corruption and related failings or jurisdictional jealousies. In this backstage role, states have made important contributions: for example, by enacting statues to reform their arbitration laws to satisfy the business users of international arbitration, or by signing the New York Convention on the Recognition and Enforcement of Arbitral Awards. The result is a strengthening and enhanced efficiency of ICA governance.

The economic-rationalist model further implies that organizational efficiency of arbitration forums is good not only for the contracting parties (by generating private gains), it also is good for the wider public. By enabling the smooth operation of global markets, ICA contributes to the optimal allocation of the world's resources, which, in turn, generates economic growth and prosperity for societies across the globe. The econometric analysis by Thomas Hale (Chapter 8) is a striking illustration of the positive impact of effective ICA governance on international trade.[17] In short, the model claims that ICA is a source of significant positive externalities (see Figure 1.6).

		Externalities on third parties	
		Positive	*Negative*
Private Gains for contractual partners	*Positive Sum*	Economic-Rationalist Model Cultural-Sociological Model	Power-based Model [Private Parties (or Private Party and Corrupt State) vs Society]
	Zero Sum/ Inequitable	Power-based Model [Powerful Private Party vs Weak Private Party]	Power-based Model [Powerful Private Party vs Weak State and Society]

Figure 1.6. Overview of the models.

[17] Thomas Hale, "What is the Effect of Commercial Arbitration on Trade?," in this book, ch. 8.

1.2 *The Cultural-Sociological Model*

The cultural-sociological model agrees with the economic-rationalist app-roach that economic incentives and rational strategies play a significant role in explaining governance arrangements, and that market competition among arbitral institutions stimulates innovation, generating rules and practices per-ceived to work effectively. However, the main charge by cultural-sociological theorists against the economic-rationalist model is that it is severely incom-plete and thus reductionist. Key factors in the analytical governance narrative are missing, conveying a false sense of "automaticity" in accounting for organizational rules and structure. The model is too thin to be accurate, use-ful, or compelling.

Cultural-sociological theorists seek to offer "a more fine-grained tool for analyzing and predicting outcomes in ICA."[18] They argue that the key to understanding ICA's emergence as a form of global governance is a legal cul-ture specific to the international arbitration community. They define govern-ance broadly as the mechanisms through which arbitral rules, procedures, and organizational structures and case law governing a community or domain of activity are adapted to the experiences and needs of those who live under them.[19] Two conditions must be met for ICA to constitute global private gov-ernance. First, legal rules must be formulated at the global level autonomous-ly from states, and apply regardless of the nationality and public or private status of the parties; and, second, ICA must have functional consistency in arbitral decision-making—no small task in the highly decentralized and com-petitive ICA world. The cultural-sociological approach, as eloquently articu-lated by Joshua Karton, posits that *legal culture* specific to the international arbitration community has helped to satisfy both conditions. Culture is defined as a complex of norms that condition behavior both by shaping the thinking of members of a community and by creating a community consen-sus or peer pressure that discourages deviation from these norms. Culture emerges from the repeated interactions among actors of a particular commu-nity. Culture-based behavior is reflexive; it operates prior to deliberative decision-making.

Several factors have facilitated the emergence of a strong legal culture among international arbitration practitioners: they were educated in elite institutions, share cosmopolitan backgrounds and multi-cultural legal training, speak multiple languages, travel in both business and academic circles, frequently meet in conferences, and work repeatedly with each

[18] Joshua Karton, "International Arbitration Culture and Global Governance," in this book, ch. 4.

[19] Alec Stone Sweet and Florian Grisel, "The Evolution of International Arbitration: Delegation, Judicialization, Governance," in this book, ch. 2.

other and on disputes within a relatively narrow range of commercial sub-jects.[20] Their community, unsurprisingly, is small. It has been described as an exclusive club, an epistemic community, a caste, cartel, gang, and even a mafia.[21]

What exactly are the normative effects of their common culture on arbitra-tion practice and governance? Three can be distinguished: first, members of the ICA community share a dedication to internationalism, a perspective detached from the national legal system, a preference for transnational sourc-es of law over national ones. "The internationalism norm drives the ICA com-munity to pursue global governance for its own sake; . . . [and] global solutions [are seen as] superior simply by virtue of the fact that they are global."[22] Sec-ond, they share normative and principled beliefs in the superiority of private over state-based adjudication and agree on the importance of autonomy from the state.[23] And, third, given their considerable commercial expertise, mem-bers of the ICA community share a disposition that is favorable toward the interests and preferences of business groups. The commercial mentality of arbitrators renders them acutely aware of the procedural and substantive legal needs of businesses. Unsurprisingly, ICA governance emphasizes flexi-ble procedures, deference to party autonomy, and rules founded in standards of commercial reasonableness.[24]

Finally, though methodologically distinct from economic-rationalism, the cultural-sociological approach agrees on two key substantive conclusions: ICA is a "positive-sum" arrangement that generates significant benefits for all implicated parties. In addition, it is a source of positive externalities for the wider society (see Figure 1.6). Arbitrators are "the guardians of a system that is imperative for the flourishing of international trade and investment."[25] Or, in the words of Michaels: "The arbitrator's private role . . . becomes a public role as well; private interests dissolve into public interests or are at least con-gruent with them."[26]

By serving the interests of the business world, ICA governance supports the providers of investment and the engines of economic growth. It is best left to its own devices; though discreet assistance—not interference—by the state is welcome and sometimes necessary.

---

[20] Karton, "International Arbitration"; Michaels, "Roles"; Yves Dezalay and Bryant G. Garth, *Dealing in Virtue: International Commercial Arbitration and the Construction of a Transnational Legal Order* (Chicago: University of Chicago Press, 1996).

[21] Michaels, "Roles."

[22] Karton, "International Arbitration."

[23] Michaels, "Roles."

[24] Karton, "International Arbitration."

[25] Susan D. Franck, "The Role of International Arbitrators," *ILSA Journal of International & Com-parative Law* 12, (2005–2006): pp. 499–523, p. 521.

[26] Michaels, "Roles."

1.3 *Power-based Models of Arbitration*

In the preceding two models, power is conspicuously absent from the analysis. "De-localization"—the detachment of international arbitration from the reach of national laws and courts—is seen as desirable, a necessary step toward greater efficiency of ICA for the benefit of all. Critical political economy theorists reject such conclusions as dangerously naïve. De-localization, they hold, is a duplicitous strategy by powerful business groups to drive a wedge ever more deeply between the political and economic domains, thereby severely limiting the possibility of democratic scrutiny of "who gets what" in ICA:

> Through claims to legitimacy as neutral experts, international commercial arbitration lawyers are able to carve out a sphere of autonomy, sustaining distinctions between economics and politics and between public and private spheres. Indeed, the belief that the settlement of international economic disputes requires a "depoliticized" environment provided by so-called impartial trade and investment experts is one of the foundational myths of the international commercial arbitration regime.[27]

Critical theorists see de-localization as part of a much wider project by powerful corporate elites—the mercatocracy—to push market fundamentalism, including privatization, liberalization, deregulation, and a much-diminished welfare role of the state. ICA governance is a central element in this project; it serves to shield global investment and trade relations from state control and oversight and subjugate public interests to those of a transnational business class. "Private transnational governance through new constitutional institutions and laws empowers the mercatocracy to recast political issues as matters of legal technique, but the terrain of this common sense is uneven."[28]

ICA governance is a scheme designed by the powerful few for their own private commercial ends. It is a mechanism of rent-extraction from the weak and poorly-organized parties in business and from society at large. In other words, far from being the "positive-sum" arrangement with positive externalities portrayed by economic-rationalist and cultural-sociological theorists, ICA governance is better understood as a "zero-sum" arrangement (for contracting parties) that, in addition, can generate extensive negative social, economic, and political externalities (see Figure 1.6).[29] The image of holistic efficiency is a mirage, a ploy by powerful business groups to silence the critics and seduce the gullible.

Critical theorists point primarily to abuses in investor-state arbitration in the context of BITs as evidence in support of their thesis. These treaties may

---

[27] A. Claire Cutler, "International Commercial Arbitration, Transnational Governance, and the New Constitutionalism," in this book, ch. 6.
[28] Cutler, "International Commercial Arbitration."
[29] "Zero-sum" implies that the gains of one party are the losses of another.

involve powerful investors (multinational corporations or "vulture" funds) and weak or corrupt governments. Some such treaties have led to harmful industrial activities and short-sighted policies dictated by investor interests. Examples of negative externalities include land-grabbing affecting access to food for the poor, pollution and other durable ecological harm, destruction of local cultural or religious heritage, discrimination in respect of local workforce, exploitation, and violence.

Horatia Muir Watt puts the problem with privatized arbitration in the context of BIT as follows: "The contractual nature of arbitration makes it ill-equipped to consider the effects of any negative externalities generated by investment-linked activities for third parties. Indeed, treaties generally lack any specific procedures whereby communities or individuals whose interests are unaligned with those of the host state may be heard."[30] This is so not by accident but by imposed design, critical theorists argue. Privatized arbitration governance maximizes the profits of the powerful few at the expense of the weak.

Are the inequities generated by power asymmetries unique to investor-state arbitration? In his critical assessment of ICA, Thomas Dietz answers the question negatively. He shows that power asymmetries are pervasive in ICA and a root-cause of the relatively ineffective or marginal role played by universal arbitral governance, as reflected in the modest growth of arbitration cases relative to the explosive growth of global trade over the last two decades: "The relatively low case load points to a limited governance function of international commercial arbitration."[31]

Dietz's argument can be put as follows: in a commercial relationship, one party is likely to be more powerful than the other. It will use its power to create an uneven legal playing field disfavoring the other party (see Figure 1.6). A particularly effective strategy is to bypass neutral transnational commercial law and choose instead a national law it knows best and the other party may know least: "Parties do not choose the law that is most efficient for both parties but the law that suits their own interests."[32] For the same reason, the powerful party may even want to drag a case to a familiar domestic court rather than have it adjudicated in a neutral international arbitration court. A domestic court is likely to confer a home advantage to the powerful party and increase the legal costs and uncertainty for the weak foreign party. As a result, and in striking contrast to the prediction of the economic-rationalist model, the vast majority of international commercial contracts, even when they

---

[30] Horatia Muir Watt, "The Contested Legitimacy of Investment Arbitration and the Human Rights Ordeal: The Missing Link," in this book, ch. 9.
[31] Thomas Dietz, "Does International Commercial Arbitration Provide Efficient Contract Enforcement Institutions for International Trade?," in this book, ch. 7.
[32] Dietz, "International Commercial Arbitration."

contain arbitration clauses, are still governed by national laws. The chosen tribunal may be international; the preferred choice of law, however, tends to be national.

The end-result, according to Dietz, is not the de-localized, autonomous, private, and efficient ICA governance portrayed by the first two models, but instead a hybrid (public–private) system that still largely depends on territorially fragmented (and sometimes dysfunctional) state law, is less than efficient, and favors the powerful at the expense of the weak.

1.4 *The Constitutionalization Model of Arbitration*

All three preceding analytical approaches are largely static. Their focus is on explaining the rules, practices, structures, and outcomes of international arbitration. Change of arbitration governance over time is beyond their principal analytical remit. Some of the studies point to changes without trying to explain them. Cutler, for example, sees signs of change in governance—greater willingness to accept submissions from non-disputing parties, permission of hearings to be opened, publication of excerpts from awards—but she is unsure whether these concessions are significant or how to account for them.

Two studies in this book are concerned primarily with mapping and explaining changes in international arbitration governance or what they call the process of constitutionalization. Moritz Renner notes that increasingly arbitral tribunals are not simply executors of the will of the contracting parties, but apply public policy norms, thereby supplementing the supposedly private nature of arbitration with broader policy objectives. Recent arbitral practice "integrates different conceptions of public policy into an overarching hierarchy of norms mimicking domestic constitutional orders."[33] Mandatory public policy norms are long established in domestic systems, where courts may enforce rules limiting freedom of contract to protect public goods or interests (e.g., market stability or fair competition) or the weaker party in a contractual arrangement (e.g., consumers or employees). An international arbitrator may now refer, for example, to domestic mandatory rules against corruption as an expression of domestic public policy, as well as to more recent rules in international anti-corruption conventions as an expression of transnational public policy.

Renner considers the rise of transnational public policy to be "the starting point of a constitutionalization of international commercial arbitration."[34] Two features characterize constitutionalization: First, a hierarchy of norms:

---

[33] Moritz Renner, "Private Justice, Public Policy: The Constitutionalization of International Commercial Arbitration," in this book, ch. 5.

[34] Renner, "Private Justice."

"Both [domestic and international] layers of public policy are reflected in a legal hierarchy which by now forms the constitutional core of the regime of transnational commercial arbitration."[35] The second feature is the structural coupling of law and politics: "By referring to policy considerations and political discourse, be it on the domestic . . . [or] international level, international arbitral tribunals "externalize" the problem of norm justification to the realm of politics."[36] It is worth noting that this characterization stands in sharp contrast to the view of critical political economy theorists, who see separation from politics rather than coupling with it as the dominant trend, and are likely to dismiss the concept of transnational public policy as largely normative or illusory in a world of power politics.

What drives constitutionalization? Renner argues that an important factor is the increasing willingness of tribunals to publish arbitral awards. Such publication enables the development of a genuinely legal form of reasoning based on precedent, generating normative expectations as well as greater doctrinal consistency, and fostering the growth of transnational law.

Alec Stone Sweet and Florian Grisel offer a more self-consciously theoretical account of constitutionalization that shares several of the insights in Renner's account. Stone and Grisel distinguish three stages: contractual, judicial, and constitutional. The more third-party dispute resolution is activated within a community of contractants, the more judicial law-making will be the driver of institutionalization. Indicators of judicialization are the development of precedent, the demand for *ex post* supervision of arbitral awards, and the use of the jurisprudence of other international judges.

> As we move from the first to the second [stage], we encounter nascent hierarchies, the development of case law, and the routine imposition of interests beyond those of the contracting parties. The constitutional [stage] . . . embed[s] . . . the arbitral legal order within an overarching legal framework that includes general principles of law, international economic law, and human rights, including property rights and guarantees of due process.[37]

At the constitutional stage, the arbitrator has become a powerful "agent" in his own right, engaged in a dialogue with other actors operating "in the network of autonomous legal orders that comprise the international economic constitution."[38]

Critical theorists may react skeptically to the constitutionalization model, insisting that power asymmetries in conjunction with narrow self-interest of the parties to an international dispute could act as overriding structural and

---

[35] Renner, "Private Justice."
[36] Renner, "Private Justice."
[37] Stone Sweet and Grisel, "The Evolution of International Arbitration."
[38] Stone Sweet and Grisel, "The Evolution of International Arbitration."

behavioral impediments to the erection of a constitutionalized arbitral architecture. Powerful actors displeased with constitutionalized structures may seek to undermine these structures by avoidance, and by using or creating alternative dispute resolution forums.[39] Renner accepts this possibility: "As arbitral dispute resolution is more and more replicating the mechanisms of domestic legal systems, it may lose its appeal as an 'alternative' forum of dispute resolution and thus jeopardize its very existence."[40] Similarly, the theory by Stone Sweet and Grisel is far from orthogonal to power considerations. It stipulates that judicialization is always contingent and can be blocked at each stage of the process. It thus is conceivable that powerful economic or political forces representing or benefitting from the old status quo may weaken, constrain, or isolate any of the three driving factors of judicialization—contracting, third-party dispute resolution, and normative institutional structure. "Judicialization proceeds only to the extent that these three factors develop in interdependent ways."[41] The precise and full modeling of the role of power in the constitutionalization model is an area for important further research.

2 A Summary of the Chapters

We proceed with more detailed and self-contained summaries of the individual project contributions.

Alec Stone Sweet and Florian Grisel argue in Chapter 2 that the arbitral world has reached a crucial point in its historical development, poised between two conflicting conceptions of its nature, purpose, and legitimacy. The standard account of arbitration emphasizes the virtues of freedom of contract, notably the contracting parties' autonomy to choose their own law and mechanisms of dispute resolution. As transnational commerce and investment has exploded, however, so too have the demands for coherent transnational governance, including more consistent awards, transparency, and even appellate supervision. Their study assesses these developments in two complementary ways. First, they present a theory of the judicialization of arbitration. With judicialization, arbitral tribunals are inevitably implicated in governance, conceived as the process through which institutions are adapted to the needs of those who live under them. Second, they consider the structure of arbitral governance in light of delegation theory, notably, the Principal-Agent (P-A) construct. To the extent that judicialization proceeds, arbitrators will act as agents of the larger transnational business and investment community, not merely of two disputing parties. As noted above,

---

[39] See Jupille, Mattli, and Snidal, *Institutional Choice.*
[40] Renner, "Private Justice."
[41] Stone Sweet and Grisel, "The Evolution of International Arbitration."

judicialization is a contingent and contested process, the outcomes of which are not preordained; indeed, it has produced opposed models of arbitral governance that are today competing for dominance. These models are illustrated and assessed in light of practices in both international commercial and investor-state arbitration.

In Chapter 3 Ralf Michaels analyzes the roles that arbitrators play and the roles they assign to themselves. This is a fascinating topic because arbitrators are, in many ways, in a curiously ambiguous position. They are judges in one way, privately contracted service providers in another. They make law, while at the same time only enforcing contracts. They transcend national legal systems, but remain embedded in the state and its laws. These tensions are reflected in their perceptions of their own role, albeit often in concealed form. Michaels examines these roles and role perceptions in three regards. The first is the position of the arbitrator between national origin and cosmopolitan community, with a strong tendency toward the latter. The second is the position of the arbitrator between legal officer, entrepreneur, and academic. The third is the position of the arbitrator between the public role of a judge and the private role of a service provider. The result is a deep ambiguity that characterizes not only the role of arbitrators in our legal system, but also the changing role of law under conditions of globalization. Methodologically, Michaels focuses not on self-descriptions and interviews, but on arbitrators' positions to doctrinal questions because these are, arguably, the most credible statements.

Joshua Karton argues, as we briefly noted above, that for international commercial arbitration to constitute a form of governance, as opposed to merely disconnected resolutions of individual disputes, there must be sufficient consistency in arbitral decision-making; a consistent adjudicative approach is a hallmark of the rule of law. In the radically decentralized international commercial arbitration system, there seems to be little to promote such consistency. In Chapter 4, Karton explains exactly how a legal culture specific to the international arbitration community provides the decisional stability necessary for arbitration to come into its own as a form of governance.

The concept of a culture shared by the legal professionals of a given jurisdiction is uncontroversial. Such a concept is more problematic in the context of international arbitration, where practitioners do not share a common nationality, language, or training, or even access to a common corpus of governing laws or precedents. However, international arbitration practitioners actually have more in common than the body of legal practitioners within any one state. They tend to share similar educational and professional backgrounds, read the same journals, attend the same conferences, and work repeatedly with each other (often exchanging roles) on disputes within a relatively narrow band of commercial subjects. When actors are placed outside existing systems of governance and interact repeatedly with each other, it is not surprising that a culture could emerge spontaneously from those interactions. Specifically, international arbitrators tend to share a conception of themselves as service providers acting within a competitive market. They identify with the interests and perspective of commercial parties and, correspondingly, give precedence to governance features that favor the needs of market actors. All these aspects of international arbitration culture shape the kind of justice provided by international arbitration and, in turn, the form of governance it creates.

In Chapter 5 Moritz Renner discusses how opting out of the domestic legal system by way of private agreements is often regarded as problematic with a view to public policy issues: While domestic courts are bound to domestic public policies and constitutions, the status of public policy in international arbitration is highly disputed. Renner argues that international commercial arbitration increasingly addresses this problem in a move of self-constitutionalization. He traces how arbitral practice has gradually established a hierarchy of norms that integrates both transnational and domestic public policy concepts. This hierarchy of norms forms the core of an emerging constitutional order beyond the nation state.

In Chapter 6 A. Claire Cutler presents international commercial arbitration in a strikingly different light, namely as an integral dimension of what she calls the new constitutionalism of disciplinary neoliberalism. Drawing upon neo-Gramscian international political economy, she conceptualizes neoliberalism as a political project that secures and advances capitalist class power through the imposition of legal disciplines on the policy and legislative autonomy of states. Legal restrictions on states' abilities to regulate international trade and foreign direct investment contribute to and facilitate the expansion of the structural power of capital. Her study reviews the contours of the new constitutionalism, examining its material, ideological, and institutional foundations. As briefly mentioned in the first section of this introduction, she argues that these foundations work to reproduce dominant conceptions about the separation of economics and politics that assist in insulating neoliberal disciplines from democratic political forces. The international commercial arbitration regime is presented as an integral component of these foundations. Her analysis closes with a consideration of the prospects for democratizing this important regime.

Arbitration is considered legally superior to litigation in state courts in terms of confidentiality, flexibility, neutrality, and costs. Thomas Dietz argues in Chapter 7 that this widely shared understanding is not necessarily wrong, but is too simplistic. His study first shows that companies engaged in cross-border exchange only very rarely rely on private arbitral institutions to safeguard the performance of cross-border contracts. This is because the costs of doing so are too high and the enforcement structures are deficient. More specifically, the institutional performance of international commercial arbitration is often severely limited due to arbitral tribunals' close links to, or dependence on, fragmented and frequently dysfunctional national legal systems. The study concludes by contrasting universal arbitration with specialized arbitration. The latter type rarely relies on state legal structures. According to Dietz, this explains why it is much more widely used and generally operates more efficiently than universal arbitration.

In Chapter 8, Thomas Hale presents a systematic empirical assessment of a wider implication of effective ICA governance. More specifically, his study offers the first large-scale econometric analysis of the effect of the 1958 New York Convention on the Enforcement of Foreign Arbitral Awards on countries' foreign trade. Hale finds that ratifying the New York Convention increases a country's trade by about half as much as joining the World Trade Organization. The ratification effect is particularly striking for countries with traditionally low-quality judicial institutions. Various alternative explanations and robustness checks are considered.

Structural inequalities within the international investment regime, along with negative distributional consequences, may be perpetuated through arbitration, which is designed to implement the applicable law on a contractual basis. The conundrum addressed in Chapter 9 by Horatia Muir Watt is how to introduce social and economic rights within the investment arbitration forum whose very design has hitherto served to exclude them. Muir Watt suggests that the key by which this forum may be opened up to a productive challenge of the applicable legal framework lies outside it, in the home state's accountability before its own domestic courts for human rights violations by its corporate investors abroad, coupled with horizontal effect. In short, the home state's enforceable commitment to ensure that the corporations which benefit from the bilateral investment treaty respect third-generation human rights in the co-contracting host state may create the external pressure required for legal contestation to enter the arbitral forum itself.

3 Further Research

Jan Paulsson notes in the preface to this book that "the international arbitral process deserves to be known in the plural, as *processes*, depending on the particular organizational frameworks and environments within which it proceeds." He also suggests that "many of the propositions advanced by the authors will encounter varied fortunes as they confront reality." These observations point to two areas of further research—one theoretical, the other empirical.

First, much of the analytical debate on international arbitration governance is still rather stylized and paradigmatic. There is virtue in simple models, including analytical clarity and tractability. And sometimes, these models are spot on—they powerfully capture the nature of a class of arbitration processes or outcomes. However, as Paulsson notes, arbitration should "be known in the plural." Different processes may require different analytical frames, and some processes or patterns are sufficiently complex to necessitate more elaborate analytical frameworks. Context-specific characteristics are likely to determine or guide the specification of the appropriate theoretical approach. Thus, the potential scope for cross-fertilization of our four simple models is considerable.

Consider, for example, the constitutionalization model. It builds on delegation and a de-contextualized view of the parties who agree to arbitrate—implicitly assuming equality. But parties are not always equal, a point forcefully made in the studies by Cutler, Dietz, and Muir Watt. And arbitrators know that powerful companies can easily reject a system of international commercial arbitration that repeatedly fails them. Arbitrators may enjoy "delegated authority," but they cannot afford to lose the allegiance of powerful global firms. Constitutionalization therefore is contingent, as noted by Stone Sweet and Grisel—strong in some contexts and weak in others. Explaining such variation requires further theoretical specification; this is work that remains to be done.

Perhaps more daunting still is the challenge of systematically testing conjectures derived from contending theories. Much international arbitration practice takes place behind the veil of confidentiality and secrecy. Unsurprisingly, authors have few options but to refer to a small number of cases in the public domain in support of their hypotheses. In the absence of a representative sample, however, it is difficult to conduct proper tests and reach firm conclusions. Consider, for example, the evidence on constitutionalization. Renner shows in his contribution that in some cases arbitrators justify their awards by referring to public policy norms not explicitly endorsed by the disputing parties. Similarly, Stone Sweet and Grisel, as well as Cutler, point to cases where arbitrators have accepted amicus curiae briefs from third parties. Are these cases exceptions, outlier cases, or do they represent a significant new trend? In the absence of comprehensive data, it is difficult to tell. Similarly, it has been suggested that variation in levels of constitutionalization may be explained, ceteris paribus, by actor-specific characteristics: arbitrators with a background in public international law may be more inclined to include public policy considerations in their decision-making than arbitrators with a private-law background. Again, without a representative sample of all relevant cases, this proposition is hard to assess.

In sum, the debate on international arbitration is raising fascinating questions of direct relevance to wider discussions on global governance. Is arbitration giving rise to private legal authority? Who are the winners and losers in global arbitration? Under what conditions is arbitration likely to lead to or contribute to the constitutionalization of global governance? The authors in this book offer stimulating thoughts on these questions. At the same time, they point to areas for further research. One urgent task is to develop more fully specified theoretical models capable of capturing striking variations across classes of arbitration processes or outcomes. Another critical task is to engage in more systematic testing of contending claims. This, in turn, will require extensive empirical work and robust data-collection—a particularly challenging but indispensable undertaking.

2

The Evolution of International Arbitration: Delegation, Judicialization, Governance

Alec Stone Sweet and Florian Grisel

The standard account of the development of international arbitration emphasizes the virtues of freedom of contract, notably, the contracting parties' autonomy to choose their own law and mode of dispute resolution. With the explosion of transnational commerce and investment that has taken place since the 1980s, the effort to make arbitration a viable alternative to national courts accelerated.[1] The result has been the steady construction of a private system of dispute resolution by a network of arbitral houses that compete with each other for business and influence.[2] The powerbrokers of the system are private actors. Large, multinational law firms have invested heavily in arbitration practice, and their lawyers argue before tribunals dominated by a

---

[1] Arbitration has a significant impact on global trade (see, *contra*, the argument made by Thomas Dietz in this volume). Although the number of cases going to international arbitration may seem negligible when compared to the number of cases filed with domestic courts, on average international arbitration largely outgrows domestic cases in terms of financial stakes. For instance, the aggregate value of all disputes pending before the ICC in 2012 amounted to approximately USD 110 billion (or an average amount of USD 43.5 million per case). "ICC Statistical Report 2012," *ICC International Court of Arbitration Bulletin*, Vol. 24, No. 1 (2013), p.13.

[2] Klaus Peter Berger, *The Creeping Codification of the Lex Mercatoria* (The Hague: Kluwer, 1999); Walter Mattli, "Private Justice in a Global Economy: From Litigation to Arbitration," *International Organization*, Vol. 55 (2001), p.919; Alec Stone Sweet, "The New *Lex Mercatoria* and Transnational Governance," *Journal of European Public Policy*, Vol. 13 (2006), pp.627–646.

relatively insular network of lawyers and law professors.[3] This elite also manages the major arbitration houses, in conjunction with representatives of an increasingly globalized business community.

This chapter focuses on the emergence of transnational arbitral governance. We conceive of governance in a generic sense: the mechanisms through which the institutions—for present purposes, arbitral rules, procedures, case law—that govern any community or domain of activity are adapted to the experiences and needs of those who live under them. Our approach does not reject the basic elements of the standard account. Arbitration's social legitimacy is firmly rooted in its capacity to resolve dyadic disputes effectively, on the basis of the consent of the contracting parties. But arbitrators are not exclusively creatures of discrete contracts. Instead, with the "judicialization" of arbitration, tribunals have strengthened their capacity to govern in the name of a larger, transnational community.

We proceed as follows. Combining judicialization theory[4] with the basics of "Principle-Agent" [PA] analysis,[5] we develop three distinct models of arbitral governance: (A) the contractual, (B) the judicial, and (C) the constitutional. As we move from model A to B, or from model B to C, we observe the judicialization of arbitration and the enhanced capacity of tribunals to act as agents of an increasingly networked community of stakeholders. Because arbitration operates in a relatively non-hierarchical environment, systemic construction of this kind cannot be presumed. Instead the legal system has developed through coordination (persuasion) among arbitrators, not through the command and control of sovereigns. In the conclusion, we briefly discuss the main empirical indicators of judicialization, as they pertain to research on both international commercial arbitration (ICA) and investor-state arbitration (ISA).

Three caveats deserve mention in advance. First, our primary objectives are conceptual and explanatory: to provide an account of how a system of transnational governance has emerged through use, rather than design. The account can be read through normative lenses—readers may support or oppose judicialization, for example—but we take no stand here on the various normative issues raised. Second, we do not claim that our approach is the only, or best, way to understand the evolution of international arbitration. Our approach, however, does focus attention on crucial issues that now confront the arbitral world. Third, there appears to be an emerging consensus on the view that ICA and ISA have developed as separate legal systems, to the

[3] Yves Dezalay and Bryant G. Garth, *Dealing in Virtue: International Commercial Arbitration and the Construction of a Transnational Legal Order* (Chicago: University of Chicago Press, 1996).
[4] Alec Stone Sweet, "Judicialization and the Construction of Governance," *Comparative Political Studies*, Vol. 31 (1999), pp.147–184.
[5] Mark Thatcher and Alec Stone Sweet, "Theory and Practice of Delegation to Non-Majoritarian Institutions," *West European Politics*, Vol. 25 (2002), pp.1–22.

extent that they are considered "systems" at all. While we see differences between ICA and ISA as a matter of degree, not kind, we do not ignore these differences but, rather, exploit them for comparative purposes. Judicialization has clearly gone faster and further in ISA, in comparison to ICA, because the mechanisms operate relatively more robustly in ISA, not because the underlying mechanisms are not shared by the two regimes.

1 Theoretical Orientations

This chapter develops a theoretical approach to explaining and charting the development of international arbitration empirically, focusing on the impact of arbitral awards on the construction of arbitral institutions. By institutions, we mean the legal rules, doctrine, procedures, customs, standards, and so on, that enable and constrain the exercise of arbitral authority.[6] Our broader aim, which goes beyond this chapter, is to assess the extent to which arbitrators are evolving capacity to govern the domains of transnational commerce and investment.

Our approach combines two strains of theory, which we briefly summarize here. The first is the theory of judicialization.[7] Judicialization refers to the process through which third-party dispute resolution (TDR) emerges and develops authority over the evolution of institutions in a community or domain of action. The theory predicts that TDR, if sustained over time, will organize institutional change, to the extent that specific causal relationships are forged between three factors: (1) social exchange—contracting; (2) the decisions of third-party dispute resolvers—case law; and (3) normative structure—institutions. It is crucial to stress that judicialization proceeds *only* to the extent that these three factors develop in interdependent ways, through the ongoing resolution of contractual disputes.

Because judicial lawmaking,[8] as registered in case law, is the crucial mechanism of institutional change, its micro-foundations deserve special attention. Consider the situation, of which arbitration is one type, in which two parties freely delegate authority to a third party to settle a contractual dispute, and each hopes to win. Once constituted, the triadic figure faces a potentially

---

[6] According to the now standard distinctions of institutionalist research in the social sciences, we distinguish "institutions" (normative structures, including rule systems, customs, and cognitive paradigms) from "organizations" (social units organized to pursue collective purposes). See Peter Hall and Rosemary Taylor, "Political science and the three new institutionalisms," *Political Studies*, Vol. 44 (1996), pp. 936–957; Douglass North, *Institutions, Institutional Change, and Economic Performance* (Cambridge: Cambridge University Press, 1990), Chapter 1.

[7] Stone Sweet, "Judicialization and the Construction of Governance."

[8] We are aware that "judicial lawmaking" is a contested concept. We use the term in a generic sense to mean any decision that supplements the corpus of normative materials that can be used in future episodes of TDR.

intractable dilemma. On the one hand, her reputation for neutrality is crucial to the legitimacy of the triad itself. Disputants would be loath to delegate disputes if it were otherwise. Yet, in resolving disputes she may compromise her reputation for neutrality by declaring one party the loser, thereby creating a two-against-one situation.[9] Each disputant may hope as much. In such a situation, the dispute resolver's priority is to settle the conflict without destroying the perception of her neutrality, with respect to both present and future disputants.

In pursuit of this objective, three basic tactics are available. First, the dispute resolver can develop procedures to uncover the relevant facts, taking care to ensure that both sides are freely able to express their version of events. Second, she can defend her decisions normatively, as meaningfully constrained by existing norms. Norms provide ready-made, presumptively legitimate rules and standards of appropriate behavior to which the dispute resolver can appeal to justify decisions. Third, she can fashion compromise decisions, in effect splitting the difference between the parties.

No known, stable system of TDR, including court systems, fails to blend these elements, if in different ratios. Nonetheless, the values underlying these tactics often contradict one another. The friction between (concrete) facts and (abstract) norms is a generic source of such tensions: getting the facts right may expose the inadequacy of existing norms, pressuring the dispute resolver to innovate. Getting the normative justification right, though, may conflict with the effort to craft a decision based more on equity. If the dispute resolver does seek to resolve the dispute by designating one party the clear "winner," and the other the "loser," then her legitimacy is likely to rest all the more on the integrity of the procedures, the "correct" determination of the facts, and the persuasiveness of normative reasoning and justification.

In any event, to the extent that TDR gains social legitimacy and institutionalizes as a taken-for-granted set of practices in any community, two basic forms of lawmaking will become inseparable from one another. The first type is particular and retrospective: the triadic figure settles an existing dispute between two parties about the terms of one dyadic contract. The terms of the settlement apply strictly to the parties. The second form is provoked if the dispute resolver justifies her decision normatively, that is, with reasons. In telling us, for example, why a given act should or should not be permitted, or how tensions between two norms or interests are to be resolved, she makes law of a general and prospective nature. This is so to the extent that her decision creates, clarifies, or alters elements that comprise institutions (the law) in ways that future disputants and dispute resolvers will credit.

---

[9] Martin Shapiro, *Courts: A Comparative and Political Analysis* (Chicago: University of Chicago Press, 1981), Chapter 1.

Given two conditions, triadic lawmaking will generate governance. First, future contractants must perceive that they are better off in a world with TDR than without it, and they must evaluate their relationships in light of the latter's decisions. Second, dispute resolvers must understand their decisions as having some prospective, pedagogical authority on future dispute resolution. Skipping a number of steps in the argument, the theory predicts that the more TDR is activated within a community of contractants—if the flow of cases is steady or rising over time—then judicial lawmaking will inexorably become a mechanism of institutional evolution, and dyadic contracting and disputing will gradually but inevitably be placed in the shadow of TDR and case law. As decisions accumulate, the corpus of applicable rules and procedures steadily deepens and expands, becoming more elaborate and differentiated, which will then help to organize future interactions, conflict, dispute resolution, and institutional change.

We emphasize that the theory of judicialization is not a teleological account of institutional evolution. Instead, it is expressed in terms of necessary conditions, variables, causal mechanisms, and "if–then" statements.[10] Indeed, judicialization is a contingent process, depending entirely on how actors identify their respective interests and behave accordingly. Actors are capable of blocking movement at crucial points. Disputants may choose to dissolve their contract rather than delegate to a third party, for example, or the dispute resolver may render capricious decisions or refuse to give reasons to justify the decision. If such behavior is, or becomes, the normal state of affairs, triadic governance will not develop.

The insights of judicialization theory[11] can be incorporated into a second strand of theory: P-A analysis. The P-A framework is an adaptation of well-known concepts of contract law and practice to explain important features of economic and political governance. Over the past three decades, the P-A construct has emerged as a standard approach to research on the firm,[12] state organs,[13] and international regimes,[14] not least because it offers ready-made, appropriate concepts that the analyst can tailor to empirical research on virtually any governance situation. The P-A framework neatly applies to arbitration, not least because arbitral power is a paradigmatic case of delegated

---

[10] Stone Sweet, "Judicialization and the Construction of Governance."

[11] The theory of judicialization was originally developed without relationship to arbitration.

[12] Jean-Jacques Laffont and David Martimort, *The Theory of Incentives: The Principal-Agent Model* (Princeton: Princeton University Press, 2001); Paul Milgrom and John Roberts, *Economics, Organization and Management* (Englewood Cliff, NJ: Prentice-Hall, 1992).

[13] Kaare Strøm, Wolfgang Müller, and Torbjörn Bergman, *Delegation and Accountability in Parliamentary Democracies* (Oxford: Oxford University Press, 2006).

[14] Mark Pollack, *The Engines of Integration: Delegation, Agency, and Agency Setting in the European Union* (Oxford: Oxford University Press, 2003).

authority through contract. We give a brief overview of the basics of delegation theory here, before applying it to arbitration in Parts 2 and 3.

The P-A approach dramatizes the relationship between Principals and Agents against the background of a specified set of governance problems. Principals are those actors who create Agents, whereupon the former confers upon the latter discretionary authority to take binding decisions. The Agent governs to the extent that her decisions influence the distribution of values and resources in the domain of her competence. By assumption, the Principals are initially in control, in that they possess the authority and resources to constitute (or not to create) the Agent. Since the Principals are willing to pay the costs of delegation, it is assumed that they expect benefits to outweigh costs, over time. The analyst typically "explains" the origin and persistence of an organization, or governance situation, in light of the specific functional demands of those who delegate.[15] Principals constitute Agents among other reasons, in order to help them settle disputes, resolve commitment problems, harness epistemic expertise in technical regulatory problems, and avoid taking blame for unpopular policies.

The Principals' capacity to control the Agent is a central preoccupation of the approach. The potential for the Agent to develop her own interests—and thereby produce unwanted outcomes that are costly to eradicate—is assumed to be an omnipresent problem. Because such "agency costs" inhere in delegation, would-be Principals face a dilemma. In order for them to achieve their goals, they have to grant meaningful discretionary authority to an Agent, yet the Agent may act in ways that undermine the rationale for delegating in the first place. In response, Principals typically seek to incentivize the Agent's work, through procedures that allow for oversight and override, for example.

Put in terms of the theory of judicialization, the move from a two-party contracting situation (the dyad) to a TDR system (the triad) creates a node of governance. The triadic entity—the arbitrator—is an Agent of the contracting parties who "need" TDR in order to resolve specific contracting dilemmas: commitment, interpretation, enforcement, and so on. Yet, unlike a situation in which a legislature creates an independent agency to help it govern in a specific domain, the arbitrator-as-Agent possesses power over the parties-as-Principals, because the latter have decided as much. The move to TDR thus inevitably raises the possibility that the arbitrator will use her power to produce outcomes that the contracting parties would find undesirable.

This account of triadic governance overlaps, if only in part, with certain economic approaches to contracting and the development of markets.

---

[15] Mark Thatcher and Alec Stone Sweet, "Theory and Practice of Delegation to Non-Majoritarian Institutions," *West European Politics*, Vol. 25 (2002), pp.1–22.

Simplifying a complex literature, modern contract theory focuses on the linked problems of how to (1) achieve optimal contracting, in which the parties maximize joint benefits, and (2) optimally balance ex ante commitment and ex post flexibility, in order to manage uncertainty and changing circumstances.[16] We assume that most formal contracts of any complexity are incomplete, in the sense that the parties are not able to fully specify their mutual rights and obligations for all contingencies. Incomplete contracting is a basic source of the demand for TDR: the dispute resolver helps to complete the contract ex post, in the face of dyadic conflict and changing circumstances. Partly for these reasons, one predictable outcome of judicialization (the institutionalization of TDR) will be to lower the costs of dyadic exchange. The dynamics of judicialization, however, will tend to undermine models of optimal dyadic contracting, to the extent that social (or policy) interests will be brought to bear on the parties. Transaction cost approaches to market-building have also heavily emphasized the significance of TDR. Indeed, TDR has been shown to be a crucial mechanism of economic expansion, both within and across borders.[17] These results depend upon the capacity of any specific system of TDR to reduce transaction costs relative to alternative, pre-existing arrangements, and not upon the maximization of efficiency for any two parties.

As this volume demonstrates, these logics apply to international arbitration. Over the past three decades, global firms, lawyers, and arbitration houses have largely displaced national courts as sites of authoritative dispute resolution for transnational commercial and investment disputes.[18] Transnational economic actors and their lawyers strongly prefer arbitration, compared to adjudicating disputes in national courts, for its politico-legal neutrality, flexibility, confidentiality, and finality. At the same time, questions such as how international arbitrators should govern, and whether too much systemic development will undermine arbitration's efficiency and legitimacy, are now central preoccupations of those who use and manage the system.

[16] For an application to ISA, see Anne Van Aaken, "International Investment Law between Commitment and Flexibility: A Contract Theory Analysis," *Journal of International Economic Law*, Vol. 12 (2009), pp.1–32.

[17] Including: Avner Greif, "Contract Enforceability and Economic Institutions in Early Trade: The Maghribi Trader's Coalition," *American Economic Review*, Vol. 83 (1993), pp.425–448; Walter Mattli, *The Logic of Regional Integration: Europe and Beyond* (New York: Cambridge University Press, 1999); Douglass North, *Institutions, Institutional Change, and Economic Performance* (Cambridge: Cambridge University Press, 1990); Neil Fligstein and Alec Stone Sweet, "Constructing Markets and Polities: An Institutionalist Account of European Integration," *American Journal of Sociology*, Vol. 107 (2002), pp.1206–1243.

[18] While complex arbitrations are often more expensive than adjudication, costs too are capable of being limited by parties that wish to do so.

2 Three Models of Arbitral Governance

In this section, we develop three distinct models of arbitration: (A) the contractual; (B) the judicial; and (C) the constitutional. The models are both descriptive and prescriptive, providing alternative notions of how legitimate arbitral power is, and should be, exercised. The contractual model is built upon the classic assumptions of freedom of contract: the source of arbitral power is a contract, which constitutes its own unique legal "system." In ISA, each Bilateral Investment Treaty (BIT) comprises an autonomous legal system. The arbitrator is an Agent of the two contracting parties—the Principals. The judicial model departs from the contractual model by considering the conditions under which the arbitrator becomes, at least in part, the Agent of a larger arbitral legal order, comprised of states, transnational firms and investors, arbitration houses, and other third-party stakeholders. Crucially, as we move from the first to the second model, we encounter nascent hierarchies, the development of case law, and the routine imposition of interests beyond those of the contracting parties. The constitutional model supplements the judicial model, embedding the arbitral legal order within an overarching legal framework that includes general principles of law, international economic law, and human rights, including property rights and guarantees of due process.

2.1 *The Contractual Model*

A P-A relationship is constituted when two contracting parties (the Principals) confer upon an arbitrator (the Agent) the authority to resolve disputes arising under the contract. The contracting parties are free to select the law governing their agreement and the procedures to be used in the dispute settlement process, and these choices bind the arbitrator. An arbitration clause comprises a commitment device that the parties use to help them resolve the collective action problems associated with dyadic exchange.

The legitimacy of arbitral power is not initially problematic, since it is based on an act of delegation to which the parties have freely consented. In the event of a dispute, the authority of the arbitrator is limited to the domain of activity governed by the contract itself. The arbitrator will typically "complete" contractual provisions in light of the contract law selected by the parties, and she will apply these interpretations to resolve the dispute. What law is made is retrospective and particular, in that it applies only to a discrete dispute involving a preexisting contract. In recent decades, arbitrators have steadily consolidated their authority over disputants. Thus, it is now settled doctrine that arbitral clauses are separable from the main contract,[19] and issues of Kompetenz-Kompetenz have been resolved in the arbitrator's favor.[20] These developments, while being important outcomes of judicialization, push in the same direction: to enhance the Agent's authority to enforce the parties' bargain. Put differently, once the arbitration begins, Principals have little (if any) means of controlling their Agent.

The contractual model conforms to the mainstream account of international arbitration. It is important to stress, however, that the contractual model can accommodate a great deal of judicialization. Here we will focus on the role of the arbitral lawmaking, the central mechanism of judicialization, which we see as partly driven by specific tensions among the disputing parties, and between the parties and arbitrators.

International arbitration today typically takes place once a commercial or investor-state relationship has been destroyed,[21] wherein the main goal of each side is to "win," that is, to obtain the best monetary settlement possible. In such a situation (Part 1), the arbitrator will be under substantial pressure to show that she is neutral with respect to the parties, not least by developing and ensuring fair procedures and giving good reasons for her decisions. Other variables push in the same direction. The greater the monetary amount at stake in the dispute, the more likely the parties will be to tolerate, or generate themselves, relatively complex and costly procedures. Further, the higher the stakes, the more likely it will be that a losing party will consider challenging an award, pushing enforcement into a national court. Thus, in so far as the parties treat arbitration as litigation, the arbitrator will be pressured to act as a judge. This is a rudimentary, but not trivial, form of judicialization.

In such circumstances, arbitral lawmaking is a predictable response to legitimacy concerns. Consider the four "principal obligations" of arbitrators that Rusty Park, the President of the London Court of International Arbitration, has recently elaborated.[22] The first is to render "an accurate award," a decision that is faithful to the "context and relevant bargain" enshrined in a contract or investment treaty. The second duty is to ensure "due process," both to fulfill the first obligation and to strengthen the perception of arbitral impartiality and independence. The third is to strive for "efficiency," in the sense of

---

[19] That is, the validity of the arbitral clause is not affected by the legal nullity of the contract of which it is a part. In essence, the doctrine forecloses moves by one of the parties to the contract to avoid arbitration by pleading the contract's nullity.

[20] Kompetenz-Kompetenz refers to the formal competence of a jurisdiction to determine its own jurisdiction, or the jurisdiction of another organ. Modern arbitration statutes and case law largely accept that the arbitrator possesses the authority to fix the scope of its own jurisdiction, subject, of course, to the will of the contracting parties.

[21] The ICC also provides mediation services.

[22] William Park, "The Four Musketeers of Arbitral Duty: Neither One-for-All nor All-for-One," *ICC Dossiers* (Paris: ICC, 2011), p.25. Park is otherwise a traditionalist who regularly expresses worries that the judicialization of arbitration is going too far.

reducing, as far as possible, "undue costs and delays" of settling the dispute. Finally, the arbitrator must produce "an enforceable award," given that one of the parties may ask a national judge either to recognize or quash it. In practice, securing judicial recognition of an award entails providing reasons to justify the award and a record of how deliberations proceeded.

As Park stresses, the good arbitrator seeks to strike a defensible balance between the values that inhere in these duties when they come into tension. Rendering an accurate award, for example, is predicated on arbitrators getting the facts right, which may conflict with efficiency concerns. Striving for accuracy and ensuring due process means building proper procedures, which the arbitrator may have to impose upon recalcitrant parties. As noted, arbitral procedures have steadily become more complex. Indeed, arbitration houses— de facto legislators in the arbitral world—regularly revise procedures and codify best practices that had already emerged through use. Reason-giving has been subject to similar dynamics. Under the rules of every major house, arbitrators must justify their awards with reasons (the ICC Court of Arbitration announced in 1924 that it would check the "phraseology of awards"[23]). But is it enough that arbitrators give a reason? Or should they worry about giving "good reasons," or even the "best reasons"? In high-stakes, high-profile cases, arbitrators will be led to develop more elaborate procedures and better reasons. Judicialization will proceed so long as "good arbitrators" resolve a steady supply of disputes in ways that fulfill their duties, including providing adequate justification for their awards.

2.2 The Judicial Model

A second type of model rejects the view that arbitral power is merely a creature of contract. The analyst adds several layers of institutional complexity to the equation to explain why arbitrators act as Agents of the transnational commercial and investment communities. In contrast to the precepts of the contractual model, the strong assumption of the judicial model is that arbitrators have a duty to resolve disputes in ways that sufficiently take into account wider social interests. Further, the "good arbitrator" in the judicial model is a professional with an interest in ensuring her arbitral career, which entails building a reputation for fairness and wisdom among the pool of future disputants, in competition with her peers. The emergence of a "distinct and cohesive legal culture" in international arbitration, as identified by Joshua Kartner in this volume, reflects this sense of duty toward building community and capacity to govern.[24]

---

[23] *The Arbitration of the International Chamber of Commerce* (Paris: ICC, 1924), p.7.
[24] See also Yves Dezalay and Bryant G. Garth, *Dealing in Virtue—International Commercial Arbitration and the Construction of a Transnational Legal Order* (Chicago: University of Chicago Press, 1996).

The judicial model explicitly acknowledges elements of hierarchy, both private and public. The major arbitration houses facilitate judicialization, by establishing mandatory procedures and supervising awards, for example. The ICC's supervisory body provides arbitrators with a check-list of their responsibilities, and it will refuse to certify an award that fails to give adequate reasons (Part 3). The ICC does so in order to maximize consistency across awards—what the ICC characterizes as promoting "justice"—and to ensure that awards rendered will be enforceable in national courts. Given that arbitration houses are in competition with each other, as well as with national courts, they have good reason to develop what is, in effect, a guarantee for the product they are selling. The fact that national courts hold the power to vacate awards also pushes the arbitral community to focus on building stable procedures and doctrine. In P-A terms, what is crucial is that the arbitrator may be subject to the authority of multiple actors, including the contracting parties, ICC officials, and national judges, who are able to exercise powers (of supervision and override) usually associated with Principals, but which the contracting parties themselves do not hold in the arbitral setting.

The judicial model also presumes that judges and arbitrators will, in practice, perform similar functions. National judges regularly engage in mediation to cajole the parties to settle,[25] for example, and arbitrators regularly apply state law to resolve conflicts. Much depends on the fact pattern of the dispute, and its interaction with national law. In ICA, when one of the parties pleads mandatory national law as a defense, the arbitrator may be compelled to impose on the parties the interest of a state. In *Mitsubishi*,[26] a major ruling of the US Supreme Court, the majority expressly delegated (if ex post) the task of interpreting and applying US anti-trust law to arbitrators seated in Japan, while retaining authority to review how international arbitrators would apply mandatory US law in future awards. Cases such as these eviscerate the claim that the arbitrator, unlike the judge, serves only the contracting parties-as-principals.

Similarly, the model casts distinctions between "private" and "public" law as relative. No national contract law, whether legislated or judge-made, is strictly private, given that it has been substantiated by state actors exercising public authority. When arbitrators resolve disputes under the contract law of a particular state, they act partly as agents of that legal order, just as they act as agents of transnational law in disputes in which the UNIDROIT Principles or any other corpus of a-national, "general principles" of contract govern. Further, the arbitrator—no less than the judge—regularly confronts law emanating from

---

[25] Section 278 of the German Civil Code, for example, requires German private law judges "to seek an amicable resolution of the legal dispute," and details procedures for doing so.
[26] *Mitsubishi Motors Corp. v. Soler Chrysler Plymouth, Inc.*, 473 US 614 (1985).

multiple sources, including national statutes and regulations that apply to performance, a situation that may lead her to adapt modes of reasoning and justification prevalent in public law adjudication.

To this point, the arbitrator's role in the judicialization process has been portrayed as essentially defensive: she develops procedures and reason-based justifications in order to secure and maintain her legitimacy with respect to present and future disputants. Whereas the contractual model emphasizes the ad hoc nature of arbitration, the field is in fact dominated by "repeat players," arbitrators seeking to build their reputations as "skilled arbitrators" in order to build and maintain careers. Put bluntly, if arbitrators strive to perform Park's four arbitral duties with an eye toward their future professional prospects, then they will in fact be led to behave as agents of the wider stakeholder community, not just of two parties in a one-shot interaction.

In sum, the judicial model focuses attention on the emergence and consolidation of structural features that enhance arbitration's autonomy as a "legal system," a regime that can be observed and evaluated on its own. While national courts and transnational arbitral tribunals remain different in significant ways, what is important is that the judicialization of arbitration has taken place despite these differences. Indeed, the judicialization of the contractual model made possible the emergence of the judicial model.

2.3 *The Constitutional Model*

A nascent—but far more speculative and controversial—model conceives the arbitrator as an Agent of a wider international legal order, at least in some circumstances. In this account, arbitration is assumed to be subject to forces that are gradually "constitutionalizing" international law and courts more generally.[27] Arbitrators will be pressed to acknowledge their roles in international governance, including rendering "justice" in accordance with higher norms.[28]

The constitutional model is rooted in a combination of two claims. First, treaty instruments of global scope have established a complex interface between arbitration, national law, and international law. The 1958 New York Convention on the Recognition and Enforcement of Foreign Arbitral Awards,

---

[27] Jan Klabbers, Anne Peters, and Geir Ulfstein, *The Constitutionalization of International Law* (Oxford: Oxford University Press, 2009); Ernst-Ulrich Petersmann, "Constitutional Theories of International Economic Adjudication and Investor-State Arbitration," in *Human Rights in International Investment Law and Arbitration*, edited by Pierre-Marie Dupuy, Francesco Francioni, and Ernst-Ulrich Petersmann (Oxford: Oxford University Press, 2009); Alec Stone Sweet, "The Structure of Constitutional Pluralism," *International Journal of Constitutional Law*, Vol. 11(2) (2013), pp.491–500.

[28] See Moritz Renner, "Towards a Hierarchy of Norms in Transnational Law?" *Journal of International Arbitration*, Vol. 26(4) (2009), pp.533–555.

which has been ratified by 149 states, made national courts the public guarantors of private arbitral authority. Under the New York Convention, parties that fail to abide by an arbitral judgment can be sued at their national bar, and national judges are, with few exceptions, required to enforce the judgment against the recalcitrant party. The 1965 Convention establishing the International Center for the Settlement of Investment Disputes (ICSID) has been ratified by more than 148 States. The Convention establishes the compulsory arbitration of disputes that come within the rubric of BITs: private investors may sue host states in ad hoc arbitral tribunals, and states are required to enforce awards.[29] The first claim, then, is that these treaties perform a constitutional function, in that they delegate authority to arbitrators and create a legal framework for enforcement of arbitral awards by national judges.

The second claim is that this framework is part of the architecture of an emerging international economic constitution. The central idea is that developments within certain key international organizations (including the WTO, the EU, NAFTA, and the ECHR) are driving the construction of pluralistic legal regimes. To the extent that this model takes hold, the "good arbitrator" will take into consideration the jurisprudence of the courts of the International Court of Justice, the World Trade Organization, the European Union, and the European Convention on Human Rights, where relevant. Put differently, one purpose of arbitration will be to build a stable interface between arbitral orders and other international economic regimes. These notions find some support in the 1969 Vienna Convention on Law of Treaties, which applies to ISA under BITs. Article 31.3, for example, requires the interpreter to take into account "any relevant rules of international law applicable in the relations between the parties." Further, international economic law is partly governed by general principles of law, comprised of a matrix of legal norms and practices that are shared among national, treaty-based, and transnational legal systems. These general principles are today routinely being "borrowed" and developed by arbitrators—as arbitral common law—which not only enhances the autonomy of the arbitral regime, but also contributes to the evolution of the international economic constitution.

A variation on the constitutional model presupposes a substantive body of "higher law" norms that are binding on all international judges, including arbitrators.[30] The most commonly invoked elements are jus cogens norms,

[29] Article 54(1) states: "Each Contracting State shall recognize an award rendered pursuant to this Convention as binding and enforce the pecuniary obligations imposed by that award within its territories as if it were a final judgment of a court in that State."

[30] Ernst-Ulrich Petersmann, "Constitutional Theories of International Economic Adjudication and Investor-State Arbitration," in *Human Rights in International Investment Law and Arbitration*, edited by Pierre-Marie Dupuy, Francesco Francioni, and Ernst-Ulrich Petersmann (Oxford: Oxford University Press, 2009).

basic human rights, including property rights, and procedural guarantees associated with due process and access to justice. Recent scholarship has emphasized the "constitutional" quality of these norms, as stable secondary rules governing transnational arbitration.[31] The international arbitrator—as much as any judge—is under an obligation to give special regard to fundamental rights when they are material to the resolution of the dispute at hand. It can be argued that the duty is reinforced by the Preamble to the 1969 Vienna Convention, which states that disputes "should be settled . . . in conformity with the principles of justice and international law." In this account, arbitrators can be said to be under a fiduciary obligation to respect fundamental rights and to pursue "justice" in other ways. Thus, the ISA arbitrator at ICSID could simultaneously be de facto an Agent of two states' parties to a BIT and the disputing parties (the contractual model), an Agent of ICSID and the greater investment community (the judicial model), and, at least at times, an Agent of a higher-law, global economic order (the constitutional model).

The model also applies to ICA. The claim is not that all disputes are inherently constitutional, but only that the arbitrator is under an obligation not to issue awards that violate "constitutional" norms, as well as to take account of rights in other ways. Under the New York Convention, the national judge is permitted to refuse to enforce an award that offends "public policy" or involves matters that are "inarbitrable" in the first place. In North America, most of Europe, and parts of Asia the public policy and inarbitrability exceptions contained in the New York Convention have been narrowed to the point of practical irrelevance. Arguably, the core exceptions that remain are linked to the types of fundamental norms just listed.

Materials from comparative contract law also support the model. In many national constitutional orders today, constitutional rights must be enforced when they are relevant to private law adjudication. In its influential Lüth ruling of 1958, the German Constitutional Court required the civil courts to strike a proper balance between constitutional rights and the values that inhere in the private law, including freedom of contract.[32] It is now the duty of German judges of the civil code to ensure the compatibility of "every provision of the private law" with rights. The basics of Lüth have now widely diffused beyond Germany, resulting in an ongoing process of "constitutionalization of the private law." Thus, proponents of the model can point to developments at both the international and domestic levels in support of their claims.

---

[31] Moritz Renner, "Towards a Hierarchy of Norms in Transnational Law?" *Journal of International Arbitration*, Vol. 26(4) (2009), pp.533–555; Pierre-Marie Dupuy, Francesco Francioni, and Ernst-Ulrich Petersmann (eds.), *Human Rights in International Investment Law and Arbitration* (Oxford: Oxford University Press, 2009).

[32] BVerfGE 7, 198 (1958).

Insofar as we move from the first to the third model, one will find arbitrators operating in an increasingly elaborate legal system which, one expects, will lead them to conceptualize their roles differently. Consider the notion of "justice." In the contractual model, the arbitrator supplies justice by settling a dyadic dispute, and an "unjust" arbitral award is merely another aspect of a business deal gone bad, with no affect beyond the dyad. In the judicial model, at a minimum rendering justice is conceived in terms of maximizing legal certainty for present and future users of the system. In the constitutional model, justice is denied when the arbitrator fails to uphold or adequately take into consideration the higher law norms that ground all modes of TDR: national, transnational, international. Further, as we move from the judicial to the constitutional model, the arbitrator is part of a process of dialogue (both cooperative and competitive) between actors operating in the network of autonomous legal orders that comprise the international economic constitution. The constitutional model therefore does not deny the pluralist structure of the system, but must accommodate pluralism.

2.4 Structural Properties

One of the major themes of this volume involves a systemic question: to what extent are ISA and ICA autonomous legal systems in their own right? The question can be addressed dogmatically (deriving an answer, in large part, deductively from first principles), empirically (through developing indicators of autonomy and collecting data on these measures), or a mixture of both (our preferred approach). Our theory focuses empirical attention on the endogenous development of arbitral institutions through the lawmaking of arbitrators themselves. The approach is designed to chart the development of a private, autonomous, and self-generating legal system.

As a structural matter, the system is inherently pluralistic, pluralism being a property of certain legal systems. International arbitration has strong forms of the two most important types of pluralism: of (A) sources of law, and (B) jurisdictional authority. First, as we have emphasized, arbitrators routinely interpret and apply diverse sources of law (national, international, and transnational) in order to resolve the disputes that come before them. Second, the arbitral world is structured by a network of competing arbitration houses, each of which has its own mandatory procedures and organizational "culture." Fragmentation is a fact of global law, and arbitration reflects as much. These points made, the world's most prominent arbitrators, as well as law firms in the area, work in both ICA and ISA, are familiar with how all of the major arbitration houses operate, and keep track of all major awards.

Nonetheless, skeptics rightly underscore the fact that arbitration would lose much of its attractiveness if national courts were not available to enforce arbitral judgments. Because states built the system of enforcement—through the 1958 New York Convention—it is possible to argue that whatever "legal" authority arbitrators exercise has been delegated to them by sovereigns. Yet it is also true that it was an arbitration house—the ICC—that generated the draft text that served as the basis of the New York Convention of 1958[33] (as it did with the Geneva Protocol of 1927[34]) and that was deeply involved in securing ratification of the Geneva Protocol of 1924.[35] Further, since 1958, national courts and legislators in major states have steadily adapted to arbitral authority as it has developed, recognizing many formal elements of arbitral autonomy, and reducing the scope of merit review of awards to virtually nil. What is indisputable is that the relative autonomy of private, transnational governance has steadily expanded, and that—when parties choose to avoid them—state courts usually perform only a residual, supervisory role. One peculiarity of arbitral authority today is that it is both dependent and parasitic on state power.

3 Mechanisms of Systemic Evolution

Much of our ongoing research involves charting and explaining the evolution from Model A (the "Contractual Model") to Model B (the "Judicial Model"), and from Model B to Model C (the "Constitutional Model"), to the extent that such movement occurs. As we have stressed, these movements are neither pre-ordained nor linear: some arbitrators are simply more comfortable working in one mode, rather than another. In addition, viewed systemically, ISA has evolved faster than has ICA. While we believe that a narrow version of Model A is now obsolete, we recognize that Model C will seem far more speculative and controversial to actors and scholars working in the field. In this section, we support our claim that the Constitutional Model is nonetheless emerging, illustrated by the example of transnational public policy, which applies to both ICA and ISA (see also Moritz Renner, Chapter 5, this volume).

"Transnational public policy" was first conceptualized by Pierre Lalive, in a seminal article of 1986.[36] Lalive understood it as a set of general principles that would both bind arbitrators and prevail over all other norms, domestic

---

[33] "Enforcement of International Arbitral Awards," *ICC International Court of Arbitration Bulletin*, Vol. 9(1) (1998), p.32.

[34] George L. Ridgeway, *Merchants of Peace: Twenty Years of Business Diplomacy through the International Chamber of Commerce 1919–1938* (New York: Columbia University Press, 1938), p.329.

[35] Ridgeway, *Merchants of Peace*, p.327.

[36] Pierre Lalive, "Ordre public transnational (ou réellement international) et arbitrage international," *Revue de l'arbitrage*, No. 3 (1986), p.329.

and international.[37] In fact, one finds that arbitrators have increasingly relied on these norms, which include the prohibition of corruption, slavery, drug trade, terrorism, genocide, the regulation of the trade of organs and weapons, as well as the various subjects over which the UN General Assembly or Security Council may pass resolutions.[38] These norms may appear uncontroversial, in the sense that their regulation does not raise much debate. Yet, arbitrations often involve business practices that infringe on these norms, as the two cases that follow demonstrate.

3.1 World Duty Free v. Kenya *(ICSID, 2006)*

The case of *World Duty Free v. Kenya* arose out of a dispute between a company incorporated on the Isle of Man, Word Duty Free Company Limited, and the Republic of Kenya in connection with an agreement concluded in 1989 for the construction, maintenance, and operation of duty-free complexes at Nairobi and Mombassa International Airports. Following the alleged expropriation of its properties by the Republic of Kenya, World Duty Free claimed restitution of the duty free complexes at both airports, and payment of damages in the amount of USD 500 million.

In the course of the proceedings, World Duty Free described in detail the circumstances under which the 1989 agreement had been concluded, including the payment of bribes to the former president of Kenya, Mr. Daniel Arap Moi. Kenya subsequently submitted an application to the arbitral tribunal requesting dismissal on the grounds that the agreement was unenforceable, having been procured through bribes. Kenya based its request on applicable English and Kenyan laws and, on a secondary basis, on international public policy. Significantly, Kenya mentioned the interests of the general public in support of its request: "[c]laims founded on illegality have to be dismissed for the benefit of the public and not for the advantage of the defendant."[39] The pleading therefore broadened the scope of the arbitration, to include public and transnational interests.

---

[37] Pierre Lalive, "Ordre public transnational (ou réellement international) et arbitrage international," p.351: "A notre avis, l'arbitre international dispose bien d'un droit international privé, et est limité par lui, et *ce droit international privé ne peut être lui-même que 'transnational,'* c'est-à-dire composé d'un certain nombre de principes généraux, soit communs à toutes les parties (et Etats) intéressés à une espèce déterminée, soit même universels." ["In our opinion, the international arbitrator has at her disposal an international private law, which constrains her, and this international private law can only be 'transnational', that is composed by a certain number of general principles, either common to all parties (and states) interested in a specific case, or even universal." Authors' translation.]

[38] See Christoph H. Schreuer, Loretta Malintoppi, August Reinisch, and Anthony Sinclair, *The ICSID Convention: A Commentary*, 2nd ed. (Cambridge: Cambridge University Press, 2009), pp.566–567.

[39] *World Duty Free Company Limited v. Republic of Kenya* (ICSID Case No. ARB/00/7), Award of September 25, 2006, para. 118.

The tribunal agreed, dismissing World Duty Free's claims primarily on the basis of transnational public policy, and only secondarily on domestic law. The tribunal took pains to define the nature of transnational public policy:

> The concept of public policy ("ordre public") is rooted in most, if not all, legal systems. Violation of the enforcing State's public policy is grounds for refusing recognition and enforcement of foreign judgments and awards. . . . In this respect, a number of legislatures and courts have decided that a narrow concept of public policy should apply to foreign awards. This narrow concept is often referred to as "international public policy" ("ordre public international"). Although this name suggests that it is in some way a supra-national principle, it is in fact no more than domestic public policy applied to foreign awards and its content and application remains subjective to each State. The term "international public policy," however, is sometimes used with another meaning, signifying an international consensus as to universal standards and accepted norms of conduct that must be applied in all fora.[40]

The tribunal thus chose a more expansive conception of public policy, whose reach extends beyond domestic public policy. The arbitrators also cited the Lalive article of 1986,[41] as well as surveying no fewer than 7 ICC awards. In doing so, the arbitrators stressed that their reasoning was rooted in ICC arbitral practice and a particular (transnational) construction of public policy.[42] Subsequent ICSID awards have adopted similar positions, thereby reinforcing the autonomous nature of transnational public policy.[43]

3.2 Supplier v. Republic of X *(ICC, 1992)*

As Moritz Renner argues in this volume, arbitrators working in the context of ICA have also developed transnational public policy. ICC Case No. 6475 (the available award is heavily redacted) arose out of contracts entered into between a European supplier and the Republic of X, namely an Agreement of Cooperation and Purchases and a Purchase Contract. Under these contracts, which were governed under Swiss law, the Supplier was to furnish agricultural products to the Republic of X. Following a dispute regarding payment, the

---

[40] *World Duty Free v. Kenya*, paras 138–139. [41] *World Duty Free v. Kenya*, para. 139.
[42] *World Duty Free v. Kenya*, para. 157.
[43] *EDF (Services) Limited v. Romania* (ICSID Case No. ARB/05/13), Award of October 8, 2009, para. 221; *Phoenix Action, Ltd. v. Czech Republic* (ICSID Case No. ARB/06/15), Award of April 15, 2009, para. 113; *Millicom International Operations B.V. and Sentel GSM SA v. Republic of Senegal* (ICSID Case No. ARB/08/20), Decision on Jurisdiction of July 16, 2010, para. 103; *Rumeli Telekom A.S. and Telsim Mobil Telekomunikasyon Hizmetleri A.S. v. Republic of Kazakhstan* (ICSID Case No. ARB/05/16), Award of July 29, 2008, paras 177 et seq.; *Gustav FW Hamester GmbH & Co KG v. Republic of Ghana* (ICSID Case No. ARB/07/24), Award of June 18, 2010 para. 123; *Fraport AG Frankfurt Airport Services Worldwide v. Republic of the Philippines* (ICSID Case No. ARB/03/25), dissenting opinion of Mr. Bernardo M. Cremades of July 19, 2007, para. 40.

Supplier initiated arbitration proceedings against the Republic of X before an ICC tribunal, which was seated in Switzerland.

In the course of the proceedings, the Republic of X mounted jurisdictional objections, arguing that arbitrating the Supplier's claims was blocked by the fact that the international community has adopted a non-recognition policy with regard to the Republic of X. In particular, the Republic of X argued that the refusal of the international community to have dealings with it defeated the jurisdiction of the arbitral tribunal.[44] Invoking the "superior interest of the international community in refusing to acknowledge in any form whatsoever the existence of the territory as a State," the Republic of X argued that "transnational public policy . . . mandates a refusal to extend the mechanisms of international arbitration to the profiteers of [discrimination] in the territory."[45]

In a partial award on jurisdiction and admissibility, the arbitral tribunal rejected the jurisdictional objection from the Republic of X following a two-step analysis. First, the arbitral tribunal held that the Republic of X had failed "to establish the existence and applicability of the principles [of transnational public policy] invoked."[46] The arbitrators, nonetheless, pointed to "a 'growing' body of 'transnational public policy' which may or should be [enforced] by international commercial arbitrators, in a proper case, in particular in ICC arbitrations."[47] Second, the tribunal held that lack of jurisdiction would violate another "clear principle of transnational public policy which is the principle of good faith,"[48] which it went on to describe as the "jus cogens" of international arbitration.[49] Thus, on behalf of the "international community," the arbitral tribunal upheld its jurisdiction on the basis of a core principle of transnational public policy. Other ICC tribunals have designated EC competition law,[50] the prohibition for a state to renege on an arbitration agreement on the basis of its own law,[51] the prohibition on secret commission

[44] Partial Award on Jurisdiction and Admissibility in ICC Case No. 6474 of 1992 in *Yearbook Commercial Arbitration 2000–Vol. XXV*, edited by Albert Jan van den Berg (The Hague: Kluwer Law International, 2000), p.281: "[T]he international community has adopted the unambiguous policy of denying any recognition to and refusing to have any dealings with the territory [of the Republic of X]. The defendant contends that this must include international arbitration."

[45] Partial Award on Jurisdiction and Admissibility in ICC Case No. 6474 of 1992 in *Yearbook Commercial Arbitration 2000–Vol. XXV*, p.282.

[46] Partial Award on Jurisdiction and Admissibility in ICC Case No. 6474 of 1992 in *Yearbook Commercial Arbitration 2000–Vol. XXV*, p.285.

[47] Partial Award on Jurisdiction and Admissibility in ICC Case No. 6474 of 1992 in *Yearbook Commercial Arbitration 2000–Vol. XXV*, p.285.

[48] Partial Award on Jurisdiction and Admissibility in ICC Case No. 6474 of 1992 in *Yearbook Commercial Arbitration 2000–Vol. XXV*, p.286.

[49] Partial Award on Jurisdiction and Admissibility in ICC Case No. 6474 of 1992 in *Yearbook Commercial Arbitration 2000–Vol. XXV*, p.286.

[50] Final award in ICC Case No. 8423 of 1994 in *Yearbook Commercial Arbitration 2001–Vol. XXVI*, p.153, p.154.

[51] Award in ICC Case No. 10,623 of 2001, *ASA Bulletin*, Vol. 21(1) (2003), p.82, pp.91–92.

agreements,[52] and the fact that a foreign law provides that a claim is not subject to any statute of limitation[53] as part of (or compatible with) transnational public policy.

3.3 Transnational Public Policy and Constitutionalization

Today, arbitral tribunals routinely recognize and apply norms of transnational public policy in commercial and investment disputes, a development that is both an outcome of judicialization and an indicator of constitutionalization. Transnational public policy results from judicialization, a process by which arbitrators create norms and governance through a self-sustaining process of exercising, building, and legitimizing arbitral authority. What is undeniable is that transnational public policy is a product of arbitral jurisprudence, a source of "higher law" that binds arbitrators, and is distinct from both the national conception of public policy enshrined in domestic law and in the 1958 New York Convention, although conceptually related to both. In this volume, Ralf Michaels and Moritz Renner also consider transnational public policy as a sign of constitutionalization, to the extent that it organizes in a hierarchical fashion what might otherwise be considered to be decentralized systems, not unlike the way jus cogens and other norms may serve to "constitutionalize" international law.[54]

If, as a matter of jurisprudence, the norms of transnational public policy prevail over contractual agreements, then Model A is no longer defensible and the contours of Model C are made visible. To take another example, the arbitral tribunal in *Niko v. Bangladesh* declared that:

> Normally, arbitral tribunals respect and give effect to contracts concluded by the parties which agreed on the arbitration clause from which they derive their powers. However, party autonomy is not without limits. In international transactions the most important of such limits is that of international public policy. A contract in conflict with international public policy cannot be given effect by arbitrators.[55]

In addition, transnational public policy may be used to correct or discard an applicable law. In ICC Case No. 6320 (1992), for instance, the arbitral

---

[52] Final Award in ICC Case No. 6248 of 1990 in *Yearbook Commercial Arbitration 1994–Vol. XIX*, p.124, p.131.

[53] Interim Award in ICC Case No. 7263 of 1994 in *Yearbook Commercial Arbitration 1997–Vol. XXII*, p.92, p.102.

[54] Godefridus J.H. van Hoof, *Rethinking Sources of International Law* (Deventer/Antwerp: Kluwer, 1983), p.151: "[...] peremptory norms of general international law serve as public order embodying material constitutional provisions of international law." See also Alec Stone Sweet, "The Structure of Constitutional Pluralism," *International Journal of Constitutional Law*, Vol. 11(2) (2013), pp.491–500.

[55] *Niko v. Bangladesh*, para. 434.

tribunal adjudicated a claim regarding the alleged unconstitutionality of the RICO statute under US law. The tribunal decided that it did not possess such authority, but that it could determine whether the same statute conformed to transnational public policy.[56] The arbitrators then proceeded to analyze transnational public policy as if it embodied a set of overarching norms comparable to constitutional law in the domestic sphere. Transnational public policy may also provide substantive norms that mandatorily apply to the merits of the dispute notwithstanding an applicable domestic law in tension with it. In ICC Case No. 6320 (1992), the tribunal decided that the treble damages rule provided under the RICO statute could not apply since it would be "contrary to the choice of law" agreed upon (Brazilian), and that the link between US law and the dispute was insufficient. However, the tribunal opined that the situation would differ if the treble damages rule had been part of transnational public policy, in which case it could have been granted notwithstanding Brazilian law: "it cannot be judged that [treble damages] are a common feature of many national laws or of international law."[57]

Our argument echoes one made earlier by founding theorists of the new *lex mercatoria*.[58] Although he avoided speaking of the "constitutionalization" of international arbitration, Berthold Goldman conceived of transnational public policy as a superior set of norms to which rules of *lex mercatoria* should conform.[59] Goldman went as far as advocating the replacement of domestic by transnational public policy, in order to ground the autonomy of arbitral law.[60] Pursuing this point further, A.V.M. Struycken showed how transnational public policy would therefore structure and organize *lex mercatoria* as a "judicial system" ("ordre juridique").[61] That these arguments were made prior to the emergence of the arbitral jurisprudence just discussed alerts us to the fact that constitutionalization is unavoidably implicated in assertions of the autonomy of international arbitration.

---

[56] Final Award in ICC Case No. 6320 (1992), *ICC International Court of Arbitration Bulletin*, Vol. 6(1) (1995), p.59.

[57] Final Award in ICC Case No. 6320 (1992), *ICC International Court of Arbitration Bulletin*, Vol. 6(1) (1995), p.59.

[58] On *lex mercatoria*, more generally, see Alec Stone Sweet, "The New *Lex Mercatoria* and Transnational Governance," *Journal of European Public Policy*, Vol. 13 (2006), pp.627–646; Florian Grisel, *L'arbitrage international ou le droit contre l'ordre juridique* (Paris: Fondation Varenne/LGDJ, 2011).

[59] Berthold Goldman, "Nouvelles Réflexions sur la Lex Mercatoria," in *Festschrift Pierre Lalive* (Basel: Frankurt a.M., 1993), p.241, p.254.

[60] *Id.*

[61] A.V.M. Struycken, "La lex mercatoria dans le droit des contrats internationaux," in *L'évolution contemporaine du droit des contrats*, Journées R. Savatier, Faculté de droit de Poitiers (1985) (Paris: PUF, 1987), p.207, p.220.

4 Conclusion

As the judicialization of arbitration proceeds, we have argued, arbitral tribunals will be increasingly implicated in the construction of transnational governance, through their awards. The claim can be evaluated by analyzing data collected on specific indicators of judicialization, the primary mechanism of which, we have argued, is arbitral lawmaking. By mechanism, we mean the underlying logic of choice that leads an actor to behave in ways that facilitate the construction of arbitral institutions and, therefore, governance. Stripped to bare essentials, the crucial mechanism is associated with the institutionalization of reason-giving, which will progressively structure argumentation (between the parties) and justification (by the arbitrators). By indicator, we mean an empirical measure of outcomes generated by the judicialization process. We conclude by briefly discussing three such indicators: the development of precedent; the demand for ex post supervision of arbitral awards; and the use of the jurisprudence of other international judges.

A first indicator is the evolution of precedent-based discourse. The authority of soft precedent—the persuasive authority accorded to some prior arbitral awards—is developing rapidly.[62] There is obvious variation between ICA and ISA. In ISA, four factors have facilitated the emergence of arbitral case law: virtually all major awards are eventually published; BITs contain similar provisions; certain repeat-player arbitrators with high prestige are engaged in building case law; and ICSID annulment committees routinely provide guidance on interpreting BITs and the ICSID statutes. Today, the dense citation of previous awards is now typical in the parties' submissions, a feedback effect which pressures arbitrators, in turn, to consider past awards as evolving law.

In contrast, the vast majority of ICA awards are not published, on confidentiality grounds, making the development of precedent-based discourse difficult to measure. There is, however, no evidence to suggest, and no good reason to believe, that lawyers would be more reticent to use published materials in ICA compared to ISA.[63] Today, some of the major arbitration houses have adopted the policy of publishing unless the parties object, and an increasing number of awards are in fact published, if in redacted form, provoking a rising tide of scholarly commentary. We know from these materials

---

[62] Irene M. Ten Cate, "The Costs of Consistency: Precedent in Investment Treaty Arbitration," *Columbia Journal of Transnational Law*, Vol. 51(2) (2013), pp.418–478; Giorgio Sacerdoti, "Precedent in the Settlement of International Economic Disputes: The WTO and Investment Arbitration Models" (unpublished, 2011, available at: <http://papers.ssrn.com/sol3/papers.cfm?abstract_id=1931560>).

[63] See Pierre Duprey, "Do Arbitral Awards Constitute Precedents? Should Commercial Arbitration Be Distinguished in this Regard from Arbitration Based on Investment Treaties?" in *Towards a Uniform International Arbitration Law?*, edited by Anne-Véronique Schlaepfer, Philippe Pinsolle, and Louis Degos (Huntington, NY: Juris Publishing, 2005).

that ICA tribunals have produced a differentiated body of "arbitral common law," procedures, and doctrine tailored to specific types of transnational business.[64] Quasi-authoritative treatises have also appeared,[65] providing practitioners with the essentials of this law, and emphasizing its autonomy from national sources. The major arbitration houses also regularly seek to build coherence, through codifying procedures, issuing white papers on problems of contracting and advocacy, and organizing conferences to discuss the evolution of "a-national" principles of contract and ICA's future.

A second indicator, directly related to the collapse of the contractual model, is the fierce debate that today surrounds the issue of whether appellate supervision is desirable or necessary for both ISA[66] and ICA.[67] ICSID rules provide for an annulment procedure, through three-member "Annulment Committees" selected by ICSID officials, not the parties. Annulment Committees possess the authority to quash awards on a set of narrow grounds, but these grounds do not include incorrect interpretation and application of the law. Nonetheless, parties seeking annulment regularly ask Committees to read the requirement that tribunals "state the reasons upon which [the award] was based" to mean a duty not to give the wrong reasons—that is, to apply the law incorrectly. Not all Committees have rejected these appeals. Others resist annulment on the grounds of "errors of law," while detailing at length the legal errors the tribunal in fact made.[68] As noted, the ICC, through its Court of Arbitration, is engaged in "scrutinizing and approving all arbitral awards, in the interests of improving their quality and enforceability."[69] One might assume that, as a result, the range of variance in argumentation and justification is narrowing, but no one has yet documented this trend beyond anecdote.

A third indicator—the sources of law to which arbitrators refer in their awards—comprises a third indicator of judicialization. The extent to which

[64] Thomas Carbonneau, *Lex Mercatoria and Arbitration: A Discussion of the New Law Merchant* (Yonkers: Juris Publishing, 1997), pp.16–18.
[65] Gary Born, *International Commercial Arbitration* (The Hague: Kluwer, 2009).
[66] Gabrielle Kaufman-Kohler, "Arbitral Precedent: Dream, Necessity or Excuse?" *Arbitration International*, Vol. 23(3) (2007), pp.357–378; Mark Weidemaier, "Toward a Theory of Precedent in Arbitration," *William and Mary Law Review*, Vol. 51 (2010), pp.1895–1958.
[67] Erin Gleason, "International Arbitral Appeals: What Are We So Afraid of?" *Pepperdine Dispute Resolution Law Journal*, Vol. 7(2) (2007), pp.269–293; William Knull and Noah Rubins, "Betting The Farm On International Arbitration: Is It Time To Offer An Appeal Option?" *American Review of International Arbitration*, Vol. 11 (2000), p.531; "Seventh Geneva Global Arbitration Forum: Reconsidering a Key Tenet of International Commercial Arbitration: Is Finality of Awards What Parties Really Need? Has the Time of an International Appellate Arbitral Body Arrived?" *Journal of International Arbitration*, Vol. 16 (1999), pp.57–114.
[68] See, e.g., *CMS Gas Transmission Company v. Argentine Republic* (ICSID Case No. ARB/01/8), Decision of the Ad Hoc Committee on the Application for Annulment of September 25, 2007.
[69] <http://www.iccwbo.org/About-ICC/Organisation/Dispute-Resolution-Services/ICC-International-Court-of-Arbitration/Functions-of-the-ICC-International-Court-of-Arbitration/> [checked on August 18, 2012].

tribunals in ICA develop and apply general principles of law, for example, is an indicator of the system's relative autonomy from state sources of law. In ISA, some tribunals are now explicitly referencing the jurisprudence of the WTO Appellate Body and the ECHR, providing evidence that ISA may be inching toward the constitutional model.[70] Among other things, the constitutional model emphasizes dialogues between arbitrators and judges in a common project. Most dramatically, recent ICSID tribunals have begun to use proportionality balancing—a mode of constitutional adjudication first developed by national constitutional courts—to deal with tensions between investor's rights on the one hand, and the state's pursuit of the public interest on the other. They did so by citing and deploying the jurisprudence of the European Court of Human Rights and the Appellate Body of the World Trade Organization.[71] The move pushes ISA away from the contractual model and into a mode of adjudication more akin to that of a public law court (administrative or constitutional), or of a German private law court under Lüth.

A final point concerns the development of the scholarly discourse on these issues. With judicialization, the discourse has begun to fragment, and support for the contractual model has dissipated. Robust scholarly attempts are underway to construct ISA as global administrative or constitutional law, for example.[72] These efforts are both empirical (the claim is that they describe better what is actually happening in ISA), and normative (claiming that the embrace of a more explicit judicial model would mitigate the growing legitimacy crisis now faced by the system). One also now finds more attention placed on the prior socialization of arbitrators. Some have argued, for example, that arbitrators who bring into ISA a commitment to the contractual model and a background in private law will produce substantively different

---

[70] See Jürgen Kurtz, "The Use and Abuse of WTO Law in Investor-State Arbitration: Competition and Its Discontents," *European Journal of International Law*, Vol. 20 (2009), p.749; Ernst-Ulrich Petersmann, "Constitutional Theories of International Economic Adjudication and Investor-State Arbitration," in *Human Rights in International Investment Law and Arbitration*, edited by Pierre-Marie Dupuy, Francesco Francioni, and Ernst-Ulrich Petersmann (Oxford: Oxford University Press, 2009); Giorgio Sacerdoti, "Precedent in the Settlement of International Economic Disputes: The WTO and Investment Arbitration Models" (unpublished, 2011, available at: <http://papers.ssrn.com/sol3/papers.cfm?abstract_id=1931560>); Alec Stone Sweet and Florian Grisel, "Transnational Investment Arbitration—From Delegation to Constitutionalization?" in *Human Rights in International Investment Law and Arbitration*, edited by Pierre-Marie Dupuy, Francesco Francioni, and Ernst-Ulrich Petersmann (Oxford: Oxford University Press, 2009).

[71] Documented in Alec Stone Sweet and Florian Grisel, "Transnational Investment Arbitration—From Delegation to Constitutionalization?" in *Human Rights in International Investment Law and Arbitration*, edited by Pierre-Marie Dupuy, Francesco Francioni, and Ernst-Ulrich Petersmann (Oxford: Oxford University Press, 2009).

[72] Gus Van Harten and Martin Loughlin, "Investment Treaty Arbitration as a Species of Global Administrative Law," *European Journal of International Law*, Vol. 17(1) (2006), pp.121–150; Benedict Kingsbury and Stephan W. Schill, "Investor-State Arbitration as Governance: Fair and Equitable Treatment, Proportionality and the Emerging Global Administrative Law," NYU School of Law, Public Law Research Paper No. 09–46 (2009).

awards.[73] A related empirical question that deserves greater attention concerns the extent to which ISA and ICA influence one another. Many have noted that ISA has drawn heavily from ICA, in the first instance,[74] but will the more extensive judicialization of ISA impact institution-building in ICA? As this volume attests, judicialization has transformed both practice and scholarly debates about arbitration's nature and purpose.

---

[73] Anthea Roberts, "Clash of Paradigms: Actors and Analogies Shaping the Investment Treaty System," *American Journal of International Law*, Vol. 107(1) (2013), pp.45–94.

[74] See Roberts, note 72, *supra*.

3

Roles and Role Perceptions of International Arbitrators

Ralf Michaels[1]

1 Introduction

International commercial arbitration is a success story in many regards. For the first time in history, an effective system of transnational commercial litigation exists. Moreover, this system exists outside of states (though not, as I will discuss later, truly without the state). As such, international commercial arbitration posits challenges for studies of law and of governance alike. Legal scholars must deal with the existence of a system that is clearly law though it is not state law—and for which, therefore, classical state-based criteria of validity and legitimacy cannot apply. Students of governance must deal with a system that performs powerful governance functions that were traditionally thought to be limited to states and state-based institutions. And yet, precisely for these reasons, the success of international commercial arbitration—and those who profit from it—is by no means certain. Arbitration constantly has to prove anew its own legitimacy and attractivity.

If international arbitration is to be scrutinized as a mode of global governance, it is important to look at its institutions and procedures, but this is not enough. At least as important is an analysis of the relevant actors involved—not necessarily the specific individuals who are active, but their roles with regard to the system of international arbitration, and to society at large. This

[1] This article is based on section II of Ralf Michaels, Rollen und Rollenverständnis im transnationalen Privatrecht (Roles and Role Perceptions in Transnational Private Law), in 45 *Berichte der Deutschen Gesellschaft für Völkerrecht* 175–227 (2012). Thanks to Diana Schawlowski, JD/LL.M. (Duke, 2014), for drafting a translation. Comments from Jan Kleinheisterkamp and Anne Peters on the German text have been helpful, as have been those by Thomas Dietz, Rachael D. Kent, Walter Mattli, Moritz Renner, Catherine A. Rogers, and Stacie I. Strong on the English version.

includes particular attention to their roles—both the roles that they play, and the perceptions that they have of their roles.

An analysis of such roles is interesting for at least three reasons. The first concerns the relation between roles and role perceptions on the one hand, and epistemic communities and disciplinary identity on the other. Disciplinary identities, that of international commercial arbitration included, are closely linked to epistemic communities: the way in which the members of arbitration define their field becomes the definition of the field at large. Such epistemic communities in turn rest on, and at the same time reinforce, certain roles played by their members.

A second interest in roles is that changes in an institution like international arbitration can most effectively be observed in the changing roles of actors within it. For example, the much-described professionalization of international arbitration is really, at its roots, a change in the roles of arbitration practitioners. The new debate on an ethical code for international arbitrators puts at the center of its analysis what these actors do and what they should be doing—in other words, their roles.

But roles do not only change over time; they are also in tension with each other. Such tensions provide the third, and most fruitful, attraction of a focus on roles. It is through such tensions that we can observe most closely the uncertain position that international commercial arbitration holds in today's world. In particular, I am interested in three types of contrasts. The first contrast exists between a national and a transnational role: To what extent is the arbitration lawyer a member of her state, and to what extent is she a member of a transnational arbitration community? The second contrast exists between the roles of counsel, arbitrator, academic, and visionary. Here, the questions are whether these roles overlap, whether they can be fulfilled by the same actors, and whether they are in conflict with each other. Finally, the third contrast concerns the relation between a public and a private role. Does the arbitration practitioner feel obliged toward the clients or toward society at large? Does he perform a private service, or is he a global governor? How private is the arbitration practitioner; how private can he be?

Such questions belong, ordinarily, to the field of sociology. And indeed, insofar as my text ventures into sociology, it can rely on a number of existing studies, first and foremost of them obviously the work by Yves Dezalay and Bryant Garth.[2] Moreover, insofar as I focus on the roles actors play, an

---

[2] Yves Dezalay and Bryant G. Garth, *Dealing in Virtue: International Commercial Arbitration and the Construction of a Transnational Legal Order* (Chicago: University of Chicago Press, 1996); summarized in part in Yves Dezalay and Bryant G. Garth, "Marketing and Selling Transnational 'Judges' and Global 'Experts': Building the Credibility of (Quasi) judicial Regulation," *Socio-Economic Review* 8, no. 1 (January 2010): pp. 113–130, at pp. 118–121.

obvious inspiration lies in role theory.[3] Methodologically, however, I take a different path from typical sociological studies. Instead of empirical studies or interviews, I am interested in the relation between responses to doctrinal questions[4] and what they reveal about the relevant roles.[5] Legal doctrine and the roles played by actors in arbitration are in an interplay—legal doctrine shapes the roles played by actors; the roles of actors in turn are reflected in positions of legal actors. Moreover, it is in doctrinal positions that legal actors must take a stance for or against a viewpoint, because consequences ensue. The law of international commercial arbitration raises a number of fundamental questions, and although their relations to the respective roles are rarely made obvious, they can be shown quite forcefully.

Such an approach should, I hope, be helpful to legal scholars and social scientists alike. Social scientists have recently shown a greatly increased interest in the functioning of the law in general, and of international commercial arbitration in particular. However, their willingness to grapple with actual doctrinal rules and discussions is still relatively limited. Without attention to such discussions, however, any analysis of a legal institution must be incomplete, because it is incapable of grasping the precise ways in which participants negotiate their respective positions. On the other hand, legal scholars, particularly in the area of international commercial arbitration, often tend to either confine their studies to doctrinal analysis, or to link such analysis with very vague and utopian theoretical concepts. Studies that combine both legal and extra-legal analysis are still rare; I hope my paper can provide a helpful combination of the two.

I limit my study to international commercial arbitration. This means, in particular, that I do not discuss investment arbitration, which, although equally fascinating, would in part raise different issues that would go beyond the scope of this chapter.

2 National Citizen and Global Citizen

I first focus on the arbitration lawyer's position between adherence to the nation state and globalization—between the roles of national citizen and global citizen. This issue can be approached using either a more doctrinal or a more sociological method.

---

[3] B.J. Biddle, "Recent Development in Role Theory," *Annual Review of Sociology* 12, no. 1 (1986): pp. 67–92.

[4] By "doctrine" I mean legal doctrine.

[5] For another link with sociological theory and jurisprudential thought, see Catherine A. Rogers, "The Vocation of the International Arbitrator," *American University International Law Review* 20, no. 5 (2005): pp. 957–1020.

2.1 Doctrine: the Transnational Regime of International Arbitration

Doctrinally, the tension between national and global identities is reflected in a number of individual questions. First and foremost among these is the question of the legal relevance of the seat *supra* of the arbitral tribunal.[6] For instance, according to a traditional position, the applicable substantive law shall be determined based on the choice of law rules of the seat country. Newer approaches, by contrast, suggest that the arbitrator shall determine the adequate choice of law rule autonomously,[7] or even determine the applicable law directly (*"voie directe"*), under exclusion of all choice of law rules.[8] A similar question is whether the procedure must conform to the law of the seat or whether procedure rules can be freely chosen by the parties or the arbitrator.[9] Yet another doctrinal question is whether the annulment of an arbitral award by the courts of the seat bars subsequent recognition of the award by foreign courts.[10]

---

[6] Another area in which national and global identity compete is the recognition of arbitral awards. This is so, for example, for attempts to complement or replace the traditional understanding of the order public as a national conflict of laws principle with an ordre public of a national or transnational nature. See, in particular: Norbert Horn, "Die Entwicklung des internationalen Wirtschaftsrechts durch Verhaltensrichtlinien. Elemente eines internationalen ordre public," *Rabels Zeitschrift für ausländisches und internationales Privatrecht* 44 (1980): pp. 423–454; Pierre Lalive, "Ordre public transnational (ou réellement international) et arbitrage international," *Revue de l'arbitrage* 1986, no. 4, pp. 329–371; Pierre Lalive, "L'ordre public transnational et l'arbitre international," in *Liber Amicorum Fausto Pocar*, vol. II (Milan: Giuffrè, 2009), pp. 599–611; comprehensively, Lotfi Chedly, *Arbitrage commercial international et ordre public transnational* (Tunis: Centre de Publications Universitaires, 2002); Richard Kreindler, "Approaches to the Application of Transnational Public Policy by Arbitrators," *Journal of World Investment* 4, no. 2 (2003): pp. 239–250.

[7] Berthold Goldman, "Les conflits de lois dans l'arbitrage international de droit privé," *Recueil des Cours* 109 (1963): pp. 347–486.

[8] *Nouveau Code de Procédure Civile*, Art. 1496; International Chamber of Commerce, *Rules of Arbitration*, Art. 17(1); cf. Gary B. Born, *International Commercial Arbitration* (The Hague: Kluwer Law International, 2009), pp. 21–23; In reality, the *voie directe* is necessarily a choice of law norm, which is not clearly labeled: Christian von Bar and Peter Mankowski, *Internationales Privatrecht* (Munich: Verlag C.H. Beck, 2003), § 5 Rn 74; differently, but based on a too narrow understanding of choice of law norms, Boris Handorn, *Das Sonderkollisionsrecht der deutschen internationalen Schiedsgerichtsbarkeit—Zur Bestimmung des anwendbaren materiellen Rechts gemäß § 1051 Abs. 1 und 2 Zivilprozessordnung* (Tübingen: Mohr Siebeck, 2005), p. 121.

[9] European Convention on International Commercial Arbitration, Art. IV(4)(d).

[10] Especially *Pabalk Ticaret Sirketic v. Norsolor* (Cass 1ᵉ Civ, 9 October 1984), *Revue de l'arbitrage* 1985, 431; Oberster Gerichtshof (Austria) (20.10.1993), SZ 66 Nr. 131 (p. 280); see also Ralf Michaels, "Anerkennung internationaler Schiedssprüche und ordre public," *Zeitschrift für Rechtsvergleichung* 40 No. 1 (1999): pp. 5–8; *Hilmarton v. OTV* (Cass 1ᵉ Civ, 23 March 1994), *Revue de l'arbitrage* 1994, 327, with note by C. Jarrosson; *Chromalloy Aeroservices v. Arab Republic of Egypt*, 939 F.Supp.907 (D.D.C. 1996); further decisions in Claudia Alfons, *Recognition and Enforcement of Annulled Foreign Arbitral Awards* (Frankfurt: Peter Lang, 2010), pp. 82–118; comprehensively, Dennis Solomon, *Die Verbindlichkeit von Schiedssprüchen in der internationalen privaten Schiedsgerichtsbarkeit. Zur Bedeutung nationaler Rechtsordnungen und der Entscheidungen nationaler Gerichte für die Wirksamkeit internationaler Schiedssprüche* (Munich: Sellier European Law Publishers, 2007); Hamid G. Gharavi, *The International Effectiveness of the Annulment of an Arbitral Award* (The Hague: Kluwer Law International, 2002); Solomon, *Die Verbindlichkeit*, p. 275, characterizes this question as "paradigm of the integration of the arbitral award into the legal system of the state where the arbitration took place" (my translation).

These positions are obviously of practical relevance. Here, however, I am less interested in their practical consequences and more in what these positions tell us about the role of the arbitral tribunal that underlies the respective position. Behind the doctrinal question of the extent to which the law of the seat (or that of the recognition state) is applicable to the arbitration and the arbitral award stands the question of the arbitrator's role: To what extent is he integrated in the legal system of the seat country? To what extent is he a national actor?

F.A. Mann, probably the last strict proponent of a necessary application of the law of the seat, argues from the proposition that the so-called international arbitral tribunal's role is in reality necessarily a national one: "In the legal sense, no international commercial arbitration exists . . . every arbitration is a national arbitration, that is to say, subject to a specific system of national law."[11] This view is now almost universally rejected; international arbitral awards are widely viewed as being delocalized or denationalized.[12] Necessarily, this view on the nature of the award extends to the role of the arbitrator: he is now similarly denationalized.

If the seat country is largely irrelevant, the question of what should fill its place remains. Proposals to delink the arbitral award from all legal systems and to submit it solely to the agreement of the parties ("*contrat sans loi*") have not been successful:[13] neither theoretically nor practically can a contract, which is necessarily incomplete, exist outside all law. Similar problems arise with a "floating" arbitral award—an award which floats above legal systems awaiting integration into one of these systems.[14] Instead, it has been proposed to integrate the arbitrator either into public international law[15] (which, as public law, is an imperfect fit) or into an autonomous legal system, based

[11] F.A. Mann, "Lex Facit Arbitrum," in *International Arbitration—Liber Amicorum for Martin Domke*, edited by Pieter Sanders (The Hague: Martinus Nijhoff, 1967), p. 159.

[12] Pierre Mayer, "The Trend Towards Delocalization in the Last 100 Years," in *The Internationalisation of International Arbitration*, edited by Martin Hunter, V.V. Veeder, and Arthur Marriott (London: Graham and Trotman, 1995), p. 37; Thilo Rensmann, *Anationale Schiedssprücke. Eine Untersuchung zu den Wirkungen anationaler Schiedssprüche im nationalen Recht* (Berlin: Duncker und Humblot, 1997), pp. 360–362; Emmanuel Gaillard, *Aspects philosophiques du droit de l'arbitrage international, Recueil des Cours* 329 (2008), pp. 49–216; Emmanuel Gaillard, *Legal Theory of International Arbitration* (Leiden: Martinus Nijhof, 2010); see also Jan Paulsson, "Arbitration in Three Dimensions," *International and Comparative Law Quarterly* 60 (2011): pp. 291–323.

[13] On the contrat sans loi, see Jean-Paul Béraudo, "Faut-il avoir peur du contrat sans loi?," in *Le droit international privé: Esprit et méthodes: Mélanges en l'honneur de Paul Lagarde* (Paris: Dalloz, 2006), pp. 93–112; Léna Gannagé, "Le contrat sans loi en droit international privé," *Electronic Journal of Comparative Law* 11.3 (December 2007), <http://www.ejcl.org/113/article113-10.pdf>.

[14] See Jan Paulsson, "Arbitration Unbound: Award Detached from the Law of its Country of Origin," *International and Comparative Law Quarterly* 30, no. 2 (April 1981): pp. 358–387. Wai has accurately described this situation as "transnational lift–off": Robert Wai, "Transnational Liftoff and Juridical Touchdown: The Regulatory Function of Private International Law in an Era of Globalization," *Columbia Journal of Transnational Law* 40, no. 2 (2002): pp. 209–274.

[15] Charalambos N. Fragistas, "Arbitrage étranger et arbitrage international en droit privé," *Revue critique de droit international privé* (1960): pp. 1–20.

either on the totality of existing systems or created by international commercial arbitration itself. Such proposals imply what Mann thought to be logically impossible,[16] namely a genuinely international arbitral award: "la sentence internationale, qui n'est rattachée à aucun ordre juridique étatique, est une décision de justice internationale."[17]

The denationalization and transnationalization of arbitration concern not only the nature of the arbitral award; they also influence the role of the actors, especially that of the arbitrator. If the arbitral award is denationalized, then, functionally, the same is true for the arbitrator: he ceases to be part of a national state and instead becomes integrated in a "global adjudication system."[18] The arbitrator is no longer obliged toward his or any other national state, nor only toward the parties themselves. Instead, he adopts a transnational role within a transnational system into which he is integrated.

2.2 Sociology: International Arbitration as Cosmopolitan Community

This doctrinal analysis is mirrored by sociological analysis. Here, the question is whether the relevant epistemic community, to which the arbitrator belongs and which influences him,[19] is primarily a national or a transnational community. Quite clearly we can speak of a transnational community of international arbitration practitioners.[20] International arbitration fulfills all criteria traditionally listed for an epistemic community.[21] We find a shared set of normative and principled beliefs in the superiority of private over state-based adjudication.

[16] Mann, "Lex Facit."
[17] "An international award that is not attached to any state's legal order is a decision of international justice." *Société PT Putrabali Adyamulia v. Société Rena Holding et Société Mnogutia Est Epices* (Cass 1ᵉ Civ, 29 June 2007), Revue de l'arbitrage 2007, 507, praised as a contribution to general legal theory by Emmanuel Gaillard, "La jurisprudence de la Cour de Cassation en matiére d'arbitrage international," *Revue de l'arbitrage* no. 4 (2007): pp. 697, 700. See already *Hilmarton v. OTV* (Cass 1ᵉ Civ, 23 March 1994), Revue de l'arbitrage 1994, 327, 328 with note by C. Jarrosson: "la sentence rendue en Suisse était une sentence internationale qui nétait pas intégrée dans l'ordre juridique de cet Etat." ("the award rendered in Switzerland was an international award that was not integrated into the legal order of that State." My translation.)
[18] Charles N. Brower, Charles H. Brower II, and Jeremy K. Sharpe, "The Coming Crisis in the Global Adjudication System," *Arbitration International* 19, no. 4 (2003): pp. 415–440.
[19] On this, see Katherine Lynch, *The Forces of Economic Globalization: Challenges to the Regime of International Commercial Arbitration* (The Hague: Kluwer Law International, 2003), pp. 94–104; Gabriele Kaufmann-Kohler, "Soft Law in International Arbitration: Codification and Normativity," *Journal of International Dispute Settlement* 1 (2010): pp. 283–299, at p. 295.
[20] Lynch, *Economic Globalization*, pp. 99–100; Thomas Schultz, "Secondary Rules of Recognition and Relative Legality in Transnational Regimes," *American Journal of Jurisprudence* 56 (September 2011): pp. 59–88; Joshua Karton, *The Culture of Arbitration and the Evolution of Contract Law* (Oxford: Oxford University Press, 2013), pp. 21–24; But cf. Reza Banakar, "Reflexive Legitimacy in International Arbitration," in *Emerging Legal Certainty: Empirical Studies on the Globalization of Law*, edited by Volkmar Gessner and Ali Cem Budak (Farnham: Ashgate Publishing Ltd., 1998), pp. 391ff.
[21] Peter M. Haas, "Introduction: Epistemic Communities and International Policy Coordination," *International Organization* 46, no. 1 (Winter 1992): pp. 1–35, at p. 3.

We find agreement on a central set of problems, in particular autonomy from the state on the one hand, the need for due process principles on the other. We find shared notions of validity—in principle—on the doctrinal treatment of problems, regardless of the applicable national law.[22] And we find a common policy enterprise: to make international arbitration more and more autonomous.[23] A transnational character is here a prerequisite of all these factors: the community is required to constitute itself as transnational in order to exist.

The role of the international arbitrator is therefore necessarily a transnational one. International arbitrators are often quite neatly separated from domestic arbitrators—organizationally (at least in US firms) and also intellectually; it is claimed that "[i]nternational arbitration is no more a 'type' of arbitration than a sea elephant is a type of elephant."[24] Differences within this group are significantly less pronounced than differences between the group and its environment. This does not contradict the conflict, described by Dezalay and Garth, between the older European type of arbitrator as "amateur" and the newer US-type of arbitrator as "professional".[25] That conflict is more a generational than a geographical one. The oft-described Americanization of international arbitration[26] has led to a convergence, but the arbitrator is not specifically American: he is cosmopolitan.[27]

This international community of arbitration lawyers is still relatively small and isolated—at least for large arbitration proceedings.[28] The majority of significant international arbitration proceedings are handled by a remarkably small number of repeat players: "a group of 'professional' arbitrators who, forming an exclusive club in the international arena, are automatically

---

[22] See Bruno Oppetit, *Théorie de l'arbitrage* (Paris: Presses Universitaires de France, 1998), pp. 113–114 ("par osmose, les idées, les pratiques, les jurisprudences, avant même les législations nationales et les conventions internationales, ont progressivement convergés . . . vers un consensus sur des principes, souvent très proches, d'organisation et de fonctionnement.") ("by osmosis, ideas, practices, jurisprudence, even before national laws and international conventions, have gradually converged . . . towards a consensus on principles, often a very close one, of organization and operation." My translation.)

[23] This does not rule out other goals, like the goal to make arbitration more efficient and effective, and for that purpose to rely on state courts.

[24] Jan Paulsson, "International Arbitration is not Arbitration," *Stockholm International Arbitration Review* 2 (2008): pp. 1–20.

[25] Dezalay and Garth, *Dealing in Virtue*, p. 52; Lynch, *Economic Globalization*, pp. 100–101; see infra section (b).

[26] Lucy Reed and Jonathan Sutcliffe, "The 'Americanization' of International Arbitration?" *Mealy's International Arbitration Report* 16 (2001): pp. 36ff; Roger P. Alford, "The Americanization of International Arbitration," *Ohio State Journal on Dispute Resolution* 19 (2003): pp. 69–88; Eric Bergsten, "The Americanization of International Arbitration," *Pace International Law Review* 18 (2005): pp. 289–301; Pedro J. Martinez-Fraga, *The American Influence on International Commercial Arbitration—Doctrinal Developments and Discovery Methods* (Cambridge: Cambridge University Press, 2009); Siegfried H. Elsing, "Incoming Tide: Die Rezeption angloamerikanischen Rechts in der Schiedsgerichtsbarkeit," *Deutscher Anwaltsspiegel* (August 5, 2010): p. 22.

[27] Shahla Ali, *Resolving Disputes in the Asia Pacific Region: International Arbitration and Mediation in East Asia and the West* (Oxford: Routledge, 2010).

[28] Rogers, "*Vocation.*"

brought into almost any major dispute by the operation of predetermined methods."[29] This group is referred to as a caste,[30] a cartel, a club, or even a gang[31] or mafia[32]—a term even used by insiders.[33] International arbitration can be compared to a cartel insofar as its participants attempt two things: they divide up proceedings and mandates among each other and, at the same time, make access for outsiders difficult. As in a guild, membership is still sometimes tied to an apprenticeship with an existing member of the club.[34]

Participation in this community requires a transnational identity. The typical international arbitrator is cosmopolitan;[35] he speaks at least English and French and frequently additional languages,[36] and appears worldwide. His national origin is frequently regarded as a handicap and may preclude him from proceedings in which his compatriots are parties. His origin and education greatly affect his ability to handle culture-specific institutes of procedural law, an area of the law marked by differences between legal cultures that are far greater than within material law. Klaus Peter Berger, for instance, identifies ten principles of German law, which inform the practice of German lawyers in German civil procedure, and, in turn, contradict the nature of international arbitration.[37] In international arbitration, national identity is ideally replaced by the function-specific

---

[29] Iran–United States, Case No. A/18, 5 Iran–U.S. Claims Tribunal Reporter 251, 336 (1984) ("an exclusive club in the international arena"), cited in Detlev F. Vagts, "The International Legal Profession. A Need for More Governance?," *American Journal of International Law* 90 (1996): pp. 250–261; cf. the quotes in Dezalay and Garth, *Dealing in Virtue*, p. 50.

[30] Thomas Clay, "Qui sont les arbitres internationaux? Approche sociologique," in *Les arbitres internationaux*, edited by J. Rosell (2005), pp. 13–32, at pp. 22–23.

[31] Clay, *Arbitres Internationaux*, pp. 22–23.

[32] Rogers, "Vocation," p. 967.

[33] See the quotes in Dezalay and Garth, *Dealing in Virtue*, p. 50 ("Now why is it a mafia? It's a mafia because people appoint one another. You always appoint your friends—people you know.") and Shahla Ali, *Resolving Disputes*, p. 92 ("You've heard about the 'arbitration mafia,' the self-perpetuating oligarchy which fortunately I seem to be a member of . . ."); According to Michael McIlwrath and John Savage, *International Arbitration and Mediation: A Practical Guide* (The Hague: Kluwer Law International, 2010), p. 255, MAFIA stands for Mutual Association For International Arbitration; critically against the term, see Jan Paulsson, "Ethics, Elitism, Eligibility," *Journal of International Arbitration* 14, no. 4 (1996): pp. 13–21, at pp. 19–20.

[34] Pierre Lalive, "Sécrétaire de Tribunaux Arbitraux—Le bon sens l'emporte," *ASA Bulletin* (1989): p. 1; Charles Brower, "W(h)ither International Commercial Arbitration?," *Arbitration International* 24 (2008): pp. 181–198, at pp. 191–192.

[35] For some individual portraits, see Dezalay and Garth, *Dealing in Virtue*, p. 139.

[36] Rogers, "Vocation," p. 958; Clay, *Arbitres Internationaux*, pp. 28–29.

[37] Klaus Peter Berger, "The International Arbitrator's Dilemma: Transnational Procedure versus Home Jurisdiction," *Arbitration International* 25 (2009): pp. 217–238; cf. Laurence Shore, "Arbitration, Rhetoric, Proof: The Unity of International Arbitration Across Cultures," in *Contemporary Issues in International Arbitration and Mediation: The Fordham Papers 2009*, edited by Arthur W. Rovine (Leiden: Koninklijke, 2010), p. 293. For accounts limited to legal rules, see Guillermo Aguilar Alvarez, "To What Extent Do Arbitrators in International Cases Disregard the Bag and Baggage of National Systems?," in *International Dispute Resolution: Towards an International Arbitration Culture*, edited by Albert Jan van den Berg (ICCA Congress Series no. 8, 1996), pp. 139–156; Malcolm Wilkey, "The Practicalities of Cross–Cultural Arbitration," in *Conflicting Legal Cultures in Commercial Arbitration: Old Issues and New Trends*, edited by Stefan N. Frommel and Barry A.K. Rider (The Hague: Kluwer Law International, 1999), pp. 79–97.

identity of the international arbitrator.[38] Yet, while discarding his own cultural identity, the arbitrator is asked to retain sensitivity for the parties' cultural backgrounds[39]—an almost impossible combination between being color-blind and being sensitive to different colors.[40] Asian arbitrators, according to a new study, value familiarity and mediation much more than their Western counterparts.[41] However, this purportedly transnational paradigm largely embodies Western principles; the cultural differences discussed are largely those within Western law, between civil law and common law.[42]

This transnational epistemic community does not emerge spontaneously; it requires active promotion. Numerous international conferences bring practitioners from all over the world into almost constant dialogue. The roots are set at a young age: The Vis International Commercial Arbitration Moot Court, for instance, the most important moot court for international arbitration, requires teams from various countries to be able in particular to switch between common law and civil law.[43] Hence, the transnationalization of future professionals is thus actively promoted. Also, the international litigation and arbitration departments of large law firms are highly diverse and encourage close cooperation between their various offices; young practitioners are commonly "loaned" to other offices or even to foreign law firms. The most striking evidence of the international arbitrator's transnational identity, however, lies in scholarship. Leading textbooks from various countries—Germany, USA, even

[38] Yasuhei Taniguchi, "Is There a Growing International Arbitration Culture? An Observation from Asia," in *International Dispute Resolution*, edited by van den Berg, pp. 38–40; Giorgio Bernini, "Is There a Growing International Arbitration Culture?," in *International Dispute Resolution*, edited by van den Berg, p. 44; Bernardo M. Cremades, "Overcoming the Clash of Legal Cultures: The Role of Interactive Arbitration," in *Conflicting Legal Cultures*, edited by Frommel and Rider, p. 165; Karl-Heinz Böckstiegel, "Past, Present, and Future Perspectives of Arbitration," *Arbitration International* 25 (2009): pp. 293–302, at p. 301.

[39] Ibrahim Fadlallah, "Arbitration Facing Conflicts of Culture," *Arbitration International* 25 (2009): pp. 303–317.

[40] Giorgio Bernini recommends "a pragmatic approach," not a very concrete proposal: "Is there a Growing International Arbitration Culture?," in *International Dispute Resolution*, edited by van den Berg, p. 43.

[41] Jonathon Crook, "Leading Arbitration Seats in the Far East: A Comparative View," in *Conflicting Legal Cultures in Commercial Arbitration: Old Issues and New Trends*, edited by Stefan N. Frommel and Barry A.K. Rider (The Hague: Kluwer Law International, 1999), p. 63; see also comprehensively Shahla F. Ali, *Resolving Disputes in the Asia-Pacific Region*.

[42] *Christian Borris*, "The Reconciliation of Conflicts between Common Law and Civil Law Principles in the Arbitration Process," in *Conflicting Legal Cultures in Commercial Arbitration*, edited by Frommel and Rider, pp. 1–18; see Thomas E. Carbonneau, "Judicial Approbation in Building the Civilization of Arbitration," in *Building the Civilization of Arbitration*, edited by Thomas E. Carbonneau and Angelica M. Sinopole (London: Wildy, Simmonds and Hill, 2010), p. 333.

[43] See Pace University School of Law, "The Annual Willem C. Vis International Commercial Arbitration Moot," accessed October 21, 2013, <http://www.cisg.law.pace.edu/vis.html>: "In the pairings of teams for each general round of the forensic and written exercises, every effort is made to have civil law schools argue against common law schools—so each may learn from approaches taken by persons trained in another legal culture. Similarly, the teams of arbitrators judging each round are from both common law and civil law backgrounds." See also Daniel Girsberger, "Internationale Schiedsgerichtsbarkeit: Ausbildung durch Moot Courts," in *Festschrift für Franz Kellerhals zum 65. Geburtstag*, edited by Greiner, Berger, and Güngerich (Berne: Stämpfli Verlag, 2005), pp. 23–33.

France—contain numerous references to different legal systems,[44] and are expressly comparative[45] or even effectively transnational; [46] many of them exist in English translations in addition to the original language.[47]

This promotion of transnationalism is not mere luxury. Such an epistemic community serves the interest of the international arbitration community: it strengthens, despite all existing competition, the internal cohesion of the arbitration world and thus also its ability to resist interventions by the states. In addition, this makes it possible to avoid the criticism sometimes brought forward against national arbitration. National arbitration may look like an evasion of access to national courts. International arbitration, by contrast, is described as necessary because international state courts do not exist.[48] Within international arbitration, actors compete. As against the external world, however, the community has a common goal to make international arbitration legitimate and indispensable.

2.3 *Excursus: Limits of Transnationalization of National Courts*

Now, transnationalization of the law has become a general trait of legal discussions, and one could conclude that international arbitration is merely a phenomenon of this more general development. On closer analysis, this is not the case: Domestic courts in most countries cannot keep up with the transnationalization of law. Admittedly, courts begin to transnationalize, too, especially through networks.[49] However, such tendencies are mostly limited to situations in which international agreement either exists or is to be created. Where such agreement does not exist, domestic courts refuse to act as

---

[44] E.g. Andrew Tweeddale and Karen Tweeddale, *Arbitration of Commercial Disputes: International and English Law and Practice* (New York: Oxford University Press, 2007) (with limits); Fouchard, Gaillard, and Goldman (eds.), *Traité de l'arbitrage commercial international* (Paris: Litec, 1996); Mauro Rubino-Sammartano, *International Arbitration Law and Practice* (The Hague: Kluwer Law International, 2001).

[45] Jean-François Poudret and Sébastien Besson, *Droit comparé de l'arbitrage* (Brussels, Bruylant/LGDJ/Schulthess, 2003); Julian D.M. Lew, Loukas A. Mistelis, and Stefan M. Kröll, *Comparative International Commercial Arbitration* (The Hague: Kluwer Law International, 2003).

[46] Especially Born, *International Commercial Arbitration*.

[47] For example, René David, *Arbitration in International Trade* (New York: Springer, 1985) (originally French); Klaus Peter Berger, *International Economic Arbitration* (Deventer/Boston: Kluwer Law and Taxation Publishers, 1993) (originally German); Emmanuel Gaillard and John Savage, *Fouchard Gaillard Goldman on International Arbitration* (The Hague: Kluwer Law International, 1999) (expanded from the French edition); Jean-François Poudret and Sébastien Besson, *Comparative Law of International Arbitration* (New York: Thomson/Sweet and Maxwell, 2007) (originally French); Rubino-Sammartano, *International Arbitration Law and Practice* (originally Italian).

[48] Paulsson, "International Arbitration is not Arbitration," pp. 3–4.

[49] See, for example, Anne-Marie Slaughter, "Court to Court," *American Journal of International Law* 92 (1998): pp. 708–808; Michael Kirby, "Transnational Judicial Dialogue, Internationalisation of Law and Australian Judges," *Melbourne Journal of International Law* 9 (2008): pp. 178–189, at p. 173. Critically now Paul Stephan, "Courts on Courts: Contracting for Engagement and Indifference in International Judicial Encounters," *Virginia Law Review* 100 (2014–2015).

bodies of the world community; they limit their regulatory reach out of respect for other states. Thus, the US Supreme Court recently abstained from applying US laws on securities liability beyond US borders.[50] Earlier, the Court limited the application of antitrust liability law to sales in the US[51]—another decision that was commended in Germany.[52] This abstention from regulation can be justified only if other regulators step in to avoid under-regulation. The Court, however, does not even mention this question.[53] Thus, transnationalization leads to restraints on courts, not to an expansion of the scope of their action. The alternative of unilateral application of domestic law as a kind of global governance[54] is, apparently, considered inappropriate.[55]

In this sense, the transnationalization of adjudication is left largely to arbitration practice. A competition between arbitration and domestic courts does not emerge. Quite to the contrary, states aim to appear friendly toward arbitration.[56] Such support of arbitration is seen as a competitive advantage vis-à-vis other states.[57] A US court gladly concedes: "The utility of the [New York] Convention [on the Recognition and Enforcement of Foreign Arbitral Awards] in promoting the process of international commercial arbitration depends upon the willingness of national courts to let go of matters they normally would think of as their own."[58] Competition with international arbitration does not take place.[59] Attempts in Germany to enable court proceedings in

[50] *Morrison v. National Australia Bank Ltd*, 130 S. Ct. 2869, 2880 (2010).

[51] *F. Hoffmann-LaRoche Ltd. v. Empagran S.A.*, 542 U.S. 155 (2004).

[52] For references and discussion, see Ralf Michaels and Daniel Zimmer, "US–Gerichte als Weltkartellgerichte?," *Praxis des Internationalen Privatrechts* 24 (2004): pp. 451–457.

[53] Ralf Michaels, "Empagran's Empire: International Law and Statutory Interpretation in the U.S. Supreme Court of the Twenty-First Century," in *International Law in the U.S. Supreme Court—Continuity and Change*, edited by David L. Sloss, Michael D. Ramsey, and William S. Dodge (Cambridge: Cambridge University Press, 2011), p. 541.

[54] Ralf Michaels, "Global Problems in Domestic Courts," in *The Law of the Future and the Future of Law*, edited by Sam Muller, Stavros Zouridis, Morly Frishman, and Laura Kistemaker (Oslo: Torkel Opsahl, 2011), pp. 167–177.

[55] See Tonya Putnam, "Courts Without Borders: Domestic Sources of US Extraterritoriality in the Regulatory Sphere," *International Organization* 63 (2009): pp. 459–490.

[56] See Catherine A. Rogers, "Fit and Function in Legal Ethics: Developing a Code of Conduct for International Arbitration," *Michigan Journal of International Law* 23 (2002): pp. 341–424, at pp. 349–350.

[57] Most recently, for example, Stefan Kröll, "Die Entwicklung des Schiedsrechts 2009–2010," *Neue Juristische Wochenschrift* 64, no. 18 (2011): pp. 1265–1271.

[58] *Baxter International, Inc. v. Abbot Laboratories*, 315 F.3d 829 (U.S. 2003); see the criticism by Richard M. Buxbaum, "Public Policy, Ordre Public and Arbitration: A Procedural Scenario and a Suggestion," in *Resolving International Conflicts: Liber Amicorum Tibor Várady*, edited by Peter Hay et al. (Budapest: CEU Press, 2009), p. 91. See also *SA Thalès Air Defense v. GIE Euromissile* (Cour d'appel Paris, 18 November 2004), *Revue de l'arbitrage* 2005, 751 and the note by Luca Radicati di Brozolo: "L'illicéité qui crève les yeux: critère de contrôle des sentences au regard de l'ordre public international (à propos de l'arrêt Thalès de la Cour d'appel de Paris)," at pp. 529ff; *SNF v. Cytec* (Cass. Civ. 1re, 4 June 2008), *Revue de l'arbitrage* 2008, 473. Thanks for these references are due to Jan Kleinheisterkamp.

[59] In an interview, Emanuel Gaillard, *Juriste d'Entreprise Magazine* no. 3 (July 2009), suggested: "Il n'y a donc aucune rivalité entre l'arbitrage et la justice étatique . . ." ("There is thus no rivalry between arbitration and the state's judiciary . . ." My translation.)

English[60] seem to be directed more against English courts and law than against international arbitration. Instead of competition, what we see is a delimitation of the functions of arbitration and courts. The more arbitration becomes transnationalized, the less pressure and desire seem to exist for state courts to do the same.[61]

Notably, even courts that themselves actively engage in international litigation—most notably courts in London and New York—do not compete with international arbitration. What we find, instead of such competition, is an overlay of functions. In London in particular, this overlay is even personal—judges often also act as arbitrators,[62] thus blurring their roles and making either institutional competition or rigorous judicial oversight rather unlikely.

3 Practice and Scholarship

3.1 *The Arbitration Lawyer as (Law) Dignitary*

I turn now to different professional role models within the world of international arbitration. For a long time—until around the 1970s—international arbitration was dominated by Europeans and was predominantly practical; legal scholarship largely ignored international arbitration. International arbitration was viewed (and advertised) as fundamentally different from national law, almost a kind of non-law: freedom from institutional constraints instead of court bureaucracy, decisions based on equity and practical needs instead of formal legal rules, confidentiality instead of public access to court proceedings, adequate decisions for the individual case instead of system of precedent and stare decisis, maximum procedural flexibility instead of formal legal remedies, speed, and low costs.[63] Arbitral awards were fulfilled not because of a legal obligation or fear of enforcement (which was extremely difficult in many countries before the New York Convention); rather, they were fulfilled as a matter of honor.[64]

---

[60] Gralf-Peter Calliess and Hermann B. Hoffmann, "Judicial Services for Global Commerce—Made in Germany?," *German Law Journal* 10 (2009): pp. 115–122; Hermann Hoffmann, *Kammern für internationale Handelssachen—Eine juristisch-ökonomische Untersuchung zu effektiven Justizdienstleistungen im Außenhandel* (Baden-Baden: Nomos, 2011), reviewed by Daniel Saam, *German Law Journal* 14 (2013): pp. 949–958.
[61] See also Hermann Hoffmann and Andreas Maurer, "Bedeutungsverlust staatlicher Zivilgerichte—Einem empirischen Nachweis auf der Spur," *Zeitschrift für Rechtssoziologie* 31 (2010): p. 279.
[62] *British Arbitration Act of 1996*, §93. In New York, the State Constitution, in §20(b)(4), bars judges from serving as arbitrators. A 2009 Delaware law that allowed Court of Chancery judges to preside over secret arbitration in business was declared unconstitutional insofar as access by public and press were barred. *Delaware Coalition for Open Government v. Strine*, 894 F.Supp.2d 493 (D.Del. 2012), affirmed, 733 F.3d 510 (C.A.3, 2013).
[63] Rogers, "Fit and Function," p. 350.
[64] Thus still Art. XX of the first edition of the International Chamber of Commerce's *Rules of Arbitration* (1923).

In such a system, the role of the arbitrator is not necessarily a specifically juridical one; credibility, personal integrity and an understanding of commercial and technical issues are more important than legal competence.[65] In this vein, Ottoarndt Glossner described the role of the arbitrator as follows:

> To be an arbitrator is to exercise an honourable function. It is no profession . . . [The arbitrator need] not be a lawyer. He can be just as well a technical expert, an engineer, but he must be a person of knowledge and high moral standards. . . . It is only natural that the parties listen more intensely to somebody who speaks to them from a higher elevation of experience, knowledge, reputation. To be an arbitrator is a noble task, which challenges the whole personality, all of its intellectual and physical capacities.[66]

If legal competence was relatively unimportant, why were jurists particularly well equipped to play the role of the arbitrator? As legal dignitaries, to use Weber's terminology, jurists enjoyed the necessary legitimacy in the Continental European tradition.[67] This is especially the case, at least in Europe, for professors and federal judges.[68] Dezalay and Garth describe how the leading international arbitrators of the older generations came to play these roles rather incidentally; their prestige stems from their positions as "grand old men,"[69] their authority was charismatic.

3.2 The Arbitrator as Professional and Entrepreneur

From about the 1970s onward, this view of the arbitrator as a dignitary began to shift, largely as a result of US practitioners' penetration of the international arbitration market.[70] In the US, arbitration, understood domestically, had for a long time been viewed as a financially and intellectually unattractive field. When the great profitability of international arbitration became evident, a small number of US law firms started to build international arbitration

---

[65] Kenneth S. Carlston, "Psychological and Sociological Aspects of the Judicial and Arbitration Processes," in *Liber Amicorum for Martin Domke*, edited by Peter Sanders, pp. 44, 47–49; Rogers, "Fit and Function," pp. 350–353.

[66] Ottoarndt Glossner, "Sociological Aspects of International Commercial Arbitration," *International Business Lawyer* 10 (1982): pp. 311–314; also in *Liber Amicorum Martin Domke*, edited by Peter Sanders, p. 143.

[67] Dezalay and Garth, *Dealing in Virtue*, pp. 46, 60; for the term, see Max Weber, *On Law in Economy and Society* (Cambridge: Harvard University Press, 1954): pp. 784–808; see also Max Rheinstein, "Die Rechtshonoratioren und ihr Einfluss auf den Charakter der Rechtsordnung," *RabelsZ* 34 (1970).

[68] For a historical-comparative perspective on the role of the jurist in Europe, see also Filippo Ranieri, "Der europäische Jurist – Rechtshistorisches Forschungsthema und rechtspolitische Aufgabe," *Ius Commune* 17 (1990): pp. 9ff.

[69] Dezalay and Garth, *Dealing in Virtue*, pp. 34–37.

[70] Jacques Werner, "International Commercial Arbitrators: From Merchant to Academic to Skilled Professional," *Dispute Resolution Magazine* 4, no. 3 (Spring 1998): pp. 22–24; Klaus Günther, "Anwaltsimperien," *Kursbuch* 155, no. 1 (2004).

departments, albeit with certain peculiar characteristics. First, international arbitration was not linked to national arbitration but to international litigation. The US arbitration practitioner is therefore originally a litigator. Second, US practitioners realized that they could not easily achieve the status of dignitaries that European arbitrators enjoyed and therefore would not be able to compete in the market under current conditions. The market for international arbitration would have to change in a way that would allow their skills to gain new prominence. Hence, the so-called Americanization of international arbitration[71]—the judicialization of international arbitration proceedings, the introduction of US-style procedures, and the tendency toward a more adversarial process—were not just responses to the increased complexity of contracts to be dealt with. Rather, that complexity was in part produced deliberately because it invited devices used to specifically enhance the competitiveness of US practitioners. This change was possible because the relatively informal character of international arbitration had been based largely on a mere tacit agreement, which proved rather powerless against the reforms.

As a result, international arbitration has ceased advertising itself as different from the national courts. Instead, it holds itself to be similar to national law,[72] only better: institutionalized arbitration procedures at the International Chamber of Commerce and others, arbitrators bound by law (especially binding legal rules), legal certainty due to rising (though still unsystematic) publication of arbitral awards, and an emerging system of precedent, standardized procedural rules such as the UNCITRAL Model Rules. The role of informal dispute resolution is now taken over by other forms of "alternative dispute resolution," especially mediation (and arbitration now competes both with state courts and with mediation).

In this system, the modern arbitration practitioner becomes exactly what Glossner opposed: a professional—that is, a professional jurist.[73] His authority is, again in Weber's words, rational; the step toward professionalization arises from Max Weber's classical paradigm.[74] What is expected of the arbitrator is not superior wisdom but effective case management.[75] The fact that Karl-Heinz Böckstiegel is frequently mentioned as a role model in this

---

[71] Dezalay and Garth, *Dealing in Virtue*, p. 52; Lynch, *Economic Globalization*, pp. 100–101.

[72] Richard B. Lillich and Charles N. Brower (eds.), *International Arbitration in the 21st Century: Towards "Judicialization" and Uniformity?* (New York: Transnational Publishers, 1994). See also Rogers, "Fit and Function," pp. 352–354; Susan D. Franck, "The Role of International Arbitrators," *ILSA Journal of International and Comparative Law* 12 (1996): pp. 499–522, at pp. 505–513.

[73] Rogers, "Vocation," pp. 960–961; Klaus-Peter Berger, *Internationale Wirtschaftsschiedsgerichtsbarkeit* (Boston: Kluwer Law and Taxation Publishers, 1993), p. 142–143.

[74] Dezalay and Garth, *Dealing in Virtue*, pp. 46, 60.

[75] Managers are, with slight exaggeration, viewed as a third generation of arbitrators (after "grand old men" and "technocrats"): Thomas Schultz and Robert Kovacs, "The Rise of a Third Generation of Arbitrators? Fifteen Years after Dezalay and Garth," *Arbitration International* 28 (2012): pp. 161–171.

context[76] demonstrates that Europeans have adapted to these new market conditions—also because younger European practitioners began to exert a similar kind of pressure as their US counterparts to value quality of work over reputation.[77] The increasing professionalization of arbitration has brought along demands for concrete ethics codes—demands which started in the 1970s and which have become more pressing to the present day—[78] and for an independent professional association (the International Bar Association).[79]

Simultaneously with its professionalization, international arbitration has shifted toward entrepreneurship:[80] the modern arbitrator is a provider of legal services in a market that is becoming increasingly competitive.[81] The field is no longer the specialty of some elite firms; more and more firms want a part of the business. For party counsel, this development largely corresponds to that of the legal profession more generally. However, the same trend is noticeable for arbitrators, who have no institutionalized position and must seek new mandates continuously. The concern that arbitrators could become biased toward parties likely to reappoint them as repeat players is well known from the national arbitration arena.[82] It seems legitimate for international arbitration as well.[83] The confidentiality of arbitration procedure makes control

---

[76] Gerald Aksen, "On Being a Pro-Active International Arbitrator," in *Liber Amicorum Karl-Heinz Böckstiegel*, edited by Robert Briner et al. (Cologne: Carl Heymanns Verlag, 2001), pp. 13–19.

[77] Berger, *Internationale Wirtschaftsschiedsgerichtsbarkeit*, p. 142 fn; Jan Paulsson, "The Timely Arbitrator: Reflections on the Böckstiegel Method," in *Liber amicorum Karl-Heinz Böckstiegel*, edited by Robert Briner et al., pp. 607–614; David W. Rivkin, "21st Cebrury Arbitration Worthy of its Name," in *Liber Amicorum Karl-Heinz Böckstiegel*, edited by Briner et al., pp. 661–669.

[78] Influentially, Michael Reisman, *Systems of Control in International Adjudication and Arbitration—Breakdown and Repair* (Durham: Duke University Press, 1992). See now Catherine A. Rogers, *Ethics in International Arbitration* (New York: Oxford University Press, 2013).

[79] Rogers, "Vocation," pp. 976–983.

[80] Rogers, "Vocation," pp. 966–967.

[81] Yves Dezalay and Bryant Garth, "Merchants of Law as Moral Entrepreneurs: Constructing International Justice from the Competition for Transnational Business Disputes," *Law and Society Review* 29 (1995): pp. 45ff.; Bernardo Cremades, "International Arbitration: A Key to Economic and Politcal Development," *International Arbitration Law Review* 5 (1999): pp. 145ff.; Lynch, *The Forces of Economic Globalization*, p. 102.

[82] Alexander J. S. Colvin, "An Empirical Study of Employment Arbitration: Case Outcomes and Processes," *Journal of Empirical Legal Studies* 8 (2011): pp. 1–23, at pp. 11–16.

[83] See Christopher R. Drahozal and Richard W. Naimark, *Towards a Science of International Commercial Arbitration: Collected Empirical Research* (New York: Kluwer Law International, 2005), p. 267; Sam Luttrell, *Bias Challenges in International Commercial Arbitration—The Need for a "Real Danger" Test* (Austin: Wolters Kluwer Law and Business, 2009), pp. 5, 86–87; in more detail: Fatima-Zahra Slaoui, "The Rising Issue of 'Repeat Arbitrators': A Call for Clarification," *Arbitration International* 25 (2009): pp. 103–119; Raphaël de Vietri and Kanaga Dharmananda, "Impartiality and the Issue of Repeat Arbitrators—A Reply to Slaoui," *Journal of International Arbitration* 38 (2011): pp. 187–200; Natalia Giraldo-Carrillo, "The 'Repeat Arbitrators' Issue: A Subjective Concept," *International Law, Revista Colombiana de Derecho Internacional* 19 (2011): pp. 75–106. See also *IBA Guidelines on Conflicts of Interest in International Arbitration*, Rule 3.1.3 (Council of the International Bar Association, 2004).

especially difficult.[84] Whether competitive pressures and cooperative efforts can make up for the lack of governmental oversight[85] is an open question.

In the end, this competition is limited by common interests in the practice of international arbitration in two ways. First, competition must not reduce the attractiveness of international arbitration altogether, because the commercial success of arbitration practitioners depends on it.[86] Second, established arbitrators are interested in maintaining their monopoly against newcomers. So far, they seem successful: Although it is sometimes suggested that a cartel can no longer succeed because leadership position can now be traced back to reputation,[87] the same actors continue to appear in the majority of large arbitration procedures. This suggests that the cartel still exists and now uses reputation to keep newcomers out. Thus, one influential practitioner openly propagates to replace the "mafia" with an "elite corps of international arbitrators" which would be open in theory, but in practice would still restrict access[88]—a kind of guild. A recent proposal has been made, in a blog, for a more transparent arbitrator information project, providing information and feedback on arbitrators.[89] Commentators on the blog disagree over whether such a system, which would not serve as an advertising platform, would open up the cartel or, rather, increase the stronghold of those who are already powerful.

3.3 *The Arbitrator as Scholar*

The professionalization of international arbitration does not imply the decrease of scholarship. On the contrary, as international arbitration becomes

---

[84] Slaoui, "Repeat Arbitrators"; Kyriaki Noussia, *Confidentiality in International Commercial Arbitration* (Berlin/New York: Springer, 2010), p. 168.

[85] Thus Catherine A. Rogers, "Transparency in International Commercial Arbitration," 54 *University of Kansas Law Review* 54 (2006): pp. 1301–1337.

[86] Unusually frank, John E. Beerbower, "International Arbitration: Can we Realize the Potential?," *Arbitration International* 17 (2011): pp. 75, 75fn ("[T]here seems to be a belief that international arbitration is facing a crisis of confidence that could jeopardise its pre-eminent status. That belief is a cause of concern for the individuals, firms, organisations and localities that have economic interests in the success and continued growth of arbitration, including lawyers, arbitrators, arbitration associations and administrative bodies and localities that have or hope to become major centres for arbitration proceedings. After all, international arbitration has become a big business (relatively speaking)"). Critical insofar Catherine Kessedjian, "Is Arbitration a Service to Business or to the Legal Profession?," in *The Fordham Papers* 2009, edited by Arthur W. Rovine, pp. 311–312. See also Clay, "Qui sont les arbitres internationaux?," at pp. 22–23. ("La philantropie est absente—ou quasiment—du monde de l'arbitrage alors qu'elle imprègne encore celui de la littérature.") ("Philanthropy is absent—almost—from the world of arbitration, even if it still permeates the world of scholarship." My translation.)

[87] R. Doak Bishop (ed.), *The Art of Advocacy in International Arbitration* (Huntington, NY: Juris Pub., 2004), pp. 3ff, at pp. 5–6.

[88] Paulsson, "Ethics," pp. 13, 19–21.

[89] Catherine A. Rogers, "The International Arbitrator Information Project: From an Ideation to Operation," Kluwer Arbitration Blog, August 10, 2012, <http://kluwerarbitrationblog.com/blog/2012/12/10/the-international-arbitrator-information-project-from-an-ideation-to-operation/>.

more prominent and is increasingly recognized in international treaties, national and model legislation, and national jurisprudence, scholarship in the field becomes more important. The reason lies both in traditional scholars' interest in this new and relevant field and the growing need for legitimization of practice by scholarship.

However, the scholarship that is developing in the area is somewhat curious. Scholarship on international commercial arbitration is predominantly positive and aims at greater efficiency and autonomy; sharply critical perspectives (which are common in writings on domestic arbitration, especially in the US) are still extremely rare. This concerns also the relation to the state—voices asking to limit influence of the state greatly outnumber those that want to expand such influence. The reason may lie in an assumption that commercial litigation between companies is not, somehow, politically relevant—though that is not an assumption we have in domestic law. And something else is peculiar: there is a vast number of publications, but many of them contribute little more that is new beyond the author's name.[90]

The main reason is this: the line between practice and scholarship is fuzzy. On the one hand, most scholarly publications, including textbooks, are written by practitioners. On the other hand, almost all scholars of international arbitration also practice as arbitrators and are thus interested in its success. Outside analyses by non-participants are still very rare—at least in legal scholarship. This can be put differently: scholarship on international arbitration is frequently also an expansion of practice and advertisement[91]—for international arbitration in general and the individual author in particular. The distinctions between practice, scholarship, and acquisition—public relations—are blurred.

This blurring of lines can be illustrated by the following statements from an article by David McLean, former co-chair of Latham & Watkins' international dispute resolution group.[92] At first, he offers what looks like a rather distant and scholarly view:

> [globalization] has necessitated a move away from traditional litigation to a new dispute resolution paradigm—international arbitration—which portends a more neutral, efficient and certain process, one which favors neither party but affords each the occasion to fully and equitably present its case, and results in an award recognized around the globe.[93]

[90] See Kessedjian, "Is Arbitration a Service?".
[91] See Clay "Qui Sont les Arbitres Internationaux?," pp. 21–22.
[92] David J. McLean, "Towards a New International Dispute Resolution Paradigm: Assessing the Congruent Evolution of Globalization and International Arbitration," *University of Pennsylvania Journal of International Law* 30 (2009): pp. 1087–1098, at p. 1089.
[93] McLean, "Dispute Resolution Paradigm," p. 1089.

While the superiority of international arbitration seems natural and its success inevitable here, a few paragraphs later the author later sees the need to fight for exactly this success from an openly normative position:

> As disputes substantively grow more complex, involve more stakeholders, and are fought for higher stakes, international arbitration must continue to offer a less time-consuming, more efficient alternative to cross-border litigation.[94]

More importantly, international arbitration must be actively advertised:

> As a result, practitioners, arbitrators, and the parties themselves will need to continue to advocate for a role in the evolution of the process to ensure its efficiency and effectiveness, in even the most complicated of circumstances.[95]

It is unclear what the stated superiority of international arbitration is in this text—an analytic or at least descriptive truth, a normative desideratum, or a mere advertising slogan by an interested party? It is also unclear who is speaking here: the practitioner, the scholar, or the advertiser. And it is not clear whether the author advertises for his field or for himself, or both.

International arbitration practitioners have three incentives to engage in scholarship. First, now that the field requires scholarly analysis, it is safer for practitioners to fulfill this task themselves and ensure that the conditions favorable to arbitration are maintained, than to leave this task to outside scholars.[96]

Second, publishing provides the practitioner with the rare opportunity to prove his competence openly. Arbitration procedure is confidential, so it is hard for young arbitrators to advertise themselves merely by performance— established arbitrators have a competitive advantage here.[97] A public reputation can be achieved, however, by scholarly activity. This may explain the large number of publications and conferences which frequently do not add any new content and have aptly been described as "beauty contests".[98] A book authored by "Leading Arbitrators" and titled *"Guide to International Arbitration,"*[99] for instance, does not merely offer students and practitioners an introduction to international arbitration; it also identifies its authors as the "leading arbitrators" in the market. The same is true for the numerous guidebooks published by large law firms.

---

[94] McLean, "Dispute Resolution Paradigm," p. 1096.
[95] McLean, "Dispute Resolution Paradigm," p. 1096.
[96] On one attempt to silence critical positions, see Clay, "Qui sont les arbitres internationaux?," p. 18; see also Thomas Schultz, "Arbitration as an iPhone, or Why Conduct Academic Research in Arbitration?," *Journal of International Dispute Settlement* 2 (2011): pp. 279–286, at pp. 280–281.
[97] Rogers, "Vocation," pp. 968–969.
[98] Kessedjian, "Is Arbitration a Service?," pp. 311–312.
[99] Lawrence W. Newman and Richard D. Hill, *The Leading Arbitrators' Guide to International Arbitration*, 2nd ed. (Huntington, NY: Juris, 2008).

Lastly, insiders have the incentive to keep the level of complexity high in order to prevent outsiders from acquiring access to the market. Complexity gives an advantage to established experts (the "elite corps"); it creates an effective restriction on entry. One is reminded of the fights in the American legal profession of the 19th century against codification of the common law, which was feared to obviate the need for legal advice.[100]

3.4 *The Arbitrator as Theorist and Philosopher of Law*

This may explain the shift to scholarship, but not the further step to legal theory and philosophy. So far, actual theories of international arbitration exist only outside of legal scholarship—sociology[101] and political theory[102] in particular. Legal theories, in contrast, pertain to the *lex mercatoria* as substantive law, and only rarely to international arbitration itself.[103] Legal philosophers are uninterested in international arbitration; arbitration scholars do not engage in philosophy of law, except some rare references to moral theory. Even experts in both international arbitration and philosophy of law, such as Norbert Horn, rarely engage in a direct exchange of ideas between the disciplines.[104]

Emmanuel Gaillard is now filling this gap with his Hague Lectures on "Philosophical Aspects of the Law of International Arbitration," meanwhile available as paperback edition in English, Arabic, Chinese, and Spanish translations.[105] Gaillard is one of the leading French practitioners and scholars of international arbitration. He is a professor in Paris, head of the litigation department at Shearman Sterling, and holds leadership positions in numerous institutions. His contributions are therefore eminently relevant to my analysis.

---

[100] See Mathias Reimann, "The Historical School against Codification: Savigny, Carter, and the Defeat of the New York Civil Code," *American Journal of Comparative Law* 37 (1989): pp. 95–115, at pp. 112–113.

[101] Dezalay and Garth, *Dealing in Virtue*.

[102] Claire A. Cutler, *Private Power and Global Authority—Transnational Merchant Law in the Global Political Economy* (Cambridge: Cambridge University Press, 2003).

[103] Early exceptions are Jerzy Jakubowski, "Reflections on the Philosophy of International Commercial Arbitration and Conciliation," in *The Art of Arbitration: Essays on International Arbitration: Liber Amicorum Pieter Sanders*, edited by Jan C. Schultsz and Albert Jan van den Berg (Boston: Kluwer Law and Taxation Publishers, 1982), pp. 175–188; Bruno Oppetit, "Philosophie de L'arbitrage commercial international," *Journal du droit international* (1993): pp. 811ff; see now also Thomas Schultz, "The Concept of Law in Transnational Arbitral Legal Orders and Some of its Consequences," *Journal of International Dispute Settlement* 2 (2011): pp. 59–85.

[104] Norbert Horn, *Einführung in die Rechtswissenschaft und Rechtsphilosophie* (Heidelberg: Huthig-Jehle Rehm, 2006) no. 179 (pp. 121–122); cf. Norbert Horn, "Enforcing Contractual Claims: From Schmitthoff to Investment Arbitration," in *Economic Law as an Economic Good: Its Rule Function and Its Tool Function in the Competition of Systems*, edited by Karl M. Meessen, Marc Bungenberg, and Adelheid Puttler (Munich: Sellier, 2009): pp. 139–148.

[105] Gaillard, *Aspects Philosophiques*, pp. 49–216; Gaillard, *Legal Theory*. See also Paulsson, "Arbitration in Three Dimensions."

Does this publication turn the arbitrator into a legal philosopher? The initial answer is no. Gaillard's book is clearly written and hence valuable, but its contribution to legal philosophy is rather basic.[106] Gaillard sees relations between two themes in international arbitration and in legal philosophy—party autonomy relates to the issue of freedom of the will; questions as to the bindingness of the arbitral award are related questions of validity in legal philosophy. These connections are rather basic. The same is true, philosophically, for his proposition to distinguish between three "representations"[107] of international arbitration—one national, one international, one transnational—and to locate these between natural law and the different version of positive law. Legal positivism is used in a very unspecific way; authors such as Kelsen, Hart, Santi Romano, Ost, and Kerchove are listed without any attempt to distinguish among their positions.[108] This does not reach the level of the respective debates in the areas of philosophy and theory of law, even to the extent that these debates focus on arbitration.[109] At the same time, the philosophical classification appears somewhat irrelevant for international arbitration as a discipline.[110] Even Gaillard himself thinks it unnecessary, indeed undesirable, for the arbitrator to think about philosophy when making a judgment.[111]

So what is really at stake? It seems plausible that arbitrators like Gaillard, rooted in the continental and French tradition, see the need for a continued scholarly basis of the field. The result, however, seems more like a gesture than an actual serious gain of knowledge (and legal philosophers have, as far as I can see, not yet been impressed).[112] What seems to matter is a display of the connections rather than a true resolution. The arbitrator does not become a philosopher of law, but he at least offers to converse with the legal philosopher.

---

[106] See also my criticism of Schultz: Ralf Michaels, "A Fuller Concept of Law Beyond the State? Thoughts on Lon Fuller's Contributions to the Jurisprudence of Transnational Dispute Resolution—A Reply to Thomas Schultz," *Journal of International Dispute Settlement* 2 (2011): pp. 417–426. See now Thomas Schultz, *Transnational Legality: Stateless Law and International Arbitration* (Oxford: Oxford University Press, 2014).

[107] Emmanuel Gaillard, "Three Representations of International Arbitration," *Journal of International Dispute Settlement* 1 (2010): pp. 271–281. His terminology shifts: he also calls these "philosophies" (Emmanuel Gaillard, "Three Philosophies of International Arbitration," in *The Fordham Papers 2009*, edited by Arthur W. Rovine, p. 305), or "mental representations" (Emmanuel Gaillard, "The Representations of International Arbitration," *Journal of International Dispute Settlement* 1 (2010): pp. 271ff).

[108] Gaillard, *Aspects philosophiques*, pp. 23, 91.

[109] See, by contrast, the extensive references in Peer Zumbansen, "Debating Autonomy and Procedural Justices: The Lex Mercatoria in the Context of Global Governance Debates—A Reply to Thomas Schultz," *Journal of International Dispute Settlement* 2 (2011): pp. 427–433.

[110] Veijo Heiskanen, Review, "Aspects Philosophiques du droit de l'arbitrage international," *European Journal of International Law* 20 (2009): pp. 945–947.

[111] Interview, *Juriste, Entreprise Magazine*, no. 3 (July 2009): pp. 14–15.

[112] But see Filippo Fontanelli, "Santi Romano and L'ordinamento Giuridico: The Relevance of a Forgotten Masterpiece for Contemporary International, Transnational and Global Legal Relations," *Transnational Legal Theory* 2 (2011): pp. 67–117.

3.5 *The Arbitrator as Visionary and Dreamer*

Gaillard's core question is an important one, namely that of the basis of validity of international arbitration. For courts, this legitimacy is directly derived from (and thus dependent on) that of the state. The arbitral tribunal lacks a similar direct basis. Remarkably, Gaillard does not offer a response. Instead, he suggests that the choice between his different "representations" does not depend on rationality or the better argument, but is a matter of visions and quasi-religious belief:

> what is at stake are not matters that may be disposed of by scientific demonstration, but rather matters that belong to the realm of belief, of faith. There is no such thing as a right or wrong representation of international arbitration. As for every other vision or ideology, one may share it or not. It may be efficient or inefficient, but never right or wrong.[113]

This sudden turn to faith and vision is surprising, but it is not an isolated case. Mauro Rubino-Sammartano begins the preface to his textbook with the following:[114]

> If I am right, the best role each of us can play is that of bearer of our beliefs and ideals. If this is so, what matters is that these beliefs and ideals continue to be carried on, irrespective of who the individual bearer is.[115]

Julian Lew, one of the leading arbitrators, provides an even more drastic quote:

> Do you dream? When do you dream? What do you dream about? Do you dream about international arbitration? Is there a dream for international arbitration? Is the concept of delocalised arbitration, or arbitration not controlled by national law, a dream or nightmare?[116]

Here, the arbitrator takes on the role of visionary, believer, dreamer, maybe even missionary. This is not irrelevant. After all, belief and vision are used here to establish no less than the autonomy of arbitration. Precisely at this point, when arbitration must be legitimized (and therefore at precisely the point at which philosophy of law should furnish answers), we find, instead of an argument, a virtually Kierkegaardian leap from rationality to faith.[117] The

---

[113] Gaillard, "Representations of International Arbitration," pp. 272–273.

[114] Rubino-Sammartano, *International Arbitration Law and Practice*, p. vii.

[115] Rubino-Sammartano, *International Arbitration Law and Practice*, p. vii.

[116] Julian D.M. Lew, "Achieving the Dream: Autonomous Arbitration," *Arbitration International* 22 (2006): pp. 179–203, cited in Julian D.M. Lew and Loukas A. Mistelis, *Arbitration Insights: Twenty Years of the Annual Lecture of the School of International Arbitration* (Netherlands: Kluwer Law International, 2007): pp. 455–486. Lew makes it clear that, for him, autonomy is the dream, control by national law is the nightmare.

[117] M. Jamie Ferreira, "Faith and the Kierkegaardian Leap," in *Cambridge Companion to Kierkegaard*, edited by Alastair Hannay and Gordon Daniel Marino (Cambridge: Cambridge University Press, 1998), p. 207.

legitimacy of arbitration itself, and thus the core of its identity, cannot be accessed by reason alone. What is presented is thus not ultimate justification. Instead, the common belief, on which the epistemic community is based and which holds it together, is formulated. Arbitration scholarship becomes utopian literature. [118]

4 Public and Private Role

With the question of legitimacy, I reach the most important tension, namely that between a private and a public role for the arbitrator. Doctrinally, this tension can be illustrated by means of the dispute about the foundation of arbitration, as it is regularly repeated in the literature.[119] The goal here is not to repeat this dispute once more, but instead to analyze it with a view to the role of the arbitrator reflected in different approaches.

4.1 *Judge or Service Provider*

Two theories of international arbitration serve as starting points for the debate. According to the contractual theory of arbitration, the basis of arbitration lies in the agreement of the parties. According to the jurisdictional theory, this basis lies in the function of the arbitrator as adjudicator. In reality, both of these theories are all but obsolete; current discussions conserve them merely for argumentative purposes. It is also doubtful whether they have any practical consequences.

However, these theories are revealing with regard to the question of whether the role of the arbitrator is a private or a public one. Doctrinally, this concerns the question of whether the arbitrator's powers are derived from state sovereignty (or an analogy thereof)[120] or from the parties' agreement. If the arbitrator's competence is derived from state sovereignty, he is a quasi-judge and thus a quasi-public actor. If his competence is derived from the parties'

[118] See, in more detail, Ralf Michaels, "Dreaming Law without a State—Scholarship on Autonomous International Arbitration as Utopian Literature," *London Review of International Law* 1, no. 1 (2013): pp. 35–62.

[119] See, e.g., Jacqueline Rubellin-Devichi, L'arbitrage: nature juridique, droit interne et droit international privé (Paris: LGDJ, 1965), pp. 10–18; Horacio A. Grigera Naón, *Choice-of-Law Problems in International Commercial Arbitration* (Tübingen: Mohr Siebeck, 1992), pp. 14–18; Lew et al., Comparative International Commercial Arbitration, pp. 71–82; Born, *International Commercial Arbitration*, pp. 184–189; Lynch, *Economic Globalization*, pp. 65–75; Solomon, *Verbindlichkeit von Schiedssprüchen*, pp. 288–310; Hong-lin Yu, "A Theoretical Overview of the Foundations of International Commercial Arbitration," *Contemporary Asia Arbitration Journal* 1 (2008): pp. 255–286.

[120] Although the jurisdictional theory is frequently equated to the derivation from state sovereignty, both concern different problems; see Solomon, *Verbindlichkeit von Schiedssprüchen*, pp. 310–334.

agreement, he is a quasi-private service provider. The quasi-judge is account-able to the state, maybe alternatively to a transnational legal system or the global community. The service provider, by contrast, is responsible only to the parties. The quasi-judge is part of global governance;[121] the service pro-vider is a mere resolver of an individual dispute.

These roles are related, to some extent, to the professional roles discussed earlier. In the traditional European paradigm, as expressed in the Glossner quote given earlier,[122] the arbitrator is a privately appointed and indebted service provider. The professionalization of international arbitration has led to an alignment at least of the function of the arbitrator to that of a judge. Contemporary arbitration procedures are frequently so adversary in nature that the common interests of the parties, which could define a service, are difficult to identify. In addition, the seamless move back and forth between positions as counsel and as arbitrator which was long typical in the field is giving way to a professional differentiation: We see more and more profes-sional arbitrators concentrate exclusively on being arbitrators. At the same time, the arbitrator remains indebted to the parties, much more so than a public judge would be. His function as a quasi-judge does not necessarily link him to a state.

4.2 The So-Called Hybrid Theory and its Shortcomings

Neither theory alone is convincing. Consequently, both theories and thus both bases for legitimacy—the public and the private one—are regularly linked, resulting in a hybrid theory. Regarding the role of the arbitrator, this approach leads to a combination of the roles of judge and of service provider.[123] More precisely, the function of the arbitrator is that of a judge;[124] the basis for this function, however, is the agreement of the parties.

The link between the two roles is affected from both the private and the public role. On the one hand, the private role is made public: because freedom of contract is made possible by the state, it is indirectly public authority.[125] This party autonomy is charged with more and more societal expectations: By enforcing the will of the parties, the arbitrator is thought to fulfill a role for the wider society, which is allegedly interested in private dispute resolution.

---

[121] Christopher A. Whytock, "Litigation, Arbitration, and the Transnational Shadow of the Law," *Duke Journal of Comparative and International Law* 18 (2008): pp. 449–476, at p. 456f.

[122] Glossner, *Sociological Aspects.*

[123] Fouchard, Gaillard, and Goldman (eds.), *Traité de l'Arbitrage Commercial International*, p. 560, para. 1017.

[124] Solomon, *Verbindlichkeit von Schiedssprüchen*, p. 330 with note 205.

[125] This is an old argument of legal realism: Morris Cohen, "The Basis of Contract," *Harvard Law Review* 46 (1933): pp. 553, 585–592.

Arbitrators are "the guardians of a system that is imperative for the flourishing of international trade and investment."[126] The arbitrator's private role in dispute resolution thus becomes a public role as well; private interests dissolve into public interests, or are at least congruent with them.

At the same time, the public role is made private. This can be seen especially in the persistent discussion about the application of mandatory norms in arbitration. In the past, the application of mandatory norms was based on the perceived need to limit private interests based on public interests: the arbitrator was hence partially responsible to the public, typically to the state. Today, the application of mandatory norms is justified with reference to private interests. The argument is that the arbitrator, by applying these mandatory norms, ensures the enforceability of the arbitration judgment and, in doing so, fulfills the ultimate interests of the parties in an enforceable award.[127] Here, the public interest dissolves into a private interest; the conflict between the autonomy of the parties and public interest is (seemingly) resolved.[128] And, remarkably, precisely for this reason judicial control is thought to be less important.

Alas, the tension between the two roles of the arbitrator is merely suppressed and not resolved. Practically, it is unclear under either conception what should happen when the arbitrator's obligation toward the parties conflicts with those toward the public. This can happen, especially, where a contractual agreement violates third party interests, or if the parties explicitly ask the arbitrator to disregard mandatory rules. Theoretically, the alleged merger of public and private role puts too much pressure on both. On the one hand, private autonomy is expected to fulfill more public functions than it legitimately can,[129] especially because it is not the same as democratic legitimacy.[130] Private autonomy, in the end, can only account for a service relationship; it alone cannot justify any judicial functions of the arbitrator which go beyond the private parties themselves. On the other hand, the protection of public interests is left

---

[126] Franck, "The Role of International Arbitrators," p. 521. On arbitration as a provider of public goods, see also Rogers, "Vocation," pp. 999–1006.

[127] See Luca Radicati di Brozolo, "Arbitrage Commercial International et Lois de Police," *Recueil des Cours* 315 (2006): pp. 265, 450ff.

[128] See, for example, the ironic remark in Alan Scott Rau, "The Arbitrator and "Mandatory Rules of Law," in *Mandatory Rules in International Arbitration*, edited by George A. Bermann and Loukas A. Mistelis (Huntington, NY: Juris, 2011), pp. 77, 79 fn. 5; towards Marc Blessing, "Mandatory Rules of Law *versus* Party Autonomy in International Arbitration," *Journal of International Arbitration* 14, no. 4 (1996): pp. 23–40. ("The 'versus' in this chapter's (*sic*) title already speaks volumes about the particular mind set here.")

[129] Too optimistically, Mark Movsesian, "International Commercial Arbitration and International Courts," *Duke Journal of Comparative and International Law* 18 (2008): pp. 423–448, at pp. 424, 432–433.

[130] See also, from widely different points of departure, Horatia Muir Watt, "'Party Autonomy' in International Contracts: From the Makings of a Myth to the Requirements of Global Governance," *European Review of Contract Law* (March 2010): pp. 250–283; Jürgen Basedow, "Theorie der Rechtswahl oder Privatautonomie als Grundlage des Internationalen Privatrechts," *RabelsZ* 75 (2011): pp. 33–59.

to the state (especially at the recognition state), even though the state can hardly fulfill transnational public interests, especially vis-à-vis arbitration.

The problem, in a nutshell, is this: On the one hand, the arbitrator now fulfills the role of judge, including a function of global governance. On the other hand, his legitimacy and his mandate are limited to those of a service provider, which especially limits his ability for governance. The state, on the other hand, which would be competent to regulate, is deprived of this competency by the private arbitration agreement. So long as state courts cannot reach the transnational sphere and arbitrators do not have the legitimacy to regulate, we face a potential regulation deficit.

4.3 *Autonomy of Arbitration?*

With globalization, this effect is amplified.[131] First, even state courts are taking on an increasingly private role.[132] Globalization limits the state's ability to regulate. In addition, national courts compete for parties:[133] National legal systems are advertised as service providers;[134] their regulation function is increasingly limited. Second, the institutionalization of international arbitration leads to an increasing independence of arbitration from the national jurisdiction and to the formation of a separate system.

A fourth theory of international arbitration responds to this development— the so-called autonomous theory. Viewed narrowly, this theory maintains merely the independence of arbitration from the state and hence from public interest, coupled with a maximum recognition of party autonomy. As such, however, arbitration would lack a legal framework within which private autonomy could unfold, as well as an internal control of correctness of arbitral decisions.[135] What is required to achieve these, in accordance with the theory, would be a constitutionalization of international arbitration.[136] To the

---

[131] Lynch, *Economic Globalization*; Bernard Hanotiau, "International Arbitration in a Global Economy: The Challenges of the Future," *Journal of International Arbitration* 28 (2011): p. 89; Hermann Hoffmann, "Schiedsgerichte als Gewinner der Globalisierung? Eine empirische Analyse zur Bedeutung staatlicher und privater Gerichtsbarkeit für den internationalen Handel," *Zeitschrift für Schiedsverfahren* 2010, no. 2: p. 96.

[132] Horatia Muir Watt, "Economie de la justice et arbitrage international (Réflexions sur la gouvernance privée dans la globalisation)," *Revue de l'arbitrage* 2008: pp. 390, 401ff.

[133] Jens Dammann and Henry Hansmann, "Globalizing Commercial Litigation," *Cornell Law Review* 94 (2008): pp. 1–71; see Muir Watt, "Economie de la Justice et Arbitrage International," pp. 404–406; Muir Watt, "Party Autonomy," pp. 278ff.

[134] See, e.g., Horst Eidenmüller, "The Transnational Law Market, Regulatory Competition and Transnational Corporations," *Indiana Journal of Global Legal Studies* 18 (2011): pp. 707–749, at p. 708.

[135] See Lynch, *Economic Globalization*, pp. 73–75.

[136] See Peer Zumbansen, "Piercing the Legal Veil: Commercial Arbitration and Transnational Law," *European Law Journal* 8 (2002): pp. 400–432, at pp. 430–432; Moritz Renner, "Towards a Hierarchy of Norms in Transnational Law?" *Journal of International Arbitration* 26 (2009): pp. 533, 554f.

extent that international arbitration emancipates itself from the state, it must independently generate the functions normally fulfilled by state law. Mandatory national norms will then be substituted by a transnational ordre public.[137]

It is noticeable that the autonomous theory, in contrast to the other three theories, does not furnish a concrete role for the arbitrator. This is not surprising. Under this theory, the arbitrator can be neither service provider nor judge—both terms belonging to the state sphere. His new role combines functions of dispute resolution with those of genuine global governance. It is a task for the future to define this role more precisely. Whether either the private or the public model as known from the state can serve as models is doubtful.

5 Conclusion

This last insight may serve as the general insight to be derived from this analysis. The analysis has shown that the arbitrator's role oscillates in many ways between different models that are familiar from traditional domestic and international law: national and transnational roles, practical and academic roles, public and private roles.

In many ways, this oscillation is not surprising: it mirrors the uncertain position that international commercial arbitration holds between the state and the global sphere. International commercial arbitration aims at being a global model, autonomous from the state. At the same time, it remains deeply embedded in the state in at least two ways. First, the state still provides the model for almost all the roles discussed in this article. Second, international arbitration—and its actors—still rely very much on the support of the state. State courts are still required at various stages of the arbitration process: to force parties to fulfill their arbitration agreement, to review arbitral awards, and to enforce them. It is not surprising, then, that we see actors in international arbitration both reject and replicate state actors at the same time.

This uncertain position is enhanced by the insight that international arbitration must fend off competition in two directions. This competition is less fierce, as I argued above, from state courts, which appear content to leave much commercial dispute litigation to arbitrators. More pressure comes from the other side, especially less law-based dispute resolution processes like mediation. Thus wedged between state courts and non-law mediators, actors

[137] For an excellent recent study informed by legal theory and sociology, see Moritz Renner, "Zwingendes transnationales Recht. Zur Struktur der Wirtschaftsverfassung jenseits des Staates," (Nomos, 2011); cf. my review, *International Journal of Constitutional Law* 10 (2012): pp. 1179–1184.26.

in international arbitration must necessarily wage a dual war: they must distinguish themselves both from state courts and from mediators at the same time. Oscillation between different roles is also a reflection of this dual competition.

Tensions between opposing roles are well known from domestic law. But they appear to be much starker, more extreme, and more foundational in the field of international commercial arbitration. These tensions between opposing and often incompatible roles may, up until now, contribute to the success of international commercial arbitrators: they can be everything to everyone. In the long run however, it is submitted, the oscillation represents a weakness of international commercial arbitration at large. Ultimately, the role of the international commercial arbitrator will need to transcend models borrowed from the state in order to be both sustainable and legitimate. The so-called autonomous theory of arbitration, discussed in the last section, could provide a starting point for the development of such a role. At present, it is more an ideology than an actual theory—a plea for independence from the state without an independent foundation of such independence. Nonetheless, it appears that this is where serious thinking about sustainable roles in international commercial arbitration will need to begin.

4

International Arbitration Culture and Global Governance

Joshua Karton[1]

1 Introduction

Academics increasingly characterize international commercial arbitration (ICA)[2] as a form of global governance or (on a less grand scale) describe ICA's international-law-generating and global regulatory aspects.[3] Relatedly, they have also produced an abundance of commentary on the new

[1] I am grateful to Walter Mattli and Thomas Dietz for their generous invitation to join this project and also for insightful comments on earlier drafts. I am also grateful for the wise advice of anonymous reviewers.

[2] Like the other chapters in this book, this chapter deals only with "general" international commercial arbitration. That is, it considers only arbitrations of disputes arising from cross-border contractual relationships between commercial entities (including state entities engaged in commerce). It does not deal with arbitration of employment or consumer disputes. Most importantly, it does not discuss arbitrations arising out of international investment treaties. Since investment treaty arbitration regulates the conduct of states in the exercise of sovereign functions, it constitutes a very different kind of global governance from that of international commercial arbitration. See, e.g., Anthea Roberts, "Divergence between Investment and Commercial Arbitration," *Proceedings of the Annual Meeting (American Society of International Law)* 106 (March 2012): pp. 297–300. Accordingly, investment treaty arbitration will not be discussed here, except to the extent that a given investment arbitration award or scholarly publication discusses matters of arbitral practice common to both investment and commercial arbitrations. It should be noted, however, that shared cultural norms are also an important factor shaping global governance in international investment arbitration. Indeed, the argument for the importance of culture is even stronger there, since the community of frequently appointed investment arbitrators is smaller and more homogeneous than the community of commercial arbitrators. See, e.g., Moshe Hirsch, "The Sociology of International Investment Law," in *The Foundations of International Investment Law: Bringing Theory into Practice*, edited by Zachary Douglas, Joost Pauwelyn, and Jorge Viñuales (Oxford: Oxford University Press, forthcoming 2014), ch. 4; Stephan Schill, "W(h)ither Fragmentation? On the literature and sociology of international investment law," *European Journal of International Law* 22, no. 3 (2011), pp. 875–908; Jeswald Salacuse, "The Emerging Global Regime for Investment," *Harvard International Law Journal* 51, no. 2 (2010): pp. 427–473.

[3] The literature is large and crosses disciplines. For some recent examples in legal publications, see, e.g., Stacie Strong, "Mass Procedures as a Form of 'Regulatory Arbitration' – Abaclat v. Argentine

lex mercatoria and the transnationalization of commercial law through arbitration.[4]

By contrast, users of ICA (parties and their counsel) tend to characterize it as a procedural alternative to litigation in national courts. They perhaps share the perspective of the US Supreme Court, which has described the difference between litigation and arbitration as purely "procedural,"[5] and arbitration agreements as simply "a specialized kind of forum-selection clause."[6] Surveys confirm that parties' specific reasons for choosing arbitration are generally procedural—most importantly, the global enforceability of arbitral awards and the neutrality of the forum, but also such matters as the ability to choose one's arbitrator, the speed and cost of the proceedings, confidentiality, and the flexibility of evidentiary rules.[7] In the ordinary case, where disputes are governed by the substantive law of a state, most people would expect an

---

Republic and the International Investment Regime," *The Journal of Corporation Law* 38 (2013): pp. 259–324; Jay Westbrook, "International Arbitration and Multinational Insolvency," *Penn State International Law Review* 29 (2011): pp. 635–649; Steven Wheatley, "A Democratic Rule of International Law," *European Journal of International Law* 22, no. 2 (2011): pp. 525–548; Salacuse, "Global Regime"; Gus van Harten and Martin Loughlin, "Investment Treaty Arbitration as a Species of Global Administrative Law," *European Journal of International Law* 17, no. 1 (2006): pp. 121–150; Stephan Schill, *The Multilateralization of International Investment Law* (Cambridge: Cambridge University Press, 2009); Florian Grizel, "Control of awards and re-centralisation of international commercial arbitration," *Civil Justice Quarterly* 25 (April 2006): pp. 166–180; Benedict Kingsbury and Stephan Schill, "Investor-State Arbitration as Governance: Fair and Equitable Treatment, Proportionality and the Emerging Global Administrative Law," in *50 Years of the New York Convention: ICAA International Arbitration Conference*, edited by Albert Jan van den Berg (Deventer: Kluwer Law International, 2009), pp. 5–68.

[4] This literature is also voluminous, and ranges in tone from utopian to highly skeptical. Some recent examples include: Cristian Gimenez Corte, "Lex Mercatoria, International Arbitration and Independent Guarantees: Transnational Law and How Nation States Lost the Monopoly of Legitimate Enforcement," *Transnational Legal Theory* 3, no. 4 (2013): pp. 345–370; Peer Zumbansen, "Debating Autonomy and Procedural Justice: The Lex Mercatoria in the Context of Global Governance Debates – A Reply to Thomas Schultz," *Journal of International Dispute Settlement* 2, no. 2 (2011): pp. 427–433; Loukas Mistelis, "General Principles of Law and Transnational Rules in International Arbitration: An English Perspective," *World Arbitration and Mediation Review* 5, no. 2 (2011), pp. 201–230; Klaus Peter Berger, *The Creeping Codification of the Lex Mercatoria*, 2nd ed. (New York: Kluwer, 2010); Laurence Ravillon et al., "Informal Sources of International Business Law," *International Business Law Journal*, no. 3 (2010): pp. 278–293.

[5] *Shearson/American Express, Inc. v. McMahon*, 482 U.S. 220, 232 (1987), reasoning that "the streamlined procedures of arbitration do not entail any consequential restriction on substantive rights."

[6] *Scherk v. Alberto-Culver Co.*, 417 U.S. 506, 519 (1974). See also *Mitsubishi Motors Corp. v. Soler Chrysler-Plymouth, Inc.*, 473 U.S. 614, 628 (1985) ("By agreeing to arbitrate a statutory claim, a party does not forgo the substantive rights afforded by the statute; it only submits to their resolution in an arbitral, rather than a judicial, forum.")

[7] See, e.g., Christopher Drahozal, "Why Arbitrate? Substantive Versus Procedural Theories of Private Judging," *American Review of International Arbitration* 22 (2011): pp. 163–186; Christopher Drahozal and Stephen Ware, "Why Do Businesses Use (or not Use) Arbitration Clauses?," *Ohio State Journal on Dispute Resolution* 25 (2010): pp. 433–476; Richard Naimark and Stephanie Keer, "International Private Commercial Arbitration: Expectations and Perceptions of Attorneys and Business People," *International Business Lawyer* 30, no. 2 (2002): pp. 203–209; Christian Bühring-Uhle, *Arbitration and Mediation in International Business*, 1st ed. (The Hague: Kluwer, 1996), pp. 129–134.

arbitral tribunal to decide issues of substantive law in roughly the same way as a court from the country whose law governs the dispute.

If ICA is just an adjunct to court litigation of commercial disputes—more neutral, more widely enforceable, perhaps faster and cheaper, but essentially the same exercise in a different venue—then ICA could constitute a form of "global governance"[8] only in a rather impoverished sense. According to such a conception, ICA could amount at most to an atomized form of governance derived from the authority of national laws and courts, a mere adapter plug that connects disparate national legal regimes with globalized businesses.

Although only a small minority of cross-border commercial disputes are resolved by arbitration,[9] ICA undoubtedly constitutes a form of "transnational governance." The standard definition of transnational law (a key aspect of transnational governance), given by Jessup in 1956, is so broad as to encompass any form of legal regulation, by any private or public entity, of any activity that crosses national boundaries: "all law which regulates actions or events that transcend national frontiers . . . [including] [b]oth public and private international law . . . [and] other rules which do not wholly fit into such categories."[10]

However, for ICA to constitute *global* governance—as opposed to merely disconnected resolutions of individual cross-border disputes according to national laws—there are at least two prerequisites. First, legal rules must be formulated at the global level and apply regardless of the nationality and public or private status of the parties.[11] Since we still live under an essentially Westphalian world order, this means that states must at minimum acquiesce to some degree of autonomy for arbitral adjudication.[12] Second, there must

---

[8] For a summary of different theories of international arbitration as governance, see Chapter 1 of this book.

[9] See Thomas Dietz, "Does International Commercial Arbitration Provide Efficient Dispute Resolution Mechanisms to Global Commerce?," Chapter 7 of this book.

[10] Phillip Jessup, *Transnational Law* (New Haven: Yale UP, 1956), p. 2.

[11] I previously made a similar distinction between global law and international law: Joshua Karton, "Global Law: The Spontaneous, Gradual Emergence of a New Legal Order," *Tilburg Law Review* 17, no. 2 (2012): pp. 276–284. See also Joost Pauwelyn et al., "The Stagnation of International Law," Leuven Centre for Global Governance Studies Working Paper No. 97 (2012), accessed April 17, 2014, <http://papers.ssrn.com/sol3/papers.cfm?abstract_id=2271862> (arguing that, whereas traditional international law is driven by state consent, new forms of cross-border rule-making are increasingly driven by a "thicker" consensus among a variety of stakeholders).

[12] As Friedman put it with respect to the promulgation of codified instruments like the INCOTERMs, "All this is supposed to constitute . . . autonomous norm creation within the international economy. . . . But in the end all such customs and practices have to be validated somehow by national courts applying what they consider to be national law or rules that national law recognizes." Lawrence Friedman, "Erewhon: The Coming Global Legal Order," *Stanford Journal of International Law* 37 (2001): pp. 347–364, 356–357 (citations omitted). The same sentiment is expressed in the International Council for Commercial Arbitration's handbook for national court judges on the application of the New York Convention: see International Council for Commercial Arbitration, *ICCA's Guide to the Interpretation of the 1958 New York Convention: A Handbook for Judges* (2012), pp. xi—xiii, accessed April 17, 2014, <http://www.arbitration-icca.org/publications/NYC_Guide.html>. ("The ultimate growth of the rule of law, the expansion of international arbitration

be a functional consistency in arbitral decision-making; a consistent adjudicative approach, such that "like cases are treated alike," is a hallmark of the rule of law. In the radically decentralized ICA system, where there is no central administrative body, no appellate hierarchy, and no common sets of procedural or substantive rules, consistency appears to be a tall order. Can there be global governance without a global governor?

The existing literature addresses ICA's character as a form of governance and explains many of its features, but does little to explain how or why ICA has emerged, or may emerge, as global governance. The literature arising from within the international arbitration community remains largely doctrinal, while the more critical literature that has developed in political science and sociological circles has focused on ICA's position within the international economic system (and has concentrated on investment rather than commercial arbitration).[13] Neither literature provides systemic explanations for the *outcomes reached* in ICA, beyond general claims that (for example) ICA decision-making tends to favor multinational corporations at the expense of developing states.[14]

A more fine-grained tool for analyzing and predicting outcomes in ICA is needed; however, it is difficult to come by. Broad confidentiality rules deprive the researcher of access to the data normally used to assess adjudicative systems: the decisions of the adjudicators. Very few ICA awards are published,[15] and there is no way of knowing whether the few extracts that are publicly available are representative of the whole body of awards. Moreover, not all of the published award extracts contain any analysis of substantive law matters, and these are difficult to compare due to variations in governing laws, facts, and membership of the tribunals. Thus, the traditional methods of legal scholarship are largely useless for explaining ICA as governance.

Several interdisciplinary perspectives have something to contribute, including the various approaches presented in this book, but I argue that the key to understanding ICA's emergence as global governance is a legal culture specific to the international arbitration community. Of course, while all sociological

---

for resolving cross-border disputes and enforcement of awards depend on the sovereign national courts. It is thus hoped that this Guide will also play its small part in assisting judges around the world to participate in this continuing harmonization process and use the Convention in a way consistent with its letter and spirit.")

[13] On the history and development of ICA scholarship, see Stavros Brekoulakis, "International Arbitration Scholarship and the Concept of Arbitration," *Fordham Journal of International Law* 36 (2013): pp. 1–42.

[14] See, e.g., several of the contributions to Michael Waibel et al., (eds.), *The Backlash Against Investment Arbitration* (Alphen aan den Rijn: Alphen, 2010).

[15] As opposed to investment arbitration awards, most of which are nominally confidential but have been published, with the consent of the parties or otherwise. See Joshua Karton, "A Conflict of Interests: Seeking a Way Forward on Publication of International Arbitral Awards," *Arbitration International* 28, no. 3 (2012): pp. 447–486, 455–456.

studies concern the effects of social norms, not all sociological theories emphasize the importance of shared cultures—that is, community dynamics. For example, two recent sociologically inflected treatments of ICA focus on the structure of ICA institutions[16] and on networks of individual practitioners.[17] However, I believe that a sociology of the whole ICA community— the field's culture—presents the best opportunities to explain its role in global governance.

The legal culture described in this chapter satisfies both of the prerequisites for ICA to become a form of global governance. A shared culture instills into international arbitration practitioners a normative commitment to establishing international arbitration as a global system of governance for cross-border commercial relationships. Arbitrators and arbitral institutions have formulated rules and established practices that are specific to globalized commerce. These rules are a long way from a complete legal system and are not self-enforcing, but the ICA community (along with the global business community it supports) has also been successful in convincing states to collaborate in the development of globalized procedural and substantive rules and practices. The same culture also provides the decisional stability necessary for arbitration to come into its own as a form of legal governance promoting the rule of law.

The notion of a culture shared by the legal professionals of a given jurisdiction is uncontroversial. After all, no legal system can be characterized solely on the basis of its rules—the rules need interpreting, and there will always be situations where no specific rule exists or where more than one rule might plausibly apply. Legal culture fills those gaps because it inculcates a collective, reflexive response that often obviates the need for argument. In ICA, it is much harder to conceive of a shared legal culture because practitioners do not share a common nationality, language, or training, or even access to a common corpus of governing laws or precedents.

However, despite their differences, international arbitration practitioners actually have *more* in common than the body of legal practitioners within any one jurisdiction.[18] As Cotterrell points out, "the distance between the work environment, career pattern and outlook of the high prestige corporation lawyer and the sole practitioner in a large American urban center is so great as to make it difficult to see any significant bonds of common

---

[16] Stavros Brekoulakis, "Systemic Bias and the Institution of Arbitration," *Journal of International Dispute Settlement* 4, no. 3 (2013): pp. 553–585.

[17] Magdalene D'Silva, "Dealing in Power: Gatekeepers in Arbitrator Appointment in International Commercial Arbitration" (2013), accessed April 17, 2014, <http://papers.ssrn.com/sol3/papers.cfm?abstract_id=2257464>.

[18] Cf. Ralf Michaels, "Roles and Role Perceptions of International Arbitrators," Chapter 3 of this book. ("Differences within this group are significantly less pronounced than differences between the group and its environment.")

experience and interest between them."[19] By contrast, most international arbitration practitioners have similar professional and educational backgrounds, including cosmopolitan and multicultural upbringings, graduate degrees from a fairly small number of elite universities, experience at multinational business law firms, and close ties with practitioner, commercial, and academic communities.[20]

The personal characteristics, values, perspectives, experiences, and modes of reasoning that ICA practitioners tend to have in common constitute a culture. That culture, along with the specific social norms that compose it, can be described, and their effects on ICA-as-governance can be assessed. A shared culture not only drives the emergence of ICA as a system of governance, but also makes it possible for ICA to achieve a measure of rule-of-law legitimacy. Although it is still a young field, ICA has reached a point in its development where its basic legal concepts are largely settled. Despite the existence of increasing numbers of international arbitrators and arbitral institutions, there is "a growing convergence in procedures and mutual goals."[21] The fact that counsel, arbitrators, and even arbitral institutions compete with each other means that beneficial innovations are quickly copied, so that the field progresses *en masse*. Even without *stare decisis* (and even without most decisions being reported), ideas and trends disseminate when arbitrators work together and when they meet in conferences and social settings.

Within the small, notoriously close-knit international arbitration community, a distinct and cohesive legal culture has emerged. This chapter looks specifically at the role that culture has played in driving the emergence of ICA as a form of global governance and in shaping the form that governance takes.

Part II evaluates "culture" as the basis for a theory of ICA-as-governance, then explains how a common culture can emerge within a heterogeneous, transnational community. Part III describes the aspects of international arbitration culture that are most relevant to ICA's development as a form of global governance. In particular, it argues that arbitrators are driven to establish ICA as an autonomous global system of governance by a shared dedication to internationalism for its own sake, and also by a belief that internationalism serves the interests of commercial parties.

To generate a cultural account of ICA as a form of global governance, I draw on a variety of previously published written sources, as well as original

---

[19] Roger Cotterrell, *The Sociology of Law: An Introduction* (London: Butterworths, 1992), p. 186 (citation omitted).

[20] The characteristics shared by leading international arbitration practitioners will be discussed in more detail in section 2(b).

[21] Russell Thirgood, "International Arbitration: The Justice Business," *Journal of International Arbitration* 21, no. 4 (2004): pp. 341–354, 342.

interview data. Written sources included anything that might express or describe standard practices in ICA or international arbitrators' values, interests, goals, or decision-making processes. These primarily include writings by arbitrators, such as academic publications, conference presentations, and lectures, as well as published arbitral awards. Academic writings are at best anecdotal evidence of one author's experiences, and only a tiny, non-representative sample of arbitral awards are published. Accordingly, such sources cannot be used for statistically valid generalizations about particular doctrines or outcomes. However, they do serve as useful sources of information about norms in ICA.

Written sources of data on ICA culture were supplemented with a series of interviews I conducted in 2012 with twenty international commercial arbitrators.[22] Most of the interviewees were selected based upon lists of leading and up-and-coming arbitration practitioners published by Chambers and Partners[23] and by Who's Who Legal;[24] additional interviewees were identified via snowball sampling.[25] It was important that the interviewees felt that they could speak freely, so all interviews are presented in an anonymized fashion. Where appropriate, interviewees are described in a general way so that the reader can put the interviewee's comments in context. No details of the interviewees' lives and careers have been changed, but information about them may have been omitted to protect their anonymity.

The interviews were conducted in person wherever possible, and otherwise by telephone. All of the interviews were recorded and transcribed for analysis. They were "semi-structured," meaning that there was not a single set of scripted questions that was posed to every interviewee; instead, a series of general topic areas, outlined in advance, was proposed for discussion, and interviewees were encouraged to speak freely on those topics or on related topics that came to mind. The semi-structured approach strikes a balance between informal and closed interview techniques. It increases the comprehensiveness of the data gathered and makes data collection more systematic, without closing off interesting areas of discussion or requiring interviewees to

---

[22] The interviews were conducted during the preparation of a recently published book: Joshua Karton, *The Culture of International Arbitration and the Evolution of Contract Law* (Oxford: Oxford University Press, 2013). That book focuses on international arbitral decision-making on matters of substantive law, and proposes that a distinct culture of international arbitration is shaping the evolution of contract law principles. However, the same research also supports the broader analysis presented in this chapter, which considers all aspects of arbitral decision-making in order to describe ICA's emergence as a form of global governance.

[23] Accessed April 17, 2014, <http://www.chambersandpartners.com/Global/Editorial/46313>.

[24] Accessed April 17, 2014, <http://www.whoswholegal.com/news/analysis/article/29384/most-highly-regarded-firms-commercial-arbitration-2012/>.

[25] That is, interviewees were asked to suggest other arbitrators who might be amenable to being interviewed and be able to share useful insights.

fit their responses into predetermined categories.[26] Semi-structured inter-
viewing therefore maximizes the opportunities for theoretically useful data
to emerge from interviews.

All twenty interviewees are active as arbitrators, but some work primarily as
counsel or as academics. They come from or currently practice in thirteen different countries,[27] and were trained in a variety of legal systems; nearly every
major region of the globe is represented.[28] They range in age from early forties
to early eighties. Some have a primarily academic background, while others
have spent their entire professional lives in law firms. Some worked for several
years in arbitral institutions, as government officials, or as national court
judges. All of them work mostly or exclusively in international arbitration, but
some are generalists and some specialize in particular types of disputes. Approximately two-thirds appear on lists of highly in-demand arbitrators, while others sit as an arbitrator less frequently or began to receive appointments as an
arbitrator only within the last few years. Only three are women, but this was
not for lack of effort to secure the participation of female interviewees: women
were more likely than men to decline requests for an interview.

Twenty interviews is a small sample, and the interviewees are not representative of all international arbitrators in a statistical sense. However, they
were chosen to represent as wide a range of backgrounds as possible; inter-
viewing arbitrators with varying characteristics presented the best opportunities to uncover similarities and differences between their adjudicative
philosophies and to identify relationships (if any) between the personal characteristics of arbitrators and their decision-making. Moreover, except on a
few well-defined issues characterized by clear differences in national legal
traditions,[29] interviewees' responses were highly consistent with each other,
regardless of differences in gender, national background, professional experience, and the like. This gives me some confidence that a larger sample would
not have yielded substantially different findings.

Of course, not everything said by arbitrators—in academic publications,
awards, or interviews—should be taken entirely at face value. In addition to
being statistically unrepresentative, the arbitral pronouncements cited in this

---

[26] See Louis Cohen et al., *Research Methods in Education*, 6th ed., (London: Routledge, 2007),
pp. 352–355.
[27] Some interviewees requested that their home states not be named because they come from
states that have produced only a few prominent international arbitrators.
[28] There were no interviewees who grew up or received their legal training in Eastern Europe,
Sub-Saharan Africa, or South Asia; however, several interviewees have extensive experience with
disputes relating to those regions.
[29] The clearest example is the appropriateness of arbitrators actively encouraging settlements
between the parties, an issue that caused some angst among interviewees. Most (but not all) of the
interviewees who indicated that it is their practice to take an active role in helping the parties to
settle were trained in jurisdictions that have a strong tradition of national court judges encouraging settlements, such as Germany, Switzerland, and various East Asian states.

chapter may simply be self-serving. After all, arbitrators work in a competitive marketplace where they must compete with other arbitrators for appointments,[30] and all of them benefit when the field as a whole expands. Indeed, much ICA scholarship has been criticized—with some justification—as amounting to little more than marketing.[31]

The fact that such sources of information may not accurately depict widespread arbitral practice does not mean that they are useless. Writings by arbitrators and interview data are important to the extent that they indicate the values with which ICA markets itself and, correspondingly, the features of ICA and characteristics of arbitrators that arbitrators themselves consider to be important. Such statements may not be statistically valid—or even accurate with respect to the individual arbitrators who wrote or said them—but they are theoretically useful. For sociological purposes, it makes little difference whether, for example, ICA actually does serve the interests of international commerce better than national court litigation. What matters is that international arbitrators passionately believe this to be the case, and that they believe serving commercial interests to be an important goal.

2 Legal Culture and Transnational Communities

Scholarly attention to ICA has thus far been dominated by traditional, doctrinal analysis that focuses on codified rules and published decisions.[32] However, "pure legal analysis" is a highly problematic concept; in any legal system, an understanding of the rules alone is insufficient to explain the outcomes

---

[30] On the role of competitive market forces in shaping ICA and in shaping international arbitrators' self-image, see Karton, *The Culture of International Arbitration*, pp. 56–75.

[31] See, e.g., Catherine Rogers, "Transparency in International Commercial Arbitration," *University of Kansas Law Review* 54 (2006): pp. 1324–1325 (observing that ICA has only "recently . . . attracted some skeptics, who are calling for . . . reforms." However, these critics remain few in number and "their proposals have demonstrated an appreciable sense of reserve.")

[32] This phenomenon may be due to the fact that so much international arbitration scholarship is published by writers who work primarily as practitioners. The purely theoretical literature on ICA (as opposed to investment treaty arbitration) is tiny and is largely focused on jurisdictional matters. See, e.g., Emmanuel Gaillard, *Legal Theory of International Arbitration* (Leiden: Martinus Nijhoff, 2010); Hong-lin Yu, "Explore the Void—An Evaluation of Arbitration Theories," *International Arbitration Law Review* 7, no. 6 (2004): pp. 180–190 (Part 1) and 8, no. 1 (2005): pp. 14–22 (Part 2). A small but increasing number of quantitative, empirical studies have been conducted. Some of these also focus on published awards, and so are either limited to investment arbitration (where most awards are publicly available) or are of very limited value because of the lack of a statistically representative sample of the total body of arbitral awards. Quantitative studies relating to international commercial arbitration mostly take the form of surveys on such easily counted matters as the relative popularity of different seats of arbitration, arbitral institutions, and governing laws. See, e.g., the surveys conducted by the School of International Arbitration at Queen Mary, University of London, with a variety of research partners. But see also Thomas Schultz and Robert Kovacs, "The Rise of a Third Generation of Arbitrators?—Fifteen Years after Dezalay and Garth," *Arbitration International* 28, no. 2 (2012): pp. 161–171. Only in the last few

reached in adjudication—the entire field of socio-legal studies is premised on this notion.[33] As Legrand writes:

> . . . the notion of "French law" cannot be reduced to that of "binding law in France." French law is much more than a compendium of rules and precepts. Accordingly, to assert that the study of French law consists in the study of French legislative texts and judicial decisions is plainly inadequate. [34]

Comparativists similarly agree that "one must take account not only of legislative rules, judicial decisions, the 'law in the books,' and also of general conditions of business, customs, and practices, but in fact of everything whatever which helps to mold human conduct in the situation under consideration."[35] In this section, I justify my focus on culture as the key component of the "everything whatever" that helps to explain international arbitral decision-making, then assess the prospects for a common culture arising in a heterogeneous, transnational community such as that of ICA practitioners.

2.1 Culture as the Basis for an Account of International Arbitration as a Form of Governance

While the existing literature discusses the interaction of multiple legal cultures in ICA,[36] it largely deals with conflicts created by differing cultural assumptions, and fails to account for the convergent effects of cultural factors on the outcomes reached in arbitrations. This is not surprising; lawyers—who, after all, make their living by working with legal rules—often resist explanations for adjudicative outcomes that discount the applicable rules (and, for that matter, cultural explanations for the creation of rules). For most lawyers,

---

years has a socio-legal literature on international arbitration begun to emerge. In addition to other chapters in this book, see also Karton, "Culture and Evolution"; Hirsch, "Investment Arbitration"; Schill, "W(h)ither Fragmentation"; D'Silva, "Dealing in Power."

[33] Also called "law and society" or "sociology of law."

[34] Pierre Legrand, *Fragments on Law-as-Culture* (Deventer: WEJ Ejeenk Willink, 1999), p. 5.

[35] Konrad Zweigert and Hein Kötz, *Introduction to Comparative Law*, translated by Toney Weir, 3rd English ed., (Oxford: Clarendon, 1998), p. 11.

[36] Most of the studies of culture in ICA that have been published focus on the divergent effects of the multiplicity of national legal cultures in which arbitrators and counsel were trained; they consider such matters as the propriety of ex parte communications, the proper scope of document production, treatment of witnesses, and the promotion of settlements by arbitrators. See, e.g., Carlos de Vera, "Arbitrating Harmony: 'Med-Arb' and the Confluence of Culture and Rule of Law in the Resolution of International Commercial Disputes in China," *Columbia Journal of Asian Law* 18 (2004): pp. 149–194; William Slate II, "Paying Attention to 'Culture' in International Commercial Arbitration," *Dispute Resolution Journal* 59 (October 2004): pp. 96–101; Laura Pair, "Cross-Cultural Arbitration: Do the Differences Between Cultures Still Influence International Commercial Arbitration Despite Harmonization?," *ILSA Journal of International and Comparative Law* 9 (2002): pp. 57–74; A. Stallard, "Joining the Culture Club: Examining Cultural Context When Implementing International Dispute Resolution," *Ohio State Journal on Dispute Resolution* 17 (2002): pp. 463–486; Stefan Frommel and Barry Rider, (eds.), *Conflicting Legal Cultures in Commercial Arbitration* (London: Kluwer, 1999).

"culture" makes for an unsatisfying account of observed behavior. It is simultaneously broad enough to be vague and narrow enough to be reductionist.[37]

Culture is also not the sole or even necessarily the prime determinant of behavior—a variety of other constraints act upon arbitrators, from legal rules to economic self-interest, to personal political or moral beliefs. Yet culture is a powerful, inescapable force shaping all aspects of human conduct, including adjudication. An explanation of arbitral justice that does not at least acknowledge cultural realities cannot hope to be complete. Despite the analytical baggage the term "culture" carries, it is the only word that adequately encompasses the various social factors that affect adjudication: standard practices, interests, values, goals, and attitudes.

Culture exists wherever members of a community share a set of norms that produce reflexive behavior conditioned by tradition or community approbation. Culture forms a feedback loop with behavior: it both shapes and is shaped by the conduct of the community's members. In other words, culture consists of a complex of norms that condition behavior both by shaping the thinking of individual members of the community and by creating a community consensus or peer pressure that discourages deviation from the community's norms. The key aspect of culture that differentiates it from other factors that shape behavior is that it is reflexive. It operates prior to— and therefore frequently obviates—deliberate decision-making. Cultural factors "make it unnecessary to think out afresh our reactions to situations. The situations become standardized. Their meaning and the appropriate way to act in relation to them become taken for granted."[38]

For analytical purposes, cultures are often broken down into their constituent social norms. The literature indicates that social norms have the same effects upon specific behaviors as culture does on behavior generally: they both condition and are conditioned by the interactions between members of the community. To put it differently, social norms and cultures are micro-level and macro-level equivalents. In the legal context, Cooter identifies three effects of social norms on law: expression, internalization, and deterrence. Norms express the customs and values of a given community, inculcate those customs and values into members of the community, and deter violations of the norms by the imposition of sanctions.[39]

---

[37] Such antipathy to culture-based explanations is hardly limited to lawyers. See, e.g., Noah Smith's derisive characterization of cultural explanations for macroeconomic patterns as "plogistonomics": Noah Smith, "Can 'Culture' Predict Economic Development?," Noahpinion Blog, April 30, 2013, <http://noahpinionblog.blogspot.ca/2013/04/can-culture-predict-economic-development.html>.

[38] Cotterrell, *Sociology of Law*, pp. 146–147.

[39] Robert Cooter, "Three Effects of Social Norms on Law: Expression, Deterrence, and Internalization," *Oregon Law Review* 79 (2000): pp. 1–22, 3.

Using norms (on the micro level) or culture (on the macro level) to explain observed behavior is a necessarily uncertain proposition. Culture is "indeterminate"—it amalgamates a "variety of activities and attributes into one common bundle"[40] and thereby may confuse different factors affecting behavior or disguise the differences between them. Culture is also "impressionistic"[41]—it lacks "sufficient analytical precision . . . to allow it to indicate a significant explanatory variable in empirical research."[42] For these reasons, it is impossible to identify direct causal relationships between specific social norms and corresponding behaviors; specific behaviors cannot be ascribed wholly to the effects of culture, let alone to any one norm. Similarly, it is impossible to separate entirely the effects of culture from other factors, such as the threat of punishment or economic self-interest. Nevertheless, so long as the researcher is careful not to indulge in false determinism, "the malleability surrounding the notion of 'culture' does not prevent the ascription of determinative efficacy and the articulation of various characteristics which can prove of direct relevance."[43]

A distinct culture is not, of course, the only thing that distinguishes international arbitral decision-making, nor is a sociologically influenced analytical method the only means by which to consider arbitral awards within their broader context. Two other fields—psychology and economics—have proven particularly useful in understanding the decision-making of national court judges, although scholars of international law have been slower to adopt interdisciplinary methods.

Psychological studies of judging—that is, studies of judges' moral and political preferences—abound in the literature on domestic litigation.[44] Similarly, many studies have been carried out that apply economic models to construct what might be called materialistic accounts of judicial

[40] Legrand, "Fragments," p. 27, quoting E. P. Thompson, *Customs in Common* (London: Penguin, 1991), p. 13.
[41] Roger Cotterrell, "The Concept of Legal Culture," in *Comparing Legal Cultures*, edited by David Nelken (Aldershot: Dartmouth, 1997), p. 21.
[42] Cotterrell, "Concept," p. 14.
[43] Legrand, "Fragments," pp. 28–29, calling the indeterminacy of culture "a handicap only for the positivist."
[44] The field has a long history, especially in the USA. An early text is Charles Haines, "General Observations on the Effects of Personal, Political, and Economic Influences in the Decisions of Judges," *Illinois Law Review* 17 (1922): p. 96 (characterized by Maveety as "the origins of what was to become behavioralism in public law": Nancy Maveety, *The Pioneers of Judicial Behavior* (Ann Arbor: University of Michigan Press, 2003), p. 8). Some prominent recent examples include Cass Sunstein et al., *Are Judges Political? An Empirical Analysis of the Federal Judiciary* (Washington: Brookings Institution Press, 2006); Richard Abel, *English Lawyers Between Market and State* (Oxford: Oxford University Press, 2003). This line of scholarship, associated at first with political scientists and later with legal scholars, is anthologized and reviewed in Maveety, *Pioneers*.

decision-making.[45] No similar studies have been conducted on ICA,[46] but in any event, for this research, the sociological approach was preferable to either economic or psychological methods. The psychological makeup and political predilections of both judges and arbitrators undoubtedly affect the way they make decisions, including their application of substantive law. However, international commercial arbitrations rarely involve the kinds of politically charged issues where differences in adjudicators' political orientations are likely to play a role. Such factors are therefore unlikely to create divergences between the ways that judges and arbitrators make decisions on the kinds of disputes that are referred to ICA.

In addition, as Tamanaha notes in his meta-study of psychological studies of judicial decision-making, the personal idiosyncrasies of judges are likely to be overshadowed by the "significant, predictable, social determinants that govern the course of judicial decision-making."[47] The "social determinants" to which Tamanaha refers include such factors as shared professional formation, mind-set, practices, and values—the kind of social norms that will be discussed below. Sociological studies are thus more likely than psychological studies to produce the kind of insights that will inform predictions about the outcomes achieved in ICA as a whole.

Economic analysis, too, has its limitations when applied to ICA. Market competition between arbitrators and between arbitral fora is one of the core institutional differences between arbitration and litigation. Indeed, some commentators have argued that the global convergence in arbitral rules and practices is best explained by economic factors. For example, Ginsburg writes that convergence is simply a case of network effects in action—like Facebook or LinkedIn, the more members in a legal network, the more valuable it is to each member. Accordingly, practices will tend toward convergence and

---

[45] See, e.g., T. Brennan, L. Epstein, and N. Staudt, "The Political Economy of Judging," *Minnesota Law Review* 93 (2009): pp. 1503–1533; Gordon Foxall, "What Judges Maximize: Toward an Economic Psychology of the Judicial Utility Function," *Liverpool Law Review* 25 (2004): pp. 177–194; Richard Posner, "What Do Judges and Justices Maximize? (The Same Thing Everybody Else Does)," *Supreme Court Economic Review* 3 (1993): pp. 1–41.

[46] Behaviorist and other psychological studies of international law have recently become more common. For a summary of this scholarship, see Tomer Broude, "Behavioral International Law," Hebrew University of Jerusalem International Law Forum Research Paper no. 12–13, accessed April 17, 2014, <http://papers.ssrn.com/sol3/papers.cfm?abstract_id=2320375>. However, to my knowledge, the only empirical psychological studies conducted on ICA are a pair of papers by Dieter Flader and Sophie Nappert, which deal with mediation of settlements and psychological factors in arbitration advocacy, respectively: Sophie Nappert and Dieter Flader, "A Psychological Perspective on the Facilitation of Settlement in International Arbitration—Examining the CEDR Rules," *Journal of International Dispute Settlement* 2, no. 2 (2011): pp. 459–470; Dieter Flader and Sophie Nappert, "Psychological Factors in the Arbitral Process," in *The Art of Advocacy in International Arbitration*, 2nd ed., edited by Doak Bishop and Edward Kehoe Huntington (NY: Juris, 2010), ch. 5.

[47] Brian Tamanaha, "The Distorting Slant in Quantitative Studies of Judging," *Boston College Law Review* 50 (2009): pp. 685–758, 697, quoting Felix Cohen, "'Transcendental Nonsense' and the Functional Approach," *Columbia Law Review* 35 (1935): pp. 809–849, 849.

newcomers will have an incentive to align themselves with existing norms.[48] However, pure economic analysis often fails to account for the influence of social norms, which constrain behavior in ways that are difficult to model in terms of economic value. For this reason, sociologists who explore economic behavior often criticize economists for ignoring the social dimension of human actions.[49]

While economic analyses often disregard the impact of social forces, the reverse is less true—sociological analyses often account for the impact of economic forces. We usually associate the word "culture" with religious, philosophical, or historical influences, but a culture may also develop out of economic forces or business practices.[50] Ogus argues that many of the characteristics of national legal cultures are explicable according to the economic value of networks.[51] As an example of legal culture developing from routine business practices, Trakman cites the informal practice of making deals over the phone, rather than relying on written contracts negotiated with the assistance of lawyers.[52] Thus, when commercial lawyers speak of "trade usages," "industry custom," or "commercial practice," they are referring to business culture.

More broadly, accounts of arbitral decision-making that emphasize arbitrators' rational self-interest (whether such accounts are based on economic models in the strict sense or on rational choice theories more generally) are unlikely to yield a complete picture. To be sure, several of the features of arbitral decision-making that are described below could be explained on the basis of arbitrators' economic self-interest. For example, as will be discussed below, arbitrators tend to defer to party autonomy on matters of procedure and choice of law; when called upon to choose the procedure or the applicable law, they are likely to select processes and laws that minimize costs and delays for the parties. Both tendencies are explicable on the basis that arbitrators want to please commercial parties and their counsel because arbitrators want to receive repeat appointments. Such analysis is accurate as far as it goes, but is incomplete in two important ways.

---

[48] Ginsburg, "Culture," p. 1342.

[49] Moshe Hirsch, "The Sociology of International Economic Law: Sociological Analysis of the Regulation of Regional Agreements in the World Trading System," *European Journal of International Law* 19, no. 2 (2008): pp. 277–299, 280, citing Mark Granovetter, "Economic Action and Social Structure: The Problem of Embeddedness," in *Economic Sociology*, edited by Richard Swedberg (Cheltenham: Edward Elgar, 1996), p. 245.

[50] Sociologists often cite market forces as underappreciated contributors to culture. See, e.g., Erhard Blankenburg, "Patterns of Legal Culture: The Netherlands Compared to Neighboring Germany," *American Journal of Comparative Law* 46 (1998): pp. 1–41.

[51] Anthony Ogus, "The Economic Basis of Legal Culture: Networks and Monopolization," *Oxford Journal of Legal Studies* 22, no. 3 (2002): pp. 419–434.

[52] Leon Trakman, "'Legal Traditions' and International Commercial Arbitration," *American Review of International Arbitration* 17, no. 1 (2006): pp. 1–43, 3.

First, even those aspects of arbitral decision-making that can be explained on the basis of economic self-interest are in some cases better explained on the basis of culture. The mere fact that a social norm has its roots in self-interested behavior does not make it any less of a norm. Over time, economic incentives yield patterns of behavior, which eventually gain normative force. If obedience to a norm is reflexive rather than the result of a deliberate choice, or is genuinely (even if inaccurately) described as a moral imperative, then the behavior is at least as much culturally determined as it is self-interested.

This phenomenon is exemplified by arbitrators' attitudes toward party autonomy. Arbitrators acknowledge that party autonomy represents a constraint on their power (for example, to determine the procedure of the arbitration),[53] but they regularly defer to the parties. One interviewee said: "I take a more deferential approach. Fundamentally, it's the parties' process." Another interviewee, a French practitioner and academic, said: "You are an arbitrator because you have been appointed as an arbitrator and it's the parties' arbitration. It's for them, so you are at their service." An American attorney put it this way:

> When I sit as an arbitrator, I think of providing a service that the parties have contracted with me to provide. I do think of myself as having a real obligation to be flexible and responsive to their needs and desires—the mode of dispute resolution that they expect when they do arbitration.

One could account for such sentiments on the basis that the parties choose the arbitrators and pay their fees, so arbitrators have a strong incentive to defer to them. In addition, many arbitral rules of procedure—binding upon arbitrators in individual cases—enshrine broad party autonomy.[54] Nevertheless, although the arbitrators I interviewed regularly (even eagerly) acknowledged that arbitration is a "business," they explained their deference to party autonomy in terms that make clear that they see party autonomy as something of inherent normative value, not simply as a rule or prudent practice.

---

[53] One interviewee said: "You are much more constrained by party autonomy than by the rules of procedure."

[54] For example, the 2013 ICC Rules of Arbitration provide that the parties may agree to join additional parties to their arbitration (Article 7), consolidate two or more arbitrations (Article 10), fix the number of arbitrators and the manner of their appointment (Article 12), replace an arbitrator (Article 15), determine the place of arbitration and the location of any hearings and meetings (Article 18), choose any rules of procedure in areas where the ICC Rules are silent (Article 19), determine the language of the arbitration (Article 20), choose the law governing the merits of the dispute, including granting the tribunal amiable composition powers (Article 21), determine the means by which case management conferences are to be conducted (Article 24), decide whether there will be an oral hearing (Article 25), exclude or admit any third parties into the hearings (Article 26), limit the power of the tribunal to grant conservatory and interim measures (Article 28), opt out of the emergency arbitrator provisions in the ICC Rules (Article 29), settle the dispute and have the settlement recorded by the tribunal in the form of an award (Article 32), set the allocation of costs of the arbitration (Article 37), and modify the time limits provided in the Rules (Article 38).

They spoke of their "duty," their "proper role," and their "moral obligation" to the parties; they characterized cases where arbitrators imposed their procedural preferences on the parties as "horror stories" where the tribunal was "riding roughshod"; they proudly gave examples of cases where they acquiesced to an agreement between the parties for procedures that the arbitrators thought were slower or more expensive than necessary.[55]

The second reason that rational choice (i.e., economic) models are necessarily incomplete is that many features of ICA governance are not explicable on the basis of arbitrators' rational self-interest. If nothing else, the choice to act as an arbitrator is itself arguably irrational, since leading practitioners can earn far more money as counsel than as arbitrators. And yet, many younger arbitration counsel aspire to "graduate" to acting as an arbitrator, and the majority of the most famous arbitrators rarely (if ever) act as counsel. Clearly, the symbolic capital they earn as arbitrators, including personal satisfaction and the esteem of their peers, is more important to them than the financial capital they earn in fees.

Another example of arbitrator conduct that is at odds with economic self-interest has to do with their application of transnational commercial law. As will be discussed below, arbitrators promote transnational law, whether in the form of codified instruments like the UNIDROIT Principles of International Commercial Contracts, or in the form of "general principles of international law" or "*lex mercatoria*." Businesses tend to be suspicious of general principles and rarely call for their application because businesses prize predictability, while general principles are notoriously malleable.[56] The continued interest in transnational commercial law, and the many scholarly writings on the subject that prominent arbitrators continue to produce, go largely against arbitrators' self-interest and are best explained by their cultural affinity for transnational contract law.

A third example relates to the principle of neutrality and the risk of bias. ICA promotes itself as a neutral forum and cannot be seen as a legitimate system of dispute resolution if arbitrators are not neutral. And yet, if self-interest were the dominant norm, individual arbitrators would be *less* neutral than national court judges. Arbitrators are both more beholden to parties (because they depend on the parties for appointments) and more likely to

---

[55] One interviewee gave the example of adjournments that violate the agreed hearing schedule: "You are much more constrained by party autonomy [than by the procedural rules]. What do the parties want to do? They'll often change their timetables by agreement. For example, let's say they wanted to go off and mediate, and they say 'May we have an adjournment of the timetable for the next four weeks?' without specifying why. You know why. A court would be much more reluctant to suddenly allow the established timetable to be ignored. But as an arbitrator, that is never a problem." Note that when arbitrators are being paid for their services in a lump sum, as is often the case, such delays directly harm their economic interests.

[56] See notes 97–99 and accompanying text.

have previously expressed opinions on factual or legal issues related to a dispute they are adjudicating (because they tend to publish in academic and trade journals). In addition, arbitrators and counsel frequently swap roles and interact freely in professional and social venues in ways that would be shocking if judges and litigators were involved. Most obviously, many arbitrators are appointed unilaterally by a single party. As Paulsson puts it, "A certain perception of reality and a distaste for hypocrisy cause some practitioners to conclude that one should simply expect that a party-appointed arbitrator will not behave as impartially as one appointed jointly or by a neutral authority."[57] If arbitrators were to act solely or primarily in their self-interest, they would systematically favor the parties that appoint them.

There is no objective evidence that such favoritism occurs in more than a handful of cases, and there is anecdotal evidence that most awards are unanimous.[58] Several interviewees said that they had never encountered a truly partial co-arbitrator, or that they had encountered one only once or twice in a hundred arbitrations. Interviewees noted that overtly partial arbitrators will lose future appointments because they will have little influence on other members of the tribunal; neutrality could therefore be seen as a function of a rational choice. However, biased arbitrators would only lose influence in tribunal deliberations if the arbitration community values neutrality. There are some arbitrations (such as some domestic arbitrations under the rules of the American Arbitration Association) where the party-appointed arbitrators are expected to be partisan and only the chair is to be neutral; such arrangements are considered anathema in ICA.

Like all social norms, neutrality is enforced by social sanctions meted out by other members of the community. Two clear examples were related by a senior arbitrator, who described two occasions where he publicly shamed co-arbitrators in investment arbitration tribunals for acting in a non-neutral manner. (He noted that such occurrences are rare, and are more common in investment than commercial arbitrations.)

> I was chairing an important investor-state panel. The party appointed by the state asked a question which was suggestive against the argument of . . . the counsel for the investor. He was a very distinguished arbitrator, but I objected to the question before any lawyer spoke. I said "I will not allow the witness to answer that question." My colleague looked at me. There was a pregnant pause, and he said "I guess you're right, Mr. Chairman. I won't insist on an answer." There is another

---

[57] Jan Paulsson, "Ethics, Elitism, Eligibility," *Journal of International Arbitration* 14, no. 4 (1997): pp. 13–22, 13–14.

[58] See Brekoulakis, "Systemic Bias." Brekoulakis concludes that, while there is little evidence that the individual biases of arbitrators have any broad-reaching impacts, decision-making in ICA in general is driven by systemic biases common to the entire ICA system. Although Brekoulakis focuses on institutions rather than social groups, the systemic biases he identifies are generally consistent with the cultural norms identified in this chapter.

case I remember . . . again the arbitrator appointed by the state showed . . . displeasure, if you wish, to a statement which was being made during the oral argument by counsel for the investor and it was obvious. I turned—and I said it loud enough for the parties to hear—I said, "So and so, please be careful with your reactions during the hearing." And [the reply came] . . . "I guess you're right. I apologize, Chairman."

In sum, a cultural account of ICA governance will highlight many of the same factors as a purely economic analysis, but will also provide insights that cannot be expressed in economic models. Culture is not the only way to explain ICA's emergence as a form of global governance, or to describe the features of that governance, but, given the limited data currently available to ICA researchers, a cultural analysis has more explanatory power than any other single theoretical model.

Only one previous large-scale cultural analysis of ICA has been conducted: Dezalay and Garth's *Dealing in Virtue*.[59] This 1996 study is well known in arbitration circles and has justly been described as "enormously successful."[60] However, *Dealing in Virtue* has both methodological and substantive limitations.

Methodologically, Dezalay and Garth relied primarily on interviews with arbitration practitioners. Their analysis generally omits arbitral awards, court decisions, and publications by arbitrators, except where they provide detailed narratives of a few historically important arbitrations. While such materials cannot necessarily be relied upon as robust in the statistical sense, they are rich sources of information about ICA. Dezalay and Garth's methodological choice to focus on interview data is consistent with their attention to personalities and relationships, as opposed to outcomes. Substantively, Dezalay and Garth focused their investigation on the kinds of people who become successful arbitrators, rather than on the decisions made by arbitrators. This was due partly to their lack of personal experience with ICA, but largely to the fact that their study is heavily influenced by the theory of social fields advanced by the French sociologist Pierre Bourdieu (who was Dezalay's mentor).

Social fields theory explains the interactions of members of a community in terms of competition for "symbolic capital."[61] It was developed to explain the internal dynamics of a community, and is not well suited to explaining the external products of those interactions, such as the outcomes reached in arbitrations. Accordingly, while social fields theory was appropriate for Dezalay

[59] Yves Dezalay and Bryant Garth, *Dealing in Virtue: International Commercial Arbitration and the Construction of a Transnational Legal Order* (Chicago: University of Chicago Press, 1996).
[60] Schultz and Kovacs, "Third Generation," p. 161.
[61] Defined as "recognized power"—the recognition that successful members of a community receive from the rest of the community. Dezalay and Garth, *Dealing in Virtue*, p. 18, quoting Pierre Bourdieu and Loic Wacquant, "Epilogue: On the Possibility of a Field of World Sociology," in *Social Theory for a Changing Society*, edited by Pierre Bourdieu and James Coleman (eds.) (Boulder: Westview, 1991), p. 72.

and Garth's purposes, it has limited utility for describing ICA's function as global governance. A broader perspective on the norms prevailing in ICA is needed, one that sheds maximum light on the core function of international arbitrators: the adjudication of disputes. This chapter therefore does not adopt Bourdieu's theory *in toto*, although it does employ some of his vocabulary, especially his notion of "symbolic capital" as defining the characteristics that members of a group find to be important. The cultural account presented here draws on interviews that focused on arbitral adjudication, and also makes use of an extensive range of written sources (in particular arbitral awards and the academic writings of arbitrators) that reveal aspects of international arbitration culture.

2.2 Emergence of a Legal Culture Specific to International Commercial Arbitration

While disagreements persist as to the particular characteristics of a particular states' legal cultures, the concept of a culture shared by legal professionals within a given jurisdiction is uncontroversial.[62] However, it is altogether more tenuous to claim that a legal culture now exists in ICA, a field that is only a few decades old, and in which practitioners do not share a common nationality, language, or training.

There are at least two good reasons to object to the notion of an ICA culture. First, arbitrators are too heterogeneous to constitute a unified community, and, second, arbitrators' actions are not reflexively conditioned by a common tradition. This section confronts these two objections and addresses the prospects for the emergence of a common legal culture in a young and heterogeneous transnational community.

Although definitions of culture vary, they all agree that a culture is a characteristic of an identifiable group.[63] Yet international arbitrators speak a variety of languages, come from different national cultures and adhere to diverse religions and ethical traditions. They were trained in different legal systems or may have no legal training whatsoever.[64] They are practicing lawyers, academics, former judges, and (though less frequently than in the past) diplomats, politicians, or industry experts such as accountants or engineers. While the most prominent arbitrators tend to be specialists in

---

[62] Cotterrell, "Concept," p. 17; Volkmar Gessner et al., (eds.), *European Legal Cultures* (Aldershot: Dartmouth, 1996), p. xvii.

[63] For a summary of different definitions of culture as the tern is used in socio-legal research, see Cotterrell, *Sociology of Law*, pp. 23–24.

[64] See Susan Bisom-Rapp, "Exceeding our Boundaries: Transnational Employment Law Practice and the Export of American Lawyering Styles to the Global Worksite," *Comparative Labor Law and Policy Journal* 25 (2004): pp. 257–337, 299–300.

arbitration law who have built their careers around ICA, others may act as an arbitrator only once or twice.[65]

What, then, are the characteristics that ICA practitioners share—the commonalities that forge ICA as a community? ICA practitioners, especially arbitrators, tend to have elite educational (if no longer socioeconomic) credentials. They have developed their careers in large, corporate, usually Anglo-American firms or major universities, and travel in both business and academic circles. They tend to share cosmopolitan, multinational backgrounds and speak multiple languages. They work repeatedly with each other and on disputes within a relatively narrow band of commercial subjects.

These commonalities will only increase as the field continues to grow; culture is a harmonizing (or at least homogenizing) force. Partly by self-selection, partly by the internalization of community norms, and partly out of a desire for esteem from other members of the community, those seeking to break into the upper echelons of international arbitral practice will emulate the résumés, practices, and perspectives of the current elite, thus reinforcing existing values and standards. These trends are reinforced by the fact that "admission" into the ranks of sitting arbitrators is controlled largely by other arbitrators and senior arbitration counsel. Counsel select party-appointed arbitrators or negotiate with each other to agree on appointments, and party-appointed arbitrators or the directing bodies of arbitral institutions (themselves composed of experienced arbitrators) make a large number of appointments.[66] In all of these scenarios, personal experience with a potential appointee is an important factor, creating incentives for ambitious younger practitioners to model their careers on those of successful members of the previous generation.[67]

In addition, the notion that so varied a group might possess a common culture is consistent with the growing importance and autonomy of transnational legal practice and private governance regimes.[68] Commerce is always

---

[65] But see: Michael Kerr, "Concord and Conflict in International Arbitration," *Arbitration International* 13, no. 2 (1997): pp. 121–144, 124 (referring to the "community of lawyers specializing in international arbitrations"); Gunther Teubner, "Breaking Frames: The Global Interplay of Legal and Social Systems," *American Journal of Comparative Law* 45 (1997): pp. 149–169, 158 (calling the international arbitral legal order a "global society").

[66] When I asked one interviewee, who has been closely involved with the governance of more than one arbitral institution, to comment on the fact that the people making appointments on behalf of institutions almost invariably are themselves active arbitrators, he replied: "Yes, but who better? You've got to know who you are appointing. The selection of arbitrators is the most important thing the institution does. . . . You look at where the parties come from, the nature of the dispute, the amount of the dispute and you discuss who would be appropriate for that case. It's the most important thing we do."

[67] On the importance of personal relationships in the selection of arbitrators see, e.g., Dezalay and Garth, *Dealing in Virtue*, p. 124; D'Silva, "Dealing in Power," pp. 51–61; Karton, *The Culture of International Arbitration*, ch. 3.

[68] Teubner, "Breaking Frames," p. 6 (arguing that ICA fulfills the criteria to constitute an epistemic community, including shared normative beliefs, shared notions of validity, and a common policy enterprise).

embedded in a mixture of public and private governance mechanisms. However, in international commerce, private governance mechanisms are relatively more important.[69] The globalization of commerce has boosted cross-border economic activity and its importance relative to domestic transacting: "as governance mechanisms become increasingly decoupled from state legal systems they are at the same time internationalized and privatized."[70]

It is only natural that internationalized legal regimes would lead to an internationalized legal practice. Modern commercial law practice has become sufficiently complex that specialization is necessary to attract clients,[71] and law firms increasingly market their international arbitration groups as specialist practices.[72] This trend has been abetted by the decoupling of legal practice from citizenship requirements, such as the elimination of educational and citizenship requirements as a bar to transborder mobility within the EU.[73] In a modern commercial practice, a lawyer of one nationality might work in a second country on a transaction governed by a third country's law, and the dispute is referred to arbitration in a fourth country. In such situations, practitioners effectively operate in a geographic limbo.[74]

When actors are placed outside existing systems of governance and interact repeatedly with each other, it is not surprising that new regimes specific to the new field of interaction might develop. As Friedman argues, transnational law "is as much a product of its times and its social context as national or local law."[75] This process has been called "auto-constitutionalization"—the phenomenon of private governance regimes that operate outside the state developing their own sets of norms.[76] In other words, where economic globalization has given rise to the establishment of a transnational corpus of specialist legal practitioners who work primarily with each other and outside the governance of any one state, autonomous professional norms will coalesce—into a culture of ICA.

[69] Gralf-Peter Calliess and Moritz Renner, "Transnationalizing Private Law: The Public and Private Dimensions of Transnational Commercial Law," *German Law Journal* 10 (2009): pp. 1341–1355, 1342.

[70] Gralf-Peter Calliess and Hermann Hoffmann, "Judicial Services for Global Governance—Made in Germany?," *German Law Journal* 10 (2009): pp. 115–122, 119 (citation omitted).

[71] J.R. Faulconbridge and D. Muzio, "Legal Education, Globalization, and Cultures of Professional Practice," *Georgetown Journal of Legal Ethics* 22 (2009): pp. 1335–1359, 1352.

[72] See, e.g., Mathias Wittinghofer, "Instead of a Foreword: What Arbitration Is About—Or: How to Win the Moot," in *The CISG—A New Textbook for Students and Practitioners, Special Edition for Participants of the 15th Willem C. Vis International Commercial Arbitration Moot*, edited by Peter Huber and Alistair Mullis (Munich: Sellier, 2007), p. 5, <http://www.cisg.law.pace.edu/cisg/moot/Wittinghofer.pdf>, accessed April 17, 2014.

[73] Patrick Glenn, "Comparative Law and Legal Practice: On Removing the Borders," *Tulane Law Review* 75 (2001): pp. 977–1002, 981.

[74] Cf. Faulconbridge and Muzio, "Legal Education," p. 1347.

[75] Lawrence Friedman, "Borders: On the Emerging Sociology of Transnational Law," *Stanford Journal of International Law* 32 (1996): pp. 65–90, 90.

[76] See, e.g., Gunther Teubner, "Global Private Regimes: Neo-Spontaneous Law and Dual Constitution of Autonomous Sectors?," in *Public Governance in the Age of Globalization*, edited by Karl-Heinz Ladeur (Aldershot: Ashgate, 2004).

A second reason to doubt that ICA possesses a culture is that the field is too new for ICA practitioners' shared values and standard practices to have become reflexively conditioned by a common tradition. Culture shapes the identity of a community through repeated interactions "over the *longue durée*."[77] In other words, culture is a function not only of the existence of shared norms, but also of time passing, so that norms become internalized—acted upon instinctively and not by conscious choice.

ICA in its modern incarnation has existed for scarcely three generations; it is still an emerging field. In the 1990s, Dezalay and Garth described two generations of arbitrators. The first, whom they called the "grand old men," were characterized by a charismatic form of authority. The second, whom Dezalay and Garth labeled "technocrats," were specialists in the law of international arbitration.[78] Schultz and Kovacs recently argued that a third generation of international arbitrators, characterized by their case management abilities, whom they dub the "managers," is now ascendant.[79] In addition, many of the practices and norms now widespread among international arbitrators result from conscious choices among competing options; they therefore stand in stark contrast to cultural norms, which are by definition reflexive. As Hirsch points out, social norms are obeyed because members of the community have internalized the norm, not because they have calculated that such behavior would be profitable.[80]

Thus, it may be argued that various social norms observable in the ICA community do not constitute a culture, and that other interdisciplinary models of arbitrator behavior (economic, psychological, etc.) must therefore have greater explanatory power. Regardless of its merits, this argument misses the point. The important question is not whether something that can properly be labeled "a culture" already exists, but whether social norms specific to the community are affecting arbitral decision-making. If they are, then regardless of any other factors affecting arbitral decision-making, understanding those norms is crucial to generating a complete understanding of whether and in what ways ICA constitutes a system of governance. The next section describes some of the social norms already prevailing in ICA and their consequences for the governance that ICA provides.

---

[77] Legrand, "Fragments," p. 27.

[78] This process has been called the "professionalization" or "judicialization" of ICA. See, e.g., Andrea Schneider, "Not Quite a World Without Trials: Why International Dispute Resolution is Increasingly Judicialized," *Journal of Dispute Resolution* (2006): pp. 119–129; Patricia Hansen, "Judicialization and Globalization in the North American Free Trade Agreement," *Texas International Law Journal* 38 (2003): pp. 489–503. An early text on this theme is Richard Lillich and Charles Brower (eds.), *International Arbitration in the 21st Century: Toward "Judicialization" and Conformity?* (New York: Transnational Publishers, 1994).

[79] Schultz and Kovacs, "Third Generation." See notes 131–132 and accompanying text.

[80] Hirsch, "International Law," p. 280.

3 International Arbitration Culture and Global Governance

This section argues that a cultural analysis shows that ICA is evolving into a form of global governance—as opposed to an atomized form of governance derived from national orders—in part because the ICA community is normatively committed to governance at the global level. This commitment can be understood in terms of a legal culture of international arbitration. That culture is composed of several norms that relate to both the institutional structure of the ICA system and the values shared by members of the community.[81] This section describes two of these norms that have the clearest effects on governance. First, members of the ICA community share a dedication to internationalism, to an ideal of global justice. The internationalism norm drives the ICA community to pursue global governance for its own sake. Second, members of the community see the purpose of ICA as serving the needs of international commerce. Since arbitrators see the interests of international commerce as being served by internationally harmonized rules and processes, the ICA community is committed to global governance for the sake of international commercial interests.

3.1 *Arbitrators' Normative Commitment to Global Governance for its Own Sake*

"Internationalism" is defined here as a point of view that reflects a dedication to subordinating national perspectives and distinctions in favor of transnational or global ideals. In practical terms, arbitral internationalism manifests itself in a desire among arbitrators to establish an international space autonomous from national legal systems and traditions. Arbitral internationalism is related to the desire to detach arbitration from interference by national courts, but it is rooted less in an instinct toward autonomy than in economic, social, and intellectual globalization. Members of the ICA community tend to see global solutions as superior simply because they are global.

Arbitrators' internationalism can be seen in their dedication to "delocalizing" ICA and in their promotion of uniform international rules and practices. Arbitrators also embody internationalism in their persons; the value that members of the community place on international *bona fides* can be seen in the cosmopolitan backgrounds and attitudes valorized in the community.

INTERNATIONALISM AND DELOCALIZATION
Arbitrators tend to share the goal of creating a coherent, unified global dispute resolution forum that is more than a hodgepodge of national laws, practices,

---

[81] See Karton, *The Culture of International Arbitration*, chs. 3 and 4.

and cultures.[82] ICA practitioners and national courts and legislatures now agree that international commerce requires "harmonized solutions . . . acceptable for parties from around the world."[83] The purpose of ICA is therefore to "provide a universal procedure for the settlement of international disputes detached, to the extent possible, from the particularities of national law."[84] Lew argues that "international arbitration is, and should be recognized to be, an autonomous process for the determination of all types of international business disputes. . . . It has its own space independent of all national jurisdictions."[85]

If ICA is to be an autonomous forum existing on a global plane, it must be supported by the national systems of enforcement that make arbitration possible—this is a reality of our Westphalian world order. However, arbitrators have worked to progressively detach ICA from the reach of national laws and courts, a process often called "delocalization."[86]

At one time, delocalization "gave rise to passionate arguments,"[87] especially in developing countries that suspected that ICA was simply another means by which multinational corporations based in developed countries could exploit natural resources without fear of legal sanction. Although these tensions and concerns persist,[88] they have diminished significantly.[89] Many aspects of delocalization are no longer controversial; parties everywhere are

---

[82] See generally Hans Smit, "The Future of International Commercial Arbitration: A Single Transnational Institution?," *Columbia Journal of Transnational Law* 25 (1986): pp. 9–33. Cf. Thomas Carbonneau, "Arbitral Law-Making," *Michigan Journal of International Law* 25 (2004): pp. 1183–1208, 1186 ("Processing international commercial claims through national courts leads to a decentralized system that is Byzantine both in its structure and operation.").

[83] Elena Helmer, "International Commercial Arbitration: Americanized, 'Civilized,' or Harmonized?," *Ohio State Journal on Dispute Resolution* 19 (2003): pp. 35–67, 57; see also Grigera Naón, "Role," p. 118.

[84] Craig et al., *ICC Arbitration*, p. 295, referring to the motivation for some of the 1998 amendments to the ICC Rules.

[85] Julian Lew, "Achieving the Dream: Autonomous Arbitration," *Arbitration International* 22, no. 2 (2006): pp. 179, 181.

[86] The term delocalization was coined to refer to the notion that a dispute need not be governed by the substantive law of the seat of the arbitration. Kaufmann-Kohler has described this as "physical delocalization," which she points out "has already been achieved." Gabrielle Kaufmann-Kohler, "Globalization of Arbitration Procedure," *Vanderbilt Journal of Transnational Law* 36 (2003): pp. 1313–1333, 1318. However, since at least the 1980s, "delocalization" has referred more broadly to the detaching of any aspect of the arbitral proceedings from national laws: Otto Sandrock, "To Continue Nationalizing or to De-Nationalize? That is Now the Question in International Arbitration," *American Review of International Arbitration* 12 (2001): pp. 301–334, 302–303.

[87] Kaufmann-Kohler, "Globalization," p. 1320.

[88] Cutler explains their persistence on the basis that international arbitration is one component of a "new constitutionalism" that maintains a separation between politics and economics, and thus shields from democratic institutions questions of "who gets what" in international commercial disputes. This democratic deficit unsurprisingly leads to dissent, especially in developing states. Claire Cutler, "International Commercial Arbitration, Transnational Governance, and the New Constitutionalism," Chapter 6 of this book.

[89] At least in commercial arbitrations. In investment treaty arbitrations, allegations of systemic bias in favor of investors or against developing countries continue to generate controversy.

now free to choose a different substantive law than that of the seat of arbitration, or to hold hearings in a different place than the seat.[90] Over roughly the last thirty years, many states have amended their arbitration-related legislation, and have done so almost uniformly in the direction of lesser state control of arbitration; a similar trend can be seen in the case law.[91]

Despite such developments, arbitrators recognize that, given the necessity of national courts as ICA's enforcement mechanism, total delocalization is as impossible as it is undesirable. In *Coppée Levalin NV v. Ken-Ren Fertilisers and Chemicals*, the House of Lords considered an application for security for costs in an arbitration administered by the International Chamber of Commerce (ICC). Lord Mustill recognized the conflict between the necessity of court involvement and arbitrators' internationalist desires:

> On the one hand the concept of arbitration as a consensual process reinforced by the ideas of transnationalism leans against the involvement of . . . a municipal court. On the other side there is the plain fact, palatable or not, that it is only a Court possessing coercive powers which could rescue the arbitration if it is in danger of foundering.[92]

This theme—a recognition of the necessity of national court involvement but a yearning for truly delocalized arbitration—has run through the international arbitration literature for decades.[93] Lew refers to a-national arbitration as "the dream,"[94] while Smit calls it "the epitome"[95] of international arbitration. The "utopian" and "mystical" cast of much of this literature shows that

---

[90] Gary Born, *International Commercial Arbitration: Commentary and Materials*, 2nd ed. (The Hague: Kluwer, 2009), p. 1675.

[91] An overview of this history is given in Karton, *The Culture of International Arbitration*, pp. 79–85, 124–134. See also Pierre Mayer, "The Trend Toward Delocalisation in the Last 100 Years," in *The Internationalisation of International Arbitration: The LCIA Centenary Conference*, edited by Martin Hunter et al. (The Hague: Kluwer, 1995); Jan Paulsson, "Delocalisation of International Commercial Arbitration: When and Why it Matters," *International and Comparative Law Quarterly* 32, no.1 (1983): pp. 53–61.

[92] *Coppée Levalin NV v. Ken-Ren Fertilisers and Chemicals* [1994] 2 Lloyd's Rep 109 (HL) (speech of Lord Mustill).

[93] See, e.g., Robert Pietrowski, "Evidence in International Arbitration," *Journal of International Arbitration* 22, no. 3 (2006): pp. 373–410, 386; William Park, "The Specificity of International Arbitration: The Case for FAA Reform," *Vanderbilt Journal of Transnational Law* 36 (2003): pp. 1241–1311, 1265; Sandrock, "De-Nationalize," p. 320; Mayer, "Delocalisation," p. 37; Hans Smit, "A-National Arbitration," *Tulane Law Review* 63 (1989): pp. 629–645, 631; Jan Paulsson, "Arbitration Unbound: Award Detached from the Law of its Country of Origin," *International and Comparative Law Quarterly* 30, no. 2 (1981): pp. 358–387; Pierre Lalive, "Les regles de conflit de lois appliqués au fond du litige par l'arbitre international siègient en Suisse," *Revue de l'arbitrage* (1976): p. 155; F.A. Mann, "Lex Facit Arbitrum," in *International Arbitration: Liber Amicorum for Martin Domke*, edited by Pieter Sanders (The Hague: Martinus Nijhoff, 1967), p. 159. Lew argues that the debate goes back at least to the 1950s, when Frédéric Eisemann, then Secretary-General of the ICC International Court of Arbitration, lobbied for the establishment of denationalized international arbitration awards that would not be subject to annulment in any jurisdiction: Lew, "Dream," p. 179.

[94] Lew, "Dream," p. 179.   [95] Smit, "A-National," p. 629.

it is motivated by more than just the "economic interests that participants in international law have in proclaiming their own autonomy."[96]

Indeed, as Kennedy puts it, delocalization is "the whole point" of constructing an international arbitral order: "If an international commercial transaction can be legally constructed in a regime detached from local legal cultures, in a place without public policy, the risks from prejudiced national public policy, intercultural misunderstandings, national elite rent seeking, or biased judiciaries can be diminished."[97] A London-based interviewee expressed this perspective in the following terms:

> Arbitration is in an area of its own, and the reason is simple: the parties have expressly excluded the courts of each other's countries, or any third country, by their agreement to arbitrate. . . . The parties are saying, in effect, "You, judge, mind your own business. Please respect what we're doing. If either of us needs your help to get evidence, help us. If either party needs interim relief, and the court thinks it's right, help that party. And when one party seeks enforcement, help that party. But don't interfere; don't second guess the arbitrators." That's what the parties want.

INTERNATIONALISM AND TRANSNATIONAL COMMERCIAL LAW

For many arbitrators, the establishment of arbitration as autonomous from both national courts and national laws calls for the establishment of a purely international commercial law. This notion encompasses codified international law instruments like the CISG and the UNIDROIT Principles. However, the desire for a substantive law that is both transnational and global is most manifest in autonomous free-floating "general principles of international law," also called *lex mercatoria* or "transnational commercial law."

Many arbitrators argue that the application of transnational commercial law is generally desired by parties engaged in international commerce. As one interviewee put it: "we see in arbitration as it develops that parties are having more confidence in the internationally minded arbitrator than they do in the nationally minded judge." To the extent that this is true, arbitral internationalism is a manifestation of respect for party autonomy and a desire to serve the interests of cross-border commerce.

But, to a large extent, it is not true. Businesses tend to be suspicious of general principles and rarely draft contracts that choose them as the governing law; businesses prize predictability, while general principles are notoriously malleable. In the vast majority of arbitrations where the contract contains a choice of law provision—97.7%, according to one study—the parties nominate the

---

[96] Ralf Michaels, "Dreaming law without a state: scholarship on autonomous international arbitration as utopian literature," *London Review of International Law* 1, no. 1 (2013): p. 37. As Michaels notes, "the literature on law without a state is replete with dreams, visions, and faith.": p. 36.

[97] David Kennedy, "New Approaches to Comparative Law: Comparativism and International Governance," *Utah Law Review* [1997]: pp. 545–647, 624.

law of some state.[98] If arbitrators simply acquiesced to the preferences of the parties, then the *lex mercatoria* would have remained merely an academic curiosity.[99] Arbitrators' continued interest in transnational commercial law is best explained by their preference for international rules over national ones, regardless of the parties' wishes.[100]

Interviewees acknowledged that commercial parties are generally suspicious of transnational law, but were adamant that transnational law maintains an important role, especially where a state law governing the contract contains gaps or is alleged to be outdated or parochial. In such circumstances, many arbitrators will at least propose to the parties that the national rule ought to be replaced with an international one. For example, one interviewee said: "I look at the applicable law and I try to find support in some international rules. Where there is a gap in the applicable law, you look at these international rules to find the right solution."

To give a concrete example, several interviewees decried the inadequacy of state laws regarding interest rates. Most (but not all) states permit the granting of prejudgment interest on damages awarded. However, state laws often award interest at a rigid statutory rate that does not take into account the actual cost of money or variations in currencies. Interviewees were blunt about the inappropriateness of such rules for modern, globalized commerce. A Swiss arbitrator recalled a case governed by Swiss law in which damages were calculated in a foreign currency:

> Does it make sense to apply the Swiss statutory interest of five percent a year to a currency . . . where the interest rate is 80 percent per year because the currency devalues so quickly that the interest rate is practically a hedge against devaluation? It has nothing to do with Swiss statutory law.

One tribunal held bluntly that, "In international arbitration, arbitrators have the broadest powers to determine interest on the basis of the most appropriate rate, without resorting to any [choice of law] rule."[101]

---

[98] Dasser, "Mouse," p. 140. See also Dietz, "Efficient Enforcement," pp. 168–170.

[99] This is another reason to discount economic self-interest as the primary determinant of arbitrator behavior.

[100] On the disconnect between arbitrators' image of the universality of the *lex mercatoria* and the small number of cases in which it is actually applied, see Piero Bernardini, "International Arbitration and A-National Rules of Law," *ICC Bulletin* 15, no. 1 (2004): pp. 58, 63.

[101] ICC Case No. 11849 of 2003, *Yearbook of Commercial Arbitration* XXXI (2006): p. 148. The contract was governed by the CISG, which provides for awards of interest but gives no guidance on how to set the rate. The parties each argued for the application of their own states' laws to determine the interest rate. However, the tribunal rejected both arguments and awarded interest at the rate it considered to be appropriate based on the facts of the case. On the setting of interest rates in international arbitration, see the various articles in a Special Issue on Compensation and Damages in International Investment Arbitration, *Transnational Dispute Management* 4, no. 6 (2009). Although they may be more sensitive to these issues than national courts are, arbitral

It appears, then, that parties' concern with transnational law is not its transnational character, but its indeterminacy. Accordingly, most arbitrators today are reluctant to apply *lex mercatoria* or general principles of international law under those names. However, they do frequently promote codified international commercial law instruments. When asked about the circumstances in which he might apply *lex mercatoria*, one interviewee, a French practitioner and academic, said: "I think it does not exist, . . . and it's a good thing that it does not exist. The UNIDROIT Principles exist. They are written, they are predictable, so why not use them?"

Tribunals have even applied codified transnational law instruments such as the CISG and the UNIDROIT Principles in circumstances where no national court would apply them, including before they went into effect[102] and when neither party submitted that they apply.[103] Even when a national law does apply, arbitrators will frequently refer to international contract law instruments as evidence of an international consensus on a point of law,[104] or as expressions of applicable trade usages,[105] or to "arrive at an internationally acceptable and economically sensible interpretation of the domestic law."[106] Witz explains that the greater use of international instruments in ICA occurs "because international arbitrators are more accustomed and more favorably

---

tribunals have nevertheless been criticized for not going far enough in calculating interest according to actual economic realities. See John Gotanda and T.J. Senechal, "Interest as Damages," *Columbia Journal of Transnational Law* 47 (2009): pp. 491–536.

[102] Klaus Berger, "International Arbitral Practice and the UNIDROIT Principles of International Commercial Contracts," *American Journal of Comparative Law* 46 (1998): pp. 129–150, 140, citing ICC Cases Nos. 5713 of 1989 *Yearbook of Commercial Arbitration* IV (1990): p. 70 and 2438 of 1975, *Journal de droit international* [1976]: p. 969 (both applying the UNIDROIT Principles). The tribunals argued that the UNIDROIT Principles applied as an expression of general principles of international law.

[103] See, e.g., ICC Case No. 11849 of 2003, *Yearbook of Commercial Arbitration* XXXI (2006): p. 148, para. 9. Even if the CISG is applicable in litigation, courts are unlikely to determine *sua sponte* that it applies; one of the parties must argue for the CISG's application. In arbitration, on the other hand, some tribunals determine on their own initiative whether the CISG or one of the other international contract law instruments applies. See, e.g., ICC Case No. 8128 of 1995, *Journal de droit international* [1996]: p. 1024. Schlechtriem also describes a case in which the contract contained an express choice of Russian law. The parties argued for conflicting interpretations of Russian domestic law but the tribunal found that the CISG applied as the Russian law pertaining to international sales contracts. Peter Schlechtriem, "Requirements of Application and Sphere of Applicability of the CISG," *Victoria University Wellington Law Review* 36 (2005): pp. 781–794, 794.

[104] See, e.g., an award reported in Michael Bonell, "Die UNIDROIT-Prinzipien der internationalen Handelsvertrage: Eine neue Lex Mercatoria?," *Zeitschrift für Rechtsvergleichung* [1996]: pp. 152, 157: "General legal rules and principles enjoying wide international consensus . . . are primarily reflected by the UNIDROIT Principles."

[105] See, e.g., ICC Case No. 5713 of 1989, *Yearbook of Commercial Arbitration* XV (1990): p. 70, where the tribunal declared there to be "no better source" than the CISG from which "to determine the prevailing trade usages." The tribunal applied the CISG on this basis, even though neither party came from a state that had ratified to the CISG.

[106] Berger, "UNIDROIT Principles," p. 138. See, e.g., the extensive use made of the UNIDROIT Principles in ICC Case No. 8486 of 1996, *Yearbook of Commercial Arbitration* XXIVa (1999): p. 162.

inclined to the application of international standards than are national judges."[107]

Indeed, the development of a transnational commercial law is an explicit project for some arbitrators. Arbitrators frequently apply general principles or *lex mercatoria* where the parties have expressed no intention to apply them, or even where the parties have expressly chosen to be governed by national laws.[108] As one tribunal noted, general principles: "apply uniformly and are independent of the peculiarities of different national laws."[109] But even where tribunals have not deliberately attempted to develop autonomous transnational commercial law, transnational legal rules may nevertheless be generated as a by-product of the heterogeneity of the ICA community and the internationalist ethos shared by many arbitrators:

> I'm not sure it's a conscious thing. . . . It's due in part to the fact . . . in international arbitration that you have actors from different backgrounds—legal, cultural. So you may have counsel from different backgrounds, you may have arbitrators on the panel who are trained in different laws, and somehow everybody wants to get to some common denominator. When you deliberate within a tribunal, you would like to get to consensus.

Arbitral internationalism can be seen most clearly in the evolution and status of what is most often called "international arbitral practice"—the standard practices of ICA practitioners reconceived as legal norms. The particularities of those standard practices are beyond the scope of this discussion; what is striking is the extent to which ICA practitioners have developed a set of procedures that are global in character and are not derived from any one national approach. They are often described as a hybrid of common law and civil law approaches, but many practices are specific to arbitration, such as the use of "Redfern Schedules" for document discovery.[110]

---

[107] Vivian Curran, "The Interpretive Challenge to Uniformity," *Journal of Law and Commerce* 15 (1995): pp. 175–199, 179 (citation omitted).

[108] See, e.g., ICC Case No. 9466 of 1999, *Yearbook of Commercial Arbitration* XXVII (2002): p. 170, para. 3, where the tribunal reasoned that: "the silence of the parties as to the law that should be applied to their contractual relationship may be construed as a significant indication of their will that their relationship be simply governed by the terms of the contract and/or . . . by the general principles of international commercial contracts." Alternatively, tribunals may avoid the controversies surrounding general principles and *lex mercatoria* but still serve internationalist values by applying the laws of the parties' home states concurrently. See, e.g., ICC Case No. 7319 of 1992, *Yearbook of Commercial Arbitration* XXIV (1999): p. 141, para. 13.

[109] ICC Case No. 8385 of 1995, *Journal de droit international* (1997): p. 1061.

[110] Redfern Schedules (named after Alan Redfern, an independent arbitrator who helped establish Freshfields' international arbitration practice group) are documents that set out, in a table format, such matters as descriptions of the documents requested, explanations of why the documents are likely to be relevant, any grounds for objection to production of the document, replies to those objections, and the tribunal's decision related to the document. See, e.g., Jeffrey Waincymer, *Procedure and Evidence in International Arbitration* (London: Kluwer, 2012), pp. 871–872.

Interviewees were unanimous in their denunciation of parties that want to have their arbitration governed by national procedural rules. Several told anecdotes of cases where they tried, with greater or lesser success, to convince the parties to adopt international procedural standards, which they equated with modernity and global acceptability. One interviewee made this broad declaration:

> I always try to apply international standards rather than any particular national standard. I understand sometimes the parties from different jurisdictions might have different positions . . . . But my practice, when I act as chairperson particularly, is to try to introduce the modern standards of international arbitration.

This internationalist approach is also being codified within ICA and in national laws. Documents like the IBA's Rules on the Taking of Evidence in International Commercial Arbitration and Guidelines on Conflicts of Interest in International Arbitration, which are in common use in ICA, were designed as crystallizations of existing practice, much in the manner that the American Restatements are intended to crystallize existing common law. Similarly, industry groups[111] and private law firms[112] have published their own compendia of best practices in international arbitration procedure.

Arbitral institutions and national legislators frequently look to international arbitral practice for guidance when updating rules and statutes. For example, the recently proposed amendments to the Dutch Arbitration Act have been described as necessary modernizations reflecting changes in international arbitral practice,[113] as were several provisions of the 2011 revisions to the French Code of Civil Procedure relating to arbitration.[114] However, the most prominent example is the UNCITRAL Model Law itself, which is often praised for codifying international arbitral practice on such basic matters as competence-competence and party autonomy in the choice of the governing law. States that have adopted the UNCITRAL Model Law often do so on the basis that the Model Law "reflects worldwide consensus on key aspects of international arbitration practice."[115]

---

[111] See, e.g., various practice guidelines and protocols issued by the Chartered Institute of Arbitrators, <http://www.ciarb.org/information-and-resources/practice-guidelines-and-protocols/list-of-guidelines-and-protocols>, accessed April 17, 2014.

[112] See, e.g., Debevoise and Plimpton LLP's "Protocol to Promote Efficiency in International Arbitration," <http://www.debevoise.com/arbitrationprotocol/>, accessed April 17, 2014.

[113] Bas van Zelst, "The Proposed New Dutch Arbitration Act," *International Arbitration Law Review* 15, no. 3 (2012): pp. 75–80.

[114] See, e.g., Guido Carducci, "The Arbitration Reform in France: Domestic and International Arbitration Law," *Arbitration International* 28, no. 1 (2012): pp. 125–157; Hong-lin Yu and Masood Ahmed, "The New French Arbitration Law: An Analysis," *International Arbitration Law Review* 15, no. 1 (2012): pp. 20–29.

[115] See, e.g., Jonathan Haydn-Williams, "International Commercial Arbitration in Barbados," *Arbitration* 77, no. 2 (2011): pp. 184–196, referring to the Barbados Arbitration Act.

Commentators reinforce these trends by evaluating institutional rules of procedure and national laws according to the extent to which they conform to international arbitral practice. For example, Luttrell and Moens praise the most recent revisions to ACICA Rules for reflecting "international best practice,"[116] while O'Reilly criticizes the English Arbitration Act 1996 for failing to "design its provisions for wide international use. . . . The time has come to review the legislation with a renewed and vigorous international outlook."[117]

INTERNATIONALISM AND ARBITRATORS' COSMOPOLITANISM

The phenomenon of globalization does not reside only in institutions.[118] Increasingly, it is a mental and cultural phenomenon, a "zeitgeist."[119] As Arthurs argues, even if institutions like the WTO were to dissolve and transnational trade and immigrant flows were to disappear, "We would still be deeply implicated in a global system driven not only by trade and economics, but also by transnational social, cultural, intellectual and ideological forces . . . a globalization of the mind."[120] ICA practitioners tend to share a perspective increasingly detached from the national legal systems and traditions in which they were trained, a preference for transnational sources of law over national ones, and a sensitivity to the issues that arise when dealing across multiple cultures and legal traditions. As one interviewee, a Swiss arbitrator who has practiced in three different countries, put it:

> There's an international dimension that . . . is absolutely key, it seems to me. There are different nationalities. You have to understand both sides. . . . You just don't handle an Italian party, a Russian party, a Polish party, a Thai party the same way. There are things you have to be aware of; otherwise, they are shocked by your behavior.

For this reason, nearly all successful international arbitration practitioners—whether arbitrators or counsel—share a kind of global cosmopolitanism that marks modern elites in a number of sectors. Rogers lists the following

[116] Sam Luttrell and G.A. Moens, "The Arbitration Rules of the Australian Centre for International Commercial Arbitration: Distinctive Features," *Arbitration* 75, no. 4 (2009): pp. 520–531, 521.
[117] Michael O'Reilly, "Provisions on Costs and Appeals: An Assessment from an International Perspective," *Arbitration* 76, no. 4 (2010): pp. 705–718.
[118] International arbitral institutions are often themselves exemplars of globalization. For example, Grigera Naón sees the ICC as exemplifying the multicultural character of international commercial arbitration. Noting the multinational makeup of the ICC Court of Arbitration and of its secretariat, he concludes: "All of this emphasizes the multicultural traits of the ICC arbitration system and guarantees the evenhanded administration of ICC arbitrations, free from cultural or other bias." Grigera Naón, "Role," p. 139.
[119] J. Flood, "Megalawyering in the Global Order: the cultural, social and economic transformation of legal practice," *International Journal of the Legal Profession* 3, no. 1/2 (1996): pp. 169–214, 200.
[120] Harry Arthurs, "Globalization of the Mind: Canadian Elites and the Restructuring of Legal Fields," *Canadian Journal of Law and Society* 12 (1997): pp. 219–240, 222.

characteristics as being shared by "leading arbitrators": linguistic ability, "multi-national educations," and "multi-faceted, multi-cultural legal training."[121] Such attributes reinforce arbitrators' image of neutrality and legitimize them to their international clientele. As Garth puts it, potential arbitrators "must demonstrate . . . an attitude that might be termed 'cosmopolitan.' . . . The 'legal nationalist' has a very difficult time making it into the international arbitration world."[122] Cremades, a prominent Spanish arbitrator, argues that professionalism in arbitration is largely defined by the arbitrator's ability to avoid legal nativism and to think internationally.[123]

Just as parties are likely to seek out arbitrators with cosmopolitan backgrounds, lawyers with cosmopolitan backgrounds are more likely to be interested in practicing international arbitration law. One arbitrator, now based in a major business capital, described leaving her home country (where she not only grew up, but also studied and practiced) in part to "get away from its parochial mentality" and "to find an international aspect to the practice of law." As Dezalay and Garth note, many of the key solicitors who developed international arbitration in England "were . . . drawn to ICC-style arbitration because of their own cosmopolitan, hybrid backgrounds—for example, they were born or educated abroad, including especially German immigrants; or they had foreign, typically French, spouses."[124] Such self-selection is self-reinforcing. Young cosmopolitan lawyers are likely to join a field populated by lawyers with similar characteristics, thus strengthening the effects of cultural norms.

These observations were supported by interviewees. While the arbitrators interviewed do not constitute a representative sample of all arbitrators, or even of highly active arbitrators, their example is illustrative of trends in ICA. All twenty interviewees speak English fluently and work regularly in English; ten speak at least three languages, and eleven are sufficiently proficient in at least two languages to conduct arbitrations in them.[125] Of the eight interviewees who are native English speakers, five are sufficiently proficient in another language to converse in it and to read legal documents in it. Ten of the interviewees studied law in at least two countries, and eight have formal training

---

[121] Rogers, "Vocation," pp. 958–959.

[122] Bryant Garth, "How to Become an International Commercial Arbitrator," *World Arbitration and Mediation Report* 8 (January 1997): pp. 10–11.

[123] Bernardo Cremades, "Overcoming the Clash of Legal Cultures: The Role of Interactive Arbitration," in *Conflicting Legal Cultures in International Arbitration*, edited by Stefan Frommel and Barry Rider (London: Kluwer, 1999), p. 165 ("The truly international arbitrator is one whose . . . professionalism leads his decision to be independent from the 'bag and baggage' of the system or national systems from which he originates.").

[124] Dezalay and Garth, *Dealing in Virtue*, p. 136.

[125] Counting Mandarin and Cantonese as different languages. They are often lumped together in arbitrators' CVs, but proficiency in one does not permit even basic understanding of the other, so they are counted separately for the present purpose.

in both common law and civil law systems. Eight practiced or taught at universities in at least two different countries.

The interviewees who speak more than one language or were trained in more than one legal system invariably pointed to their multinational backgrounds as a reason for their effectiveness as arbitrators and their success in garnering appointments. A London-based arbitrator who speaks English, French, and Russian, and was trained in both civil law and common law, said that these are significant assets:

> It's absolutely essential in this field to have, if not languages, certainly the cultural awareness at the very, very least . . . . In the big firms nowadays I don't think they even consider you if you have only one language . . . That certainly wasn't the case in my day. I think also that my civil law-common law background was invaluable.

An Australian arbitrator, who has significant experience with Asian legal systems and also studied in Europe, made a similar point about cultural awareness:

> Firstly, it's desirable to have experience in more than one legal system. But beyond that, it's desirable to have a broader, cross-cultural sensitivity and experience. It's not simply the fact that laws differ from place to place. The significance of the contract, and the approach to the law and the role of law differ from place to place. One has to understand that they come from a different system and you have to make allowances and be fair.

The theme of cross-cultural sensitivity was raised by every interviewee. For example, interviewees said that they might alter the way they manage an arbitration depending on the nationality of the parties and their counsel. When asked whether it is appropriate to encourage the parties to settle, a Swiss arbitrator said that the appropriate course of action depends in part on the parties' backgrounds:

> I'm not among those who say that's out of the question; an arbitrator shouldn't do it. But you do have to be careful; you really have to choose where it will be well received and where it will not, and that may depend on the cultural background and the legal background of counsel and the parties. If I proposed it to Swiss and German parties, they will find it very natural, but if I have English and Australian counsel they will think it's totally outrageous.

Several interviewees articulated their role as including helping parties from different traditions and counsel from different legal systems to understand each other. Said one interviewee: "It's part of my job to make, not necessarily make the parties converse, because obviously often they are no longer able to do that, but certainly to make sure that they have a conduit." Interviewees gave examples of circumstances in which they acted as "cultural translators" (in the words of one interviewee), either between the parties or between one party and other members of the tribunal.

All of these characteristics—cultural sensitivity, training in multiple systems, and facility with multiple languages—constitute forms of symbolic capital in the ICA community. Symbolic capital constitutes the recognition, institutionalized or not, that successful members of a community receive from the rest of the group.[126] The forms of symbolic capital which members of the field try to accumulate are closely related to shared cultural norms. Leaders in the field have become leaders because of their stores of symbolic capital, while those seeking entrance to the field must conform to accepted norms and practices, thus reinforcing prevailing orthodoxies. In ICA, such global cosmopolitan *bona fides* are important sources of symbolic capital. Their prevalence among members of the community is evidence of ICA's normative commitment to internationalism.

3.2 Arbitrators' Commitment to Global Governance Because it Serves the Needs of Business

Arbitrators are private contractors. They provide a service (resolution of disputes) and are compensated for that service by their clients (the disputing parties). As Gélinas puts it: "International arbitration exists to serve the needs of international business."[127] Lord Mustill takes the argument a step further: "Commercial arbitration exists for one purpose only: to serve the commercial man. If it fails in this, it is unworthy of serious study."[128] The same principle applies to individual arbitrators:

> The idea that . . . the arbitrator is bound to respect the parties' will in exercising his or her role and, more generally, in discharging his or her duties, has prevailed for a long time. That the arbitrator is the servant of the parties is . . . a widespread view.[129]

ICA is characterized by two social norms that relate to the service of business: an ideal of client service, and an orientation toward the interests of the international commercial system.

At its heart, arbitration is a service industry. As one interviewee put it: "I do think of myself as somebody who is providing paid service to the parties. When I'm sitting as an arbitrator, the parties are entitled to the service they are paying you for." The relationship between arbitrators and disputing

---

[126] Bourdieu and Wacquant, "Epilogue," p. 72.

[127] Fabien Gélinas, "Arbitration and the Challenge of Globalization," *Journal of International Arbitration* 17, no. 4 (2000): pp. 117–122, 117.

[128] Mustill, "New Lex Mercatoria," p. 86. See also Fortier, "Back to the Future," p. 121 (characterizing Mustill's statement as "the essential creed of the commercial arbitrator)."

[129] Piero Bernardini, "The Role of the International Arbitrator," *Arbitration International* 20, no. 2 (2004): pp. 113–122, 114.

parties (and their counsel) is one characterized by collegiality, informality, and an identification by the arbitrators with the mutual interests of the parties before them.[130] Arbitrators work to ensure that the parties see the arbitration process as serving their needs: "Unlike judges, arbitrators must inevitably treat the parties and their lawyers as having something of the aura of a clientele, whose goodwill, understanding and respect for the tribunal's authority must be cultivated and preserved."[131]

The clearest way in which arbitrators act as service providers is by actively managing disputes so as to serve the interests of the parties, especially with respect to minimizing costs and delays. A survey conducted by Schultz and Kovacs indicated that the current generation of arbitration practitioners particularly prizes "case management abilities" when selecting arbitrators.[132] My interviews support this survey data. Interviewees were unanimous in their belief that arbitrators should actively manage the proceedings so as to serve the collective interests of the parties. They rejected the notion that an arbitrator should act purely as an umpire in the manner of a common law judge. One observed:

> I'm a great believer in getting my hands right in the mud, right up to here [gestures at her elbow], and I think the parties appreciate the fact that you care about their dispute and that you show that you care by getting down to the nitty gritty with them, rather than just sitting there.

More generally, as one interviewee related: "You need a decent office, you need an organization. Robert Briner used to say that 'arbitration is mostly logistics,' and he's absolutely right. It's getting organized, having a system."[133] Such abilities are particularly important for sole arbitrators and chairs.

In particular, interviewees emphasized the importance of tailoring the procedure of each arbitration to the needs of the parties and the particularities of the case, which usually involves acceding to the parties' agreement on matters of procedure unless the agreed processes are manifestly inappropriate.[134]

---

[130] But see Michaels, "Roles," p. 62 (arguing that "Contemporary arbitration procedures are frequently so adversary in nature that the common interests of the parties, which could define a service, are difficult to identify.").

[131] Kerr, "Concord," p. 124.

[132] Schultz and Kovacs, "Third Generation," p. 170.

[133] This interviewee proudly pointed out the low, wheeled cabinets that cluttered his office and the color-coded filing system he had developed for his own use: "I have a nifty system for these kinds of things. A lot of others have probably similar systems."

[134] One interviewee pointed out that most disagreements on procedure between the tribunal and the parties should be resolved in the parties' favor: "After all . . . in case management, you are guiding the parties in a direction in which they are not unhappy to go. In arbitration essentially, you start off with what the parties agreed to as the procedure and you build on that. You don't normally tear up what they've written. . . . If the practitioners are experienced, they will tell you why it was agreed in this way, and you will pipe down, settle down and say, 'That's fine. If that's what you want, that's what you'll get.'"

Interviewees invariably stated that their practice is to hold a procedural conference as early in the proceedings as possible, not only to determine how the arbitration will go forward, but also to establish a good working relationship. They noted that it is helpful to have not just counsel, but also party representatives at this meeting:

> It is useful to have a very good first session where you discuss procedure. You have counsel there, and you also have party representatives. . . . They may not be used to this process [and] it's important that they get a good impression . . . of the way the tribunal handles matters. That is what I mean by management skills: practically and technically, how do you draft a calendar; what comes first, what comes next; what do you do if there is an issue that disrupts the calendar; these kinds of things.[135]

The emphasis currently placed on case management can be traced in part to a backlash against the arguably more legalistic style of arbitration employed by the technocratic "second generation" of arbitrators identified by Dezalay and Garth.[136] Commercial parties (and many arbitration lawyers) frequently complain that arbitration has become too technical and rule-bound, too slow and expensive—in short, too much like litigation.[137] The modern-day valorization of case management skills is an example of the field adapting to ensure that it continues to serve the needs of commercial parties.

Arbitrators' dedication to their "clientele" goes beyond such matters as deferring to the parties' agreement in matters of procedure or taking steps to minimize costs and delays. The entire field is oriented toward the interests and perspectives of businesses engaged in cross-border commerce. ICA practitioners tend to see arbitration as part of the international commercial system, rather than sitting separate from it, as national courts do.

In a much-quoted passage, Justice White of the US Supreme Court wrote that arbitrators should not be held to standards of "judicial decorum" because arbitrators' effectiveness depends on them being "men of affairs, not apart from

---

[135] Another interviewee gave an example of the benefit of bringing party representatives to the procedural conference. When counsel ask for an extension due to a schedule conflict, "the arbitrators peer over at the party on the other side, the in-house lawyer, and say, 'Is that the schedule you want or do you want this over sooner?' Often, you get a different response."

[136] See notes 131–132 and accompanying text.

[137] See, e.g., Thomas Stipanowich, "Arbitration: The 'New Litigation'," *University of Illinois Law Review* (2010): pp. 1–59; Steven Seidenberg, "International Arbitration Loses Its Grip," *ABA Journal* (April 2010), <http://www.abajournal.com/magazine/article/international_arbitration_loses_its_grip>, accessed April 17, 2014. Many of these critics associate greater legalism and procedural complexity with an Americanization of ICA; see, e.g., Pedro Martinez-Fraga, *The American Influence on International Commercial Arbitration: Doctrinal Developments and Discovery Methods* (Cambridge: Cambridge University Press, 2009). Some commentators appear to identify "Americanization" with something more specific: expansive document discovery. See, e.g., Lucy Reed and Jonathan Sutcliffe, "The 'Americanization' of International Arbitration?," *Mealey's International Arbitration Report* 16, no. 4 (2001): p. 37; Nicholas Ulmer, "A Comment on 'The 'Americanization' of International Arbitration?," *Mealey's International Arbitration Report* 15, no. 6 (2001): p. 24.

the marketplace."[138] Arbitrators have come to see themselves as actors not just in an international legal system, but in international commerce as well. One interviewee contrasted the arbitral and judicial roles on the basis that arbitrators play a constructive role in improving commercial relationships:

> What you want when you are an arbitrator is somehow to be constructive, as opposed to a judge, which I think can be quite a destructive way of acting, in the sense that you keep breaking relationships. As an arbitrator . . . in certain cases there is scope for a role to allow business to carry on, or just generally to be part of the wheels of business.

As Lew puts it, arbitration has "survived the test of time . . . because it has served the users well. It has met the needs of those business entities which have considered national courts to be unsuited to their needs."[139] Many arbitrators believe passionately in the essential role of arbitration within international business and, in particular, in arbitration's superiority over litigation for the resolution of international commercial disputes. Arguments for arbitration's indispensability often take the form of lists of the general deficiencies of litigation in national courts, such as its purported slowness and expense in comparison with arbitration. However, arbitrators are most likely to cite the "inability" of litigation to respond to the "specific needs" of international commerce.[140]

Arbitrators often go out of their way to highlight various ways in which national laws are inadequate to the task of regulating modern international commerce. For example, in ICC Case No. 9427 of 1998, the dispute concerned an on-demand guarantee. The governing law, that of a Baltic state, had no provisions dealing specifically with on-demand guarantees. Instead of applying broader contract law principles, as a national court would have done, the tribunal applied "such legal principles relating to on-demand guarantees which are generally applied in international banking practice."[141] Thus, faced with an apparent gap in the applicable national law, the tribunal applied general principles specific to the particular industry, notwithstanding that neither party had asked the tribunal to do so. It did not, as a national court would likely have done, reason by analogy to other provisions of the governing law.

Aside from the perceived inadequacies of national laws, in pursuing global governance the ICA community is also responding to commercial parties'

---

[138] *Commonwealth Coatings Corp. v. Cont'l Casualty Corp.*, 393 U.S. 145, 150 (1968), reh'g denied, 393 U.S. 1112 (1969).

[139] Lew, "Dream," p. 180.

[140] Markus Petsche, *The Growing Autonomy of International Commercial Arbitration* (Frankfurt: QUADIS, 2005), p. 10; Gilles Cuniberti, "Beyond Contract—The Case for Default Arbitration in International Commercial Disputes," *Fordham International Law Journal* 32 (2009): pp. 417–488.

[141] ICC Case No. 9427 of 1998, *Yearbook of Commercial Arbitration* XXVII (2002): p. 153, para. 7.

interest in predictable, non-discretionary rules.[142] With respect to cross-border commerce, certainty and predictability can best be achieved by a unification or harmonization of the law; otherwise, when disputes arise, parties may face an unpredictable choice of law process, and be surprised to find themselves subject to unfamiliar foreign laws.[143] Since the movement to unify national commercial laws has achieved at best partial success, harmonization of commercial law on a global scale may best be accomplished by the organic development of global commercial law outside of state law-making processes. It is this intuition that has driven the development of the various non-state codifications like the UNIDROIT Principles.

Arbitrators also distinguish themselves from national court judges by touting what they see as their superior commercial expertise. Interviewees were unanimous in expressing their view that commercial experience and a commercial perspective are essential for effective arbitration. To be effective, arbitrators must understand the commercial context of disputes. One interviewee, a partner at a Swiss law firm, expressed this idea:

> You have to have good analytical skills, so that in a short time you get to know what the case is about, you're able to discern the interests of the parties that lie behind their positions and that means you have to have a certain commercial experience. I think that the best arbitrators are those that have a long career behind them as advisors to parties to commercial transactions.[144]

A London-based barrister, with extensive experience in both arbitration and litigation, put the point in these terms:

> Parties want you to understand that they've got a big commercial dispute which is a real burden for them and they're trying to cope with it as best they can. It's costing them a lot of money, it's taking up huge amounts of management time and

---

[142] See, e.g., Joshua Karton and Lorraine de Germiny, "Has the CISG Advisory Council Come of Age?," *Berkeley Journal of International Law* 27 (2009): pp. 448–495, 448–449 ("A well-functioning commercial system requires a high degree of legal certainty; businesses will hesitate to enter into contractual relationships if they are unable to forecast the risks associated with breakdowns in those relationships."); Robert Bejesky, "The Evolution in and International Convergence of the Doctrine of Specific Performance in Three Types of States," *Indiana International and Comparative Law Review* 13 (2003): pp. 353–404, 398 ("private sector actors demand enhanced certainty in transnational business dealings"); James Callaghan, "UN Convention on Contracts for the International Sale of Goods: Examining the Gap-Filling Role of CISG in Two French Decisions," *Journal of Law and Commerce* 14 (1995): pp. 183–200, 185 ("Enhancing certainty in the realm of international sales will greatly facilitate the flow of international trade and serve the interests of all parties engaged in commerce.").

[143] See, e.g., Larry DiMatteo et al., *International Sales Law: A Critical Analysis of CISG Jurisprudence* (Cambridge: Cambridge University Press, 2005), p. 11 (decrying the "panoply of different domestic laws and systems that commercial parties face"); Hannu Honka, "Harmonization of Contract Law Through International Trade: A Nordic Perspective," *Tulane European and Civil Law Forum* 11 (1996): pp. 111–184, 117 ("Free international trade functions better in a legally harmonized environment than in the opposite situation.").

[144] A similar point was made by a Canadian interviewee, who observed that facility with numbers is an important but underrated skill.

you need to be sympathetic to the commercial background that both parties will be experiencing in fighting a major case. Judges in my experience are often quite oblivious to all this commercial background.[145]

To some extent, such denigration of judges' expertise may be motivated by arbitrators' interest in promoting ICA over national court litigation. After all, in many jurisdictions, complex commercial cases are heard only by judges sitting on a "commercial court" or named to a "commercial list," who presumably have significant relevant experience. However, as noted above, reactions that begin as economic self-interest (or continue to coincide with self-interest) may become internalized as social norms. Almost universally, commentators on ICA—including, but not limited to, my interviewees—aver that a commercial mentality exists alongside a legal mentality in the minds of arbitrators. One interviewee said simply: "I like to think my approach would be fact-based and commercial in nature. In other words, if at all possible, to focus on the basic business aspects of the case." Hermann declares more broadly: "It is fundamental to arbitration that it should solve disputes according to commercial practice and common sense, arriving at a result considered fair in a particular business community."[146] Collins contrasts what he sees as the "commercial reasoning" employed by arbitrators with the "private law reasoning" employed by courts:

> Private law reasoning is relatively closed to the competing normative considerations governing contractual behavior outside the discrete communications system provided by the formal contract itself. As a result, it cannot translate expectations grounded in business relations . . . into its default standards for regulation. Commercial arbitration appears to be favored precisely because it can provide . . . reasoning which marries adjudicated outcomes with business expectations more closely. [147]

This mind-set is exemplified by one interviewee, who said that there are really only two rules of contractual interpretation: "Common sense is one. Commercial sense is the other."

The primary practical manifestation of this purported commercial mentality is the primacy given in arbitral awards to arguments based on trade usages and commercial reasonableness. As Schmitthoff notes: "The interaction between international commercial usage and international arbitration is very

---

[145] This claim—that national court judges often make for poor arbitrators—was made by many interviewees, all without any prompting. One said, "The fact that someone has been a very distinguished judge by no means qualifies that person as a good international arbitrator. I've seen this many times." In general, the retired judges who have had the most success in gaining appointments are those with significant experience as counsel in international arbitrations prior to their elevation to the bench (Lord Mustill might be the paradigmatic example).

[146] A.H. Hermann, *Judges, Law and Businessmen* (Deventer: Kluwer, 1983), p. 221.

[147] Hugh Collins, *Regulating Contracts* (Oxford: OUP, 1999), p. 187.

close."[148] Arbitrators thus oblige what they see as the preference of businesses to be judged according to the standards of their industries, and not according to a priori rules of general contract law imposed upon them by the legal system.

In an apparent exception to their usual deference to party autonomy, arbitral tribunals sometimes apply trade usages when the parties have not raised them, and may find that a trade usage governs even absent evidence that the parties were aware of it.[149] For example, in ICC Case No. 7661 of 1995, the tribunal reasoned that it was "unlikely that a seller would accept a lower price to account for an event, known or unknown, that may never happen." Consequently, the tribunal found that the contract did not include a guarantee against certain unforeseen financial contingencies.[150] In ICC Case No. 9443 of 1998, the tribunal considered a contractual obligation that, on its plain language, was perpetually renewable unless both parties expressly repudiated it. The tribunal interpreted the term differently, on the ground that "such an obligation is irreconcilable with general principles of international commerce. It is unimaginable that two corporations will be obliged to cooperate eternally without one or the other being able to put a stop to the cooperation."[151]

There are even cases where arbitral tribunals disregarded express contractual or statutory terms in light of trade usages. Such cases are explicable on the basis that the norm in favor of trade usages is consistent with party autonomy; tribunals appear to assume that, regardless of their express agreement, parties also intend to be bound by applicable trade usages. For example, ICC

---

[148] Clive Schmitthoff, "The Codification of the Law of International Trade," *Journal of Business Law* (January 1985): pp. 34–44, 34. Cremades makes a similar observation: "International arbitrators have always been closer, and thus more familiar with, the usages and practices of international commercial trade than local judges." Cremades, "Clash," p. 167.

[149] Under the major international contract law instruments, parties are deemed to be aware of relevant trade usages and must take active steps to inform themselves. With respect to the CISG, see Martin Schmidt-Kessel, "Article 9," in *Schlechtriem & Schwenzer Commentary on the UN Convention on Contracts for the International Sale of Goods (CISG)*, edited by Ingeborg Schwenzer, 3rd English ed. (Oxford: OUP, 2010), p. 191. (Under CISG art. 9(2), if it can be shown that a relevant usage is "objectively known," then a "lack of due care" is imputed to a party that claims ignorance of the usage.) With respect to general principles, the online CENTRAL compilation of *lex mercatoria* rules, Principle I.2.2, adopts a similar position: <http://www.trans-lex.org/903000/>, accessed April 17, 2014. This reversal of the standard posture in domestic legal systems indicates the greater deference to trade usages in international than in national commercial laws.

[150] ICC Case No. 7661 of 1995, *Yearbook of Commercial Arbitration* XXII (1997): p. 149, para. 17. While this can be seen as simply an application of common sense, and not a specific trade usage, it remains that such arguments are made from the point of view of practice rather than law. Another example of interpretation of a party's intent based on commercial reasonableness is consolidated ICC Cases Nos. 6515 and 6516 of 1994, *Yearbook of Commercial Arbitration* XXIVa (1999): p. 80, para. 15.

[151] ICC Case No. 9443 of 1998, Journal de droit international (2002): p. 1106 (author's translation): "Un tel engagement serait également inconciliable avec les principes généraux du commerce international. Il est par exemple inimaginable que deux sociétés puissent s'obliger à coopérer éternellement sans que l'une ou l'autre puisse mettre fin à la coopération."

Case No. 3820 of 1981 involved a sale of food products in installments. Payment was to be by documentary credit, which provided that the seller could draw down the credit "provided goods have been received by opener." The buyer refused the goods and argued that this meant that it had not received the goods, so the preconditions for payment had not been met. The Dutch sole arbitrator wrote that documentary credits must be interpreted "not . . . in accordance with specific national laws . . . but in accordance with the practices that apply on this subject in international trade." He held that, contrary to its express terms, the letter of credit must be read to include situations where "the opener could have received the goods if he had wanted to."[152]

Institutional rules of arbitration and national arbitration laws reflect arbitrators' desire to ensure that applicable trade usages are enforced. In a 2000 survey of arbitral institutions, Drahozal found that thirty-two of the forty-four largest commercial arbitration institutions require arbitrators to take trade usages into account, regardless of the applicable law.[153] As for national arbitration laws, prior to 1985 references to trade usages were rare.[154] Since 1985, the situation has changed dramatically; most statutes enacted or amended after that date contain provisions requiring arbitrators to take trade usages into account.[155] These changes are part of a broader phenomenon in which states compete to attract arbitration business to their jurisdictions, largely by limiting the means by which state courts and state laws will intrude into the arbitration.[156] The trend toward greater emphasis on trade usages is likely to continue because businesses are served by processes that judge their behavior according to the standards specific to their industries.

---

[152] ICC Case No. 3820 of 1981, *Yearbook of Commercial Arbitration* VII (1982): p. 134, 136. See also ICC Case No. 7063 of 1993, *Yearbook of Commercial Arbitration* XXII (1997): p. 87, awarding interest at the prevailing rate of inflation despite acknowledging that an applicable provision of Saudi law prohibited an award of interest; ICC Case No. 3316 of 1979, *Yearbook of Commercial Arbitration* VII (1982): p. 106, holding that, in a documentary credit, "unconditional" should not be interpreted literally, since in banking practice it is often used as a synonym for "irrevocable."

[153] Christopher Drahozal, "Commercial Norms, Commercial Codes, and International Commercial Arbitration," *Vanderbilt Journal of Transnational Law* 33 (2000): pp. 79–146, 112.

[154] Drahozal, "Commercial Norms," p. 118.

[155] English translations of these statutes are collected in Jan Paulsson, ed., *International Handbook on Commercial Arbitration* (The Hague: Kluwer, 2010). This trend is traceable in part to the enactment since 1985 of approximately seventy statutes based on the UNCITRAL Model Law on International Commercial Arbitration, which includes a provision to this effect, art. 28(4).

[156] Beginning in the 1970s, when the arbitration field began to grow rapidly, states engaged in "open rivalry" to provide attractive venues for arbitration: Michael Kerr, "Arbitration and the Court: The UNCITRAL Model Law," *International and Comparative Law Quarterly* 34, no. 1 (1985): pp. 1–24, 7. This process is exemplified by the 1979 and 1996 revisions to the English Arbitration Act, the "main object" of which was "to attract arbitration to London." William Park, "The *Lex Loci Arbitri* and International Commercial Arbitration," *International and Comparative Law Quarterly* 32, no. 1 (1983): pp. 21–37, 21 (referring to the 1979 Act). After the 1979 Act was passed, there ensued a "scramble among western European nations" to compete for arbitration business: William Park, "National Law and Commercial Justice: Safeguarding Procedural Integrity in International Arbitration," *Tulane Law Review* 63 (1989): pp. 647–709, 680.

The *lex mercatoria* is also partly a manifestation of arbitrators' preference for trade usages, and of their belief that the parties also prefer to be governed by trade usages. A common characterization of the *lex mercatoria* is as the set of trade usages specifically "adapted to the conditions of international commerce."[157] Tribunals have invoked this notion when they apply *lex mercatoria* without the express authorization (and sometimes over the objections) of the parties. For example, in ICC Case No. 8873 of 1997, the contract contained an express term that it was governed entirely by Spanish law to the exclusion of all other laws.[158] Nevertheless, the tribunal found that it also had to consider *lex mercatoria*, which is not a "law," but rather applies to all international commercial disputes because it embodies international trade usages.[159] Indeed, proponents of *lex mercatoria* argue that the universalized, formalized language of *lex mercatoria* gives a patina of law to what are essentially trade usages, thus enhancing their legitimacy as a basis for arbitral decision-making.[160]

4 Conclusion

It is not a teleological inevitability that ICA should come to constitute a form of global governance. It could amount to no more than what domestic commercial arbitration is in many jurisdictions: a more informal and flexible adjunct to court litigation. However, ICA is in fact evolving into a genuine system of global governance—one that (unlike national courts) is limited in the ambit of its subject-matter jurisdiction but (also unlike national courts) is global in its reach. Despite the variety of laws that apply to international arbitrations and the variety of backgrounds possessed by international arbitrators,

---

[157] ICC Case No. 8385 of 1995, *Journal de droit international* [1997]: p. 1061 (author's translation); Petsche (n 124) 15; see also Flood, "Megalawyering," p. 170; Catherine Rogers, "Fit and Function in Legal Ethics: Developing a Code of Conduct for International Arbitration," *Michigan Journal of International Law* 23 (2002): pp. 341–423, 351–352. For a similar characterization of the medieval *lex mercatoria*, see Harold Berman and Colin Kaufman, "The Law of International Transactions (Lex Mercatoria)" *Harvard International Law Journal* 19 (1978): pp. 221–277, 225.

[158] ICC Case No. 8873 of 1997, *Journal de droit international*(1998): p. 1017 ("Ce Contrat sera entièrement régi par le droit espagnol, à l'exclusion de tout autre droit.").

[159] ICC Case No. 8873, "On devra prendre en considération également, dans le contexte de la loi nationale choisie par les parties, les usages de commerce international." ("One must also take into consideration, in the context of the national law chosen by the parties, the usages of international commerce. " Author's translation.) Another example is ICC Case No. 8365 of 1996, where the respondent contested the applicability of *lex mercatoria* on the ground that it is not a complete system of law, and can therefore serve only to interpret the applicable national law and fill gaps in it. Nevertheless, in the absence of a choice of law by the parties, the tribunal decided to apply "the terms of the contract and trade usages." It also referred to "international arbitral precedent," which it characterized as "largely applying . . . general principles of law, trade usages and international customary law, or lex mercatoria": ICC Case No. 8365 of 1996, *Journal de droit international* (1997): p. 1078, 1079 (author's translation).

[160] Cf. Flood, "Megalawyering," p. 170.

a common legal culture knits together the members of this distinct international community. This shared culture makes it possible for ICA to emerge as a kind of global governance and at the same time propels that emergence.

In domestic legal communities, culture provides a shared frame of reference on the applicable laws and rules and also fills the inevitable gaps in those laws and rules. The same is true in the transnational sphere. Arbitrators' normative commitment to an ideal of global justice guides them to seek internationally harmonized rules of both procedure and substance. The field's orientation toward serving the needs of international business shapes those rules. As would be expected based on the cultural analysis presented above, the governance provided by international arbitration emphasizes legal and cultural neutrality, flexible and efficient procedures, deference to party autonomy, and substantive rules founded in standards of commercial reasonableness.

5

Private Justice, Public Policy: The Constitutionalization of International Commercial Arbitration

Moritz Renner[1]

"International commercial arbitration has become big legal business, the accepted method for resolving international business disputes," Dezalay and Garth wrote in 1995.[2] It is even bigger legal business today, and the number of disputes resolved by arbitral tribunals is steadily growing.[3] Commercial actors prefer arbitration over litigation because they consider the arbitral procedure superior in terms of confidentiality, efficiency, flexibility, neutrality, and costs.[4] There is a growing competition between different mechanisms of dispute resolution—domestic and international, public and private. Economic actors forum-shop for "law as a product,"[5] tailored to their individual needs.

[1] The author is greatly indebted to Claire Cutler, Thomas Dietz, Ralf Michaels, and Walter Mattli for their comments on earlier versions of this paper.

[2] Yves Dezalay and Bryant G. Garth, "Merchants of Law as Moral Entrepreneurs: Constructing International Justice from the Competition for Transnational Business Disputes," *Law & Society Review* 29, no. 1 (1995): pp. 27–64.

[3] For up-to-date figures see <http://www.iccwbo.org/court/arbitration/id5531/index.html>, accessed October 31, 2013.

[4] Julian D. Lew et al., *Comparative International Commercial Arbitration*, (Den Haag: Kluwer Law International, 2003), paras 1–13 *et seq.*; Alan Redfern and Martin Hunter, *Law and Practice of International Commercial Arbitration*, (London: Sweet & Maxwell, 2004), paras 1–41 *et seq.*

[5] Roberta Romano, "Law as a Product. Some Pieces of the Incorporation Puzzle," *Journal of Law, Economics, and Organization* 1, no. 2 (1985): pp. 225–283.

However, the possibility of "opting out of the domestic legal system"[6] by way of private agreements raises questions with a view to public-policy concerns: While domestic courts are bound to national public policies and constitutions, the status of public policy in international arbitration as a "private justice system"[7] is highly disputed.[8] Thus, the "opting out of the legal system" by private actors going to arbitration may very well entail—or even be aimed at—a simultaneous "opting out of regulation."[9] Under the conditions of a fierce competition between domestic legal systems and alternative dispute-resolution mechanisms, this might lead to a "race to the bottom" between courts and tribunals with regard to public-policy standards. Some authors, such as Claire Cutler, harshly criticize the emerging transnational legal order as being formed by a global "mercatocracy" and curtailing the potential for necessary nation-state regulation.[10]

The problem is a direct consequence of the far-reaching autonomy of international commercial arbitration vis-à-vis domestic legal systems. The reach of public policy in arbitration proceedings is not determined by domestic law, but by the conflict-of-laws rules applied by arbitral tribunals, i.e., the meta-rules which determine the applicable substantive law in arbitration (*infra* I). But conflict-of-laws rules not only lie at the core of the problem, they may at the same time indicate its solution. This is evidenced by an empirical survey of the practice of arbitral tribunals, which shows that such tribunals are not simply executors of the will of the parties, but do apply public-policy norms, both domestic and international (*infra* II). Arbitral practice integrates different conceptions of public policy into an overarching hierarchy of norms mimicking domestic constitutional orders. This self-constitutionalizing move can be explained, on a macro-sociological level, as a consequence of the juridification of arbitral dispute resolution (*infra* III). Effectively, it both expands and limits the reach of international commercial arbitration as a governance instrument: It supplements the supposedly private nature of arbitration with broader policy objectives—yet this approximation to domestic legal systems might also lessen the appeal of arbitration to potential claimants (*infra* IV).

---

[6] Lisa Bernstein, "Opting Out of the Legal System: Extralegal Contractual Relations in the Diamond Industry," *Journal of Legal Studies* 21, no. 1 (1992): pp. 115–157.

[7] Cf. Lew et al., *Comparative International Commercial Arbitration*, paras 5–20.

[8] For a paradigmatic account of the problem see Marc Blessing, "Mandatory Rules of Law versus Party Autonomy in International Arbitration," *Journal of International Arbitration* 14, no. 4 (1997): pp. 23–40; for a more recent survey see Moritz Renner, "Towards a Hierarchy of Norms in Transnational Law?" *Journal of International Arbitration* 26, no. 4 (2009): pp. 533–555.

[9] Erin Ann O'Hara, "Opting Out of Regulation: A Public Choice Analysis of Contractual Choice of Law," *Vanderbilt Law Review* 53 (2000): pp. 1551–1604.

[10] A. Claire Cutler, *Private Power and Global Authority. Transnational Merchant Law in the Global Political Economy*, (Cambridge: Cambridge University Press, 2003).

This chapter analyzes the role and reach of public-policy norms with a view to international commercial arbitration. Similar problems arise in other fields of international arbitration as diverse as investment arbitration and domain-name dispute resolution. I have discussed these examples elsewhere.[11] International commercial arbitration has been chosen as an example for this chapter because it reflects the tension between the parties' contractual autonomy and public-policy issues in a particularly pointed manner. The research leading to this chapter is based on an empirical survey of more than 400 arbitral awards, the results of which are referred here in a very condensed form.[12]

1 The Problem

International commercial arbitration is firmly founded on the principle of party autonomy. Parties may choose the arbitrators, the venue, the rules of procedure, as well as the applicable substantive law. This freedom of choice is what chiefly distinguishes arbitration from litigation in domestic courts. Domestic courts limit the parties' freedom of choice in several ways, most importantly with regard to the applicable substantive law. Even though national conflict-of-laws rules usually allow for a choice of law in cross-border contractual disputes (e.g., art. 3 Rome I Regulation[13]), the court will apply "overriding mandatory provisions" (e.g., art. 9 Rome I Regulation) as well as the "public policy of the forum" (e.g., art. 21 Rome I Regulation) regardless of the law otherwise applicable.[14]

These limitations of party autonomy result from the fact that every legal order is deeply embedded in a historically grown conception of shared values and social order.[15] They are based on the assumption that certain fundamental norms of society must not be left at the parties' disposal. It is therefore well established that state courts, when they enforce commercial contracts and protect property rights, at the same time exercise public control functions by

---

[11] Moritz Renner "Towards a Hierarchy of Norms in Transnational Law?"

[12] For the whole survey cf. Moritz Renner, *Zwingendes transnationales Recht. Zur Struktur der Wirtschaftsverfassung jenseits des Staates*, (Baden-Baden: Nomos, 2011). The survey includes published arbitral awards rendered within the ambit of the Court of Arbitration of the International Chamber of Commerce, the Uniform Dispute Resolution Policy of the Internet Corporation for Assigned Names and Numbers, and the International Center for the Settlement of Investment Disputes between 1990 and 2006.

[13] Regulation EC No. 593/2008 on the Law Applicable to Contractual Obligations.

[14] For the objectives of overriding mandatory provisions and public policy see, e.g., Moritz Renner, "art. 9 Rome I" and "art. 21 Rome I," in *The Rome Regulations. Commentary on the European Rules of the Conflict of Laws*, edited by Gralf-Peter Calliess (Alphen aan den Rijn: Kluwer Law International, 2011).

[15] Moritz Renner "art. 21 Rome I," in *The Rome Regulations*, edited by Gralf-Peter Calliess, para. 1.

limiting the legal autonomy of commercial actors with regard to certain policy considerations (*infra* II).

However, in enforcing such norms, domestic courts generally show a rather lenient attitude toward cross-border contracts, as compared to purely domestic contracts.[16] Furthermore, there is disagreement as to the question of whether domestic courts should only apply the overriding mandatory provisions of the forum state or also those of third states.

Nonetheless, it is well established under every domestic system of conflict-of-laws that certain mandatory norms protecting public policy must be applied to cross-border contracts as well (so-called "overriding" mandatory provisions).[17] In contrast, international commercial arbitration as a mechanism of alternative dispute resolution is not bound by domestic conflict-of-laws rules (*infra* III). Instead, international arbitral tribunals develop their own conflicts rules—and thus decidedly enhance the reach of party autonomy, while the applicability and reach of mandatory norms remain largely unresolved (*infra* IV).

2 Private Law and Public Policy

Freedom of contract is the cornerstone of every modern system of private law. The concept is based on the liberal ideal that individuals can best manage their own affairs if there is as little government interference as possible. Yet even in the private law codifications of the 19th century, as well as in the natural law tradition, it was generally accepted that freedom of contract has certain necessary limits. Already under Roman law, commentators had argued that there should be a number of norms which could not be derogated by way of private agreement: "ius publicum quod privatorum pactis mutari non potest."[18]

The question of which norms in a given legal order should be mandatory has always been subject to dispute. In the dispute about the reach and content of public-policy considerations in private law, different conceptions of individual freedom and the role of the state come to the fore.

The private law codifications of the 19th century, as well as the state of the common law of the time, reflected the urge for freedom from the bonds of

---

[16] Moritz Renner "art. 9 Rome I," in *The Rome Regulations*, edited by Gralf-Peter Calliess, paras 13–20. Cf. Gralf-Peter Calliess and Moritz Renner, "The Public and the Private Dimensions of Transnational Commercial Law," *German Law Journal* 10 (2009): pp. 1341–1356.

[17] For the status of mandatory rules in conflict of laws see especially Thomas G. Guedj, "The Theory of the Lois de Police, A Functional Trend in Continental Private International Law—A Comparative Analysis with Modern American Theories," *American Journal of Comparative Law* 39, no. 4 (1991): pp. 661–697, as well as Trevor Clayton Hartley, "Mandatory Rules in International Contracts: The Common Law Approach," *Recueil des Cours* 266 (1997): pp. 337–426.

[18] Dig. 2.14.38.

monarchic and corporative societies (freedom of contract) and the striving for more social equality (abolishment of feudal privileges).[19] Yet the principles of freedom of contract and formal equality realized their liberating potential only in a brief historical moment—and only for a small group of people. Since the middle of the 19th century, particularly for small trade and the growing working class, the promise of freedom and equality has not always fulfilled itself in the way it did for the propertied classes. Small trade was soon choked by the competition of larger factories, and for the working class freedom of contract, as yet unbalanced by the freedom of coalition, soon became an instrument of oppression.[20]

These injustices not only fueled socialist critiques of private law, they also led to fundamental changes in law-making. The merely formal and procedural provisions of private law were gradually supplemented and replaced by substantive standards of justice; public-policy considerations became more and more important. And these considerations were usually framed as mandatory rules of law. In Germany, for example, the natural law concepts of *iustium pretium, laesio enormis,* and *clausula rebus sic stantibus* (amounting to equity standards for price control) which had been abolished in the codifications of the 19th century, were re-integrated into the doctrine of private law under the impression of the hyper-inflation of the 1920s. They effectively superseded freedom of contract and the principle of *pacta sunt servanda.* At the same time, the legislature reacted to social inequalities through new laws in the fields of labor and tenancy law. Here, too, the content of private contracts was no longer left for the parties alone to agree, but certain minimum standards, e.g., with regard to cancellation periods, were laid down as mandatory rules of law.

Thus, the liberal private law codifications have been transformed, step by step, into a body of law which openly pursues public-policy objectives.[21] This is also apparent in the field of competition and antitrust law, where private agreements are considered invalid and can give rise to fines and claims for damages if they entail an abuse of economic power.[22] Since the 1970s, this instrumentalization of private law has been further reinforced by European law, particularly in the field of consumer law.[23] After the recent financial

---

[19] Franz Wieacker, *Das Sozialmodell der klassischen Privatrechtsgesetzbücher und die Entwicklung der modernen Gesellschaft,* (Karlsruhe: C.F. Müller, 1963), pp. 8–9.

[20] Id at 11–12.

[21] Patrick S. Atiyah, *The Rise and Fall of Freedom of Contract,* (Oxford: Clarendon Press, 1979).

[22] Ground-breaking Franz Böhm, "Das Problem der privaten Macht," *Die Justiz* (1928): pp. 324–345.

[23] On the critique of this process and potential alternatives to instrumentalized private law, see: Gunther Teubner, "Substantive and Reflexive Elements in Modern Private Law," *Law & Society Review* 17, no. 2 (1983): pp. 239–285; Jürgen Habermas, "Paradigms of Law," *Cardozo Law Review* 17, no. 4–5 (1995–1996): pp. 771–784.

crisis, similar developments can be observed in the fields of banking law and capital markets supervision. [24]

As a consequence, today it is well established in every legal system that courts can limit the freedom of contract for a number of reasons, specifically by enforcing mandatory rules of law pertaining to (1) public interests or public goods such as a workable competition or market stability, (2) the effects of contracts on third parties, e.g., on creditors outside the contractual relationship, and (3) the protection of weaker parties within the contract itself, such as the protection of consumers or employees against the unilateral exercise of private autonomy by economically dominant actors.[25]

3 The Autonomy of International Commercial Arbitration

But while a certain balance between freedom of contract and mandatory law has, over a long time, been established in domestic courts, it is still unclear whether and how this matters for international arbitral tribunals. This lack of clarity is a direct consequence of the highly tenuous legal status of such tribunals. In commercial matters, the status of international arbitral tribunals—as well as their interaction with domestic courts—is circumscribed by the 1958 New York Convention on the Recognition and Enforcement of Foreign Arbitral Awards (New York Convention),[26] which enjoys almost universal membership. The New York Convention foresees that all State Parties to the Convention must enforce awards rendered by international arbitral tribunals on their territory without *de novo* review as to their substance (Art. III). Recognition and enforcement may be refused only in a strictly limited number of situations, especially if such enforcement were contrary to the public policy of the country where enforcement is sought (Art. V para. 2 b). For the same reason, an arbitral award may be set aside by domestic courts under Art. 34 para. 2 b ii of the UNCITRAL Model Law on International Commercial Arbitration (UNCITRAL Model Law), on which the procedural law concerning arbitration is based in most states.

Thus, the New York Convention and the UNCITRAL Model Law establish a limited oversight over international arbitration by state courts with regard

---

[24] Oren Bar-Gill and Elizabeth Warren, "Making Credit Safer," *University of Pennsylvania Law Review* 157, no. 1 (2008): pp. 1–101.

[25] For an instance of weaker-party protection through overriding mandatory provisions see Case C-381/98 *Ingmar GB Ltd v. Eaton Leonard Technologies Inc.* [2000] ECR I-9305; for other limitations on party autonomy in the name of weaker-party protection see Ralf Michaels, "Zur Struktur der kollisionsrechtlichen Durchsetzung einfach zwingender Normen," in *Liber Amicorum Klaus Schurig*, edited by Ralf Michaels and Dennis Solomon (München: Sellier, 2012), pp. 191–200.

[26] New York Convention on the Recognition and Enforcement of Foreign Arbitral Awards, June 10, 1958, 330 U.N.T.S. 38.

to public-policy concerns. On the one hand, arbitral tribunals remain free to make decisions according to those rules of substantive law that seem appropriate for transnational commercial relations, especially based on the parties' choice of law and their legitimate expectations. But on the other hand, they are bound to take into account potential obstacles to the validity and enforceability of the resulting arbitral awards. The arbitration rules of the International Chamber of Commerce (ICC) in Paris, which is the leading provider of international commercial arbitration services worldwide, reflect this tension. According to Art. 17 para. 1 of the ICC Rules of Arbitration (ICC Rules):

> [T]he parties shall be free to agree upon the rules of law to be applied by the Arbitral Tribunal to the merits of the dispute. In the absence of any such agreement, the Arbitral Tribunal shall apply the rules of law which it determines to be appropriate.

Article 35 of the Rules, in contrast, provides that "[i]n all matters not expressly provided for in these Rules, the Court and the Arbitral Tribunal shall . . . make every effort to make sure that the Award is enforceable at law." In addition, Art. 6 of the Internal Rules of the ICC Court of Arbitration foresees that all ICC arbitral awards are scrutinized by the ICC's central administrative body with regard to requirements of the "law of the place of arbitration."

Against this background, the status of public-policy related norms in international commercial arbitration is highly tenuous. First, it can be argued that the international arbitrator is (by contract) bound to respect the will of the parties, but is not to be the guardian of any state's public policy.[27] Not only can the seat of the arbitral tribunal be freely chosen by the parties, it is also "virtual" to the extent that it need not be the place where the arbitral proceedings actually take place. And from a practical perspective, it seems hardly possible for an arbitral tribunal to take into consideration the public policy of every state where enforcement of the award might potentially be sought. Second, it is fundamentally unclear which legal system might serve as the point of reference for the arbitrator applying mandatory rules in the first place. Given that international arbitral tribunals do not have a *lex fori* in the conflict-of-laws sense of the term, to the international arbitrator "there is no foreign law"[28]—but at the same time "every law is foreign law."[29]

---

[27] Yves Derains, "Public Policy and the Law Applicable to the Dispute in International Arbitration," in *Comparative Arbitration Practice and Public Policy in Arbitration*, edited by Pieter Sanders (Deventer: Kluwer, 1987), pp. 227–256, 240–241.

[28] Id, 232.

[29] Nathalie Voser, "Mandatory Rules of Law as a Limitation on the Law Applicable in International Commercial Arbitration," *American Review of International Arbitration* 7, no. 3–4 (1996): pp. 319–357, 330.

Accordingly, international arbitration has developed its own rules of conflicts, based on the "general principles of conflict of laws"[30] common to all domestic systems.[31]

4 Party Autonomy and Mandatory Norms in International Arbitration

As a consequence, the decision-making perspective of international arbitrators is indeed an autonomous one—although international arbitration is by no means disconnected from domestic law. Whereas current discussions might suggest otherwise, the autonomy of international commercial arbitration is not primarily related to the "private" or "transnational" nature of the applicable substantive law. The practical relevance of non-state norms in international arbitration is much more limited than is generally assumed. Empirical surveys show that most disputes in international arbitration are based on rules of domestic law, which are only punctually supplemented by non-state norms, *lex mercatoria*, and the "trades and usages of international commerce."[32] But even when arbitral tribunals apply domestic law, they do so according to a very peculiar "method of decision-making"[33] which, through self-made conflict-of-laws rules, eclectically combines legal norms from different legal systems: domestic, international and transnational, public and private.

The starting point of any analysis of the applicable law in commercial arbitration is the principle of party autonomy, as evidenced, e.g., by the aforementioned Article 17 of the ICC Rules, which can be understood as a codification of the customary rules of conflict-of-laws in international commercial arbitration. Just like the arbitration rules of other institutions (e.g., Art. 42 ICSID Convention), the provision leaves much leeway for the parties' choice of law in the first place and for the arbitrator's discretion in the second place. As a consequence, any arbitral decision is based on the

---

[30] For a good illustration of this approach see ICC case no. 5953, *Revue de l'arbitrage* (1990): pp. 701–711.

[31] Cf. Berthold Goldman, "Les conflits de lois dans l'arbitrage international de droit privé," *Recueil des Cours* 109 (1963): pp. 347–485.

[32] For empirical surveys, see e.g., Gralf-Peter Calliess et al., "Transformations of Commercial Law: New Forms of Legal Certainty for Globalized Exchange Processes?" in *Transforming the Golden Age Nation State*, edited by Achim Hurrelmann et al. (Hampshire: Palgrave Macmillan, 2007), pp. 83–108, 98 (table 5.2); Stefan Voigt, "Are International Merchants Stupid? Their Choice of Law Sheds Doubt on the Legal Origin Theory," *Journal of Empirical Legal Studies* 5, no. 1 (2008): pp. 1–20.

[33] Emmanuel Gaillard, "Transnational Law: A Legal System or a Method of Decision-Making?" *Arbitration International* 17, no. 1 (2001): pp. 59–72.

rules of law that are either directly chosen by the parties to a commercial transaction or are at least meant to take account of their "legitimate expectations."[34]

Many commentators therefore argue—quite paradoxically—that even the application of mandatory norms can, in international commercial arbitration, only be justified by recourse to the will of the parties themselves. Accordingly, mandatory norms should only be applied to the extent that they form part of the law chosen by the parties as applicable to their contract (*lex causae* approach).[35] This approach is problematic, however, when the parties have expressly excluded the application of mandatory norms in their contract: In such a case, an arbitral tribunal would be entirely barred from applying mandatory norms.[36] Therefore, others argue that certain "overriding" mandatory provisions should be applied in commercial arbitration, in much the same way as if they were applied by a domestic court.[37] Yet this second approach poses considerable practical problems. Even in domestic conflict-of-laws systems, the "overriding" mandatory character of certain norms may be hard to determine;[38] but under domestic law, at least some guidance is provided by standing case-law and constitutional principles. In international commercial arbitration, there is no such guidance.

How do arbitral tribunals react to this situation? Two different answers seem conceivable: either, arbitral tribunals could entirely refrain from applying mandatory norms—or they could develop their own strategies for applying such norms.

---

[34] Yves Derains, "L'ordre public et le droit applicable au fond du litige dans l'arbitrage international," *Revue de l'Arbitrage*, no. 3 (1986): pp. 375–414, 380 *et seq.*; see also Arthur Taylor von Mehren, "To what Extent Is International Commercial Arbitration Autonomous?" in *Le droit des relations économiques internationales. Études offertes à Berthold Goldman*, edited by Philippe Fouchard, Philippe Khan, and Antoine Lyon-Caen (Paris: Litec, 1982), pp. 217–227, 227.

[35] Eric Loquin, "Les pouvoirs des arbitres internationaux à la lumière de l'evolution récente du droit de l'arbitrage international," *Journal du droit international*, no. 2 (1983): pp. 293–359, 342; Klaus-Peter Berger, *Internationale Wirtschaftsschiedsgerichtsbarkeit* (Berlin, New York: de Gruyter, 1992), p. 486; Julian D. Lew et al., *Comparative International Commercial Arbitration* (Den Haag: Kluwer Law International, 2003), paras 17–27.

[36] Yves Derains, "L'ordre public et le droit applicable," p. 391: "Si les parties ont expressément écarté certaines règles de ce droit, les arbitres ne sauraient, au nom d'un ordre public dont ils ne sont pas les gardiens, en imposer l'application." ("If the parties have expressly excluded certain rules of law, arbitrators cannot, in the name of a public policy which is not theirs to guard, impose their application"; my translation.)

[37] *et seq.*; Nathalie Voser, "Mandatory Rules of Law," p. 345 *et seq.*; Anton K. Schnyder, "Anwendung ausländischer Eingriffsnormen durch Schiedsgerichte. Überlegungen zu einem Grundsatzentscheid des Schweizer Bundesgerichts," *RabelsZ* 59 (1995): pp. 293–308, 302 *et seq.*; Marc Blessing, "Mandatory Rules of Law," p. 31 *et seq.*; Jette Beulker, *Die Eingriffsnormenproblematik in internationalen Schiedsverfahren: Parallelen und Besonderheiten im Vergleich zur staatlichen Gerichtsbarkeit*, (Tübingen: Mohr Siebeck, 2005), pp. 276 *et seq.*

[38] For details see Moritz Renner "art. 9 Rome I," in *The Rome Regulations*, edited by Gralf-Peter Calliess, paras 9–20.

5 Practice

As a survey of ICC arbitral awards[39] published between 1990 and 2006 demonstrates,[40] arbitral practice has chosen the latter path. The strategies developed in ICC arbitration for applying mandatory norms, however, differ widely. Common to all arbitral awards is a conflict-of-laws approach which starts from an extensive understanding of party autonomy: "In an international contract . . ., involving parties of different nationalities, the choice of law is entirely free."[41] The choice of the applicable law is always based on a "test objectif révélant ce qu'aurait du être l'intention et l'attente raisonnable des parties concernant le droit applicable."[42]

5.1 *The Paradox of Party Autonomy*

Starting from here, many tribunals at least implicitly follow the above-sketched *lex causae* approach: Mandatory norms are not applied because they are mandatory, but because (and only to the extent that) they form part of the law chosen as applicable by the parties to the contract themselves.[43] In most cases, the applicability of such mandatory norms is either not expressly discussed at all, or the discussion is kept very short: "there is no need to invoke *loi de police* or *fraude à la loi*: any provision contrary to the mandatory character of the applicable law is simply void on the basis of the law itself."[44] The doctrinal

---

[39] The survey was based on awards published in the *Yearbook of Commercial of Arbitration*, the *Revue de l'arbitrage*, and the *Journal du droit international* (Clunet), as well as the *ASA Bulletin*.

[40] Excerpts from the study have been published as Moritz Renner, "Towards a Hierarchy of Norms in Transnational Law?" pp. 539–543; for a more complete account see Moritz Renner, *Zwingendes transnationales Recht*, pp. 110–126.

[41] ICC case no. 4629 (1989), *Y.B. Comm. Arb.* XVIII (1993), p. 11.

[42] ICC case no. 7710 (1995), *Clunet* (2001), p. 1147 with further references from arbitral practice: "objective test based on what must have been the intention and reasonable expectation of the parties with regard to the applicable law" (my translation).

[43] Exclusively concerned with mandatory norms of the *lex causae* are ICC cases nos. 5730 (1988), *Clunet* (1990), p. 1029; 6497 (1994), *Y.B. Comm. Arb.* XXIVa (1990), p. 71; 6515/6 (1994), *Y.B. Comm. Arb.* XXIVa (1999), p. 80; 6754 (1993), *Clunet* (1995), p. 1009; 6998 (1994), *Y.B. Comm. Arb.* XXI (1996), p. 54; 7063 (1993), *Y.B. Comm. Arb.* XXII (1997), p. 87; 7146 (1992), *Y.B. Comm. Arb.* XXVI (2001), p. 119; 7181 (1992), *Y.B. Comm. Arb.* XXI (1996); 7314 (1995), *Clunet* (1996), p. 1045; 7528 (1993), *Y.B. Comm. Arb.* XXII (1997); 7639 (1994), *Y.B. Comm. Arb.* XXIII (1998), p. 80; 8385 (1995), *Clunet* (1997), p. 1061; 8423 (1994), *Y.B. Comm. Arb.* XXVI (2001), p. 153; 8486 (1996), *Clunet* (1998), p. 1047; 10060 (1999), *Y.B. Comm. Arb.* XXX (2005), p. 42; 10947 (2002), *ASA Bulletin* (2004), p. 308; 10988 (2003), *Clunet* (2006), p. 1408. The applicability of such norms is also discussed in ICC cases no. 5617 (1989), *Clunet* (1994), p. 1041; 5943 (1990), *Clunet* (1996), p. 1014; 6248 (1990), *Y.B. Comm. Arb.* XIX (1994), p. 124; 6286 (1991), *Y.B. Comm. Arb.* XIX (1994), p. 141; 6320 (1992), *Y.B. Comm. Arb.* XX (1995), p. 62; 6474 (1992), *Y.B. Comm. Arb.* XXV (2000), p. 279; 7047 (1994), *Y.B. Comm. Arb.* XXI (1996), p. 79; 7518 (1994), *Clunet* (1998), p. 1034; 7893 (1994), *Clunet* (1998), p. 1069; 8420 (1996), *Y.B. Comm. Arb.* XXV (2000), p. 328; 8626 (1996), *Clunet* (1996), p. 1073; 9333 (1998), *ASA Bulletin* (2001), p. 757; 10671 (2006), *Clunet* (2005), p. 1268.

[44] ICC case no. 6998 (1994), *Y.B. Comm. Arb.* XXI (1996), p. 54.

intricacies of "overriding mandatory provisions" or "public policy" in traditional conflict-of-laws discussions are thus elegantly bypassed. Only hesitantly, some tribunals' reasoning departs from the chosen law, e.g., by stating that a certain mandatory rule "is also admitted in most legal systems."[45]

The justificatory paradox of a position which justifies the limitations of party autonomy with reference to the will of the parties, however, can hardly be avoided. Not surprisingly, arbitral tribunals come to contradictory conclusions when contractual provisions conflict with mandatory norms of the *lex causae*. Some tribunals hold that the contractual choice of law trumps all other provisions of the contract;[46] the paradox of party autonomy is thus resolved through establishing a hierarchy of norms within the contract itself. Other tribunals, in contrast, refer to the French doctrine of *contrat international* and argue that the parties should be assumed to have excluded from their choice of law those norms of the *lex causae* which would invalidate—as a whole or in part—their contract: "The primary consequence of party autonomy in international contracts . . . is that the contract should be performed as agreed."[47] According to this line of thought, even those norms which are considered "overriding mandatory provisions" or "public policy" under domestic law might be abrogated by the parties. In such a vein, one tribunal argues:

> It would . . . run counter to the common intention of the parties at the time when they entered into the . . . sales contracts, if the arbitral tribunal would apply [sic] a public policy provision of Jordanian law while there had been a clear intention of the parties to remove this subject-matter from Jordanian domestic jurisdiction.[48]

5.2 State Interests

Many tribunals,[49] however, argue that the question of the applicable law in international arbitration must not only accommodate the autonomy of the parties, but also all state regulatory interests concerned:

> [I]n general, the will and autonomy of the parties are particularly relevant . . . with respect to applicable law and contractual issues . . . . This priority of the will

[45] ICC case no. 6497, *Y.B. Comm. Arb.* XXIVa (1999), p. 71.
[46] See, e.g., ICC case no. 6998 (1994), *Y.B. Comm. Arb.* XXI (1996), p. 54.
[47] ICC case no. 7528 (1993), *Y.B. Comm. Arb.* XXII (1997), p. 125.
[48] ICC case no. 6149 (1990), *Y.B. Comm. Arb.* XX (1995), p. 41.
[49] ICC cases nos. 5030 (1992), *Clunet* (1993), p. 1004; 5617 (1989), *Clunet* (1994), p. 1041; 5864 (1989), *Clunet* (1997), p. 1073; 6294 (1991), *Clunet* (1991), p. 1050; 6320 (1992), *Y.B. Comm. Arb.* XX (1995), p. 62; 7539 (1995), *Clunet* (1996), p. 1030; 5622 (1988), *Y.B. Comm. Arb.* XIX (1994), p. 105; 6149 (1990), *Y.B. Comm. Arb.* XX (1995), p. 41; 6286 (1991), *Y.B. Comm. Arb.* XIX (1994), p. 141; 6363 (1991), *Y.B. Comm. Arb.* XVII (1992), p. 186; 6379 (1990), *Y.B. Comm. Arb.* XVII (1992), 212; 6752 (1991), *Y.B. Comm. Arb.* XVIII (1993), p. 54; 7047 (1994), *Y.B. Comm. Arb.* XXI (1996), p. 79; 7893 (1994), *Clunet* (1998), p. 1069; 8420 (1996), *Y.B. Comm. Arb.* XXV (2000), p. 328; 8528 (1996), *Y.B. Comm. Arb.* XXV (2000), p. 341; 8817 (1996), Clunet (1999), p. 1080; 9333 (1998), *ASA Bulletin* (2001), p. 757; 12045 (2003), *Clunet* (2006), p. 1434.

of the parties must, however, be construed to be subordinate to the . . . application of . . . the mandatory law of a particular state, [if] such state [has] a strong and legitimate interest to justify the application of such a law in international arbitration.[50]

As a consequence, not only might mandatory norms of the *lex causae* be applied by the arbitral tribunal, but also mandatory norms from other legal systems. The rationale for their application is sought not in the will of the parties, but in the regulatory interests of the states potentially concerned by the case at hand: If there is a strong enough (and justifiable) regulatory interest of any state, its mandatory norms are applied as "overriding."[51] Just as under traditional conflict-of-laws doctrine, two different avenues are taken by arbitral tribunals for applying such "overriding" mandatory norms.[52]

On the one hand, there are tribunals which try to give effect to mandatory norms from legal systems other than the chosen law by way of extensively interpreting certain *lex causae* provisions, such as rules on *force majeure*[53] or good faith principles. This approach assumes a merely "indirect applicability" of mandatory norms. For example, the tribunal in ICC case no. 5864 held that the respondent had become free from its contractual obligations when a US Presidential order prohibited exports to Libya, because the Presidential order constituted *force majeure* under the Libyan *lex causae*.[54] Mandatory norms outside the *lex causae* are indirectly applied by considering their factual effects,[55] and thus the doctrinal consistency of an autonomy-based conflict-of-laws approach is preserved.

On the other hand, some—if only a few—arbitral tribunals apply mandatory norms outside the *lex causae* by their own right, mostly referring to the French doctrine of *lois de police* and thus following a "direct applicability" approach.[56] For example, ICC case no. 8528 deals with the transferability of tax reliefs that the respondent is entitled to under (mandatory) Turkish law, the *lex causae* being Swiss law. The tribunal decides in favor of a direct applicability of Turkish law, considering that such a direct applicability of mandatory

[50] ICC case no. 6320 (1992), *Y.B. Comm. Arb.* XX (1995), p. 62, para. 153.
[51] This is the terminology employed by art. 9 Rome I Convention; traditionally such norms have been termed *lois de police*, *Eingriffsnormen*, *leggi di applicazione immediata*; for an overview see Thomas G. Guedj, "The Theory of the Lois de Police, A Functional Trend in Continental Private International Law—A Comparative Analysis with Modern American Theories," *American Journal of Comparative Law* 39, no. 4 (1991): pp. 661–697.
[52] Cf. Moritz Renner "art. 9 and art. 21 Rome I," in *The Rome Regulations*, edited by Gralf-Peter Calliess, art. 9 Rome I, paras 30–31.
[53] ICC cases nos. 5864 (1989), *Clunet* (1997), p. 1073 and 7539 (1995), *Clunet* (1996), p. 1030; similarly ICC case no. 5617 (1989), *Clunet* (1994), p. 1041.
[54] ICC case no. 5864 (1989), *Clunet* (1997), p. 1073.
[55] Cf. Albert A. Ehrenzweig, "Local and Moral Data in the Conflict of Laws," *Buffalo Law Review* 16, no. 1 (1966): pp. 55–60.
[56] ICC case nos. 6320 (1992), *Y.B. Comm. Arb.* XX (1995), p. 62; 8528 (1996), *Y.B. Comm. Arb.* XXV (2000), p. 341; 9333 (1998), *ASA Bulletin* (2001), p. 757.

law was widely recognized, e.g., by Art. 19 of the Swiss conflict-of-laws code and by Art. 7 of the Rome Convention (preceding the Rome I Regulation). The tribunal reasons that it was a general principle of law that mandatory rules of law should be applied irrespective of the law otherwise applicable whenever (1) there was a sufficiently close connection to the case at hand, (2) an overarching interest of at least one of the parties called for its application, and (3) the legislative purpose of the norm demanded its application to the case.[57]

However, this kind of reasoning, which demands a close consideration of state regulatory interests, is far from being accepted by all arbitral tribunals. Many tribunals see it as contradictory to the very purposes of international commercial arbitration. For example, ICC case no. 6379, based on the Italian *lex causae,* clearly rejects such an approach: "It is a very interesting concept, but it is not a universally accepted norm of Italian law, which should be applied by the arbitrator in the present case." Furthermore: "An arbitral tribunal is not an instrumentality of any particular state."[58] Faced with such fierce resistance, most arbitral tribunals either do not at all consider the application of mandatory norms beyond the *lex causae,*[59] or they decline their applicability to the case at hand.[60] Some decisions evade the problem by simply stating that the mandatory norm in question was accepted in all legal systems possibly concerned.[61]

5.3 Territorial Ties

The reluctance to apply mandatory norms beyond the *lex causae,* i.e., such mandatory norms whose application cannot be justified by the will of the parties, even extends to the mandatory law of the seat of arbitration and of the potential countries of enforcement. The "consideration" of such norms, therefore, which is asked for by the ICC Rules and the internal rules of the ICC Court of Arbitration, remains pure theory.

Only seldom do arbitral tribunals expressly refer to the mandatory law of their seat, such as one tribunal sitting in Switzerland, which is concerned with the validity of a contractual punitive damages clause:

> Damages that go beyond compensatory damages to constitute a punishment of the wrongdoer (punitive or exemplary damages) are considered contrary to Swiss public policy, which must be respected by an arbitral tribunal sitting in Switzerland

---

[57] ICC case no. 8528 (1996), *Y.B. Comm. Arb.* XXV (2000), p. 341.
[58] ICC case no. 6379 (1990), *Y.B. Comm. Arb.* XVII (1992), p. 212.
[59] See, e.g., ICC case no. 6149 (1990), *Y.B. Comm. Arb.* XX (1995), p. 41.
[60] ICC cases nos. 6320 (1990), *Y.B. Comm. Arb.* XX (1995), p. 62; 6363 (1991), *Y.B. Comm. Arb.* XVII (1992), p. 186; 6752 (1991), *Y.B. Comm. Arb.* XVIII (1993), p. 54; 7047 (1994), *Y.B. Comm. Arb.* XXI (1996), p. 79; 9333 (1998), *ASA Bulletin* (2001), p. 757.
[61] See, e.g., ICC case no. 8817 (1997), Clunet (1999), p. 1080.

even if the arbitral tribunal must decide a dispute according to a law that may allow punitive or exemplary damages as such. . . .[62]

However, the tribunal in this case makes no attempt to justify the decision under its own conflict-of-laws rules; rather, it relies on practical considerations. Other tribunals take into consideration the public-policy provisions of potential enforcement states, but do so merely in *obiter dicta*:[63] "nous sommes d'avis que le tribunal arbitral devrait toujours se préoccuper de l'efficacité de sa décision. Ceci est expressément prévu par l'Article 26 [now Art. 35 ICC Rules, MR]."[64]

5.4 *International Community*

Thus, it seems that neither the concept of party autonomy and the *lex causae* approach nor state interests can successfully be employed for justifying the application of mandatory norms in international commercial arbitration. While arguing with the principle of party autonomy inevitably leads to a justificatory paradox, balancing state interests poses a more than difficult task to commercial arbitrators. It is not surprising that arbitrators often shy away from this task, because—differently from state judges—they lack a constitutional order as frame of reference for such balancing processes.

To overcome this difficulty, arbitral tribunals ever more often refer to the values of a genuinely transnational community, a "truly international"[65] or transnational public policy when applying mandatory rules of law.[66] Thus, they try to translate the domestic concept of *public policy* into an embodiment of the shared values of the international community. In this context, one arbitral tribunal quotes Lalive's ground-breaking article on the *ordre public transnational*:[67]

[62] ICC case no. 5946 (1990), *Y.B. Comm. Arb.* XVI (1991), p. 97, para. 51.

[63] ICC cases nos. 8528 (1996), *Y.B. Comm. Arb.* XXV (2000), p. 341; 8626 (1996), *Clunet* (1999), p. 1073.

[64] ICC case no. 8626 (1996), *Clunet* (1999), p. 1073: "We think that the arbitral tribunal should always be concerned with the enforceability of its decision. This is expressly foreseen by Article 26 [now Art. 35 ICC Rules, MR]" (my translation).

[65] Pierre Lalive, "Transnational (or Truly International) Public Policy in International Arbitration," in *Comparative Arbitration Practice and Public Policy in Arbitration, ICCA Congress Series No. 3,* edited by Pieter Sanders (Deventer: Kluwer, 1987), pp. 257–318.

[66] ICC cases nos. 5030 (1992), *Clunet* (1993), p. 1004; 5622 (1988), *Y.B. Comm. Arb.* XIX (1994), p. 105; 5943 (1990), *Clunet* (1996), p. 1014; 6248 (1990), *Y.B. Comm. Arb.* XIX (1994), p. 124; 6320 (1992), *Y.B. Comm. Arb.* XX (1995), p. 62; 6474 (1992), *Y.B. Comm. Arb.* XXV (2000), p. 279; 6503 (1990), *Clunet* (1995), p. 1022; 6754 (1993), *Clunet* (1995), p. 1009; 7047 (1994), *Y.B. Comm. Arb.* XXI (1996), p. 79; 7518 (1994), *Clunet* (1998), p. 1034; 8420 (1996), *Y.B. Comm. Arb.* XXV (2000), p. 328; 8891 (1998), *Clunet* (2001), p. 1076; 9333 (1998), *ASA Bulletin* (2001), p. 757; 10671 (2006), *Clunet* (2005), p. 1268; 10947 (2002), *ASA Bulletin* (2004), p. 308; 12045 (2003), *Clunet* (2006), p. 1434.

[67] Pierre Lalive, "Ordre public transnational (ou réellement international) et arbitrage internationale," *Revue de l'arbitrage*, no. 3 (1986): pp. 327–373.

It is true that the notion of morality is as fluid and vague in international commercial relationships as it is, mutatis mutandis, in national law, although to a lesser degree since the national community is more homogenous than the international community. However, it can be said that transnational public policy is jeopardized . . . by a hostile behaviour against principles which are generally held to be fundamental from an ethical-juridical point of view.[68]

However, it often remains rather unclear to which form of "international community" the concept of transnational public policy might actually refer. Sometimes it seems to denote the international community of states in the public international law sense of the term,[69] sometimes it describes legal concepts shared by different legal systems,[70] and sometimes it refers to the values of "international commerce."[71] Not surprisingly, the content and reach of the concept of transnational public policy remain equally unclear. In this context, many tribunals distinguish between negative and positive functions of transnational public policy.

The negative function of transnational public policy determines which mandatory norms, in the *lex causae* and beyond, should *not* be applied to the case at hand. For example, ICC case no. 6248 applies mandatory norms of the *lex causae* (concerning *boni mores*) only after stating that these do not run counter to transnational public policy.[72] ICC case no. 6320 argues similarly with regard to mandatory norms from a legal system other than the chosen law.[73] In other arbitral awards, this argument is radicalized: Transnational public policy, they reason, excludes the application of any mandatory law beyond the *lex causae*—unless this law is itself an expression of transnational public policy.[74]

The latter turn in the argument points to the positive function that is increasingly attributed to the concept of transnational public policy. This positive function comes into play when arbitral tribunals try to justify the application of mandatory norms which do not form part of the *lex causae*— or part of any domestic legal system at all. Arbitral tribunals necessarily do so in the rare cases in which they decide *ex aequo et bono*,[75] i.e., without recourse to legal rules at all, or when the parties have chosen *lex mercatoria* as the law applicable to their contract.[76] For example, in ICC case no. 8891 the

---

[68] ICC case no. 5622 (1988), *Y.B. Comm. Arb.* XIX (1994), p. 105, para. 33.
[69] ICC case no. 6474 (1992), *Y.B. Comm. Arb.* XXV (2000), p. 279.
[70] ICC case no. 8891 (1998), *Clunet* (2001), p. 1076.
[71] ICC case no. 6320 (1992), *Y.B. Comm. Arb.* XX (1995), p. 62.
[72] ICC case no. 6248 (1990), *Y.B. Comm. Arb.* XIX (1994), p. 124.
[73] ICC case no. 6320 (1992), *Y.B. Comm. Arb.* XX (1995), p. 62.
[74] ICC cases nos. 7047 (1994), *Y.B. Comm. Arb.* XXI (1996), p. 79 and 12045 (2003), *Clunet* (2006), p. 1434.
[75] ICC cases nos. 6503 (1990), *Clunet* (1995), p. 1022 and 8891 (1998), *Clunet* (2001), p. 1076.
[76] ICC case no. 5030 (1992), *Clunet* (1993), p. 1004.

arbitrators in an *ex aequo et bono* arbitration have to rule on the validity of a "consulting contract" entailing the bribing of public officers. The arbitrators, who are barred from applying mandatory provisions of any domestic legal order, refer to general principles of fairness: "[les] arbitres . . . rendent la justice, même s'il s'agit de justice privée."[77] They further argue with the ICC's code of conduct for arbitrators, arbitral precedent, doctrinal debate, and also with reference to international political discourse:

> [L]a lutte contre la corruption se renforce à l'heure actuelle, comme en témoignent notamment les débats lors de l'Assemblée annuelle des institutions de Bretton Woods . . . ou encore les négociations au sein de l'OCDE en vue d'une convention anticorruption.[78]

The arbitral tribunal in ICC case no. 5030, deciding on a contract under *lex mercatoria* ("principes généraux du droit des contrats internationaux"), refers to transnational public policy in the "usages of international commerce" and—quite surprisingly—postulates a general principle of weaker party protection in international contracts:

> Le tribunal est d'avis que la pratique consistant de la part du partenaire développé à laisser son cocontractant s'engager dans des liens contractuels sans le moindre avis technique sérieux, et même en le pressant expressément de conclure, constitue un abus de sa faiblesse, sa légèreté ou son inexpérience, contraire aux usages normaux du commerce international.[79]

But also some arbitral decisions with a particular domestic law chosen as *lex causae* refer to positive transnational public policy. They usually do so, however, only in *obiter dicta* in order to justify a result already found under the *lex causae*. This may concern general private law principles such as *pacta sunt servanda*[80] and good faith,[81] but also more specific rules such as the prohibition of corruption. Nevertheless, this move toward transnational public policy arguments—even in cases where it would not be necessary from a strictly doctrinal point of view—indicates that the tribunals are willing and able to justify limitations of party autonomy without recourse to domestic legal

---

[77] "Arbitrators render justice, even if it is private justice." (My translation.)

[78] ICC case no. 8891 (1998), *Clunet* (2001), p. 1076: "The fight against corruption is currently being reinforced, as evidenced by the debates on the occasion of the annual assembly of the Bretton Woods institution . . . or the negotiations within the OECD framework regarding an anti-bribery convention." (My translation.)

[79] ICC case no. 5030 (1992), *Clunet* (1993), p. 1004: "The tribunal holds that a practice which consists in the developed partner letting his co-contractor enter into a contractual relationship without the slightest reliable technical advice, and even urging him expressly to conclude the contract, constitutes an abuse of the co-contractor's weakness, improvidence or his lack of experience. This runs counter to the normal usages of international commerce." (My translation.)

[80] ICC case no. 7518 (1994), *Clunet* (1998), p. 1034.

[81] ICC cases nos. 6474 (1992), *Y.B. Comm. Arb.* XXV (2000), p. 279; 10671 (2006), *Clunet* (2005), p. 1268.

systems. At the same time, the positive content of transnational public policy is thus gradually gaining a clearer shape in arbitral practice.

5.5 Constitutionalization

The concept of transnational public policy can be considered the starting point of a constitutionalization of international commercial arbitration, and it is exactly the interplay between its negative and its positive functions which enables the process of constitutionalization. Clearly, the term "constitutionalization" lends itself to many different understandings and misunderstandings—this abundant discussion shall not be reproduced in this article.[82] Instead, the term shall be used in a functional way as referring to two distinct features of modern legal orders: (1) a hierarchy of norms, and (2) the "structural coupling" of law and politics.[83] Both features are present in arbitral reasoning relying on transnational public policy.

This is well illustrated by ICC case no. 9333, which deals with the validity of a contractual obligation to pay a commission in relation to a pipeline project in a North African country.[84] The parties have chosen Swiss law as the law applicable to their contract. The respondent argues that the contractual provision is void as being contrary to the prohibition of corruption. The arbitral tribunal first analyzes this allegation under the *lex causa*, i.e., Swiss private law, but sees no grounds for an invalidity of the clause. Then, the tribunal turns to the US Foreign Corrupt Practices Act as a potentially applicable "overriding" mandatory law, whose applicability is also denied. In a last step, the tribunal analyzes the applicability of the OECD Convention on Combating Corruption as an expression of transnational public policy.

Thus, the tribunal not only deals with different conceptions of public policy by referring to different political contexts, both national and international, but also relates those different sources of public policy in a hierarchical manner, with transnational public policy standing at the top of an emerging transnational hierarchy of norms: First, the applicability of mandatory norms in the *lex causae* is discussed, then, second, the applicability of mandatory norms from other legal systems. Both are checked against negative transna-

[82] For an overview of the positions in the debate see, e.g., Erika de Wet, "The International Constitutional Order," *International & Comparative Law Quarterly* 55, no. 1 (2006): pp. 51–76; Anne Peters, "Global Constitutionalism in a Nutshell," in *Weltinnenrecht. Liber amicorum Jost Delbrück*, edited by Klaus Dicke et al., (Berlin: Duncker & Humblot, 2005), pp. 535–550; Gunther Teubner, "Global Private Regimes: Neo-spontaneous Law and Dual Constitution of Autonomous Sectors in World Society," in *Globalization and Public Governance*, edited by Gunther Teubner and Karl-Heinz Ladeur, (Aldershot: Ashgate, 2004), p. 71.

[83] For an in-depth discussion of this concept of constitutionalization relying on *Luhmannian* systems theory see Moritz Renner, *Zwingendes transnationales Recht*, pp. 230–248.

[84] ICC case no. 9333 (1998), *ASA Bulletin* (2001), p. 757.

tional public policy. In a third and last step, the positive content of transnational public policy is brought to bear on the case.

This approach is even more apparent in the example of ICC case no. 6320.[85] Here, the parties have chosen Brazilian law as the law applicable to their construction contract. Nonetheless, the tribunal discusses the applicability of the US Racketeer Influenced and Corrupt Organizations Act (RICO Act) as "overriding" mandatory law. In this context, the tribunal first analyzes the "constitutionality" (sic) of the RICO Act under (negative) transnational public policy, before stating that the RICO Act itself does not form part of (positive) transnational public policy. Transnational public policy, thus, becomes the Archimedean point of a rudimentary constitutional order which comprises mandatory norms reflecting both domestic and "genuinely" international public policies.

At this point, it also becomes apparent that the two layers of public policy reflect an internal differentiation of the political system: While the world economy already operates as a global system, political discourse largely remains fragmented into the institutions of the nation-state, on the one hand, and the—still rather rudimentary—fora of international politics, on the other.[86] Arbitral tribunals, therefore, might refer to domestic laws combating corruption as an expression of domestic public policy and then turn to an OECD Convention as expressing transnational public policy. Both layers of public policy are reflected in a legal hierarchy, which by now forms the constitutional core of the regime of transnational commercial arbitration.

6 Tentative Explanations

Given the paramount importance of the principle of party autonomy in international commercial arbitration—and the ensuing doctrinal difficulties—it seems almost surprising that arbitral tribunals apply mandatory rules of law at all. But arbitral tribunals have good reasons for doing so. In the first place, it should not be forgotten that in most procedural constellations at least one of the disputing parties has a manifest interest in the application of mandatory norms. In contractual disputes, it is usually the alleged non-performance of one of the parties which gives rise to the dispute. The non-performing party, then, is likely to argue that its contractual obligations are void, specifically because they violate mandatory rules of law (such as competition law, anti-corruption provisions, etc.). Thus, in terms of economic theory it is the

---

[85] ICC case no. 6320 (1992), *Y.B. Comm. Arb.* XX (1995), p. 62.
[86] Niklas Luhmann, *Die Politik der Gesellschaft*, (Frankfurt a.M.: Suhrkamp, 2002).

ex post opportunism of rational actors[87] which guarantees that mandatory norms are applied. Secondly, the procedural framework of the New York Convention (depicted above) enables the losing party to seek an annulment of the arbitral award or to oppose its enforcement on public policy grounds. This provides arbitrators with an incentive to respect public policy rules, as the enforceability of awards is of paramount importance for the attractiveness of arbitral dispute resolution.

Yet as convincing as these explanations might seem, they do not take sufficient account of the distinctive features of international commercial arbitration. On the one hand, it may very well be that both parties to the arbitration want to avoid an application of mandatory norms even from an ex post perspective. Most often this happens with regard to competition law, where both parties to an anti-competitive agreement want to preserve the agreement's validity, even in cases of dispute over specific provisions of the agreement. On the other hand, the public policy control by domestic courts is limited in reach—and often evaded. In this context, it is important to note that the vast majority of commercial arbitral awards are never enforced by domestic courts because the parties comply with the award voluntarily.[88] Again, there are good economic reasons for the parties to do so: reputation mechanisms as well as informal and relational norms provide for an enforcement mechanism which is far more effective than any domestic legal system could be.[89]

From this perspective, it remains a conundrum why arbitral tribunals apply mandatory norms even against the express will of the parties (*ex officio* application). The conundrum can only be resolved by taking a perspective that departs from the immediate interests of the parties to the arbitral procedure. This perspective might be based on micro-sociological insights into the socialization and legal education of the arbitrators; methodologically it would then have to employ expert interviews and similar techniques of qualitative

[87] Cf. Oliver E. Williamson, "The Economics of Governance," *American Economic Review* 95, no. 2 (2005): pp. 1–18, 7.

[88] See, e.g., Volker Triebel and Eckart Petzold, "Grenzen der lex mercatoria in der internationalen Schiedsgerichtsbarkeit," *RIW* 34, no. 4 (1988): pp. 245–250, 250 footnote 106. This may include the conclusion of a settlement agreement in the enforcement stage. Furthermore, most arbitration proceedings are not concluded with an arbitral award at all, but only with a settlement agreement of the parties, Hilmar Raeschke-Kessler, "Der Vergleich im Schiedsverfahren—Anmerkungen zu § 19 DIS-SchiedsO," in *Festschrift für Ottoarndt Glossner zum 70. Geburtstag*, edited by Ottoarndt Glossner et al., (Heidelberg: Verlag Recht und Wirtschaft, 1994), pp. 255–270, 265.

[89] This insight is well established in legal sociology: Stewart Macaulay, "Non-Contractual Relations in Business: A Preliminary Study," *American Sociological Review* 28, no. 1 (1963): pp. 55–67; Ian MacNeil, "Relational Contract: What We Do and Do Not Know," *Wisconsin Law Review* 3 (1985): pp. 483–525. It is corroborated by empirical research focusing on transnational commercial relations: Gralf-Peter Calliess et al., "Transformations of Commercial Law: New Forms of Legal Certainty for Globalized Exchange Processes?" in *Transforming the Golden Age Nation State*, edited by Achim Hurrelmann et al., (Hampshire: Palgrave Macmillan, 2007), pp. 83–108.

research.[90] Alternatively, one might follow a macro-sociological, or social theory, approach focusing on the systemic features of international commercial arbitration.[91] The main advantage of such a systemic perspective on the field of international arbitration as compared to actor-based approaches—be they rational-choice based, game-theoretical, or "critical"—is that it takes seriously the institutional and discursive constraints of the field. It focuses on the immanent rationality and evolution of legal discourse, while necessarily fading out individual motives and dispositions.[92]

It is specifically from a systemic perspective that the above-depicted constitutionalization process can be explained as a by-product of the juridification of international commercial arbitration. Valuable insights in this respect are provided by systems theory.[93] Systems theory shows that, under certain conditions, any mechanism of dispute resolution may develop into a legal system effectively stabilizing social expectations. These conditions are fulfilled whenever a dispute-resolution procedure (1) allows for a verbalization of social conflicts and (2) establishes an institutionalized form of "remembering and forgetting" rules and decisions.[94] While international commercial arbitration has always provided a court-like procedure for the verbalization of conflicts (condition 1), it is only in recent years that arbitral dispute resolution has also begun to publish arbitral awards on a broader basis (condition 2). The publication of arbitral awards, however, is crucial for the development of a genuinely legal form of reasoning, specifically based on arbitral precedent.[95]

As soon as arbitral tribunals begin to rely on past decisions and base their reasoning on established rules and principles of law rather than mere equity, one can speak of an evolving "transnational law," a "law beyond the state" in international commercial arbitration. And it is at this point that commercial arbitration has to face a "complexity problem": Like any other legal process, it must reach an adequate level of complexity vis-à-vis its societal environment

---

[90] The benchmark for such an endeavor is provided by Yves Dezalay and Bryant G. Garth, *Dealing in Virtue: International Commercial Arbitration and the Construction of a Transnational Legal Order*, (University of Chicago Press, 1996).

[91] See, e.g., Gralf-Peter Calliess and Moritz Renner, "Between Law and Social Norms: The Evolution of Global Governance," *Ratio Juris* 22, no. 2 (2009): pp. 260–280.

[92] Gralf-Peter Calliess et al., "Law, The State, and Private Ordering," *German Law Journal* 9, no. 4 (2008): pp. 397–410, 406–408.

[93] Niklas Luhmann, *Law as a Social System*, (Oxford: Oxford University Press, 2004); for the most influential translation of *Luhmannian* systems theory to (transnational) law see Gunther Teubner, *Law as an Autopoietic System*, (Oxford, UK/Cambridge, USA: Blackwell, 1993) and Gunther Teubner, "Global Bukowina: Legal Pluralism in the World Society," in *Global Law without a State*, edited by Gunther Teubner, (Aldershot: Dartmouth, 1997), p. 3.

[94] Gralf-Peter Calliess and Moritz Renner, "Between Law and Social Norms," pp. 268–269; similarly Stone Sweet and Grisel, in this volume.

[95] Gabrielle Kaufmann-Kohler, "Arbitral Precedent: Dream, Necessity or Excuse?" *Arbitration International* 23, no. 3 (2007): pp. 357–378.

lest it become irrelevant.[96] In order to attract potential claimants, the legal system needs to respond to individual demands and social change, but at the same time it must maintain a certain degree of durability in order to fulfill its stabilizing function.[97]

This balance is especially hard to strike in transnational legal processes. Here, the evolution of law is, through the contractual basis of arbitration, closely linked to economic processes. It is the flexibility and adaptability of the arbitral procedure which explains its attractiveness for cross-border exchange. In the terms of systems theory, international arbitration is marked by *cognitive* expectation structures. Cognitive expectations are defined as social knowledge which is modified in cases of disappointment and thus enables learning processes.[98] This is what party autonomy chiefly stands for: an adaptation of legal structures according to the needs of individual actors.

But at the same time, this very adaptability threatens to undermine the build-up of adequately complex normative structures within legal discourse as the law can barely keep up with the development of an increasingly over-complex economy.[99] Even more, keeping up with these developments would most probably end in a self-destruction of the legal system,[100] as any concept of law builds on the idea that rules are (generally) valid even if they are (individually) disadvantageous.[101] Thus, legal processes are defined by the fact that they generate *normative* expectations, i.e., expectations which are counterfactually upheld even in cases of non-compliance.

Both cognitive and normative expectations are necessary for guaranteeing an adequate complexity of the legal system toward its environment. But while knowledge in the form of cognitive expectations is produced in any social context, normative expectations can only be created within the legal process itself. International arbitration can very well rely on standard from contracts, customs, and usages of international commerce in order to remain sufficiently responsive to economic needs. But when it comes to the creation of normative expectations, the legal system cannot rely on the decentralized knowledge produced in the social fields which it seeks to regulate. Instead, the legal system itself must ultimately produce the very norms

---

[96] Moritz Renner, "Death By Complexity. The Financial Crisis and the Crisis of Law in World Society," in *The Financial Crisis in Constitutional Perspective: The Dark Side of Functional Differentiation*, edited by Poul Kjaer et al., (Oxford: Hart, 2011), pp. 93–111, 94–96.

[97] Niklas Luhmann, *Law as a Social System*, (Oxford: Oxford University Press, 2004), pp. 147–148.

[98] Niklas Luhmann, "Die Weltgesellschaft," *ARSP* 57, no. 1 (1971): pp. 1–35, 11.

[99] Moritz Renner, "Death By Complexity. The Financial Crisis and the Crisis of Law in World Society," in Poul Kjaer et al. (eds.), *The Financial Crisis in Constitutional Perspective: The Dark Side of Functional Differentiation*, (Oxford: Hart, 2011), pp. 93–111.

[100] Niklas Luhmann, "Die Weltgesellschaft," p. 14.

[101] Stone Sweet and Grisel, in this volume.

upon which it relies.[102] This circularity of the legal process necessarily leads to problems of justification with a view to the regulated sector: Why should the parties of a commercial contract, after having voluntarily opted for arbitration, obey any rules of law beyond the contract and their explicit choice of law at all?

In the case of international arbitration, this problem of justification is addressed by two distinct but interrelated mechanisms—and those are the two features of constitutionalization identified above: the structural coupling of law and politics, and an emerging hierarchy of norms. In a first step, by referring to policy considerations and political discourse, be it on the domestic, international, or transnational level, international arbitral tribunals "externalize" the problem of norm justification to the realm of politics.[103] In a second step, public policy considerations are integrated into an overarching transnational hierarchy of norms.[104]

Thus, the strong interaction of the legal and the economic system through the mechanism of party autonomy ("arbitration privileges contract, not politics"[105]) is counter-balanced by an increasing openness for policy considerations in the emerging transnational constitutional order.[106]

7 Perspectives

The constitutionalization of international commercial arbitration analyzed in this chapter seems to open up a perspective for integrating public policy concerns into the transnational legal process. The juridification of international arbitration leads to the emergence of a hierarchical order of conflict-of-laws rules which not only structure the internal complexity of the transnational legal process, but also reconcile the mechanisms of a globalizing economy with the rationality of political discourse.

With regard to the governance function of international commercial arbitration,[107] this assimilation of arbitral practice to domestic legal systems is of foremost importance. The application of public policy norms directly addresses the issue of potential *negative externalities* following from arbitral dispute resolution.[108] From an economic-rationalist point of view, whether or

---

[102] Niklas Luhmann, *Law as a Social System*, pp. 108–109.

[103] Niklas Luhmann, "Verfassung als evolutionäre Errungenschaft," *RJ* 9 (1990): pp. 176–220.

[104] Moritz Renner, "Towards a Hierarchy of Norms in Transnational Law?".

[105] Amr Shalakany, "Arbitration and the Third World: A Plea for Reassessing Bias Under the Specter of Neoliberalism," *Harvard International Law Journal* 41 (2001): pp. 419–468, 459.

[106] Moritz Renner, "The Dialectics of Transnational Economic Constitutionalism," in *Karl Polanyi, Globalisation and the Potential of Law in Transnational Markets*, edited by Christian Joerges and Josef Falke, (Oxford: Hart, 2011), pp. 419–433.

[107] Mattli and Dietz, Chapter 1, this volume.

[108] Mattli and Dietz, Chapter 1, this volume.

not arbitration produces private gains as compared to domestic adjudication, the application of public policy norms serves to prevent negative effects on third parties or the general public. This is most apparent in the application of competition law, where a circumvention of mandatory norms might serve the disputing parties, but at the same time be detrimental to other market participants.

However, a closer look reveals the highly ambivalent nature of this constitutionalization process. As arbitral dispute resolution increasingly replicates the mechanisms of domestic legal systems, it may lose its appeal as an "alternative" form of dispute resolution and thus jeopardize its very existence. As arbitral dispute resolution gains both in doctrinal consistency and in responsiveness to political concerns, it loses in flexibility and adaptability to the parties' concerns.[109] *Private gains* which are usually expected from arbitration vis-à-vis domestic court proceedings[110] might thus be cancelled out. As a result, economic actors may prefer to settle their conflicts by more informal means from the outset. The "opting out of the legal system" might thus be followed by an "opting out of arbitration."

In this regard, it remains to be seen whether potential claimants might not, after all, prefer a highly consistent system of legal rules which also reflects public policy concerns over the idiosyncratic arbitral "method of decision-making"[111] of the olden days. It is not unlikely that the public-policy orientation of arbitral bodies is seen by potential claimants as reinforcing the autonomous authority of arbitrators as adjudicators. But it will then depend on the ability of arbitral institutions to present themselves as legal actors not only equivalent to, but also sufficiently distinct from, domestic courts as to safeguard its comparative attractiveness.[112] The expectation of private gains, which has so far fueled the rise of international commercial arbitration, is, after all, a matter of perception.[113]

---

[109] On this debate cf., e.g., the contributions in *International arbitration in the 21st Century. Towards "Judicialization" and Uniformity?*, edited by Richard B. Lillich and Charles N. Brower (Irvington, NY: Transnational Publishers, 1994).

[110] Mattli and Dietz, Chapter 1, this volume.

[111] Emmanuel Gaillard, "Transnational Law: A Legal System or a Method of Decision-Making?".

[112] Cf. Michaels, Chapter 3, this volume.   [113] Cf. Karton, Chapter 4, this volume.

6

International Commercial Arbitration, Transnational Governance, and the New Constitutionalism

A. Claire Cutler

1 Introduction

Transnational governance is a mode of regulation that structures local and global political economies and comprises a multiplicity of actors and institutions.[1] Its development was anticipated in Philip Jessup's volume on the subject, which defines transnational law as "all law which regulates actions or events that transcend national frontiers . . . [including] [b]oth public and private international law . . . [and] other rules which do not wholly fit into such categories."[2] This broad definition would seem to include any cross-border transaction, including those involving both public/state and private/non-state participants. Indeed, Harold Koh characterizes transnational law as a "hybrid of private and public, domestic and international law," and emphasizes the permeability of local and global legal systems.[3] International commercial arbitration plays a central role in transnational governance and similarly partakes of both private and public international law. International commercial arbitrations range from the highly confidential and private hearings held under the auspices of the International Chamber of Commerce (ICC) International Court of Arbitration to the quasi-public proceedings held under the World Trade Organization (WTO) and the investor-state proceedings of Chapter 11 of the North American Free Trade Agreement (NAFTA) and the World Bank's International Centre for the

---

[1] Marie-Laure Djelic and Kerstin Sahlin-Andersson, eds., *Transnational Governance*. (Cambridge: Cambridge University Press, 2006), p. 6.

[2] Philip Jessup, *Transnational Law*. (New Haven: Yale University Press, 1956), p. 2.

[3] Harold Koh, "Transnational Public Litigation," *Yale Law Journal* 100, no. 8 (1991): pp. 2347–2402 at p. 2349.

Settlement of Investment Disputes (ICSID). While this chapter refers to these institutions as forming a system, it is important to note considerable differentiation in their nature and operation. In addition, the hybrid nature of the investor-state treaty regime, which grafts private international law dispute resolution mechanisms onto public international law treaties, creates considerable uncertainty and ambiguity as to the nature and function of arbitration proceedings.[4] The private law origins of international commercial arbitration have given rise to concerns about the propriety and adequacy of employing private law concepts and practices when arbitral proceedings involve matters of public interest and concern.[5] One commentator notes the clash of legal cultures emanating from this public/private law hybridization:

> Private commercial and public international lawyers have different perspectives on and different philosophies about the role of law, the state, and the function of dispute resolution. Also, their audiences and conceptual approaches are often different. Whereas public international lawyers embed international investment law firmly in general international law and approach the topic against that background, commercial arbitral lawyers focus on dispute settlement and see investment treaty arbitration as a subset of international (commercial) arbitration.[6]

Indeed, the privatization of authority is increasingly recognized as a significant development in international relations that raises challenging concerns about the analytical adequacy of conventional distinctions between public and private authority.[7] In addition, private law-making and dispute resolution processes are regarded as transforming the fields of public and private international law and giving rise to a new transnational legal order.[8] Private individuals and business associations have a long history in the constitution of transnational merchant law, dating back at least a millennium.[9] However,

[4] Zachary Douglas, "The Hybrid Foundations of Investment Treaty Arbitration," *British Yearbook of International Law* 74, no. 1 (2003): pp. 151–289.

[5] William Burke-White and Andreas Von Staden, "Private Litigation in a Public Law Sphere: The Standard of Review in Investor-State Arbitrations," *The Yale Journal of International Law* 35, no. 2 (2010): pp. 283–346.

[6] Stephan Schill, "W(h)ither Fragmentation? On the Literature and Sociology of International Investment Law," *European Journal of International Law* 22, no. 2 (2011): pp. 875–908 at p. 888.

[7] A. Claire Cutler, Virginia Haufler, and Tony Porter, eds., *Private Authority and International Affairs*. (New York: Suny Press, 1999); Rodney Hall and Thomas Biersteker, eds., *The Emergence of Private Authority in Global Governance*. (Cambridge: Cambridge University Press, 2002); Jean-Christophe Graz, and Andreas Nölke, eds., *Transnational Private Governance and Its Limits*. (London and New York: Routledge, 2008).

[8] Ralph Steinhardt, "The Privatization of Public International Law," *George Washington Journal of International Law and Economics*, 25, no. 2 (1991): pp. 523–553; John Spanogle, "The Arrival of Private Law," *George Washington Journal of International Law and Economics* 25 (2), 1991: pp. 477–522; Gunther Teubner, "Breaking Frames: Economic Globalization and the Emergence of *Lex Mercatoria*," *European Journal of Social Theory* 5, no. 2 (2002): pp. 199–217.

[9] A. Claire Cutler, "Global Capitalism and Liberal Myths: Dispute Settlement in Private International Trade Relations," *Millennium: Journal of International Studies* 24, no. 3 (1995): 377–395; Norbert Horn and Clive Schmitthoff, eds., *The Transnational Law of International Commercial Transactions*. (Deventer: Kluwer, 1982).

the focus here is on the expansion and deepening of private systems of ordering attending the restructuring of local and global political economies over the past few decades according to the logic of the new constitutionalism. New constitutionalism advances market fundamentalism, neoliberal economic discipline, and neoconservative politico-military strategy by locking states into binding legal agreements that are of a constitutional order because they set significant limits on states' rights to govern themselves.[10] Privatized systems of rule form the normative underbelly for transnational capitalism and have expanded both extensively and intensively with the deregulation and globalization of capitalism and its increasingly deeper reach into local political economies and societies.[11] It is here argued that the international commercial arbitration system is a key element in the new constitutionalism, in that it functions to both constitute the material conditions for the continuing expansion of capitalism and to legitimize strategies of private accumulation as the dominant regime of accumulation. The private ordering of international dispute settlement through international commercial arbitration both structures and rules local and global political economies, and consequently it may be analyzed as a normative system comprised by principles, rules, and decision-making structures. It may also be conceptualized as a material system that makes possible and constitutes trade, investment, production, financial, and other socio-economic relations. It is further argued that these normative and material characteristics of transnational governance may be usefully analyzed through the lenses of critical political economy theory and the analysis of the central role played by international commercial arbitration lawyers as central agents in transnational governance.

It will be argued that today international commercial arbitration lawyers are central members of the *mercatocracy*, which forms a transnational merchant class and the "organic intellectuals" of a nascent transnational business civilization. Derived from the medieval term, *lex mercatoria*, or the law merchant, the *mercatocracy* "is comprised of transnational merchants, private international lawyers and other professionals and their associations, government officials, and representatives of international organizations" who operate locally and globally to develop, harmonize, and universalize systems of commercial laws and dispute resolution practices.[12]

---

[10] Stephen Gill, ed. *Power and Resistance in the New World Order*. Second revised edition. (Houndsmill: Palgrave Macmillan, 2008); David Harvey, *The New Imperialism*. (Oxford: Oxford University Press, 2003) and *A Brief History of Neoliberalism* (Oxford: Oxford University Press, 2005); David Schneiderman, *Constitutionalizing Economic Globalization: Investment Rules and Democracy's Promise*. (Cambridge: Cambridge University Press, 2008).

[11] Tim Büthe and Mattli Walter, *The New Global Rulers*. (Princeton and Oxford: Princeton University Press, 2011).

[12] A. Claire Cutler, *Private Power and Global Authority: Transnational Merchant Law in the Global Political Economy*. (Cambridge: Cambridge University Press: 2003), pp. 4–5.

The next section introduces the concept of hegemony as crucial to understanding the centrality of the *mercatocracy*, as the organic intellectuals of transnational civil society, to the operation of global capitalism. Noting that hegemony is a process that requires continuous reproduction and legitimation, the discussion addresses the role that international commercial arbitration lawyers and law play in maintaining and strengthening the structural power of capital.[13] This is achieved, in part, by legitimizing new constitutional disciplines that subordinate public interests to the protection of private interests as the necessary costs incurred to advance the general public welfare. However, theorizing that dominant power structures always give rise to resistance, the analysis identifies weaknesses or gaps in the hold of the *mercatocracy* and its privatized system of justice. These holes provide openings for practices that have the potential to undermine the structural power of capital and advance progressive transformations of the international arbitration system.

The following section examines the role that international commercial arbitration lawyers play in the articulation and legitimation of the international commercial arbitration system as an integral dimension of new constitutionalism and a central mechanism for governing global capitalism. The analysis reveals significant developments in international commercial arbitration that suggest that there are fractures in the hegemony of the *mercatocracy*. Conflicting arbitral decisions concerning the balancing of public and private interests and changes in arbitral rules and practices governing the openness and inclusivity of certain arbitral regimes suggest important shifts in arbitral culture.

The conclusion then advances a *praxis* conception of international law, arguing that the continuing success of the *mercatocracy* as the organic intellectuals of transnational capitalism will turn on its ability to continuously construct and represent its private interests as public in nature and effect, and questions whether the current global financial crisis puts this capacity in doubt.

[13] The structural power of capital refers to the "ability of capital to shape policy and beneficial conditions for accumulation in the long–term associated with the structural features of capitalism and the capitalist state. Under capitalism, governments usually operate from the premise that it is private investment that provides growth, prosperity and jobs, and seek to foster a hospitable investment climate. However if policies are perceived by business as undermining such a climate, individual investors may spontaneously decide to postpone investment or to invest in other countries. The investment strike is a case of structural power, uniquely available to business to discipline governments and unions, a power strengthened by free capital mobility across jurisdictions. It works primarily through the market mechanism in capitalist economies. By contrast, if organized labor opposed government policies and collectively organized a general strike, the strike would likely be treated as if it was an attack upon society itself and be met with opposition from and possibly coercion on the part of the capitalist state" (see Stephen Gill and A. Claire Cutler, eds., *New Constitutionalism and World Order.* (Cambridge: Cambridge University Press, 2014), pp. 323–324).

2 New Constitutionalism and the Constitution of Hegemony

New constitutionalism is a political project aimed at the continuous expansion of capitalism through the entrenchment into national and international legal frameworks of neoliberal, market-oriented laws and policies that favor privatization, liberalization, and deregulation of trade, investment, finance, services and a host of economic, social, and cultural activities.[14] New constitutional disciplines of trade and investment activities are evident in three characteristics of these legal regimes: the significant insulation of foreign investment and trade relations from interference by states; the agreement to standards of behavior that limit the policy and legislative autonomy of states; and the commitment to dispute settlement in private arbitral proceedings subject to no or minimal legal review by states.

The first characteristic of typical bilateral and multilateral investment agreements is the protection of the trade and investment activities of private individuals and corporations from interference by local, national, political, and legal authorities. Under these agreements governments agree to refrain from activities that might impair or harm the economic activities covered by the agreements. Governments agree to observe certain standards of behavior that set broad limits on their legislative and policy autonomy. The typical bilateral investment treaty (BIT), for example, contains three main elements: definitions, substantive obligations for host states, and provision for binding investor-state arbitration. Investment is typically broadly defined to include a range of agreements as investments that are governed by the BIT, and often "umbrella clauses" are used to bring all contractual arrangements entered into between the investor and host state under the jurisdiction of the BIT. This works to internationalize and delocalize many contracts that would otherwise be subject to the jurisdiction of the host state.[15] Arbitration tribunals have held that consent to arbitration under a BIT prevails over contractual provisions providing for dispute resolution in local or national courts of law.[16]

In addition to providing definitions of investment, the typical BIT will establish general standards of behavior for the host state. The common standards include "fair and equitable treatment," "full protection and security," "national treatment," "most-favored-nation treatment," and "treatment in

---

[14] Gill and Cutler, *New Constitutionalism*.

[15] Rudolf Dolzer, "The Impact of International Investment Treaties on Domestic Administrative Law," *New York University Journal of International Law and Politics* 37, no. 4 (2005): pp. 953–972 at p. 965.

[16] *(Lanco) Lanco International Inc. v. The Argentine Republic*, Preliminary Decision on Jurisdiction of 8 December 1988, ILM 40 (2001): 457; *(Vivendi v. Argentina) Compañía de Aquas del Aconquija S.A. and Vivendi Universal v. Argentine Republic*, ICSID Case No. ARB/97/3, Decision on Annulment (July 2, 2002).

accordance with international law." The BIT will also include specific standards concerning the investment, such as dealing with monetary transfers, expropriation, and investor rights during war, revolution, or civil unrest. The BIT rarely states specific consequences of a breach, but arbitration tribunals have uniformly held that compensation is due upon breaches resulting in injury on the basis of customary international law. Finally, the BIT will provide for a binding enforcement mechanism for investors and will often designate the arbitration institutions and rules to be adopted.

Chapter 11 of NAFTA provides for similar standards of conduct for the host state, as well as binding investor-state dispute resolution. Binding dispute resolution through international arbitration allows foreign investors to sue host states directly if they believe that the BIT governing their investment or Chapter 11 standards of conduct have been violated. The ability for a foreign corporation to sue a host state directly has been described as a "revolutionary innovation" that has caused a "paradigm shift" in and "profound transformation" of international law, which was unprecedented.[17] This is because the rules of public international law governing international legal personality identify states as the "subjects" of international law. Only subjects are capable of taking claims before international legal tribunals. Private persons and corporations have no inherent legal rights, save for those granted to them by states.[18] Even in the WTO, which possesses one of the most developed dispute settlement systems, private actors do not have legal standing—only states may bring actions. The granting of the right for foreign investors to sue states directly is thus a new development in international law. In fact, investor-state arbitration is described by a leading arbitration lawyer, Jan Paulsson, as "not a sub-genre of an existing discipline. It is dramatically different from anything previously known in the international sphere."[19]

It is difficult to overstate the significance of the institutionalization of investor-state arbitration. Prior to this, foreign corporations basically had two options if they had a dispute with the host country: they could take legal action under the local laws of the host state, or they could approach their home state to make a claim for them and depend upon politics and diplomacy. Neither option was adequate. The first did not guarantee an impartial hearing, while the second did not guarantee compensation. States are under no duty to make claims on behalf of their citizens, and in any case the

---

[17] Tillmann Braun, "Investors as Subjects of Public International Law," *General Public International Law and International Investment Law*. ILA German Branch Working Group. (March 2011), p. 46, note 175.

[18] A. Claire Cutler, "Critical Reflections on Westphalian Assumptions of International Law and Organization: A Crisis of Legitimacy," *Review of International Studies* 27, no. 2 (2001): pp. 133–150.

[19] Jan Paulsson, "Arbitration Without Privity," *ICSID Review Foreign Investment Law Journal* 10, no. 2 (Fall 1995): pp. 232–257 at p. 256.

customary international law governing standards of compensation was uncertain. The provision of a direct legal action against the host state raises foreign investors to the legal status of states for the purposes of investor-state proceedings. This is indeed transformative of the statist foundations of public international law.

Investor-state dispute resolution thus delocalizes the proceedings by removing them from the jurisdiction of the local legal system and placing them in private commercial arbitration settings. The matters at issue may have significant public policy dimensions, including the protection of human rights or the environment.[20] BITs identify international arbitration as the method for dispute settlement and usually identify the institution to be utilized, such as ICSID, or other private arbitration tribunals. Often the arbitration rules to be utilized will also be specified, such as those of the ICC or the United National Commission on International Trade Law (UNCITRAL). NAFTA provides for ICSID or UNCITRAL as the dispute settlement rules available to the parties under the Chapter 11 investor-state provision.

What is important to note is that this delocalization of investor-state dispute settlement through binding dispute resolution in specialized tribunals tends to stabilize and legitimize the status quo by enabling foreign corporations to enforce their BIT or NAFTA rights into the future without regard for changing circumstances. BITs and NAFTA lock states into accepting limitations on their policy autonomy, a crucial function of neoliberal discipline under new constitutionalism.[21]

In a ruling that has generated much controversy, a tribunal interpreted the host state's obligation to provide the foreign investor with "fair and equitable treatment" as acting

> in a consistent manner, free from ambiguity, and totally transparently in its relations with the foreign investor, so that it may know beforehand any and all rules and regulations that will govern its investments, as well as the goals of the relevant policies and administrative practices or directives, to be able to plan its investments and comply with such regulations.[22]

---

[20] The extent to which new constitutional discipline limits Canadian public policy autonomy and is articulated within the Canadian state is revealed in an interesting NAFTA case. An American company that manufactures a fuel additive that was banned by a Canadian regulation banning the inter-provincial transport and import of fuel containing the additive on public health and environmental grounds made a claim under Chapter 11 of breach of Canada's NAFTA obligations (expropriation, national treatment, performance requirements). Canada settled the claim with the company, agreed to remove the ban and paid the company $19 million in compensation after an internal review revealed that the ban was also inconsistent with an internal interprovincial trade agreement modelled on NAFTA-like principles. See Schneiderman, *Constitutionalizing Economic Globalization*, pp. 129–133.

[21] Gill, *Power and Resistance*.

[22] *(Tecmed) TécnicasMedioambientales Tecmed S.A. v. United Mexican States*. ARB (AF)/00/02, dated May 29, 2003. p. 2.

Arguably, the broad scope of disclosure required and the level of specificity contemplated leave little public policy space or flexibility for the host state.

In addition to delocalizing investment disputes, the investor-state regime privatizes dispute settlement by identifying specialized arbitration institutions that operate like a private justice system, with significant autonomy from national legal systems.[23] For example, many BITs provide that the parties do not have to exhaust local remedies, which is a standard rule in other areas of international law, such as international human rights law. In addition, BITs that do not provide exclusively for binding arbitration will often contain "fork-in-the-road" clauses that require an investor to choose either to submit a claim to arbitration or to dispute resolution in local courts. Once the choice has been made the investor is bound by it.[24] NAFTA Chapter 11 requires that investors initiating arbitration waive their right to initiate or continue proceedings in a national tribunal or court of law.[25]

As mentioned previously, NAFTA identifies ICSID and UNCITRAL rules as the dispute settlement mechanisms available to foreign investors. The ICSID system is "self-contained," whereby review and annulment proceedings take place within the regime.[26] ICSID awards may then be enforced under the New York Convention on the Enforcement of Foreign Arbitral Awards (New York Convention). The New York Convention provides that awards may not be enforced if contrary to public policy in the enforcing country. However, courts regularly adopt a restrictive approach limiting policy concerns to matters of "morality and justice" and not permitting substantive review of awards on their merits.[27] UNCITRAL awards may be reviewed by national courts at the seat of arbitration, but most countries have adopted the UNCITRAL Model Law that limits grounds for review to jurisdictional and procedural matters.[28] While the Model rules do provide for the public policy exception, this does not permit substantive review of the award on its merits.[29]

The rules governing investor-state arbitration are modelled on the principles governing private commercial arbitration between two parties where confidentiality has been a driving concern. Moreover, the origins of the investor-state

---

[23] Cutler, *Private Power*.

[24] Andrea Bjorklund, "Private Rights and Public International Law: Why Competition Among International Economic Law Tribunals Is Not Working," *Hastings Law Journal* 59 (December 2007): pp. 101–163 at p. 153.

[25] Bjorklund, "Private Rights," p. 154.

[26] Judith Levine, "Navigating the parallel universe of investor-State arbitration under the UNCITRAL Rules," in *Evolution in Investment Treaty Law and Arbitration*, edited by Chester Brown and Kate Mills (Cambridge: Cambridge University Press, 2011), p. 401.

[27] Joseph McLaughlin and Laurie Genevro, "Enforcement of Arbitral Awards Under the New York Convention—Practice in U.S. Courts," *Berkeley Journal of International Law* 3, no. 2 (Winter 1986): pp. 249–272 at p. 258.

[28] Levine, "Navigating the parallel universe," p. 402.

[29] Thomas Webster, "Review of Substantive Reasoning of International Arbitral Awards by National Courts: Ensuring One-Stop Adjudication," *Kluwer Law International* 22, no. 3 (2006): pp. 431–462.

dispute resolution system in the laws and culture of private international commercial arbitration have proved very challenging for domestic democratic forces seeking to gain access to and information about the proceedings. The tendency of WTO dispute settlement panels to exhibit a "liberalizing bias" when there is a conflict between foreign investment or trade interests and domestic interests suggests that the arbitral system does not operate neutral-ly.[30] Indeed, Gus Van Harten identifies a structural bias of investor-state arbitration in favor of "those states and other actors that wield power over appointing authorities or the system as a whole."[31] On the basis of a recent study, he further notes evidence of a systemic bias that favors "legal interpretations that tend to benefit claimants by expanding the authority of the tribunals and by allowing more claims to proceed, especially where the claim is from a Western capital-exporting state."[32] Indeed, arbitration institutions are very competitive and often produce inconsistent awards, reflecting contesting social forces and considerable fragmentation and duplication of proceedings.[33] Analysts further observe that the extension of commercial arbitration to the settlement of disputes involving public authorities is producing a clash of legal cultures between public international law traditions, emphasizing the protection of human rights, the environment, and other matters of public interest and concern, and private international law, emphasizing freedom of contract and the autonomy of commercial actors to conduct their private affairs as they see fit.[34] Many believe that general consent[35] to delocalized and privatized dispute resolution produces a "democratic deficit":

[30] Judith Goldstein and Richard Steinberg, "Regulatory Shift: The Rise of Judicial Liberalization," in *The Politics of Global Regulation*, edited by Walter Mattli and Ngaire Woods (Princeton and Oxford: Princeton University Press, 2009), pp. 211–241.

[31] Gus Van Harten, "Investment Treaty Arbitration, Procedural Fairness, and the Rule of Law," in *International Investment Law and Comparative Law*, edited by Stephan Schill (Oxford: Oxford University Press, 2010).

[32] Gus Van Harten, "Pro-Investor or Pro-State Bias in Investment-Treaty Arbitration? Forthcoming Study Gives Cause for Concern," *Investment Treaty News* (April 13, 2012) available at <http://www.iisd.org/itn/2012/04/13/pro-investor-or-pro-state-bias-in-investment-treaty-arbitration-forthcoming-study-gives-cause-for-concern/>, p. 4.

[33] Bjorklund, "Private Rights," identifies the US-Canada Softwood Lumber dispute as a classic example of fragmented and duplicative proceedings that were initiated by different parties in the WTO, NAFTA, and domestic arbitral panels over the course of the dispute.

[34] Schill, "W(h)ither Fragmentation."

[35] Most BITs give *general consent* to delocalized, binding arbitration, as opposed to specific consent in a contract to arbitrate where the parties will be governed by the domestic rules of contract under the applicable system of private international law. The general consent given by a host state in a BIT "is general because it authorizes the arbitration of *any* future dispute with *any* foreign investor [of the state party] in the state's territory" and operates like a "blank cheque which may be cashed for an unknown amount at a future, and as yet unknown, date" transforming "investor-state arbitration from a modified form of commercial arbitration into a system to control the state's exercise of regulatory authority with respect to investors as a group" (Gus Van Harten, "Private authority and transnational governance: the contours of the international system of investor protection," *Review of International Political Economy* 12 no. 4 (2005): pp. 600–623 at pp. 607–608, quoting A. Redfern and M. Hunter, *Law and Practice of Commercial Arbitration* 3rd edition (London: Sweet & Maxwell, 1999), pp. 21–22).

State parties to investment agreements can no longer legislate at will in the public interest without concern that an arbitral tribunal will determine that the legislation constitutes interference with an investment. Thus investment arbitration may result in an overall loss of state independence and sovereignty, which has implications for democratic governance. . .

. . .the question arises whether state exercises of public authority should be adjudicated by foreigners, largely on the basis of commercial principles, when the adjudicators are unconcerned with the wider effects of their decisions.[36]

These agreements contribute to deepening the structural power of transnational capital by privileging international economic relations over local relations. In Polanyian terms, they work to disembed economic activity from domestic social and political controls.[37] How did this come about? How is it that governments would agree in advance to lock themselves into binding limits on their sovereignty and autonomy when it comes to regulating trade and foreign investment activities? For the answer, we must turn to the insights offered by critical international political economy.

Most students of critical political economy recognize that capitalism does not simply reproduce itself of its own accord, but requires certain dispositions, institutions, and apparatuses to enable its continuing reproduction and expansion.[38] State theories, for example, recognize the analytical distinction between functions of accumulation and legitimation, recording the need of capitalist states for material, institutional, and normative or ideological reproduction. Robert Jessop, for example, differentiates between the "accumulation strategies" of a state and its "hegemonic project," suggesting that achieving the material conditions for capitalism is insufficient, for these conditions must be generally accepted by society.[39] Jessop articulates Gramscian understandings of hegemony and the idea that the dominant class achieves dominance or "hegemony" through the combined influence of coercion and consent. Gramsci believed that hegemony—the process by which the ruling class establishes the conditions necessary for achieving leadership—could not be secured solely through coercion, but required the ideological capture of popular support. This involves the acceptance and internalization by the masses of the interests and values of the ruling class as their own. Indeed, as Adam Morton observes, "hegemony is the articulation

[36] Barnali Choudhury, "Recapturing Public Power: Is Investment Arbitration's Engagement of the Public Interest Contributing to the Democratic Deficit?" *Vanderbilt Journal of Transnational Law* 41, no. 2 (2008): pp. 775–832 at p. 779.

[37] Karl Polanyi, *The Great Transformation: The Political and Economic Origins of Our Time*. (Boston: Beacon Press, 1944).

[38] Karl Marx, *Capital: A Critique of Political Economy*, vol. 1. trans B. Fowkes. (London: Penguin, 1976. [1867]); Louis Althusser, "Ideology and Ideological Sate Apparatuses: Notes Towards an Investigation," in *Lenin and Philosophy*, trans. by Ben Brewster (London: New Left Books, 1971).

[39] Robert Jessop, *State Theory: Putting the Capitalist State in its Place*. (Pennsylvania: Pennsylvania State Press, 1990), p. 216.

and justification of a particular set of interests as general interests. It appears as an expression of broadly based consent, manifested in the acceptance of ideas and supported by material resources and institutions."[40]

The acceptance by civil society of relations of dominance is thus a crucial dimension of hegemony. So too is the work of the "organic intellectuals" who facilitate the internalization of the interests of the ruling class as the common interest and, indeed, as the "common sense" of the time. Antonio Gramsci observes that the acceptance by the masses of the dominant ethos as "common sense" is not a result of "self-deception [*malafede*]" but "the expression of profounder contrasts of a social historical order" associated with its subjugation as a group.[41] Organic intellectuals are able to garner both the "spontaneous" consent of the masses and the legal enforcement of coercive discipline. In this latter respect, Gramsci regarded the law and legal institutions as playing a particular role in producing the common sense understandings which undergird hegemony.[42] Although Gramsci wrote very little about law, his fragmentary analysis of law coupled with his understanding of hegemony inspires a *praxis conception of law* of great relevance to this analysis.[43] This conception derives from Gramsci's theorization of Marxism as a philosophy of praxis: as a unity resulting from the dialectical development of contradictions between theoretical and practical activity. Gramsci contemplated this unity as "immanent" in capitalist society and as realizable through practices informed by critical inquiry.[44] The role of the organic intellectual is linked to the processes of establishing the hegemony or leadership of the dominant social forces. The process of achieving hegemony and "colonizing the internal world of the dominated classes" involves three related developments in which organic intellectuals and law play leading roles: universalization, naturalization, and rationalization.[45] Universalization involves the representation by the dominant group of its parochial and private interests as common and public in nature, while naturalization and rationalization concern processes of reification that present the existing order as fully consistent with the natural and rational order of things. Law facilitates these processes by interpellating individuals as equal legal subjects, obscuring their actual subordination and inequality, and rationalizing this appearance as part of the universal and

---

[40] Adam Morton, *Unravelling Gramsci: Hegemony and Passive Revolution in the Global Political Economy.* (London: Pluto Press, 2007), p. 113.

[41] Antonio Gramsci, *Selections from Prison Notebooks of Antonio Gramsci*, edited by Q. Hoare and G. Nowell Smith (New York: International Publishers, 1971), pp. 326–327.

[42] Mark Benney, "Gramsci on Law, Morality and Power," *International Journal of the Sociology of the Law* 11 (1983): pp. 191–208.

[43] A. Claire Cutler, "Gramsci, Law, and the Culture of Global Capitalism," *Critical Review of International Social and Political Philosophy* 8, no. 4 (2005): pp. 527–542.

[44] Gramsci, *Selections*, pp. 400, 450.

[45] Douglas Litowitz, "Gramsci, Hegemony, and the Law," *Brigham Young University Law Review* 2, no. 2 (2000), pp. 515–551 at p. 525.

natural order of things.[46] These processes may be achieved through *trasformismo*, being the absorption of opposition into the dominant group,[47] which involves the work of organic intellectuals who "perpetuate the existing way of life at the level of theory."[48]

Today we may conceptualize international commercial arbitration lawyers and the various arbitral regimes as the organic intellectuals of global capitalism. They participate in the creation of the ideational, material, and institutional conditions—what Louis Althusser refers to as the ideological and state apparatuses—which enable the continuing reproduction of capitalism.[49] In this the legal expert excels, for it is the legal technocrat that crafts the laws framing civil society and the private sphere. Gramsci identifies as the "entire "juridical problem" that of "assimilating," "educating," and "adapting" the masses to the goals of the ruling class.[50] This is achieved through laws of private property and contract that establish the normative framework for capitalism according to understandings of individual autonomy and freedom of contract, carving out the private sphere of "civil society" as distinct from the public sphere of the state and "political society."[51] The international commercial arbitration system and the investor-state regimes participate in the construction of hegemony by universalizing, naturalizing, and rationalizing distinctions between the private and public spheres transnationally.[52] They advance the need to discipline societies according to neoliberal market discipline as the common sense of our time. However, as theorized by many critical thinkers, disciplinary power is always accompanied by resistance.[53] Common sense, like hegemony, is never monolithic, but is fragmentary and contested and must be continuously reproduced.[54] As we turn to consider the contribution of the *mercatocracy* to transnational hegemony, apparent cracks and fractures in common sense suggest that hegemony has not been fully achieved.

---

[46] Althusser, *Ideology.*

[47] Gramsci, *Selections*, pp. 57, 58–59.

[48] Litowitz, *"Gramsci,"* p. 526; See A. Claire Cutler, "Unthinking the GATS: a radical political economy critique of private transnational governance," in *Business and Global Governance*, edited by Morten Ougaard and Anna Leander (London and New York: Routledge, 2010), pp. 78–96, for an Althusserian reading of the interpellation of transnational corporations as neoliberal subjects under global capitalism.

[49] Althusser, *Ideology.*

[50] Gramsci, *Selections*, p. 195.

[51] Gramsci, *Selections*, p. 160.

[52] Cutler, "Global Capitalism"; A. Claire Cutler, "Artifice, Ideology, and Paradox: The Public/Private Distinction in International Law," *Review of International Political Economy* 4 no. 2 (1997): pp. 261–285.

[53] See Michel Foucault, *"Society Must Be Defended": Lectures at the Collège De France 1975–1976*, edited by Mauro Bertani and Arnold Davidson, trans. David Macey (New York: Picador, 1997); Gill and Cutler, *New Constitutionalism.*

[54] Mark Rupert, "Globalising common sense: a Marxian-Gramscian (re)vision of the politics of governance/resistance," *Review of International Studies*, 29, no. 1 (2003): pp. 181–198 at p. 185.

3 The *Mercatocracy*, International Commercial Arbitration, and Transnational Legal Apparatuses

Gramscian formulations of hegemony direct attention to conditions that enable the ruling class—the *mercatocracy*—to achieve leadership, forming what Gramsci called a *"blocco storico"* or "historical bloc."[55] Wolfgang Haug describes the historical bloc as "certainly a phenomenon of the present, which aims at a sociopolitical aggregated agency and potency to shape this on-going process [of history in the making]."[56] Neo-Gramscians, such as Robert Cox, conceptualize the historical bloc as an assemblage of material, institutional, and ideological forces that cements political and civil societies together through a mix of coercive and consensual social relations.[57] In international commerce, the *mercatocracy* provides this leadership, crafting the material, institutional, and normative conditions and apparatuses that enable the continuing expansion of capitalism. The ascendancy of this transnational business class is associated with transformations in the mode of production of capitalism and the advent of patterns of flexible production that are altering state-society relations by reconfiguring the domains of public and private authority.[58] While historically law has figured prominently in the constitution and regulation of trade and investment relations, legal forms and institutions have today taken on an historical specificity that is related to the changing nature of capitalism as a transnational force that is increasingly competitive.[59] New constitutional policies and practices facilitate the reach of transnational legal forms deep into the domestic sphere of states, where they discipline local social, political, and economic relations according to neoliberal principles privileging privatized governance through free market mechanisms, self-regulation, and radically diminished welfare and regulatory roles of states. In the areas of global trade and foreign investment, transnational law serves to delocalize and denationalize legal forms, processes, and institutions for law creation and for dispute resolution. Indeed, the international commercial arbitration system forms a crucial foundation for de-linking legal enforcement from the state by submitting commercial disputes to the discipline of transnationalized laws and practices.

---

[55] Gramsci, *Selections*, pp. 377, 418.

[56] Wolfgang Haug, "Rethinking Gramsci's philosophy of praxis from one century to the next," *Boundary 2* 26, no. 2 (Summer 1999): pp. 101–117 at p. 111.

[57] Robert Cox with Timothy Sinclair, *Approaches to World Order*. (Cambridge: Cambridge University Press, 1996).

[58] Gill, *Power and Resistance*; David Harvey, *The Condition of Postmodernity: An Enquiry into the Origins of Cultural Change*. (Cambridge, MA and Oxford: Blackwell, 1990).

[59] Cutler, *Private Power*; Yves Dezalay and Bryant Garth, *Dealing in Virtue: International Commercial Arbitration and the Construction of a Transnational Legal Order*. (Chicago: University of Chicago Press, 1996).

The international commercial arbitration system comprises a complex mix of public and private laws, institutions, and actors and so is probably best described as a transnational rather than an international legal order.[60] In a seminal study published almost twenty years ago, Yves Dezalay and Bryant Garth describe the international commercial arbitration system as an "arcane domain," "mysterious," but foundational to advancing and perpetuating the rule of law in the form of a highly autonomous global system of "private justice."[61] They trace its efficacy to the legitimacy generated by the claims of international arbitration law to universality as a rationalized system of law and practice that functions more-or-less autonomously from state control to uphold private commercial agreements. However, "[a]utonomy is never complete and must be reaffirmed constantly" and be inscribed and re-inscribed in "institutions and mentalities" so as to become "nearly natural and self-evident."[62] In Gramscian terms, international commercial arbitration laws and practices must be rationalized, universalized, and naturalized as serving valued public purposes in order to become regarded as "common sense." Moreover, as noted already, the production of common sense, like the production of hegemony, is a process that must be continuously pursued. This is achieved by the international commercial arbitration community of arbitration lawyers, judges, multinational law firms, and related professionals who form what has been described as an "epistemic community" that advances international commercial arbitration as an indispensable public good.[63] As the regime's organic intellectuals, they have accumulated significant "symbolic capital" as recognized experts in the impartial settlement of commercial disputes and are able to present the private settlement of commercial disputes as a legitimate dimension of the public domain.[64] Just as national domestic courts of law uphold the contracts of private parties, international arbitrations tribunals uphold international commercial contracts, which are then enforced in domestic courts of law.[65] Through a process of de-localizing and de-nationalizing rule-creation and dispute settlement, but then re-localizing and re-nationalizing the enforcement of

---

[60] A. Claire Cutler, "Toward a radical political economy critique of transnational economic law," in *International Law on the Left: Re-examining Marxist Legacies*, edited by Susan Marks (Cambridge: Cambridge University Press, 2008).

[61] Dezalay and Garth, *Dealing in Virtue*, p. 4.

[62] Dezalay and Garth, *Dealing in Virtue*, p. 281.

[63] Jeswald Salacuse, "The Emerging Global Regime for Investment," *Harvard International Law Journal* 51, no. 2 (Summer 2010): pp. 427–467.

[64] Dezalay and Garth, *Dealing in Virtue*, p. 18.

[65] David Trubeck, Yves Dezalay, Ruth Buchanan, and John Davis, "Global restructuring and the law: Studies in the internationalisation of the legal fields and transnational arenas," *Case Western Law Review*, 44, no. 2 (1994): pp. 407–498; John Brathwaite and Peter Drahos, *Global Business Regulation*. (Cambridge: Cambridge University Press, 2000).

commercial arbitral awards as part of the public judicial function,[66] international commercial arbitration is integrated into local politico-legal fields and serves to condition local state-society relations with an internal logic that privileges private, opaque, secretive, and closed proceedings. This process is an integral dimension of the constitution of hegemony through the apparent transformation of the private enforcement of commercial agreements into a matter of public interest and responsibility. This process has, in fact, become the new common sense and is widely accepted as a "public good" benefiting the world community.

However, in order to sustain the belief that the public enforcement of private accumulation is a "public good," there must be general acceptance of the efficacy and legitimacy of distinctions between economics and politics, as well as between the private and public spheres. In this, the *mercatocracy* excels. Through claims to legitimacy as neutral experts, international commercial arbitration lawyers are able to carve out a sphere of autonomy, sustaining distinctions between economics and politics and between public and private spheres. Indeed, the belief that the settlement of international economic disputes requires a "depoliticized" environment provided by so-called impartial trade and investment experts is one of the foundational myths of the international commercial arbitration regime.[67]

However, as Dezalay and Garth noted, the system is characterized by a clash of legal cultures and generations, suggesting that there are fractures in this common sense.[68] The European "grand old men" who embodied the informality of the ancient *lex mercatoria* have been successfully challenged by Anglo-American technocrats, who, as newer arrivals to the field, brought increasingly litigious, aggressive, and competitive practices. These challenges have contributed over time to the increasing judicialization, bureaucratization, and formalization of the regime. They also noted a clash between academics and practitioners that today combines with the clash in cultures between public and private international lawyers to reflect further ruptures in common sense.

More recently Dezalay and Garth observe a shifting emphasis in public and private law norms.[69] They describe contemporary law firms as modern-day "compradors" who act locally and globally to advance the ventures of dominant states and as "double agents . . . situated between global corporate law and local structures of power." Their function is to manage this relationship,

---

[66] See Robert Wai, "Transnational liftoff and juridical touchdown: The regulatory function of private international law in an era of globalization," *Columbia Journal of Transnational Law* 40, no. 1 (2001): pp. 209–274.
[67] Cutler, *Private Power*.
[68] Dezalay and Garth, *Dealing in Virtue*, p. 52.
[69] Yves Dezalay and Bryant G. Garth, "Corporate Law Firms, NGOs, and Issues of Legitimacy for a Global Legal Order," *Fordham Law Review* 80, no. 6 (2012): pp. 2309–2345.

"continuously reproducing and reinventing the social legitimacy of law-yers."[70] In doing so, through "spillover" and "contagion" from other legal decisions or systems, lawyers have become "modernizers" as public interest norms enter into private law practices and reshape expectations about the role of law in society. This appears to be happening in the investor-state regimes, where some tribunals are challenging dominant conceptions about arbitration, recognizing the public dimension of many disputes, and drawing on changing practices in other dispute settlement institutions.

Indeed, fragmentation and fractures in common sense are evident in the following comparison of practices in the ICC, the WTO, and investor-state arbitration under Chapter 11 of the NAFTA and the ICSID.

4 ICC, WTO, NAFTA, ICSID, and Transnational Hegemony

The principle of "party autonomy" has long been a *grundnorm* for the inter-national commercial arbitration regime. Party autonomy in the choice of law to govern commercial agreements, party autonomy in the choice of institu-tions and arbitrators to adjudicate disputes, and party autonomy from the interference of local national courts of law (save for in the enforcement of foreign arbitral awards) are bedrocks of the regime. The idea that private par-ties should be free to govern their private relations *in privacy* is a foundation of liberal political economy and liberal theories of government, and rests upon assumed and "common sense" distinctions between the public and private spheres, as well as between public and private international law.[71] However, a comparison of international commercial arbitration practices in different institutional contexts reflects fractures in these common sense understandings. A comparison of the balance struck between public and priv-ate interests and differences in the openness of these institutions to chal-lenges from non-parties—be they civil society human rights or environmental groups, interested governments, corporations, or industry representatives—suggest some interesting innovations in arbitral practices. These innovations may be indicative of emerging challenges to the new constitutionalism and neoliberal discipline in the form of new practices and an emerging "innova-tive form of global praxis, intimating potentials for a transformation of global politics."[72] They also raise exciting opportunities for future development of a praxis conception of international law.

---

[70] Dezalay and Garth, "Corporate Law Firms," p. 2316.

[71] See Cutler, "Artifice, Ideology, and Paradox."

[72] Stephen Gill, "Towards a Radical Conception of Praxis: Imperial 'common sense' Versus the Post-modern Prince," *Millennium: Journal of International Studies* 40, no. 3 (June 2012): pp. 505–524 at p. 517.

4.1 *Comparing the ICC, WTO, NAFTA Chapter 11, and ICSID*

The ICC is a private organization founded in 1919 by national business organizations and corporations to promote international trade and market economies based on free competition and economic growth. The ICC International Court of Arbitration is the leading international commercial arbitration center in the world and its practices and procedures are informed by principles of private law. International commercial arbitration is conceived of as "a private form of adjudication authorized by the will of the disputing parties" and "is subject to the principles of private law, beginning with the supremacy of party autonomy."[73] Indeed, the "authority for commercial arbitration is rooted in contract," and so understandably ICC arbitrations give priority to the agreement established by the parties to the arbitration agreement.[74] Moreover, the "conceptual framework" informing international commercial arbitration regards commercial arbitration as "an autonomous system" that should be free from political or judicial interference and whose awards should be recognized by and executable before national courts of law. In keeping with this private law culture, ICC arbitrations are confidential and open only to the parties. The governing rules make no provision for the participation of non-parties, such as governments, non-governmental organizations (NGOs), and civil society groups, as in the case of third party participation or the submission of *amici curiae* ("friends of the court") briefs. As Van Harten and Loughlin note, this conceptual framework might make logical sense "so long as a dispute exists within the private sphere," but it loses meaning when disputes involve the constraint of governmental authority.[75] Thus, when we examine commercial arbitration under the WTO and under the investor-state regimes of NAFTA (Chapter 11) and ICSID, the private law conceptualization becomes problematic. Indeed, it is in these quasi-public arbitration tribunals that voices informed by public law principles of transparency, representation, and participation began to create fractures in the logic and common sense of private law conceptions. In addition, legal academics challenged practitioners to recognize the fundamentally public nature of proceedings that seek to review, discipline, and constrain state actions dealing with environmental, taxation, labor, or human rights matters raised by trade and foreign investment arbitrations.[76]

---

[73] Gus Van Harten and Martin Loughlin, "Investment Treaty Arbitration as a Species of Global Administrative Law," *European Journal of International Law* 17, no. 1 (2006): pp. 1–150 at p. 140.

[74] Van Harten and Loughlin, "Investment Treaty Arbitration," p. 140.

[75] Van Harten and Loughlin, "Investment Treaty Arbitration," p. 141.

[76] Cutler, "Global Capitalism"; Van Harten and Loughlin, "Investment Treaty Arbitration"; Gus Van Harten, *Investment Treaty Arbitration and Public Law.* (Oxford: Oxford University Press, 2007); Schneiderman, *Constitutionalizing Economic Globalization.*

The dispute resolution system of the WTO was established in 1994 under the Uruguay Round of multilateral trade negotiations that lead to the creation of the WTO. The Dispute Settlement Body (DSB), ad hoc panels to adjudicate individual disputes, and the Appellate Body are thus institutions of public international law. Only WTO member states are authorized to initiate claims under the Dispute Settlement Understanding (DSU) or to participate as third parties in disputes before adjudicative panels. In *US-Shrimp*, the Appellate Body observed:

[i]t may be well to stress at the outset that access to the dispute settlement process of the WTO is limited to Members of the WTO. This access is not available, under the WTO Agreement and the covered agreements as they currently exist, to individuals or international organizations, whether governmental or non-governmental.[77]

The limitation of access to member states reflects the state-based nature of public international law.

Although the WTO is an institution of public international law, the private law foundations of international commercial arbitration have provided the conceptual template for the dispute settlement regime. This has infused WTO dispute settlement proceedings with private arbitral legal foundations that emphasize the consent-based and contractual nature of dispute settlement proceedings between member states. However, these foundations have come under pressure from a number of external sources, including civil society groups, corporations, and states, who have mobilized around public interest concerns and sought to participate in WTO proceedings. Environmentalists, for example, were motivated to challenge the outcome of the *Tuna-Dolphin*[78] decisions that were products of GATT deliberations that took place during the negotiations for the Uruguay Round and NAFTA. In these cases the U.S. Marine Mammal Protection Act was found to be inconsistent with GATT trade rules, which sent a chill through environmental groups who believed that trade disciplines would trump all environmental concerns. As John Knox notes,

[m]ost panel members were trade experts with no apparent knowledge of environmental issues, they construed the trade/environment conflict in the context of an agreement designed to liberalize trade, and the proceedings were closed to non-governmental input. It was unsurprising that the panels seemed to dismiss environmental concerns out of hand.[79]

[77] (*US-Shrimp*) United States-Import Prohibition of Certain Shrimp and Shrimp Products (Report of the Appellate Body, WT/DS58/AB/R, October 12, 1998).

[78] (*Tuna-Dolphin*) United States-GATT Dispute Panel Report on Restrictions on Imports of Tuna, September 3, 1991, GATT B.I.S.D. (39th Supp.) at 155 (1993).

[79] John Knox, "The Judicial Resolution of Conflicts Between Trade and the Environment," *Harvard Environmental Review* 28, no. 1 (2004): pp. 1–78 at p. 24.

Subsequent efforts to ensure that the provisions of the WTO and NAFTA were friendly to environmental interests failed as the WTO DSU and NAFTA basically adopted the GATT framework. However, Knox argues that while the political process failed to address environmental interests, subsequent rulings under the WTO Appellate Body did, resulting in a "greening of trade jurisprudence."[80] This has been achieved, he argues, with the adoption of three substantive principles that have been imported into the trade rules: the principle that WTO members have the right to determine levels of health and safety protection, that natural resources include living natural resources, and that international environmental protections should generally be based on multilateral agreements.[81] For example, In *EC-Asbestos* Canada challenged a French ban on products containing asbestos.[82] The Appellate Body ruled in favor of the EC, over-ruling significant limitations in *Tuna-Dolphin* and opening the window for environmental considerations to be taken into account in the interpretation of trade rules. Notably, some seventeen applications to submit *amici curiae* briefs were made by NGOs, but ultimately were not admitted.

While the DSU and Working Procedures for the Appellate Body are silent regarding *amici curiae* participation, the Appellate Body in *US-Shrimp* (paras 101–110) interpreted the general right of panels to seek information from any source as conferring a discretion to receive and consider *amici curiae* submissions. This case involved a United States government ban on the import of shrimp from several states. The US did not deny that the ban violated the trade rules, but sought to legitimize the ban under the GATT General Exception provided for the protection of human, animal, or plant life or health or the conservation of natural resources. In support of the ban, the US submission included comments from a number of NGOs supporting the US claim that the fisheries practices of these countries was endangering sea turtle populations. The Appellate Body held that the dispute settlement panel was authorized by the DSU to receive *amicus curiae* briefs directly from the NGOs and that the parties could attach the materials to their submissions. This was the first WTO case to accept such submissions. However, neither the US nor the NGOs achieved their goals. The ruling has been subject to much public criticism for requiring that the US environmental rules "cleave to the existing structures of trade law" and representing "the triumph of economic globalization over the protection of endangered species."[83] However, the Appellate Report removed restrictions imposed by *Tuna-Dolphin* and signaled what is required to make trade rules more environmentally friendly.

[80] Knox, "The Judicial Resolution," p. 29.
[81] Knox, "The Judicial Resolution," p. 53.
[82] (*EC-Asbestos*) European Communities-Measures Affecting Asbestos and Asbestos-Containing Products (Report of the Appellate Body, WT/DS135/AB/R, March 12, 2001).
[83] Ian Hurd, *International Organizations: Politics, Law, Practice*. (Cambridge: Cambridge University Press, 2011), p. 58.

The *US-Shrimp* decision on *amicus curiae* has been affirmed in other cases. In the *Australia Salmon* dispute, concerning quarantine measures banning the import of salmon products, the panel accepted submissions from two Australian fishermen on Australian sanitary standards.[84] In *US-Lead*, concerning countervailing measures imposed by the United States, submissions from two industry groups representing the steel industry and steel workers' interests were considered.[85] Although both were ultimately rejected, the Appellate Body expanded on its decision in *US-Shrimp*, finding that the DSU itself and not just the WTO Panel had the authority to accept submissions from third parties. At issue in the *US-Lead* case was the admissibility of *amici curiae* briefs from the American Iron and Steel Institute and the Speciality Steel Industry of North America. The Appellate Body (paras. 41–42) clarified that the ruling in *US-Shrimp* applied to the Appellate Body as well as panels, and that the authority to receive *amici curiae* briefs was discretionary, a discretion the Appellate Body in fact chose not to exercise in this case.

To date, only a few panels have accepted unsolicited *amici curiae* briefs and the Appellate Body has not done so at all, except where they have been attached as exhibits to the submissions of a party, their inclusion being viewed as a prerogative of the parties to determine the content of their own submissions. The issue remains extremely controversial among WTO members, many of whom have expressed their opposition to the Appellate Body's interpretation, particularly in respect of NGO submissions.

Similar pressures to broaden participation in dispute settlement proceedings have occurred in the investor-state regimes established under NAFTA Chapter 11 and ICSID. In these bodies the private law culture of international commercial law has provided the conceptual foundations. However, this foundation is increasingly regarded by many as inadequate to address the important public interest issues arising in investor-state arbitrations.[86] Unlike commercial arbitrations that typically involve disputes between private parties, investor-state arbitrations involve actions against states and frequently concern a government's right to regulate its economy, environment, public utilities, health, safety, or human rights.

The NAFTA is a preferential trade agreement entered into in 1994 by Canada, Mexico and the United States, together with two concurrent agreements on the environment and labor. In response to severe criticism of the private

[84] (*Australia Salmon*) Australia-Measures Affecting the Importation of Salmon, complaint by Canada, (Report of the Panel and Appellate Body, WT/DS18, March 19, 1999).

[85] (*US-Lead*) United States-Imposition of Countervailing Duties on Certain Hot-Rolled Lead and Bismuth Carbon Steel products originating in the United Kingdom (Report of the Appellate Body, WT/DS138/AB/R, May 10, 2000).

[86] Van Harten, *Investment Treaty Arbitration*.

and confidential nature of initial proceedings, inclusiveness and transparency have increased over the evolution of NAFTA's dispute settlement processes. As Anthony De Palma commented about NAFTA arbitral panels:

> Their meetings are secret. Their members are generally unknown. The decisions they reach need not be fully disclosed. Yet the way a group of international tribunals handles disputes between investors and foreign governments can lead to national laws being revoked and environmental regulations changed. And it is all in the name of protecting foreign investors under NAFTA.[87]

Chapter 11 of NAFTA outlines the dispute resolution mechanism available to investors who believe a host state has contravened its obligations under the agreement and which has resulted in loss or damage. The investor has the option to submit a claim for arbitration to ICSID or under the United Nations Commission on International Trade Law (UNCITRAL) Arbitration Rules. ICSID was established in 1966 under the auspices of the World Bank by the Convention on the Settlement of Investment Disputes between States and Nationals of Other States (Washington Convention) for the purpose of providing institutional facilities for the conciliation and arbitration of international investment disputes. Today over 150 states are signatories to the Convention,[88] and the Centre has handled over 300 cases since inception.[89]

NAFTA, ICSID, and UNCITRAL exhibit limited receptivity to broadening participation and openness through the admission of *amici curiae* briefs. Several NAFTA cases involved environmental and public health measures, while others arose out of failed privatization initiatives and Argentina's economic crisis. *Methanex* is the first NAFTA tribunal under UNCITRAL rules to allow NGOs to submit written briefs as *amici curiae*.[90] The tribunal relied heavily on decisions of the WTO DSB admitting the submission and consideration of NGO briefs in the *US-Shrimp* case. Methanex Corporation is a Canadian company that was claiming compensation for damages resulting from the imposition ban imposed by California on the use of MTBE, a fuel additive produced by the company. California argued that the ban was necessary because the additive poses a risk to human health and safety and the environment. Methanex submitted that the ban was tantamount to an expropriation of their investment and thus a violation of NAFTA, and sought close to $1 billion in compensation. The International Institute for Sustainable Development, NGOs for a Better Environment, and the Earth Institute requested rights to

---

[87] Anthony De Palma, "NAFTA's Powerful Little Secret: Obscure Tribunals Settle Disputes, But Go Too Far, Critics Say," *New York Times* (March 11, 2001). BU 1., p. 11.

[88] Statistic from ICSID web site: <http://icsid.worldbank.org/ICSID>.

[89] ICSID, "2010 Annual Report," available at: <http://icsid.worldbank.org/ICSID>, p. 21.

[90] *(Methanex) Methanex Corporation v. The United States of America*, UNCITRAL (NAFTA) Decision of the Tribunal on Petitions from Third Persons to Intervene as Amici Curiae dated January 15, 2001.

submit briefs, to be granted observer status, and to receive documentary materials. The tribunal allowed the submission of briefs, but not observer status or access to materials on the basis of confidentiality and privilege. It arrived at this decision after inviting comments from the parties and other NAFTA states on the *amicus* petition. Methanex and Mexico initially opposed the submission of briefs, while the United States and Canada supported the petition. The tribunal differentiated between the filing of an *amicus* submission and the adding of a party to the dispute, stressed the importance of the parties consent, and adopted a statement on the participation of non-disputing parties provided by the NAFTA Free Trade Commission (FTC). Subsequently two briefs were filed by the NGOs, which were accepted by the parties. While NAFTA does not contain the General Exception clause found in the GATT/WTO rules, the tribunal went beyond the NAFTA text and appealed to general principles of international law to find that the ban was a regulation enacted for a public purpose, in a non-discriminatory way, and in accordance with due process. The International Institute for Sustainable Development has concluded that "the Methanex case has been pivotal in beginning the transition of international investment arbitrations from a secret and secretive process into a more transparent, accessible and thus accountable process."[91]

This *Methanex* decision was followed in *United Parcel*, when two unions submitted briefs in a dispute filed by UPS for damages they claimed resulted from the monopoly granted by Canada to Canada Post.[92]

The FTC issued an interpretive note to the effect that Chapter 11 rules do not impose "a general duty of confidentiality or preclude the parties from providing public access to documents" and that the parties "agree to make available to the public in a timely manner all documents submitted" subject to confidential material which is privileged or protected by law from disclosure.[93] Subsequently, Canada and the United States issued statements supporting opening NAFTA hearings to the public using the appropriate technology (closed-circuit television, Internet webcasting). Mexico later adopted this position as well. It is important to note, however, that the scope of *amicus* participation remains very narrow and is regarded as performing a public information function for the tribunals. It does not include participation as an observer or access to documents, unless the parties consent.

[91] Howard Mann, "The Final decision in Methanex v. United States: Some New Wine in New Bottles," International Institute for Sustainable Development, (2005). Available at <http://www.iisd.org/pdf/2005/commentary_methanex.pdf>.

[92] *(United Parcel) United Parcel Service of America Inc. v. Government of Canada* (UNCITRAL/NAFT) Decision of the Tribunal on Petitions for the Intervention and Participation as Amicus Curiae, dated October 17, 2001.

[93] NAFTA Free Trade Commission, 2001. Notes of Interpretation on Access to Documents and Minimum Standard of Treatment in Accordance with International Law (July 31).

The issue of *amicus* participation also arose in ICSID proceedings. ICSID has traditionally observed confidentiality in its proceedings, reflecting the view that "arbitral awards . . . constitute by inference, a contract between the parties,"[94] whereby "the parties privatize their dispute and take a form of market ownership of their disputing procedure."[95] The matter of *amicus* participation arose in a number of cases involving services privatization initiatives where public interest and civil society groups mobilized in asserting the public policy dimensions of these initiatives. Many of the cases involve concessions granted to foreign investors to operate public water and sewage systems and raised environmental and human rights concerns. A number of NGOs filed petitions for *amici curiae* participation, arguing that the people affected by the soaring water prices were being denied the human right to water. *Bechtel v. Bolivia* was an ICSID case involving a claim by Bechtel, an American company operating the water and sewage system for Cochabamba, Bolivia, through its subsidiary, Aguas del Tunari, under a 40-year lease as part of a World Bank inspired privatization scheme.[96] Within weeks of taking over the operation of the water system the rates were increased by so much that families living on the minimum wage were being billed up to 25 percent of their monthly income.[97] The rate increases resulted in massive protests, the declaration of martial law, and the injury of many people. Protests continued, and in 2000 Bechtel abandoned the project and filed a claim for lost profits. The claim was filed with ICSID under the Dutch-Bolivian BIT and, despite Bolivia's opposition, the tribunal ruled that it had jurisdiction over the dispute through Bechtel's subsidiary in The Netherlands. Petitioners asked the Tribunal "to decide whether an international investment agreement requires Bolivia to upset the balance, established by Bolivia's democratic political processes, between property rights and governmental authority to implement public health and sanitation regulations."[98] The Tribunal rejected the petition of several NGOs to submit *amici* briefs, but left the door open for such submissions in other cases. The case remained in arbitration for some years until Bechtel, responding to pressure to drop the case, settled the $50 million claim for a symbolic 30 cents.[99]

---

[94] Benjamin Tahyar, "Confidentiality in ICSID Arbitration after *Amco Asia v. Indonesia*: Watchword or White Elephant?" *Fordham International Law Journal* 10 (1986): pp. 93–122 at p. 109.

[95] Edward Brunet, *Arbitration Law in America: A Critical Assessment*. (Cambridge: Cambridge University Press, 2006), pp. 7–8.

[96] *(Bechtel v. Bolivia) Aguas del Tunari SA v. The Republic of Bolivia*, ICSID Case No. ARB/03/2.

[97] Tim Johnson, "'Water War': A Test Case on Trade Transparency," *Miami Herald* (October 13, 2002).

[98] Amanda Norris and Katina Metzidakis, "Public Protests, Private Contracts: Confidentiality in ICSID Arbitration and the Cochabamba Water War," *Harvard Negotiation Law Review* 15, (Spring 2010): pp. 31–75 at p. 67.

[99] Elena Blanco and Jona Razzaque, *Globalization and Natural Resources Law: Challenges, Key Issues and Perspectives*. (Cheltenham, UK: Edward Elgar, 2011), p. 261.

ICSID subsequently revised its rules in response to concerns about the impact of investor-state arbitration on public interests, providing for the intervention of non-parties and providing for the submission of *amicus curiae* briefs.[100] Subsequently, an ICSID Tribunal in *Biwater v. Tanzania* permitted five NGOs to submit written briefs under the new rules, but denied their request for access to documents and to attend the hearings.[101]

A similar result occurred in *Vivendi v. Argentina,* which is a significant case in that it raised the "public interest factor" as an appropriate consideration in investor-state arbitration.[102] This case involved a consortium of French, Spanish, and UK investors operating the water and sewage systems for Buenos Aires that provided services for over 10 million people. Over the course of the relationship a number of disputes arose; with the intensification of the Argentine financial crisis the parties were at odds over the tariff-rates charged to consumers, and the investors wanted to modify the rates under the economic equilibrium clause in the concession agreement. However, Argentina resisted. The human right to water was invoked by Argentina as one argument in its defense of necessity to its termination of the water concession, supported by an *amici curiae* submission filed by five NGOs. This is the first case under ICSID in which such submissions were accepted despite the objections of one of the parties. In reviewing the criteria to consider in admitting *amici* briefs, the tribunal invoked the *Methanex* ruling and noted the special public interest dimensions of the dispute and the need for increased transparency in investor-state arbitration:

> [t]he factor that gives this case particular public interest is that the investment dispute centers around the water distribution and sewage systems of a large metropolitan area, the city of Buenos Aires and surrounding municipalities. These systems provide basic public services to millions of people and as a result may raise a variety of complex public and international law questions, including human rights considerations.[103]

However, the tribunal did not grant the NGOs the right to participate as observers or access to the case documentary materials without the consent of the parties. In general, the tribunal emphasized the "defense's exceptional nature and of the strict conditions surrounding its application"[104] and

---

[100] Andrew McDougal and Ank Santens, "ICSID Tribunals Apply New Rules on Amicus Curiae," *Mealey's International Arbitration Report* 22 (February 2007), p. 2.

[101] *(Biwater) Biwater Gauff (Tanzania) v. United Republic of Tanzania*, ICSID Case No. ARB/05/22.

[102] Epaminontas Triantafilou, "Is a Connection to the 'Public Interest' a Meaningful Prerequisite of Third Party Participation in Investment Arbitration?" *Berkeley Journal of International Law Publicist* 5 (2010): pp. 38–46.

[103] *(Vivendi v. Argentina) Compañid de Aquas del Aconquija S.A. and Vivendi Universal v. Argentine Republic*, ICSID Case No. ARB/97/3, Decision on Annulment (July 2, 2002).

[104] *Vivendi*, para. 258.

rejected Argentina's defense "because Argentina's measures in violation of the BITs were not the only means to satisfy its essential interests and because Argentina itself contributed to the emergency situation that it was facing."[105]

The *Vivendi* case has significant implications concerning the legal capacity of states to develop adequate protections in times of economic emergencies. This is of particular significance for developing states with constrained resources to withstand economic crises. However, the case does mark an important development in its recognition of the *public* dimension of investor-state arbitrations and the need for transparency in these proceedings. To what extent is this recognition an indication of changing praxis?

4.2 A Praxis Conception of International Commercial Arbitration?

The ongoing financial crisis indicates a deeper crisis of leadership in the governance of global capitalism: "at issue is how basic conditions of existence are increasingly mediated by the world capitalist market system under neoliberal governance arrangements."[106] Indeed, the present world (dis)order is characterized by multiple crises which signal the existence of fractures in common sense understandings of governance. An important rupture concerns the authority wielded by experts as the organic intellectuals of new constitutionalism.[107] An important role of the expert/organic intellectual "is to depoliticize fundamental questions relating to the nature of capitalism, transforming political debates into technical questions directed at appropriate means rather than at questioning the fundamental ends of the capitalist system."[108] Private transnational governance through new constitutional institutions and laws empowers the *mercatocracy* to recast political issues as matters of legal technique, but the terrain of this common sense is uneven and contested.[109]

Contestation is evident in the Public Statement issued by some fifty-three academics, this author included, that strongly criticized the existing international investment regime.[110] The signatories represent diverse disciplinary

---

[104] *Vivendi*, para. 258.

[105] *Vivendi*, para. 265.

[106] Stephen Gill, "Introduction: global crises and the crisis of global leadership," in *Global Crises and the Crisis of Global Leadership*, edited by Stephen Gill (Cambridge: Cambridge University Press, 2011), p. 5.

[107] A. Claire Cutler "The legitimacy of private transnational governance: experts and the transnational market for force," *Socio-Economic Review* 8, no. 1 (2010): pp. 157–185.

[108] Gill, "Leaders and led in an era of global crises," in *Global Crises*, p. 30.

[109] A. Claire Cutler, "Private transnational governance and the crisis of global leadership," in *Global Crises*, pp. 56–70.

[110] Public Statement on the International Investment Regime. (August 2010). Available at <http://www.osgoode.yorku.ca/public_statement>.

and professional backgrounds, including public international law, private international law, administrative law, human rights law, international investment and trade law, political science, international relations, international politics, economics, sociology, and development studies. The Public Statement identifies significant inequities in the existing system, including the prioritization of "the protection of the property and economic interests of transnational corporations over the right to regulate of states and the right to self-determination of peoples"[111] and a problematic "reorientation of the balance between investor protection and public regulation in international law."[112] The Statement articulates the "fundamental right" of states "to regulate on behalf of the public welfare," which "right must not be subordinated to the interests of the investors where the right to regulate is exercised in good faith for a legitimate purpose."[113] It recommends a number of measures to attempt to reorient the regime, but, most importantly, it advises states to review their investment treaties and to withdraw or renegotiate if they are experiencing unfair or unfavorable conditions.[114] The Statement also declares efforts to conclude a multilateral investment treaty as "misguided because they risk entrenching and legitimizing an international investment regime that lacks fairness and balance, including basic requirements of openness and judicial independence." This is a damning indictment that raises the profoundly political and public nature of investment arbitration and challenges claims to arbitral neutrality and impartiality. These criticisms have not been well-received by many arbitration lawyers.[115] To what extent is there movement in the direction identified by the Statement?

On one hand, the developments that this chapter has identified are fairly marginal in terms of fundamentally reorienting the regime. Participation as a "friend of the court" is not at all full, meaningful participation and is most certainly not going to revolutionize the regime. On the other hand, contestation over the openness and transparency of arbitration practices and the publicness of the issues at stake do reflect fissures in common sense and present openings for changing practices by challenging dominant assumptions about the nature of trade and investment arbitration. The lawyers making the case for broadening participation and transparency succeeded in some cases, and some governments have responded by broadening participation rules: the United States, Canada, and Mexico have done so. The ICSID Arbitration Rules were amended to permit tribunals to accept submissions from non-disputing

---

[111] Public Statement, para. 5.
[112] Public Statement, para. 5.
[113] Public Statement, para. 4.
[114] Public Statement, para. 13.
[115] Tom Toulson, "Investment treaty arbitration is 'unfair' say academics," *Global Arbitration Review* (September 10, 2010).

parties, to permit hearings to be opened, and to require publication of excerpts from the awards. UNCITRAL is considering rule modification for investor-state arbitrations.

Some states, such as Bolivia, Ecuador, and Venezuela, have actually withdrawn from investor-state arbitration, while others have redrafted their investment treaties, curtailing limits on public policy regulations and exempting certain activities from the purview of the investment agreement altogether.[116] Canada and the United States were already moving in this direction. The new Canadian model Foreign Investment Protection Agreement (FIPA) refers to sustainable development in its preamble and contains a GATT-like General Exception that applies to all of the obligations in the model treaty. This exception covers measures adopted for the protection of human animal or plant life or health and conservation purposes. The model also provides for public access to all documents, and arbitral hearings are open to the public. In addition, it provides a procedure for non-disputing parties to file written submissions.[117] The US Model BIT goes further and addresses relations between investment and labor rights and expands the scope for state policy autonomy. The Australia-US Free Trade Agreement does not provide for investor-state arbitration, and in 2011 Australia announced that it would no longer include such provision in its trade agreements due to concerns about sovereignty.[118]

These developments suggest a rethinking of assumptions concerning the neutrality of international commercial law and practice and suggest a more critical understanding of the nature of the separations between economics and politics and the private and public spheres. Mindful that "common sense" is not "good sense" and that it must be continually reproduced in order to maintain hegemony, these developments suggest that there are openings for challenging and resisting unfair and inequitable dimensions of the international commercial investment regime. In a lecture entitled *The Future of Global Leadership?* Richard Falk observed that "academic discipline lacks an appropriate horizon for considering the future of global governance." It is dominated by "horizons of feasibility" that regard the future as an

[116] Michael Nolan, "Venezuela Withdraws from the World Bank's International Centre for Settlement of Investment Disputes," *Milbank's Litigation Group* (January 30, 2012).

[117] However, the recently negotiated Canada-China FIPA departs from this practice and does not provide for public access to documents and hearings in arbitration proceedings, as a general rule. See Catherine Walsh and Michael Woods, "The Canada-China Foreign Investment Promotion and Protection Agreement: Part II: Investor-State Dispute Settlement Provisions," *Focus* (January 2–13) available at: <http://www.heenanblaikie.com/en/Publications/2013/The-Canada-China-Foreign-Investment-Promotion-and-Protection-Agreement-Part-II-Investor-State-Dispute-Settlement-Provisions.pdf>, accessed November 2, 2013.

[118] Gillard Government Trade Policy Statement: *Trading Our Way to More Jobs and Prosperity*, April 4, 2011, available at <http://www.acci.asn.au/getattachment/b9d3cfae-fc0c-4c2a-a3df-3f58228daf6d/Gillard-Government-Trade-Policy-Statement.aspx>.

inevitable continuation of the past and excludes both "horizons of necessity" and "horizons of desire."[119] Falk appealed to horizons of necessity in order to get to grips with the ecological crisis facing the world and horizons of desire to displace "the present logic of world order which is premised essentially on inequality and domination." He appealed to Gramsci's famous line concerning "pessimism of the intellect and optimism of the will," and to St. Francis, who said "start by doing what's necessary, then what's possible and suddenly you are doing the impossible." A praxis conception of international commercial arbitration requires the creative exploration of horizons of desire and a refusal to let horizons of feasibility block the type of praxis that so many people recognize as fundamentally necessary for a more just world order.

---

[119] Richard Falk, "Horizons of Desire," Lecture to *Future of Global Governance? Toronto*: York University. (May 25, 2011). Available at <http://yorku.ca/lefutur/>.

7

Does International Commercial Arbitration Provide Efficient Contract Enforcement Institutions For International Trade?

Thomas Dietz[1]

It is a commonplace to note that arbitration has evolved into the main method of dispute resolution in international trade. Explicitly or implicitly, most scholars explain the rise of arbitration by competitive pressures shaping legal developments at both the national and transnational levels. Recognizing the limitation of their own national legal systems, states enacted pro-arbitration laws and committed their courts and jurisdictions to enforce both contractual arbitration clauses and arbitral awards in order to attract foreign business. In doing so, states created a global market for arbitration. Today many arbitration houses compete for the business of resolving conflicts in cross-border trade. Competition presses arbitration houses to improve their legal services continuously. Facing a choice between delegating conflicts to litigation in state courts or private arbitration, parties choose the latter because it maximizes their joint welfare. Arbitration is capable of equipping global exchange with efficient dispute resolution mechanisms because they are not shaped by rent-seeking governments, but

[1] Comments and suggestions by William Burke-White, Gralf-Peter Calliess, Patrick Emmenegger, Dirk Lehmkuhl, and Walter Mattli are gratefully acknowledged. Financial Support was provided by the Volkswagen Foundation.

evolve bottom-up in response to the legal demands of an emerging global business community.[2]

In the following I intend to critically discuss the prevailing view on the upsurge of arbitration. The chapter proceeds in three steps: *Part one* is descriptive. It starts by looking at the caseload of international commercial arbitration. Most pundits consider the increasing number of cases filed at major international arbitration houses, such as the ICC in Paris, as clear evidence for the increasing economic significance of international commercial arbitration. Part one discusses this view. In a deviation from the prevailing assumption, it will be concluded that the case numbers filed at major arbitration houses are still too small to suggest a vibrant governance role for these private legal institutions in international trade. Particularly when compared to the tremendous growth rates for international trade as such, the rise of international commercial arbitration over the last decades appears rather modest.

Part two aims to explain these empirical findings. It will be argued that any formal dispute resolution mechanism consists of three different constitutive institutional elements: (A) legal rules, (B) courts or tribunals applying these rules, and (C) effective sanctions to enforce the courts' or tribunals' decisions.[3] For each of the three institutional elements, this chapter explains, firstly, why states fall short of providing a workable legal infrastructure for global commerce, and, secondly, to what extent international commercial arbitration is able to overcome these shortcomings. In part two, it will become clear that arbitration is a hybrid legal mechanism. The tribunals (element B) are private, yet both the legal rules (element A) that these courts apply and the sanctions (element C) that they rely on to enforce their awards are usually provided by the state. The chapter shows that when it comes to those elements in which arbitration operates in close tandem with state legal systems, this mechanism is restrained in its ability to provide reliable dispute resolution mechanisms for global commerce. Most importantly, it will be argued that the close link between arbitration and territorially fragmented and, therefore, dysfunctional national legal structures block the evolution of international commercial arbitration into a more vibrant and effective mechanism of global economic governance. The dominant view that states, by committing their courts to enforce both contractual arbitration clauses and foreign arbitral awards, have actively promoted the rise of arbitration is

---

[2] Bruce L. Benson, "The Spontaenous Evolution of Commercial Law," *Southern Economic Journal* 55, no. 3 (January 1989): pp. 644–661; Erin A. O'Hara and Larry E. Ribstein, *The Law Market* (Oxford/New York: Oxford University Press, 2009).

[3] Gralf-Peter Calliess, Thomas Dietz, Wioletta Konradi, Holger Nieswandt, and Fabian Sosa, "Transformations of Commercial Law: New Forms of Legal Certainty for Globalized Exchange Processes," in *Transforming the Golden-Age Nation State*, edited by Achim Hurrelmann, Stephan Leibfried, Kerstin Martens, and Peter Mayer (Basingstoke: Palgrave Macmillan, 2007), pp. 83–108.

certainly correct, but it needs qualification, as national legal structures not only facilitate, but at the same time also hamper arbitration.

Finally, *part three* illustrates these arguments further. In parts one and two the chapter focuses on what is in the following called "universal arbitration." The major arbitration houses such as the ICC in Paris accept cases from all kinds of companies and industries. From these arbitration houses we can distinguish a small but interesting number of so-called specialized international arbitration courts, which are established in specific industries by the respective international trade associations for their members only. Specialized arbitration houses differ from universal arbitration houses in two significant ways. First of all, their caseload suggests that these institutions play a more important economic role in supporting trade in their respective industries than universal arbitration does in international trade in general. Secondly, a closer institutional analysis indicates that specialized arbitration, in contrast to universal arbitration, works largely in independence from state legal structures. Part three therefore substantiates the argument that efficient arbitral services can only emerge, when they are capable of overcoming the profound institutional shortcomings that are caused by the territorial fragmentation of national legal orders.

The conclusion summarizes this chapter's argument. I will advocate that not only state courts, but also arbitral tribunals face profound institutional shortcomings in their dispute resolution functions. Most importantly, this chapter suggests that the transformation of international commercial arbitration into an efficient mechanism of global economic governance is considerably less clear and more difficult than prevailing theories about arbitration would propose.

1 The Caseload of International Commercial Arbitration

In order to prove the rise of international commercial arbitration as the central legal institution for conflict resolution in cross-border trade scholars usually refer to the increasing number of cases filed at these private legal institutions. Dezalay and Garth, for example, specify the growth trend of international commercial arbitration by the fact that the ICC (as the biggest and oldest arbitration house) dealt with 333 cases in 1991, 337 cases in 1992, and 352 in 1993.[4] More generally, Walter Mattli states that the caseload of major arbitration houses, which as well as the ICC include the LCIA in London and the SCC in Stockholm, doubled between the 1970s and the 1990s;[5] Alec Stone

---

[4] Yves Dezalay and Bryant G. Garth, *Dealing in Virtue: International Commercial Arbitration and the Construction of Transnational Legal Order* (Chicago: University of Chicago Press, 1996), p. 6 (footnote 4).

[5] Walter Mattli, "Private Justice in a Global Economy: From Litigation to Arbitration," *International Organization* 55, no. 4 (Autumn 2001): p. 920.

Table 7.1. Arbitration requests filed at the ICC, LCIA, and SCC between 2000 and 2010[8]

Court/Year	2003	2004	2005	2006	2007	2008	2009	2010
ICC[9]	580	561	521	593	599	663	817	793
LCIA[10]	99	83	110	130	127	163	272	246
SCC[11]	82	50	56	74	87	85	96	91
AAA/ICDR[12]	646	614	580	586	621	703	836	801
HKIAC[13]	287	280	281	394	448	602	429	401
CIETAC[14]	422	462	427	442	429	548	559	531
DIS[15]	81	76	72	75	100	122	156	176
Total	2197	2126	2047	2294	2411	2886	3065	3039
8 year av.	2508							

Sweet shows that, from a long-term perspective, traders filed about 3,000 disputes during the period from 1920 to 1980, whereas in the 1990s they filed more than 3,500 disputes. Finally, 5,250 disputes were filed at the ICC between 1996 and 2005.[6] Table 7.1, which provides a very detailed picture of the international commercial arbitration activities of the seven most important arbitration houses,[7] confirms this trend of a rising caseload between 2003 and 2010. In total we see a rise from 2197 cases in 2003 to 3039 in 2009, which means growth of around 38 percent.

I initially started to doubt the economic relevance of these numbers in the course of a study on the global software industry which I completed in 2012. In this study a total of 51 qualitative interviews were conducted with software companies from Germany, India, Bulgaria, and Romania. Against all expectations the empirical results of this study showed that international commercial arbitration at best plays a minor role in the resolution of conflicts and the enforcement of contracts in cross-border trade.[16]

Given this finding, questions arose as to why the results of the empirical study on the global software industry differ so significantly from the widely

---

[6] Alec Stone Sweet, "The New Lex Mercatoria and Transnational governance," *Journal of European Public Policy* 13, no. 5 (2006): p. 636.

[7] The seven major courts handle around 85 percent of the total global caseload. This can be concluded from a comprehensive worldwide list of international commercial courts, and their caseload is provided by an international arbitration study published by the School of International Arbitration of Queen Mary University London in cooperation with PricewaterhouseCoopers. See: "International Arbitration Study 2008—Corporate Attitudes and Practices: Recognition and Enforcement of Foreign Awards," Queen Mary, University of London—School of International Arbitration, 2008, <http://www.arbitrationonline.org/docs/IAstudy_2008.pdf>.

[8] The numbers are taken from the homepages of the eight major international commercial arbitration courts.

[9] International Court of Arbitration.   [10] London Court of International Arbitration.

[11] Arbitration Institute of the Stockholm Chamber of Commerce.

[12] American Arbitration Association/International Centre for Dispute Resolution.

[13] Hong Kong International Arbitration Centre.

[14] China International Economic and Trade Arbitration.   [15] German Institute of Arbitration.

[16] Thomas Dietz, *Global Order without Law* (Oxford: Hart Publishing, forthcoming).

supported view that international commercial arbitration plays a pivotal role in providing the legal infrastructure for globalized exchange. At first glance, the most plausible answer to this puzzle seems to attribute the deviant results to the research design of the study. Various factors could have an impact: the interviewed experts might want to keep the use of these institutions confidential; the software industry might be an exceptional case where arbitration in general tends to play a minor role; or the surprising result of a non-use of international arbitration could be explained by the small number of companies interviewed in the qualitative study. However, the following closer critical look at the statistical figures for international commercial arbitration shows these concerns to be irrelevant. Instead it will become clear that the results of the qualitative study of the software industry in fact represent an adequate picture of the significance of private arbitration in international trade, whereas the general view on this subject is vastly exaggerated.

Three of the major arbitration courts—namely the ICC, LCIA, and SCC—publish detailed annual reports about their activity on their websites. Besides the caseload, which is already shown in Table 7.1, these reports include information about the parties that actually used these arbitration courts. Since, as mentioned above, the empirical study about cross-border software contracts focused on companies from Germany, India, Bulgaria, and Romania, the first interesting area of information concerns the number of parties involved in international arbitration based in these countries. The ICC statistics for 2005 (the year when the interviews for the empirical study were conducted) show the involvement of a total of 102 German parties, 42 Indian parties, seven Bulgarian, and six Romanian parties.[17] For the same year the figures for the SCC include eleven German parties and zero parties from India, Bulgaria, or Romania.[18] To be clear, these numbers do not represent software companies, but all companies from all industries existing in these four countries that are involved in international commercial arbitration. Different from the other two major arbitration houses, the LCIA provides data about the involved parties in percentages. The figures for 2005 show a share of 4.75 percent for German parties, 4 percent for Indian parties, and 1.5 percent for Eastern European parties (excluding Russia).[19] If we now take into account the total number of 110 cases handled by the LCIA in 2005,[20] it becomes apparent that the numbers of parties that are based in the four countries from the empirical study

---

[17] Please see the statistics provided by the ICC, available at: <http://www.iccwbo.org/Products-and-Services/Arbitration-and-ADR/Arbitration/Introduction-to-ICC-Arbitration/Statistics>.

[18] Please see the statistics provided by the SCC, available at: <http://www.sccinstitute.com/?id=23700>.

[19] Please see: "Director General's Review of 2005," LCIA, available at: <http://www.lcia.org/LCIA/Casework_Report.aspx>.

[20] Please see Table 7.1.

are also very small. Particularly in the case of Germany and India, the numbers are even much smaller than the numbers of the ICC.

What can be concluded from these figures? It is fair to assume that, in total, hundreds of thousands of German, Indian, Bulgarian, and Indian companies from all different kinds of industries are engaged in cross-border trade on global markets. Yet, compared to these huge numbers, the number of companies from the four countries in the empirical study that are actually engaged in cross-border arbitration is marginal. A further look at the statistics shows that this result can even be generalized. In all three courts' statistics (ICC, LCIA, SCC) Germany is among the countries with the highest number of parties involved in international commercial arbitration worldwide. Only the USA presents with slightly higher numbers.[21] India shows the highest degree of party involvement in Asia.[22] Romania and Bulgaria lie in the midfield of their region, Eastern and South-Eastern Europe.[23] This means that, as a matter of fact, there are no countries with significantly higher party involvements than those investigated in the empirical study about the global software industry. The marginal use of international commercial arbitration is therefore not a country-specific phenomenon, but can be asserted for international trade in general. Against the background of very large numbers of companies that are engaged in international trade, the caseload for international arbitration courts appears to be very small.

The following example will make this point even clearer: As noted above, the USA shows the highest absolute numbers of companies involved in international commercial arbitration. According to the ICC statistics, in 2009 10 percent of the parties were based in the USA.[24] Unfortunately, most arbitration houses do not provide detailed statistics about the country of origin of the parties, but let us assume that around 15 percent of all worldwide arbitration cases involve a party from the USA. Most probably this number is too high. Considering Table 7.1, which contains the caseload for the seven major arbitration houses, we can then assume for the year 2009 a total number of international commercial arbitration cases of 4000. Most likely this number is also too high; 15 percent of 4000 cases mean that in 2009 around 600 US parties were involved in international commercial arbitration cases.

Please note that in the same year (2009) the U.S. Department of Commerce identified a number of 285,843 US companies exporting goods or services

[21] In 2005, for example, 164 parties from the USA were involved in ICC arbitration procedures, compared to 102 companies from Germany (statistics provided by the ICC).
[22] This means that even more Indian companies use international arbitration courts than companies from China. Looking again at the ICC caseload statistics for 2005, we see that only 34 companies from China were involved in arbitration, compared to 42 companies from India.
[23] With 34 parties, the ICC statistics show Turkey as the country from this region with the highest party involvement at the ICC in 2005.
[24] Please see the statistics provided by the ICC.

across borders.[25] If we take this number and divide it by the number of 600 parties that were involved in international commercial arbitration cases, we see that in 2009 only one out of 476 companies—or around 0.2 percent—of all exporting US companies were involved in international commercial arbitration. If we now extrapolate this number to a longer-term perspective this result indicates that in ten years not more than 2 percent of all American exporters were involved in an international arbitration court case. Clearly, this number is very insignificant.

At this point it could be objected that sole numbers of court usage do not provide an adequate indicator to determine the real impact of legal systems. Sometimes, courts function like peace armies that do not need to take real action in order to have a strong bearing on individual behavior. If companies in global markets believe that international commercial arbitration courts were effective, they will also believe that cheating in contractual relations would lead to sanctions and thus to undesired outcomes. Since rational contractual parties aim to avoid undesired outcomes, they would not cheat, which in turn means that fewer court cases would occur.

The problem is that the number of cases filed at international commercial arbitration courts is just too marginal to render this effect. A short comparison of the caseload of international commercial courts with the caseload of German commercial courts makes this point very clear. If we look again at Table 7.1 we see that on average 2,508 annual cases were filed at the seven major international commercial courts in the years 2003 to 2010.[26] But, throughout the same period (2003–2010) each year the German commercial courts (*Kammern für Handelssachen*), which are specialized courts for business-to-business contractual matters only, handled an average case load of about 50,000 domestic cases.[27] According to Gary Born, another interesting figure shows that the American Arbitration Association, under its commercial rules, handles about 12,000 domestic cases yearly.[28] These numbers make clear that economic exchange invariably involves disputes among contractual parties,

[25] Please see: "A Profile of U.S. Importing and Exporting Companies, 2008-2009," U.S. Census Bureau, Department of Commerce, April 12, 2011, available at: <http://www.census.gov/foreign-trade/Press-Release/edb/2009/edbrel.pdf>.

[26] Please also note that each year usually around 20 percent of these total cases are withdrawn again, and that around 15 percent of the cases involve exclusively domestic parties and are thus not linked to international trade. In other words, the real number of international commercial arbitration cases is even significantly lower than suggested in the table.

[27] Statistisches Bundesamt, Justizstatistik der Zivilgerichte 2009 (Fachserie 10 Reihe 2.1), September 6, 2010, available at: <https://www.destatis.de/DE/Publikationen/Thematisch/Rechtspflege/GerichtePersonal/Zivilgerichte2100210097004.pdf?__blob=publicationFile>; please see also: Hermann Hoffmann and Andreas Maurer, "Entstaatlichung der Justiz: Empirische Belege zum Bedeutungsverlust staatlicher Gerichte für internationale Wirtschaftsstreitigkeiten," *Zeitschrift für Rechtssoziologie* 31, no. 2 (2010): pp. 279–302.

[28] See: Gary Brian Born, *International Commercial Arbitration* (Alphen aan den Rijn: Kluwer Law International, 2009), p. 162.

and as workable legal infrastructures exist a significant number of these disputes will end up in courts, be they arbitration or state courts. However, what applies to domestic contexts obviously does not apply to the same degree to international contexts. World trade has grown tremendously in recent decades. In 2010 world exports amounted to a sum of 15.235 trillion USD,[29] which is around 4.6 times the German GDP. However, what is almost entirely missing is the involvement of international commercial arbitration to correspond with these enormous economic figures.

The following simple model further illustrates this point. The model is set up to compare the governance function of national commercial courts for national economic value creation with the governance function of international commercial arbitration for international economic value creation. The model is far too rough to generate exact results, but nevertheless it gives us a tentative impression of how economically important national courts and international arbitration are. To keep the model simple it is only applied to Germany.

In the first step, the German GDP for 2010 (3.3 trillion USD[30]) is divided by the number of domestic commercial cases (around 50,000). The result is around 66 million, which means that on average one German commercial court case corresponds to a German economic value creation of 66 million USD.

In the second step, we divide the volume of world exports 2010 (15.2 trillion USD) by the number of international commercial cases filed in 2010 at the seven major courts (3039): the result is around 5 billion, which means that one case in international commercial arbitration falls upon an international economic value creation of 5 billion USD. If we now divide 5 billion by 66 million the result is 76, which means that if international arbitration courts were to play a similar role for the international economy as the German commercial courts play for the German economy, their caseload would have to be 76 times higher—instead of around 3500 annual cases, it would have to be 266,000 annual cases.

Even as international commercial arbitration courts have grown by more than 40 percent in the last seven years, they started from such a low level that these growth rates are not suitable for drawing relevant conclusions about their significance as a legal support structure for global exchange. Although much more empirical research is needed to determine the exact scope of international commercial arbitration, it seems fair to assume that compared to the role

[29] Please see the numbers provided by the International Monetary Fund, available at: <http://www.imf.org/external/pubs/ft/weo/2010/01/weodata/index.aspx>.

[30] Please see the numbers provided by the International Monetary Fund, available at: <http://www.imf.org/external/pubs/ft/weo/2010/01/weodata/weorept.aspx?sy=2008&ey=2010&scsm=1&ssd=1&sort=country&ds=.&br=1&c=134&s=NGDPD&grp=0&a=&pr.x=41&pr.y=8>.

domestic courts play for domestic markets, the role of international commercial arbitration courts for global markets is rather unimportant. Given the tremendous growth of world trade over recent decades the rise of international commercial arbitration appears rather modest. The relatively low case load points to a limited governance function for international commercial arbitration. The next part deals with the question of how this limited governance role can be explained.

2 State Legal Structures Constraining International Commercial Arbitration

Scholars of arbitration do not usually focus on the limits of international commercial arbitration; Rather, they concentrate on the institutional shortcomings of litigation in state courts and explain the rise of arbitration as a direct reaction to the incapability of states to adapt their national legal systems to the demands of global commerce for the purpose of effective dispute resolution mechanisms. In extending the theory of regulatory competition and the legal market to private legal actors, this view provides important insights into the dynamics of current transnational legal processes. On the other hand, this view lacks complexity. In the following part, it will become clear that not only state courts, but also international commercial arbitration face profound limitations in providing a workable legal infrastructure for global commerce.

Generally, efficient formal dispute resolution institutions need to combine three constitutive elements successfully: (A) legal rules, (B) courts applying these rules, and (C) effective sanctions to enforce the courts' decisions. Due to territorial fragmentation, national legal systems fall short of providing all three elements. However, international commercial arbitration is only partly able to overcome the limitations of state legal systems. If we take into account its entire institutional structure, we have to recognize that international commercial arbitration is a hybrid, combining private and public structures. The courts are private (element B), yet both the legal rules that arbitral tribunals apply (element A) and the sanctions for enforcing arbitral awards (element C) are usually provided by the state. The following paragraphs will highlight that according to its hybrid structure, arbitration is only capable of overcoming shortcoming B. Arbitral tribunals are indeed better equipped to deal with international cases than state courts. Yet, with regard to elements A and C, international arbitration tribunals face institutional shortcomings similar to those of litigation in state courts. They neither work on the basis of efficient legal rules, nor do they dispose of universally effective sanctioning mechanisms. In the end, the close institutional link to dysfunctional state legal structures hampers international commercial arbitration in performing its governance functions of resolving disputes in international trade.

2.1 Courts—Element B

At the time that an economic transaction crosses the borders of nation states the rules of more than one national legal system might apply to this transaction, which in turn means that different, territorially fragmented national contracts laws are likely to collide. Among other things, collision problems might result in uncertainty about the actual place of jurisdiction. Which court has jurisdiction when a transaction involves more than one state? States have created private international laws to address this problem. Private international law is essentially a set of procedural rules that determines which country's laws and courts are to be used in a given cross-border dispute. However, international private law has a reputation for working rather badly in practice. The problem is this: Private international laws are national laws; they are just as fragmented as national legal systems in general. Each state has developed its own conflict-of-laws techniques. It can therefore even happen that uncertainties emerge about which country's private international law has to be used in the first place in order to determine a place of jurisdiction. Other consequences of flawed conflict-of-laws techniques might be that more than one court requires jurisdiction, or none. Generally, cross-border litigation that involves the application of present conflict-of-laws techniques is time-consuming and highly unpredictable, and therefore causes very high transaction costs for the disputing parties.[31]

Given these shortcomings of private international laws, it is not surprising that states allow an extensive use of choice-of-forum clauses in cross-border contracts. In doing so, they enable the parties to avoid inefficient conflict-of-laws techniques, since they can choose the place of jurisdiction already in their contract. According to traditional law and economics, choice-of-law clauses in international trade support the parties in contractually agreeing on an efficient place of jurisdiction, which maximizes their joint welfare.[32] The practice, however, looks rather different. Many empirical and theoretical studies show that the problem of complexity and related information costs make it impossible for the parties to choose the optimal available national

---

[31] See for example: Klaus Peter Berger, *The Creeping Codification of the Lex Mercatoria* (Alphen aan den Rijn: Kluwer Law International, 1999); Friedrich K. Juenger, "The Lex Mercatoria and the conflict of laws," in *Lex Mercatoria and Arbitration: A Discussion of the New Law Merchant*, edited by Thomas E. Carbonneau (Yonkers: Juris, 1998), pp. 213–224; Stone Sweet, "The New Lex Mercatoria."

[32] O'Hara and Ribstein, The Law Market.

forum.[33] Rather, routines and familiarity with a court system play crucial roles in negotiating the place of jurisdiction. Put differently, parties to international contracts have generally strong incentives to select their home courts, and it is usually the party with the superior power which dominates the bargaining process.

Whenever a party manages to choose familiar national courts to govern a cross-border transaction, it saves legal information costs and thereby achieves a strategic advantage over its contractual partner, who has to carry the higher costs of using courts in a foreign legal system.[34] In addition, the foreign party might fear that the courts are biased in favor of the local party. Consequently, companies that conduct their transactions under the jurisdiction of foreign courts face a strategic disadvantage vis-à-vis their contractual partners. From their perspective, state legal systems do not provide a level playing field for them and their contractual parties, but rather increase uncertainty, legal costs, and, finally, the imbalances between the contractual partners.[35]

On the supply side, the imperfect cross-border law market provides few incentives for national courts to adopt their dispute resolution mechanisms to the demands of global commerce. National judges, therefore, remain well trained in applying their national laws but often lack the knowledge for applying foreign laws, which often leads to unpredictable court decisions, plus additional time and costs for the often required drafts of legal opinions on foreign laws. Above that, language barriers and related costs for translations decrease the attractiveness of national courts significantly: for example, in Germany, one of the leading export nations, court procedures are still not allowed to be conducted in English. To sum up, national courts in general are still badly equipped to handle international cases efficiently.

It would take time and significant government efforts to adopt a state's national court system to the needs of global commerce. Given this, it seems rational that states, in aiming to attract foreign business, opened up their legal systems for arbitration by committing their courts to enforce both contractual arbitration clauses and arbitral awards. States thereby created a global market for arbitral services. In contrast to litigation in state courts, arbitration is private business. Competition forces arbitrators to adapt their legal services to the demand of global commerce. Arbitrators are therefore specialists in resolving cross-border

---

[33] For a very good summary of all theoretical and empirical arguments see: Stefan Vogenauer, "Regulatory Competition through Choice of Contract Law and Choice of Forum in Europe: Theory and Evidence," *European Review of Private Law* 21, no. 1 (2013): pp. 13–78.

[34] Peter Mankowski, "Überlegungen zur sach- und interessengerechten Rechtswahl für Verträge des internationalen Wirtschaftsverkehrs," Recht der internationalen Wirtschaft 2003, no. 1 (2003): pp. 2–15.

[35] Dieter Schmidtchen, "International Contracting and Territorial Control: The Boundary Question. Comment on B.V. Yarbrough and R.M. Yarbrough's article of the same name," *Journal of Institutional and Theoretical Economics* 150, no. 1 (1994): pp. 272–278.

contractual disputes. Arbitral procedures can be conducted in English or other languages, if the parties so wish. Moreover, the location of the arbitration specified in the contract might be a legal fiction, in the sense that the factual hearings take place at a location that can easily be reached by both parties. International commercial arbitration houses only define the broad framework of their arbitral work. Otherwise, the parties are free to choose the procedural norms they want to govern their disputes. Often this means that arbitration can avoid time-consuming and complex procedures in favor of fast and cost-effective decisions.

Moreover, in arbitration, none of the involved parties needs to fear that courts are biased in favor of local parties. The parties are free to choose their arbitrators. Arbitration is therefore neutral, which makes it attractive for the parties to agree on this private dispute resolution mechanism. Sure, the parties could also delegate their conflicts to a court in a neutral third state, and, in fact, they sometimes do so. However, since international arbitration far better serves the needs of global commerce for effective dispute resolution, in many cases arbitration is preferred over litigation in state courts. In sum, arbitration does indeed seem able to overcome the problem of dysfunctional conflict-of-laws techniques and inefficient courts in cross-border trade.[36]

2.2 Legal Rules—Element A

In cross-border transactions, however, collision problems not only concern the place of jurisdiction, but also the applicable law. If a transaction involves more than one legal system, it remains open which country's law applies to a given contract? For the same reasons as outlined above, it also holds for this question that neither present conflict-of-laws techniques nor choice-of-law clauses are able to deal with this question efficiently. Even when states implement uniform laws that the transacting parties can choose to govern their contractual relationship, such as the United Nations Convention on Contracts for the International Sale of Goods (CISG), their relevance is insignificant. In practice, parties to international contracts not only strongly prefer their home courts, but also their home laws, and, again, it is usually the party with the greater bargaining power that dominates the bargaining process, thereby creating an uneven legal playing field for the actors involved.

Interestingly, international commercial arbitration is often assumed to also provide a solution for this second legal problem of international trade. Note that the scope of choice-of-law possibilities is principally greater in international arbitration than in state litigation. National courts restrict the choice of law to

---

[36] Moritz Renner, "Towards a Hierarchy of Norms in Transnational Law?" *Journal of International Arbitration* 26, no. 4 (2009): pp. 533–555.

national laws, whereas the legal practice in international arbitration allows the choice of both national laws and private transnational law codifications, such as, for example, the UNIDROIT Principles of International Commercial Courts. Many scholars of international commercial arbitration argue that the extensive choice-of-law possibilities provided in international arbitration would trigger the frequent application of transnational commercial laws to international contracts. Transnational commercial law is based on customary norms and generated by the merchants themselves. Thus, this private body of laws is far better adapted to the demands of the global trading community than national laws, which are created by rent-seeking national governments.[37] Transnational commercial law is conceptualized as a system that works in favor of contracting global business parties. Consequently, it is widely expected that parties will choose transnational commercial law in their contracts.[38]

However, according to Christopher R. Drahozal, who in 2005 summarized the available empirical data on choice of law in international commercial arbitration, this expectation seems to be misleading. In fact, parties to international contracts very rarely use the possibility of referring to transnational private codifications, but almost exclusively choose national laws to govern their contracts.[39]

This picture is confirmed by a recent study at Queen Mary University, London, which is based on online questionnaires comprising 78 questions, which were completed by 136 respondents from February to August 2010. The respondents were mostly legal counsels or heads of legal departments of large- or medium-sized international companies from all kinds of industries and regions. A further 68 qualitative interviews were conducted with the same group of interviewees. The study differentiates between four different categories of transnational commercial law:

> first, unwritten international principles (e.g. broad concepts fairness and equity, determination ex aequo et bono); second, international treaties and conventions (e.g. the United Nations Convention on Contracts for the International Sale of Goods (CISG)); third, commercial law rules relating to trade and international contracts (e.g. UNIDROIT Principles of International Commercial Contracts 2004 (UNIDROIT Principles) and INCOTERMS); fourth, other international rules (e.g. Uniform Customs and Practice for Documentary Credits (UCP)).[40]

[37] Harold J. Berman, "World Law Essay: Roll of International Law in the Twenty-First Century," *Fordham International Law Journal* 18, no. 5 (May 1995): pp. 1617–1622.
[38] Benson, "The Spontaenous Evolution"; Berger, *The Creeping Codification*; Klaus Peter Berger, "The New Law Merchant and the Global Marketplace, A 21st Century View of Transnational Commercial Law," *International Arbitration Law Review* 3, no. 4 (2000): pp. 91–102.
[39] Christopher R. Drahozal, "Contracting Out of National Law: An Empirical Look at the New Law Marchant," *Notre Dame Law Review* 80, no. 2 (2005): pp. 536–544.
[40] "International Arbitration Study 2010—International Arbitration Survey: Choices in International Arbitration," Queen Mary, University of London—School of International Arbitration, 2010, <http://www.arbitrationonline.org/docs/2010_InternationalArbitrationSurveyReport.pdf>.

Overall, the vast majority of interviewees stated that they never or only sometimes use one of the four categories of transnational commercial law. Furthermore, the study makes clear that even when parties do rely on transnational commercial law, they do so to supplement, rather than displace, national law. In sum, transnational commercial law is used in international contracts considerably less frequently than is often assumed.[41]

In order to explain this finding, it is mostly argued that the benefits of transnational law come "at the price of certainty."[42] General principles that characterize this type of law "may on occasion, be useful to fill a gap but in essence they are too elementary . . . . to permit detached evaluation of conflicting interests, the specifically legal appreciations of the implications of a given situation."[43] Thus, national laws are preferred over transnational laws, because they offer better predictability and legal certainty. A second reason is that more powerful parties to an international contract are not interested in creating a level playing field by choosing a neutral transnational law, but insist on choosing a national law with which they are familiar and their contractual partners are not. In doing so, the stronger party puts itself in an even better strategic position should conflicts arise. From a rational choice point of view, it is clear that parties do not choose the law that is most efficient for both parties, but the law that best suits their own interests. Finally, one could argue that transnational commercial law, as it existed to govern trade in the middle ages, has not survived in modern times. As a matter of fact, in the 19th and 20th centuries, societies went through fundamental modernization processes which were primarily driven by the emerging nation states. States developed their own contract laws and abolished the idea of universally applicable rules and norms created by the merchants themselves. Being a lawyer in the 19th and 20th centuries implied studying national law plus, in exceptional cases, the laws of other nation states in a comparative fashion. However, the use of any kind of transnational law beyond the legal framework of nation states was not part of the prevailing cognitive framework. Certainly, since the 1950s there have been increasing academic efforts to reintroduce transnational commercial law into legal practice as a third category of law beyond national and international law. Thus, it might turn out that in the near future transnational commercial law becomes routine practice and a regularly applied legal tool to guide the conduct of cross-border transactions. However, looking at the currently available empirical data, we also need to understand that, for the time being, transitional law has not achieved this status: up to now transnational commercial law has played only a minor role

---

[41] "International Arbitration Study 2010," Queen Mary, University of London.
[42] "International Arbitration Study 2010," Queen Mary, University of London.
[43] "International Arbitration Study 2010," Queen Mary, University of London.

in transnational commercial arbitration. Thus, international commercial arbitration has not accomplished the evolution of a common transnational law so far that it would be capable of establishing a level legal playing field for companies engaged in global trade. The vast majority of cross-border contracts, even when they contain arbitration clauses, are still governed by national laws because these laws still determine the cognitive framework of legal professionals.

The fact that international commercial arbitration courts predominantly apply national laws to solve disputes in cross-border exchanges clearly has a negative impact upon the efficiency of these institutions. As explained above, the territorial fragmentation of national legal systems leads to structural problems for state courts and enforcement authorities when dealing with cross-border transactions. A global legal system that only accepts state law as an operating unit has the effect that contracts invariably need to be attached to existing laws and jurisdictions. Consequently, one of the parties is very likely to perform its contractual obligations under a foreign, unfamiliar law, which in turn leads to increasing uncertainty, high legal costs, and, finally, deepening imbalances between the contractual partners. In theory international commercial arbitration courts could solve this fragmentation problem because, in contrast to state courts, these private courts extend the freedom of the choice-of-law to transnational bodies of law. Yet, for the above-mentioned reasons, transnational commercial laws are in practice rarely chosen by the contracting parties, and this leads international commercial arbitration courts, like national courts, to operate on the basis of a normative system shaped by fragmented national private laws. Thus, in international commercial arbitration those parties who perform their contractual obligations under foreign, unfamiliar laws also face uncertainty and high legal costs. In sum, the significant role of fragmented national laws in international commercial arbitration presents a first crucial factor for understanding the limits—and thus the relatively small caseload—of these private courts in the context of the immense growth of international trade.

2.3 Enforcement—Element C

The final shortcoming of state legal systems in providing a reliable legal infrastructure for cross-border transactions concerns the enforcement of court judgements. In contrast to domestic conditions, where authorities are directly committed to enforce court judgements, foreign judgments must be recognized by the local courts of the foreign country before they can be enforced. In order to enhance the reliability of these procedures, states may conclude international treaties that agree on the reciprocal recognition and the enforcement of court judgments. However, even where they exist, merely bilateral reciprocal treaties are not enough. The parties can determine the respective applicable law and the place of jurisdiction, but often not the place of enforcement. Since money and other types of assets can be moved around the globe, the prevailing party often might not know where the judgment will need to be enforced until it is issued. Losing parties might also move assets strategically to a state that has not entered into a bilateral agreement with the state in which the judgment is rendered. The multilateral agreements necessary to overcome these problems are still lacking.[44]

Effective cross-border enforcement is not only limited through a lack of international agreements. In order to cover all aspects of the problem, we also need to look at the domestic level. If we take a brief look at comparative analyses of state legal systems—as, for example, provided by the World Bank—we can discern great differences in the efficiency of different national contracts laws. In some countries contracts can be enforced fast and at low cost, whereas in other countries the legal system turns out to be dysfunctional.[45] It was mentioned in the previous paragraph that parties to an international contract are principally free to choose the respective applicable law and jurisdiction. At least in theory, parties are thus in the position to circumvent inefficient institutions and to choose those laws and jurisdiction that suit their purposes best. It has also been mentioned that in practice parties rarely engage in rational decision-making to determine the best available law, but tend to aim at stipulating their home laws in the contracts. However, this is not the decisive point here; the point is that even when parties are free to choose the applicable law and jurisdiction, they still cannot fully exclude inefficient or unreliable national legal units from cross-border contract enforcement. The following quotation, which is taken from an empirical study that investigates contractual relations between German and Indian firms, makes this point very clear: When asked about the importance of state law in the enforcement of contracts across borders, the interviewed German expert stated:

> In India it is much harder to sue [than in Germany] and which law do you apply? If I apply Indian law, I run into the issue that an Indian court might be more inclined to decide in favour of an Indian company rather than a German one. If I

[44] These exist within the EU. By setting into force the so-called Brussels I-Regulation, Member States commit their courts to automatically recognize and enforce judgments from other Member State's courts. The Brussels I-Regulation, however, is an exception. In general, states remain hostile to enforcing foreign judgments, because it profoundly undermines their authority and reduces their judges' power.

[45] "Doing Business Report 2011: Making a difference for entrepreneurs," The World Bank, November 4, 2010, pp. 70–76, <http://www.doingbusiness.org/~/media/GIAWB/Doing%20Business/Documents/Annual-Reports/English/DB11-FullReport.pdf>; *Worldwide Governance Indicators*, The World Bank, <http://info.worldbank.org/governance/wgi/index.aspx?fileName=wgidataset.xlsx#reports>.

choose German law, I get my right; but if I appear with this ruling in India and want to enforce it, the Indians might just laugh at me.[46]

At least when it comes to the stage of enforcement, companies have no choice but to rely on local courts and authorities. Whenever an unreliable legal unit is involved in the process of enforcing cross-border contracts, the performance of state enforced contract law will be reduced. Sure, in many constellations trade occurs between companies of states with sufficiently reliable legal systems. However, in many other and ever more numerous constellations cross-border transactions involve companies that have their main assets in states like China, Brazil, India, and many other smaller emerging market economies, which still possess rather inefficient legal systems, if one follows various comparative governance report.[47] To sum up, the cross-border enforcement of court judgments is limited by two factors: missing international agreements that facilitate the emergence of a multilateral enforcement order and partly dysfunctional legal conditions at the domestic level.

Now, we can ask again: Is international commercial arbitration able to overcome these enforcement problems? According to most pundits, this is indeed the case. The arbitration literature highlights a number of multilateral international conventions that facilitate the recognition and enforcement of foreign arbitral awards,[48] most importantly the 1958 United Nations New York Convention on the Recognition and Enforcement of Foreign Arbitral Awards[49], to which almost 150 states are signatories.[50] The New York Convention gives foreign arbitral awards a far better chance of becoming successfully enforced across borders than judgments by state courts. This advantage in turn induces companies engaged in international trade to favor international commercial arbitration over state courts. The New York Convention has therefore triggered the rise of international commercial arbitration as the most important contract-enforcement institution in international trade.[51]

---

[46] Thomas Dietz, "Contract Law, Relational Contracts and Reputational Networks in International Trade: An Empirical Investigation into Cross-Border Contracts in the Software Industry," *Law & Social Inquiry* 37, no. 1 (Winter 2012): p. 36.

[47] "International Arbitration Study 2010," Queen Mary, University of London.

[48] See for example: Nigel Blackaby, Constantine Partisides, Alan Redfern, and Martin Hunter, *Redfern and Hunter on international arbitration* (Oxford/New York: Oxford University Press, 2009), p. 631.

[49] The Convention on the Recognition and Enforcement of Foreign Arbitral Awards (in short: "New York Convention") was signed on July 10, 1958 and it entered into force on June 7, 1959. See: "United Nations Conference on International Commercial Arbitration: Convention on the Recognition and Enforcement of Foreign Arbitral Awards," United Nations, <http://www.uncitral.org/pdf/english/texts/arbitration/NY-conv/XXII_1_e.pdf>.

[50] Please see for example: Born, *International Commercial Arbitration*, p. 209; Alan Redfern and Martin Hunter, *Law and practice of international commercial arbitration* (London: Sweet & Maxwell, 2004), p. 69.

[51] See for example: Blackaby, Partisides, Redfern, and Hunter, *Redfern and Hunter on international arbitration*, p. 631.

Yet, scholars of international commercial arbitration tend to overlook the fact that the second problem—the unreliable legal structures at the domestic level—also applies to the enforcement of foreign arbitral awards. The widely shared notion that arbitral awards are reliably enforceable only because a state has become a member of the New York Convention is rather naïve. Indonesia provides a good illustration of this point. The country became a party to the New York Convention in 1981. However, according to Robert N. Hornick, even after accession it was practically impossible to successfully enforce a foreign arbitral award in Indonesia.[52] It took the Indonesian government almost ten years to implement the New York Convention. Throughout this period the Indonesian courts refused to enforce arbitral awards that came under the New York Convention on the grounds that the regulations implementing the Convention were not yet issued by the relevant Indonesian authorities. But even when the necessary regulations finally entered into force, the situation did not change. The local courts refused to enforce arbitral awards. In every case the courts identified unclear legal matters that inhibited prompt enforcement, unless superior courts or state authorities provided further guidance. At the time that Hornick published his article in 1991, not a single foreign arbitral award was successfully enforced in Indonesia, eleven years after the country became a member of the New York Convention.[53]

International commercial arbitration tribunals usually do not utilize private sanctions to enforce their arbitral awards, but ultimately rely on state enforcement. This means that at the end of the legal chain international commercial arbitration courts are also restrained by corrupt, slow, or expensive national enforcement procedures in many regions of world trade.[54] The 2008 study of Queen Mary University is again very helpful in illustrating this point. When asked about the recognition and enforcement of foreign arbitral awards, companies reported a range of difficulties. Unsurprisingly, the main difficulty (46 percent) was hostility to foreign arbitral awards in the place of enforcement. When questioned further about the kind of difficulties they had experienced at the place of enforcement, 56 percent of company lawyers cited local recognition and enforcement procedures or execution procedures. The majority of company lawyers linked both of these problems with the attitudes of local

---

[52] Robert N. Hornick, "Indonesian Arbitration in Theory and Practice," *The American Journal of Comparative Law* 39, no. 3 (Summer 1991): pp. 559–597.

[53] Hornick, "Indonesian Arbitration."

[54] "International commercial arbitration still very much relies on the support of national legal systems. The ultimate authority for arbitration procedures is that they are recognized and supported by national legislative and judicial processes. Without the power of state legal systems behind them, a party who expects to do poorly in the arbitration will have no incentive to comply [. . .]. Consequently, international commercial arbitration operates very much in the 'shadow of the law' and national laws continue to impose important limits": Robert Wai, "Transnational Liftoff and Juridical Touchdown: The Regulatory Function of Private International Law in an Era of Globalization," *Columbia Journal of Transnational Law* 40, no. 2 (2002): p. 267.

bureaucrats and courts. Ten percent of the interviewees cited difficulties with corruption at local courts. When asked about particular countries, the most frequently mentioned regions where difficulties are likely to appear in enforcement or execution proceedings were Central America, South America (including Brazil), and Africa. China was the country mentioned most often, with India and Russia also considered potentially problematic territories.[55] These results show that despite the New York Convention, international commercial arbitration in its universal form lacks an efficacious worldwide enforcement system. However, without effective enforcement a legal institution has no bearing on human behavior. From a transaction cost perspective, the fact that foreign arbitral rewards cannot reliably be enforced in many parts of the world, which are today deeply integrated into the world market, severely constrains the capability of international commercial arbitration courts to provide a universally viable legal infrastructure for global exchange.

2.4 Overall Results

Efficient formal dispute resolution institutions need to successfully combine three constitutive elements: (A) legal rules, (B) courts applying these rules, and (C) effective sanctions to enforce the courts' decisions. As Table 7.2 illustrates, litigation fails in all three elements. Arbitration therefore clearly outperforms state courts. However, outperforming litigation is only one aspect of arbitration, and does not allow the conclusion that arbitration automatically evolves into an efficient and powerful mechanism of global economic governance. As a matter of fact, arbitration also faces profound institutional limitations. Element (B)—*courts*—is the only element of the whole institutional structure of international commercial arbitration that is entirely private. Regarding elements (A)—*legal rules*—and (C)—*enforcement*—arbitration operates on the basis of legal structures provided by the state. In the end, these connections to dysfunctional state legal structures also exert a negative impact upon international commercial arbitration. Clearly, arbitration works better than litigation in state courts. But, on the other hand, international

Table 7.2. Institutional performance of litigation and arbitration

	(A) Courts	(B) Rules	(C) Enforcement
Litigation	–	–	–
Arbitration	+	–	+/ –

[55] See: "International Arbitration Study 2008," Queen Mary, University of London, pp. 10–12.

commercial arbitration seems far away from offering economic agents engaged in global commerce a viable universal legal infrastructure.

3 Private Governance Regimes

Seeing these results, it is interesting to note that not all types of international commercial arbitration are hybrids in the sense that they are closely embedded into state legal structures. Up to now the analysis has focused on what in the following is called universal or non-specialized international commercial arbitration. All courts listed in the table above are open to accept cases from all kinds of different companies and industries engaged in international commercial transactions. From these courts we can distinguish a small number of so-called specialized international arbitration courts,[56] which are provided by international trade associations specializing in particular business sectors for their members only. Berkowitz and colleagues have identified three international trade associations offering arbitration services to their members: The Grain and Feed Trade Association (GAFTA), the Federation of Coca Commerce (FCC), Coca Association of London, and the Liverpool Cotton Association (LCA).[57] The London Metal Exchange[58] (LME) provides another example in this field and, last but not least, Lisa Bernstein has described the international diamond industry as a federation of commercial associations using industry-specific arbitration courts to adjudicate disputes and enforce contracts.[59]

Although the above-mentioned specialized arbitration courts do not make their caseload public, so we cannot exactly determine their economic relevance, it seems very likely that in contrast to the universal type, specialized international commercial arbitration courts are indeed capable of providing a workable legal infrastructure for cross-border exchange within their particular areas of trade. In each of the respective industries the vast majority of the total worldwide trade volume is governed by model contracts that are administered by the different above-mentioned associations and their arbitral bodies. As the following example of the diamond industry illustrates, this practice has a significant impact upon the caseload of specialized arbitration courts.

---

[56] Christopher R. Drahozal, "Private Ordering and International Commercial Arbitration," *Penn State Law Review* 113, no. 4 (Spring 2009): p. 1045.

[57] Daniel Berkowitz, Johannes Moenius, and Katharina Pistor, "Legal Institutions and International Trade Flows," *Michigan Journal of International Law* 26, no. 1 (Fall 2005): pp. 163–198.

[58] Please see: <http://www.lme.com>.

[59] Lisa Bernstein, "Opting out of the Legal System: Extralegal Contractual Relations in the Diamond Industry," *The Journal of Legal Studies* 21, no. 1 (January 1992): pp. 115–158.

International diamond trade is organized within a federation of 29 world-wide diamond bourses.[60] To take part in this organized worldwide diamond market one has to be a member of one of these bourses. Each member can trade at each bourse worldwide, and each bourse is governed by a local arbitration court. The New York Diamond Dealers Club (DDC) which Lisa Bernstein mainly focuses on is one of these 29 bourses. In 1992 Bernstein counted a total of 150 cases submitted to the DDC's arbitration systems.[61] Unfortunately, arbitration courts in the diamond industry do not make their caseload public. However, given the fact that diamonds are traded internationally in 28 further bourses, and that each of these bourses provides its own arbitration court, it is obvious that arbitration courts play a much more vibrant role in this particular business sector than in international trade in general.

Specialized arbitration courts are different from universal arbitration courts in two central aspects: First, contractual parties cannot choose the applicable law. When two parties use a model contract that is administered by a particular business association then this contract stipulates that in the case of a conflict the specialized arbitration court has jurisdiction. Furthermore, the parties automatically agree that the work of the arbitral bodies is governed by both industry-specific procedural and substantial rules. The above-mentioned international business associations formalized their private legal systems roughly between the last 30 years of the 19th century and the first 30 years of the 20th century. However, the trading associations and bourses usually look back on much longer trading histories. The formalization of rules at the end of 19th century and the beginning of the 20th century was thus merely an act of writing down traditional practices and trade customs that merchants in these particular branches had been continuously using for centuries. Different from universal arbitration, the practice of applying uniform *lex mercatoria* norms to given conflicts has survived in specialized arbitration. Here economic agents are not exposed to unfamiliar foreign national norms systems, but conduct their businesses on a level legal playing field. From a transaction cost perspective these unitary normative structures clearly reduce information costs and thus enhance the institutional performance of specialized arbitration courts.

Second, international trade associations and bourses not only provide private norms that operate independently from territorially fragmented state law, but also set up their own systems of sanctions to enforce the awards of their specialized arbitration courts. When, for example, it comes to sanction

---

[60] It was 20 bourses in 1992 when Bernstein published her article. See: Bernstein, "Opting out of the Legal System," p. 121.
[61] Bernstein, "Opting out of the Legal System," p. 124.

a defaulting party in the international diamond industry, the bylaws of the diamond bourses provide that "[a]ll decisions of arbitration panels [. . .] which are not complied with within 10 working days, together with the picture of the non-complying member, shall be posted in a conspicuous room in the Club rooms."[62]

This information is communicated to all bourses in the world federation. Membership in the federation requires each bourse to enforce the judgments of all member bourses worldwide. Since most dealers frequently transact in foreign bourses, this reciprocity of enforcement greatly increases the penalty for failing to voluntarily comply with arbitration judgments. The local bourses usually exclude the non-complying party from the trading floor.[63] Bernstein defines this enforcement structure as an "information intermediary regime"[64] in which technology and markets link the rapid and low-cost dissemination of information and reputation.

Similar to the diamond bourses' arbitration courts the other four specialized international commercial arbitration courts mentioned above are also embedded in organized reputational systems. GAFTA and LME arbitration courts are entitled to inform their members about a party that refuses to carry out an arbitral award. The LCA goes even further. Its directors might pass the name of the defaulting party not only to members but also to:

> Registered Firms, Associate Members, Member Associations of the Committee for International Co-operation between Cotton Associations (CICCA) or any other organisation or person by any method it chooses, including the listing of the name of the defaulter and appropriate details in the publicly accessible area of the Association's website.[65]

The decisive point is, again, that these systems of private sanctions considerably enhance the institutional performance of specialized arbitration courts. Economic agents do not have to engage in additional potentially uncertain legal procedures to enforce their arbitral awards, but can rely on well-organized reputational effects which, like the global economy, operate even beyond national borders.

At this stage, it is interesting to note that parts of the arbitration literature emphasize that most universal arbitral awards rendered are voluntarily complied with and do therefore not require judicial enforcement. In other words, universal arbitration also evolves even without effective state enforcement supported by private sanctions. At an initial glance, this argument seems

---

[62] Cited in Bernstein, "Opting out of the Legal System," p. 128.

[63] Bernstein, "Opting out of the Legal System," p. 128.

[64] Bernstein, "Opting out of the Legal System," p. 116.

[65] "Bylaws and Rules of The International Cotton Association," International Cotton Association (ICA), approved by the Members December 9, 2010, p. 36, <http://www.ica-ltd.org/media/layout/documents/rulebooks/rulebook_english_jan11.pdf>.

plausible. However, on closer inspection this view is too simplistic. Since universal arbitration is not supported by organized reputational systems, voluntary enforcement in this case means that losing parties comply with the arbitral award because they fear informal sanctions, like the ending of a business relationship or the exclusion from business networks. These sanctions are very effective; however, as institutional economics and game theorists have demonstrated many times, they are also restricted to long-term relations or close-knit groups, i.e., relational contracting.[66] Dispute resolution mechanisms that aim at providing a viable legal infrastructure for modern, globalized markets with high numbers of impersonal market participants need to be supported by either coercive state sanctions or systems of organized blacklisting.[67] Given this, the practice of voluntary enforcement in arbitration is rather an indicator for the limits of arbitration than proof of its efficiency. Note, the relatively low caseload of international commercial arbitration compared to the tremendous growth of international trade also points to the fact that enforcement mechanisms capable of supporting anonymous exchange are still missing in universal arbitration.

3.1 *Maritime Arbitration*

The impact of effective sanctions on the economic performance of international commercial arbitration also becomes evident in the case of maritime arbitration. Maritime arbitration presents a unique case. On the one hand, it only accepts maritime cases and therefore belongs to the group of specialized international commercial arbitration. On the other hand, maritime arbitration is not embedded into privately organized blacklisting systems, but, like universal arbitration, ultimately relies on state authorities to enforce their awards.

However, state enforcement of maritime arbitral awards differs from state enforcement of normal universal arbitral awards because of the so-called ship or vessel arrest: A ship arrest is a legal procedure administered by state courts and state enforcement authorities that cannot directly be ordered by maritime

[66] Douglass C. North, *Institutions, Institutional Change and Economic Performance* (Cambridge: Cambridge University Press, 1990); Avinash K. Dixit, *Lawlessness and economics: alternative modes of governance* (Princeton/Oxford: Princeton University Press, 2004); Avinash K. Dixit, "Governance Institutions and Economic Activity," *The American Economic Review* 99, no. 1 (March 2009): pp. 5–24.
[67] Paul R. Milgrom, Douglass C. North, and Berry R. Weingast, "The Role of Institutions in the Revival of Trade: The Law Merchant, Private Judges and the Champagne Fairs," *Economics and Politics* 2, no. 1 (March 1990): pp. 1–21.

arbitration courts.[68] The most important facet of a ship arrest is the following. If a party has a certain type of claim relating to a vessel, then that party can issue proceedings directly against this vessel or usually also a sister vessel belonging to the same owner. The party can have the vessel arrested until the claim is settled. If the debtor is unable to settle the claim the courts can be directed to sell the vessel under certain legal procedures.[69]

Ship arrests are parts of national laws; hence, legal details vary from state to state. However, a substantial number of coastal states are party to the 1952 International Convention for Unification of Certain Rules Relating to the Arrest of Sea-Going Ships (Arrest Convention). The convention specifically sets out a list of maritime claims for which a vessel may be arrested. Generally speaking this list includes all possible claims related to using, renting, selling, buying, or financing sea ships.[70]

It was noted earlier that enforcing arbitral awards is often uncertain because of corrupt or unreliable legal systems in many regions of the world that today play vibrant roles in world trade. The crucial point is that given the enforcement tool of the ship arrest maritime arbitration is capable of overcoming this problem. Practically all countries with harbors have integrated the ship arrest into their legal systems. The claimant can therefore choose where to file the case. If, for example, a Greek ship-owner wants to enforce an arbitral award against a Chinese shipping company, he can file the case in the Netherlands or Singapore. Both countries have a reputation for particularly efficient enforcement procedures, which means that the claimant can fully avoid the inefficient Chinese authorities. Sooner or later a vessel of the Chinese shipping company will have to enter a port with an efficient jurisdiction because no shipping company can afford to run ships that are unable to call at some of the most economically important harbors in world trade. Thus, for the Chinese company the incentives to pay the debt to the Greek ship-owner are very strong. Since in the case of the ship arrests assets that can be used for enforcement travel borderless around the world seas, national differences in territorially fragmented legal systems have no significant impact upon the efficiency on the whole system.

Certainly, according to the New York Convention an arbitral award, rendered by a universal arbitration court, can be enforced in any signatory country. In many cases, globally operating companies will have assets in multiple countries. However, in other cases they do not—or at least no assets of significant

---

[68] Georgius I. Zekos, *International commercial and marine arbitration* (London: Routledge-Cavendish, 2008), pp. 380–383.

[69] Zekos, *International commercial*, p. 382.

[70] The text of the convention is available at: <http://treaties.un.org/doc/publication/unts/volume%20439/volume-439-i-6330-english.pdf>; see also: Robert W. Lynn, "A Comment on the New International Convention on Arrest of Ships, 1999," *University of Miami Law Review* 55, no. 3 (April 2001): pp. 453–485.

value. Moreover, valuable assets, like bank accounts or licenses, are mobile in the sense that the losing party can easily move them to locations where enforcement is problematic. It might also involve significant costs and time for the prevailing party to locate enforceable assets and to hire local lawyers to start the procedures. These legal uncertainties and enforcement costs do not exist in maritime arbitration. The territorial fragmentation of national legal systems therefore does constrain the institutional performance of maritime arbitration considerably less than the institutional performance of universal arbitration in general.

In social sciences it is often difficult to make clear-cut casual references. Yet, the fact that maritime arbitration plays a considerably more significant role in providing a legal infrastructure for maritime trade than universal arbitration plays for international trade in general clearly supports this chapter's analysis. Maritime arbitration courts are very active, particularly in the area of charter business.[71] In maritime trade the most important arbitration courts are the London Maritime Arbitrators Association (LMAA) and the Society of Maritime Arbitrators in New York (SMA). Together these two courts handle around 90 percent of the worldwide caseload.[72] Both the LMAA and the SMA only accept maritime cases for arbitration. However, despite this limitation, with around 4500 requests in 2009,[73] these courts handle a significantly higher caseload than all universal arbitration tribunals together—although universal arbitration, since it accepts cases from all industries involved in global trade, operates in a potentially far greater market.[74] Again this example suggests a strong impact of the institutional features of different types of international commercial arbitration upon their economic performance. The less a particular type of arbitration depends upon dysfunctional territorially fragmented state legal structure, the more efficient this type works in practice.

4 Conclusion

This chapter was set up to critically assess the oft-repeated hypothesis that in the absence of a viable state legal infrastructure international commercial arbitration increasingly provides economic agents engaged in cross-border trade with reliable dispute resolution mechanisms and, therefore, performs an economically important governance function. First of all, it was made clear that the caseload of universal arbitration houses, such as the ICC, the

[71] See: Andreas Maurer, *Lex Maritima* (Tübingen: Mohr Siebeck, 2012).
[72] See: Maurer, *Lex Maritima*.
[73] For detailed statistical numbers on maritime arbitration please see: Hoffmann and Maurer, "Entstaatlichung der Justiz"; Maurer, *Lex Maritima*.
[74] See: Maurer, *Lex Maritima*.

LCIA, or the SCC, is still very low compared to the tremendous growth of international trade over recent decades.

In a detailed institutional analysis, the chapter then aimed at explaining these findings. Overall, the analysis supports the view that international commercial arbitration works more efficiently than litigation in state courts. Legal developments in the field of cross-border dispute resolution are largely driven by global economic forces. States that aim at improving their legal systems in order to attract foreign business have recognized that it is very costly to adapt their national court systems to the demands of firms engaged in cross-border trade; therefore, they opened their legal systems to the services of private international commercial arbitration and thus created a huge global market for the business of resolving disputes in cross-border exchange. Arbitration tribunals have indeed adapted their legal services to the demands of global commerce and therefore outperform state courts. Yet, the privatization of arbitration remains incomplete. The tribunals are private, yet both the legal rules that arbitral tribunals apply and the sanctions of enforcing arbitral awards are usually provided by the state. International commercial arbitration is thus only partly able to overcome the limits of territorially fragmented national legal systems. In other respects, its performance is limited by institutional shortcomings that are similar to those that limit the performance of state courts in international trade.

In practice, the contracting parties rarely choose bottom-up evolving unitary transnational commercial laws. Like national courts, universal international commercial arbitration tribunals mostly operate also on the basis of a normative system that is shaped by fragmented national private law. Proponents of a law market and regulatory competition perspective claim that the choice between different norm systems would trigger the effect that parties select those legal systems that suit their purposes most efficiently.[75] However, this conclusion seems rather simplistic. In fact, empirical evidence proves that most contractual parties try to stipulate their home laws in their contracts, either because of continued routines or in order to gain a strategic advantage over their contractual partners. The effect is that those parties who perform their contractual obligations under foreign, unfamiliar laws face great normative risks and high legal costs. In this respect, it holds true for both state courts and arbitral tribunals that they not only fail in reducing transaction costs in international trade, but that they also deepen imbalances between the contracting parties in many situations, which in turn results in even greater legal uncertainties. From a normative perspective, one could

---

[75] Wolfgang Kerber, "Transnational Commercial Law, Multi-Level Legal Systems, and Evolutionary Economics," in *Law, Economics and Evolutionary Theory*, edited by Peer Zumbansen and Gralf-Peter Calliess (Cheltenham: Edward Elgar, 2011).

argue here that powerful arbitration houses, like the ICC, should try to press for the use of unitary *lex mercatoria* norms in order to enhance the efficiency of their legal services.

In contrast to specialized arbitration courts, universal arbitration does not dispose of systems of private sanctions. Instead, the ultimate sanction of arbitral awards is enforcement before a state court. This link to state legal systems entails a major shortcoming. Similar to national courts, international commercial arbitral tribunals are at the end of the legal chain constrained by corrupt, slow, or expensive national enforcement procedures that exist in many states which play significant roles in current international trade. International commercial arbitration in its universal form cannot avoid the inclusion of inefficient national legal systems into its legal operations. Empirical data show that companies engaged in cross-border transactions are well aware of this fact. They know that in many circumstances they might end up with foreign arbitral awards that they cannot enforce.

In this context, maritime arbitration presents a very interesting exception. Although maritime arbitration courts are specialized, they are not embedded in completely private governance regimes. Maritime arbitration courts rely on state enforcement. Nevertheless, their caseload is significantly higher than the caseload of universal arbitration courts in general. Maritime arbitration courts are more effective than universal arbitration courts because they can rely on a special enforcement tool—ship arrest. Profitable ships that carry goods and passengers around the globe sooner or later need to call at a harbor with a reliable and cost-effective jurisdiction. Given this, the winning party can avoid unreliable national enforcement systems. In maritime arbitration, it is indeed possible to exclude inefficient national legal units from the operation of the arbitral system. Again, this point reinforces the argument that the performance of arbitration courts crucially depends upon effective enforcement structures. When such structures are absent, as in international commercial arbitration in general, the institutional performance is clearly limited.

Proponents of international commercial arbitration often highlight the role of the voluntary enforcement of arbitral rewards. Informal sanctions networks work within close-knit groups, in which information spreads easily. However, reputational information is not sufficient to guarantee enforcement in a broad impersonal global legal system. Note, these constraints of informal reputational networks do not imply that reputation is entirely incapable of playing a pivotal role in the enforcement of arbitral awards. It can, in fact, play a role, but only when it organizes systems of blacklisting. Specialized arbitration courts provide a very good example in this respect. They are already embedded in organized reputational systems. Certainly, one has to take into account that it is comparatively easy to inform the members of a particular international trade organization of the failure of a losing party to fulfil an arbitral award. On the other hand, given the possibilities of modern information and communication technologies, it should be a relatively easy task to publish a blacklist on the Internet detailing all defaulting parties; this could then be checked by companies in the run-up phase of a cross-border business transaction. Since a good reputation is crucial for global business success, such a list clearly has the potential to evolve into a powerful global sanctioning mechanism.

Yet, these are only normative suggestions that are not part of the present system of international commercial arbitration. Up to now, the provision of companies engaged in cross-trade with efficient contract-enforcement institutions has been severely restricted by the close connection to state legal structures. More efficient arbitral institutions only exist within a few international trade associations. In contrast to universal arbitration, specialized arbitration mainly works independently of deficient state legal structures. In future, universal arbitration houses should, therefore, ponder new ways of overcoming the legal problems that arise from the territorial fragmentation of national legal systems.

8

What is the Effect of Commercial Arbitration on Trade?

Thomas Hale

1 Introduction

Economic exchanges require credibility. For simple, face-to-face transactions, credibility is guaranteed by the physical presence of the goods to be exchanged in the outstretched palms of the two parties to a deal. But few exchanges in the modern economy are so straightforward. Transactions take place across time and space, meaning that a merchant has no guarantee that an obligation fulfilled at a certain time, in a certain place, will be reciprocated later on, elsewhere. Moreover, the nature of the good or service exchanged may be highly complex—e.g., a financial instrument, an intellectual property license, a service agreement, etc.—making it difficult to ascertain its value *ex ante* or determine contract compliance *ex post*, and therefore to hold the seller to account. When these types of risks and informational asymmetries are present, beneficial deals will not be made unless there is some way to ensure that both parties can credibly fulfill their commitments.

For this reason, the rule of law is widely seen as the *sine qua non* of economic exchange.[1] Specifically, a system is required to adjudicate disputes over a contract and then enforce the terms of the deal. Typically we think of public courts as fulfilling this key function. But many disputes, particularly those involving firms from different countries, are in fact adjudicated by private arbitral bodies. In almost all major trading countries, the decisions of these

---

[1] North, D. (1981). *Structure and Change in Economic History*. New York, W. W. Norton and Company; Acemoglu, D. and J. A. Robinson (2012). *Why Nations Fail: The Origins of Power, Prosperity and Poverty*. New York, Profile Books.

private, transnational tribunals have been made enforceable in public courts under domestic and international law, principally the 1958 New York Convention on the Enforcement of Private Arbitral Awards (hereafter NYC).

Advocates of commercial arbitration often stress the practical benefits firms can obtain by choosing to resolve disputes via private tribunals. Arbitration is said to resolve disputes more efficiently, professionally, secretly, and with more enforceable results, than court proceedings.[2] These claims have been at least partially corroborated by surveys of large multinational firms.[3]

These arguments typically focus on the private benefits that individual firms obtain from arbitration. But facilitating economic exchange can also be thought of as a public good, as private transactions aggregate into broader prosperity and may have wide-ranging positive externalities. Indeed, arbitration can be seen as one institutional "technology" through which the key function of the rule of law—or at least contract enforcement—is provided. In the context of cross-border trade, dispute settlement mechanisms can therefore be seen as providers of both private goods to firms, and, in the aggregate, the larger global public good of facilitating global economic exchange.

In this way the system of transnational commercial arbitration (TCA) is analogous to the World Trade Organization (WTO), or other public, intergovernmental institutions through which states cooperate to provide global public (or club) goods by subjecting economic relations to legal rules and, crucially, independent dispute settlement bodies. Of course, TCA performs a distinct function from the other institutions that underpin the global economy. It allows firms to credibly commit to uphold their deals with other firms, while the WTO allows countries to uphold their agreements (to not adopt protectionist measures) with other countries. TCA is also distinguishable from the system of investment protection under bilateral investment treaties (BITs), in which states commit not to expropriate firms' investments, though both use arbitration as a dispute settlement technique.

Do these institutions work? More specifically, do they provide the global public goods that observers ascribe to them? Surprisingly, the academic literature on the WTO ran to many pages before scholars addressed this fundamental question rigorously. Following Rose's provocative finding that the WTO did *not* increase trade, scholars across international relations and economics have explored the connection between the world body and trade flows.[4]

---

[2] Born, G. (2009). *International Commercial Arbitration*. The Hague, Kluwer.

[3] Mistelis, L. and C. Baltag (2008). "Recognition and Enforcement of Arbitral Awards and Settlement in International Arbitration: Corporate Attitudes and Practices." *The American Review of International Arbitration* 19(3–4): 319–375, Mistelis, L. and P. Martin (2010). *2010 International Arbitration Survey: Choices in International Arbitration*. London, Queen Mary School of Law, School of International Arbitration.

[4] A. K. Rose (2004). "Do We Really Know the WTO Increases Trade?" *The American Economic Review* **94**(1): 98–114.

While the subject remains an active topic of study, a rough consensus has emerged that the WTO does in fact increase trade, although much more for some kinds of countries than for others.[5] Studies of the economic effects of BITs are similarly in flux, in part because investment data are patchier.[6]

Along similar lines, this chapter assesses the impact of the system of transnational commercial arbitration on trade flows. I build on Leeson (2008), who found that ratifying the NYC increased trade between two countries by 15 percent if one was a member and 38 percent if both were members, and Hale (2012), who found the effects to be 20 percent and 57 percent, respectively.[7] The present study offers three primary improvements over these studies. First, it employs a larger and more accurate dataset that elides an important form of selection bias present in previous studies. Second, it ameliorates the endogeneity concerns of previous studies by using instruments to control for the factors that lead countries to ratify the NYC. Third, it explores the interchangeability of private arbitration and public courts.

On average, I find that delegating judicial authority to private arbitration, as measured by membership in the NYC, exerts a strong positive effect on trade, increasing the flow between two countries by 30 percent if one is a member and 63 percent if both are members. Once endogeneity concerns have been addressed, this effect is found to be much stronger, increasing to 172 percent. While less than the effect of the WTO on trade, these results suggest that the NYC has played a key role in the post-war trade regime. I also find that the effect of NYC ratification differs substantially for countries with high and low quality judicial institutions; countries with weak public courts see a larger boost in trade following ratification than countries with strong judiciaries. These results suggest that private transnational arbitration and public courts are to some extent substitutable for each other.

These results stand in contrast to Chapter 7 of this volume, which argues that TCA plays too small a role in transborder commerce, and is too dependent on national courts for enforcement, to have a substantial impact upon cross-border trade. Possible explanations for this divergence are discussed below.

---

[5] Anderson, J. E. and E. van Wincoop (2003). "Gravity with Gravitas: A Solution to the Border Puzzle." *American Economic Review* 93: 170–192; Subramanian, A. and S.-W. Wei (2007). "The WTO Promotes Trade Strongly, but Unevenly." *Journal of International Economics* 72: 151–175; Liu, X. (2009). "GATT/WTO Promotes Trade Strongly: Sample Selection and Model Specification." *Review of International Economics* 70: 428–446; Eicher, T. S. and C. Henn (2011). "In Search of WTO Trade Effects: Preferential Trade Agreements Promote Trade Strongly, but Unevenly." *Journal of International Economics* 19: 137–153; Rose, "Do We Really Know the WTO Increases Trade?" 2004.

[6] Sauvant, K. P. and L. E. Sachs (2009). *The Effect of Treaties on Foreign Direct Investment: Bilateral Investment Treaties, Double Taxation Treaties, and Investment Flows.* Oxford, Oxford University Press.

[7] Leeson, P. T. (2008). "How Important is State Enforcement for Trade?" *American Law and Economics Review* 10(1): 61–89; Hale, T. (2012). "The Rule of Law in the Global Economy: Explaining Institutional Variation in Commercial Dispute Resolution." PhD dissertation. Department of Politics. Princeton University.

The chapter proceeds as follows. Section 2 outlines a set of theoretical expectations between the rule of law and global commerce based in the existing literature. Section 3 outlines the analytical approach developed in the present chapter. Section 4 presents the results of the econometric analysis and section 5 concludes.

2 The Rule of Law and Global Commerce

There are few areas of greater consensus among students of political economy than around the importance of the rule of law for economic exchange. For North, the "provision of a set of public (or semi-public) goods and services designed to lower the cost of specifying, negotiating, and enforcing contracts which underlie economic exchange" is the central task of the state, so much so that "the creation of the state in the millennia following the first economic revolution was the necessary condition for all subsequent economic development."[8] In subsequent years this argument has expanded into a broader "institutionalist revolution" in economics, transforming the conventional wisdom from a minimalist neoclassical view into the idea that "it's the politics." While initially focused exclusively on the state, the institutionalist turn has also recognized how so-called "private orderings" can undergird economic exchange, be they general social norms or more institutionalized forms of adjudication and contract enforcement such as private tribunals.[9]

The importance of domestic institutions to national economic development raises a crucial question for students of international political economy. Absent a world state, how can the "rule of law" be provided to sustain global trade and investment? Several institutional solutions can be observed.

First, domestic institutions, principally public courts, may adjudicate and enforce contracts for nationals and foreigners alike. Of course, such courts regularly intervene in questions of global commerce, tackling disputes relating not just to commercial contracts, but also to investment protection, intellectual property protection, corporate governance, etc. In many cases they perform the required function efficiently, providing the global public good in a decentralized, state-based manner. It is therefore commonly assumed that

---

[8] North 1981, p. 24.
[9] Barkun, M. (1968). *Law without Sanctions: Order in Primitive Societies and the World Community.* New Haven, Yale University Press; North 1981; MacMillan, J. and A. Linklater, Eds. (1995). *Boundaries in Question: New Directions in International Relations.* New York, Pinter Publishers; McMillan, J. and C. Woodruff (2000). "Private Order under Dysfunctional Public Order." *Michigan Law Review* **98**(8): 2421–2458. Milgrom, P., D. North, et al. (1990). "The Role of Institutions in the Revival of Trade: the Law Merchant, Private Judges, and the Champagne Fairs." *Economics and Politics* **2**: 1–23; Greif, A. (2006). *Institutions and the Path to the Modern Economy: Lessons from Medieval Trade.* Cambridge, Cambridge University Press.

countries with strong contract enforcement institutions will be more involved in trade. Section 4 presents additional evidence that the quality of domestic judicial institutions stimulates international trade.

But national courts also face important limitations. Not all countries possess technically adept, efficient, independent judicial bodies. Explicit or indirect bias toward co-nationals cannot be ruled out, nor can corruption or political interference. And even if adjudication can be done fairly, national courts may find it difficult to enforce judgments against parties whose assets lie beyond their jurisdictions.

When domestic institutions face limitations of this kind, states often turn to a second type of institutional arrangement: intergovernmental treaties and organizations that coordinate policies across countries. States have created these types of entities to provide the "rule of law" for two important types of disputes in global commerce: state-state disputes over trade rules and investor-state disputes over expropriation of foreign capital.[10] The principal institution governing the former is the WTO's Dispute Settlement Mechanism, an international, public adjudication body that determines whether states meet their obligations to one another under international trade laws. For investment protection, in turn, commitments typically take the form of BITs or regional treaties, like the North American Free Trade Agreement, that commit states to not unfairly expropriate the investments of foreign entities. Most of these disputes are also handled by a public, intergovernmental adjudication body, the World Bank's International Centre for Settlement of Investment Disputes, although others are dealt with via private arbitration or, more rarely, domestic courts.

As noted above, the effect of these intergovernmental agreements has been a subject of significant research over the past decade. Departing from Rose's negative finding, scholars of the WTO have presented a range of estimates for that organization's effectiveness.[11] Tomz et al.[12] show how proper specification of WTO membership is important to understanding its effects, arguing that including de facto members alongside de jure members substantially increases the organization's effect upon trade.[13] Subramanian and Wei concur, but show that the benefits of the WTO have been unevenly distributed,

---

[10] Interestingly, states have not created public intergovernmental courts to resolve commercial disputes between private traders in the modern era, though historical precedents exist. See Jupille, J., W. Mattli, et al. (2013). *Institutional Choice and Global Commerce.* Cambridge, Cambridge University Press.

[11] For a useful summary and additional results, see Gil-Pareja, S., R. Llorca-Vivero, et al. (2013). "A Re-examination of the Impact of GATT/WTO on Trade." Forthcoming.

[12] Tomz, M., J. L. Goldstein, et al. (2007). "Do We Really Know that the WTO Increases Trade? Comment." *The American Economic Review* **97**(5): 2005–2018.

[13] Goldstein, J. L., D. Rivers, et al. (2007). "Institutions in International Relations: Understanding the Effects of the GATT and the WTO on World Trade." *International Organization* **61**(1): 37–67.

with industrialized countries benefiting much more than developing ones.[14] These results are largely confirmed by Gowa and Kim, who find that benefits flow chiefly to great powers and that alliances play an important mediating role.[15] Eicher and Henn, instead, find that the effect of the WTO on bilateral trade washes out once countries' trade relations with the rest of the world are properly considered (the so-called "multilateral resistance" effect; see section 3b).[16] Finally, Liu shows how an expanded set of data—which considers not just how the WTO increases trade amongst existing trading partners, but also promotes the development of new trading relationships—provides strong evidence that the WTO positively affects trade.[17]

The literature on BITs is more mixed. Several studies find that BITs increase investment, but qualifications abound. The poor quality of investment data limits what can be learned from such studies.[18]

In sum, by allowing states to commit to uphold trade rules and to safeguard investments, the WTO (and perhaps BITs) have facilitated global commerce. But scholars have paid far less attention to an arguably more fundamental rule of law function in the global economy: dispute resolution between individual traders (Reinstein 2005).[19] A deal between two companies to exchange goods or services across borders is the most basic transactional unit of the global economy, yet few studies have investigated how effective one of the chief institutions that provides this function—transnational commercial arbitration—actually is. This third type of institutional "solution" is the focus of the present study.

One key difficulty in measuring the effect of commercial arbitration on trade is that the extent of a country's participation in the practice is not possible to measure. Because commercial arbitration occurs at hundreds of private arbitral tribunals around the world, almost always in secret, we have no reliable way of estimating the number of global transactions that rely on TCA, much less the extent to which traders from a given country employ it.[20]

---

[14] Subramanian, A. and S.-W. Wei (2007). "The WTO Promotes Trade Strongly, but Unevenly." *Journal of International Economics* 72: 151–175.

[15] Gowa, J. and S. Y. Kim (2005). "The Effects of the GATT on Trade, 1950–1994." *World Politics* 57(4): 453–478; Gowa, J. (2010). "Alliances, market power, and postwar trade: explaining the GATT/WTO." *World Trade Review* 9: 487–504.

[16] Eicher, T. S. and C. Henn (2011). "In Search of WTO Trade Effects: Preferential Trade Agreements Promote Trade Strongly, but Unevenly." *Journal of International Economics* 19: 137–153.

[17] Liu, X. (2009). "GATT/WTO Promotes Trade Strongly: Sample Selection and Model Specification." *Review of International Economics* 70: 428–446.

[18] Sauvant, K. P. and L. E. Sachs (2009). *The Effect of Treaties on Foreign Direct Investment: Bilateral Investment Treaties, Double Taxation Treaties, and Investment Flows.* Oxford, Oxford University Press.

[19] Reinstein, E. (2005). "Finding a Happy Ending for Foreign Investors: The Enforcement of Arbitration Awards in the People's Republic of China." *Indiana International and Comparative Law Review* 16(1): 37–72.

[20] The existence of ad hoc arbitration, which is outside a permanent tribunal, makes the challenge even greater.

Dietz's contribution looks at the caseloads of several major arbitration providers and concludes that these are too small for the institution to play a major role in the global economy. Other evaluations have used samples of private contracts[21] or surveys of firms[22] to answer the same question. While informative, none of these approaches allows us to capture the total universe of global arbitration cases, or to draw representative samples from the even larger set of transborder contracts or firms that trade across borders. It is therefore unsurprising that they arrive at conflicting conclusions.[23]

The present analysis takes a different approach. As an approximation of the effect of TCA on trade, this study measures the effect on trade of a country's policies regarding arbitration. As Dietz (Chapter 7, this volume) argues, arbitration often relies, at least formally, on enforcement by public courts. But the extent to which countries back arbitration in this way varies. The research question to answer is therefore: what is the effect on trade when countries delegate judicial authority to private tribunals?

Note that this more restricted question likely *underestimates* the total effect of arbitration on trade, as it only measures the additional effect of public enforcement. Most (perhaps as many as 90 percent) of private arbitration awards are complied with voluntarily.[24] This high rate of compliance is likely only partially due to the "shadow" of public enforcement in courts, as market forces and reputational concerns will often promote compliance even in the absence of judicial enforceability, especially in the commodity trades or other areas of exchange in which markets are well organized and arbitration has a long history.[25] By measuring just the effect of public support for arbitration on trade, the present analysis is therefore not considering how purely private dispute settlement systems contribute to the rule of law that underpins global commerce.

---

[21] Eisenberg, T. and G. P. Miller (2007). "The Flight from Arbitration: An Empirical Study of Ex Ante Arbitration Clauses in the Contracts of Publically Held Companies." *DePaul Law Review* **56**: 335–352; Drahozal, C. R. and S. J. Ware (2010). "Why Do Businesses Use (or Not Use) Arbitration Clauses?" *Ohio State Journal on Dispute Resolution* **25**.

[22] Mistelis, L. (2004). "International Arbitration—Corporate Attitudes and Practices —12 Perceptions Tested: Myths, Data and Analysis Research Report." *The American Review of International Arbitration* 15(3–4): 525–591; Mistelis, L. and C. Baltag (2008). "Recognition and Enforcement of Arbitral Awards and Settlement in International Arbitration: Corporate Attitudes and Practices." *The American Review of International Arbitration* 19(3–4): 319–375; Mistelis, L. and P. Martin (2010). *2010 International Arbitration Survey: Choices in International Arbitration.* London, Queen Mary School of Law, School of International Arbitration.

[23] For a discussion, see Hale, T. (2012). "The Rule of Law in the Global Economy: Explaining Institutional Variation in Commercial Dispute Resolution." PhD dissertation. Department of Politics. Princeton University.

[24] Mistelis, L. and C. Baltag (2008). "Recognition and Enforcement of Arbitral Awards and Settlement in International Arbitration: Corporate Attitudes and Practices." *The American Review of International Arbitration* 19(3–4): 319–375.

[25] For an extended discussion of private enforcement, see Hale (2012).

Finally, note that even this less direct question is difficult to answer, because the degree to which national policies empower private tribunals is nuanced and complex, involving not just international treaty commitments such as ratifying the New York Convention, but also national arbitration laws, national jurisprudence, and the actual practices and behaviors of firms, lawyers, and judges. Ideally, one would like a quantitative measure to capture all of these factors in a comparable fashion across countries. In practice, the present study, like previous ones, relies on the most observable, objective, and comparable proxy of national backing for private tribunals: ratification of the NYC. The treaty commits countries to enforce foreign arbitral decisions in their own courts and largely bars countries from re-hearing or altering arbitral decisions. Today 146 countries are members (Figure 8.1). Membership in the NYC, therefore, can be considered a rough approximation of a country's involvement in the commercial arbitration regime generally.

Leeson was the first to analyze the effect of the NYC on trade, building on the research design and data that Rose employed to analyze the effect of the WTO.[26] Leeson found that ratifying the NYC increases a country's trade by 15–38 percent. Leeson characterizes this effect as "modest," given how central contract enforcement is thought to be to economic exchange, but this is a misleading interpretation. After all, countries that do not participate in the New York Convention do not render contracts unenforceable. Rather, they simply retain that function in public courts, or rely on exclusively private

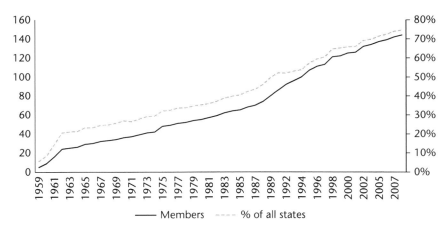

Figure 8.1. Participation in the 1958 New York Convention (source: UN Treaty Database).

[26] Leeson, P. T. (2008). "How Important is State Enforcement for Trade?" *American Law and Economics Review* 10(1): 61–89.

systems. The increase in trade that Leeson attributes to public backing for private courts is, in fact, remarkable.

Hale argues that Leeson actually underestimates the impact of TCA on trade.[27] Leeson's model, like Rose's, does not accurately measure participation in the GATT/WTO by excluding so-called "non-member participants"—de facto members—from the analysis.[28] There are also some straightforward errors in the Rose data that Tomz et al. correct. Hale's study, employing the refined model and data, found ratifying the NYC to have a larger impact upon trade. On average, two countries' bilateral trade would be 20 percent higher if one of countries joined the New York Convention, and 57 percent higher if both did. The comparable figures for the WTO from the Tomz et al. study were 28 and 61 percent, respectively, suggesting that the NYC was just as important to global trade flows at the WTO.

3 Analysis

The present study improves on previous analyses in three important ways. First, it draws on Liu[29] to employ a larger and more refined dataset that allows us to examine not just how the NYC affects existing trade flows, but how it may also lead to new trading relationships. Second, it considers the relationship between delegation to arbitration and the quality of domestic courts. Finally, it employs a recent study that analyzed the causes of NYC ratification— why countries choose to delegate judicial authority to private tribunals—to address endogeneity concerns.

3.1 *Data*

The data form a panel of country pairs by year, meaning that the unit of analysis is the dyad-year. The present study benefits from several data improvements that previous studies could not. First, I employ a larger dataset. Following Rose and Tomz et al., respectively, Leeson considers a panel that includes 150 countries and 50 years while Hale considers 177 countries and 51 years. Using data from Liu, the present study covers 210 countries and regions (note that countries have come and gone over the period of analysis) from 1958 to 2003.

Second, the Liu data also use a more accurate measure of trade than the Rose and Tomz et al. data that served as the basis of the Leeson and Hale

---

[27] Hale, T. (2012). "The Rule of Law in the Global Economy."
[28] Tomz, M., J. L. Goldstein, et al. "Do We Really Know that the WTO Increases Trade? Comment."
[29] I am grateful to Dr. Liu for sharing his data and for discussing methodological considerations.

studies. While those studies measure bilateral trade as the average of four trade flows (A's imports from B, A's exports to B, B's exports to A, B's imports from A), the present study measures only the sum of A's imports from B and B's imports from A. Because imports are thought to be measured more accurately by governments (not least because they often tax them), the present study likely captures the dependent variable more precisely. Each dyad therefore appears twice for each year, with an observation both for A's imports from B and B's imports from A (i.e., directed dyads).

Finally, as noted above, Liu's chief contribution is to eliminate an important source of selection bias from previous studies. Liu notes that the traditional log-linear gravity model used to estimate trade flows excludes observations for which no trade occurs, effectively treating them as missing data. In other words, they only measure the effect of the WTO on trade amongst countries that already trade at least a little, or what economists call the "intensive margin of trade." Liu's data, instead, allow us to measure the "extensive margin of trade" as well—that is, the new trading relationships that develop after countries join the WTO or, in our case, the NYC. To do so, Liu adds one dollar to each of the existing observations. The resulting measurement error is negligible (trade flows run to the billions of dollars), and very worthwhile considering that this small adjustment effectively doubles the number of observations that can inform the log-linear specification of the gravity model (observations increase from approximately 566k to 1.1m). This advance allows the present study to measure how the NYC may create new trade flows, in addition to measuring how it may expand existing flows.

The trade data are taken from the IMF's *Direction of Trade Statistics*, with missing values filled in with information from the World Trade Flows data and the World Export Dataset (together these latter two sources contribute less than 5 percent of the total data). GDP and population data are built from a number of sources,[30] with GDP measured by purchasing power parity and converted into constant 1995 USD. WTO and RTA membership are taken from the WTO website, and GSP participation is borrowed from Liu. The *2003 CIA Fact Book* provides data on geographic area, distance, border contiguity, language, religion, and landlocked or island status. Data on military conflicts are taken from the MID dataset, while alliance data come from the Formal Alliance data. Finally, I employ Liu's measure of remoteness, which measures how far a country is from every other country in the world, weighted by each country's GDP. For each dyad the value of the remoteness variable is simply

---

[30] PWT6.1, PWT5.6, WDI2003, *Historical Statistics*, *International Financial Statistics*, and *United Nations Statistical Yearbooks*. See Liu (2009, p. 436) for further details regarding the mis-measurement of GDP in previous studies.

Table **8.1.** Summary statistics

Variable	Obs	Mean	Std Dev	Min	Max
Both NYC	1373620	0.15	0.35	0.00	1.00
One NYC	1373620	0.36	0.48	0.00	1.00
Both GATT/WTO	1373620	0.29	0.45	0.00	1.00
One GATT/WTO	1373620	0.47	0.50	0.00	1.00
Log GDP A	1262342	9.87	2.19	0.12	16.10
Log GDP B	1264412	9.91	2.18	0.12	16.10
Log GDP/Pop A	1262128	1.31	1.07	−1.97	3.90
Log GDP/Pop B	1264127	1.31	1.07	−1.97	3.90
Log distance	1373620	8.72	0.78	4.15	9.91
Log area of A	1373620	11.54	2.71	1.95	16.92
Log area of B	1373620	11.57	2.69	1.95	16.92
Land border	1373620	0.02	0.14	0.00	1.00
Landlocked	1373620	0.28	0.49	0.00	2.00
Islands	1373620	0.45	0.60	0.00	2.00
Same language	1373620	0.12	0.32	0.00	1.00
Same religion	1373620	0.52	0.50	0.00	1.00
Hostility	1373620	0.01	0.09	0.00	3.33
Com. colony	1373620	0.16	0.37	0.00	1.00
Colony	1373620	0.01	0.08	0.00	1.00
Colonizer	1373620	0.01	0.08	0.00	1.00
Cur. colony	1373620	0.00	0.04	0.00	1.00
Cur colonizer	1373620	0.00	0.04	0.00	1.00
Remote	1373618	0.81	1.70	0.00	4.51
Alliance	1373620	0.06	0.23	0.00	1.00
Customs union	1373620	0.02	0.15	0.00	1.00
Pref. trade agreement	1373620	0.06	0.24	0.00	1.00
GSP from A to B	1373620	0.08	0.27	0.00	1.00
GSP from B to A	1373620	0.08	0.27	0.00	1.00
ICSID A	1373620	0.37	0.48	0.00	1.00
ICSID B	1373620	0.37	0.48	0.00	1.00
BITs A	934106	0.64	1.67	0.00	19.00
BITs B	937331	0.64	1.67	0.00	19.00
Judicial indep. A	963555	0.47	0.31	0.02	0.99
Judicial indep. B	967077	0.46	0.31	0.02	0.99
Same legal order A	977206	20.33991	18.85639	0	68
Same legal order B	981675	20.14296	18.80957	0	68
UNCITRAL A	1373620	0.2221204	0.4156718	0	1
UNCITRAL B	1373620	0.2242534	0.4170899	0	1

the product of the two countries' remoteness. A summary of the key variables is given in Table 8.1.

3.2 *Model*

In the present study I employ various specifications of the log-linear gravity model to determine the effect of the NYC on trade. The basic functional form is:

$$\ln T_{ijt} = \beta_0 + \beta_1 BothNYC_{ijt} + \beta_2 OneNYC_{ijt} + \beta_3 lnGDP_{it} + \beta_4 lnGDP_{jt}$$
$$+ \beta_5 \ln\left(\frac{GDP}{pop}\right)_{it} + \beta_6 \ln\left(\frac{GDP}{pop}\right)_{jt} + \beta_7 lnDist_{ij} + \beta_8 lnArea_i + \beta_9 lnArea_j$$
$$+ \beta_{10} Border_{ij} + \beta_{11} Landlock_{ij} + \beta_{12} Island_{ij} + \beta_{13} ComLang_{ij}$$
$$+ \beta_{14} ComRelig_{ij} + \beta_{15} Colony_{ij} + \beta_{16} Colonizer_{ij} + \beta_{17} ComColony_{ij}$$
$$+ \beta_{18} CurColonizer_{ijt} + \beta_{19} CurColony_{ijt} + \beta_{20} Remote_{ijt}$$
$$+ \beta_{21} Hostility_{ij} + \beta_{22} Alliance_{ijt} + \beta_{23} CU_{ijt} + \beta_{24} RTA_{ijt} + \beta_{25} GSP_{ijt}$$
$$+ \beta_{26} GSP_{jit} + \beta_{27} BothWTO_{ijt} + \beta_{28} OneWTO_{ijt} + a_t + a_{ij} + \varepsilon_{ijt}$$

The key parameters to estimate are β_1 and β_2, the effect on bilateral trade if both countries are members of the NYC and if one is, respectively. β_{27} and β_{28} instead capture the effect of the WTO on bilateral trade flows, which is both a useful control variable and a reference point for interpreting the relative importance of the NYC. Note that, following Liu, the dependent variable is actually ln $(T_{ijt} + 1)$.

In additional to the usual explanatory variables, I consider both year and dyad fixed effects, a_t and a_{ij}, respectively. Year fixed effects allow us to control for specific events in the business cycle or world politics that may affect trade idiosyncratically in any given year. Dyad fixed effects, in turn, control for any omitted variables that are inherent in the trading relationships between countries, but are not captured by the standard gravity model. Finally, the inclusion of the remoteness variable, as well as the fixed effects, controls for the so-called "multilateral resistance effect,"[31] the idea that bilateral trade depends not only on trade barriers between the members of any given dyad, but also on their trading relationships with the rest of the world.

3.3 The Conditional Effect of Arbitration: Three-Level Games

As discussed above, commercial arbitration is just one way in which firms may resolve disputes, and therefore just one of the institutional forms in which the "rule of law" can be provided for global commerce. Domestic courts, to the extent that they are fair and efficient, can also play this role, at least to some degree. Hale argues that firms arbitrage across various sites of governance—domestic, intergovernmental, and transnational—to obtain the outcomes that best suit their goals, a process he terms "three-level games." Given that no public intergovernmental bodies for commercial dispute resolution exist

---

[31] Anderson, J. E. and E. van Wincoop (2003). "Gravity with Gravitas: A Solution to the Border Puzzle." *American Economic Review* **93**: 170–192.

today, firms effectively face a choice between arbitration and litigation for contract enforcement.[32]

This idea caries an observable implication for trade flows. We should observe some degree of substitutability between public courts and delegation to private arbitration—that is, trade flows should benefit more from arbitration when public courts are weak, and less from arbitration when they are strong.

Measuring the quality of public courts across a wide range of countries and years has traditionally vexed students of political economy. While recently created datasets now collect a rich range of information about national judicial systems, they do not extend sufficiently back in time to help estimate trade flows. However, the present study is able to benefit from a recently created dataset that fixes many of these errors and provides information on judicial independence for 200 countries over 50 years.[33] Judicial independence is estimated from a number of indexes that overcome many of the missing data limitations of previous studies.

3.4 Omitted Variables and Endogeneity: What Explains NYC Ratification?

Endogeneity is a primary concern for studies that attempt to analyze the effects of international institutions.[34] Does institutional membership drive an outcome like trade? Or is causation instead reversed, with trade causing countries to be more likely to join the WTO? Strikingly, the literature on the effect of the WTO on trade has largely avoided this question.

In the context of the NYC, we may have a similar concern. Rising trade may make countries more likely to ratify the NYC for any number of reasons: the value of doing so becomes greater, policymakers have more opportunities to learn from other countries' experiences, pro-trade interest groups may be strengthened, etc. If these types of effects are significant, the error term will be correlated with our dependent variable, and the gravity model will not accurately estimate the effect of NYC membership on trade.

A related concern is the potential for omitted variables. It is often difficult to determine quantitatively if an outcome is the result of a country's membership in an institution, or of some other factor, known or unknown, that explains both institutional membership and the outcome in question. Again,

---

[32] Note that firms often rely on a third option, mediation, to resolve disputes as well. This practice is typically adopted before the more conflictive and expensive process of arbitration or litigation. The decision to either arbitrate or litigate therefore typically follows the failure of mediation efforts.

[33] Linzer, D. A. and J. K. Staton (2012). *A Measurement Model for Synthesizing Multiple Comparative Indicators: The Case of Judicial Independence.* Atlanta, Emory University.

[34] Downs, G., D. M. Rocke, et al. (1996). "Is the Good News about Compliance Good News about Cooperation?" *International Organization* 50(2): 379–406; Simmons, B. and D. Hopkins (2005). "The Constraining Power of International Treaties: Theory and Methods." *American Political Science Review* 99(4): 2005.

the existing literature looking at the role of the WTO in trade only partially addresses this concern.

In the context of the NYC, we might be concerned that ratifying the NYC is associated with, for example, a general interest amongst policymakers in liberalizing the economy or integrating with world markets. If this were true, it might then be the case that this political project is the real driver of trade, with NYC membership playing on an epiphenomenal or, at best, mediating role.

We can mitigate both endogeneity and potential omitted variables by understanding the reasons why countries ratify the NYC and controlling for them in the gravity model. A recent study strives to do just that, testing a range of both material and ideational explanations for why countries ratify the NYC.[35] Notably, a set of seemingly important material factors are *not* in fact associated with ratifying the NYC, including the amount a country trades, GDP per capita, the amount a country trades with other NYC members, and the extent to which a country competes with NYC members for the same export markets. Instead, the study finds that *legal* networks are the primary drivers of countries' decisions to ratify. Specifically, the following factors are associated with increased propensity to ratify: the independence of the judiciary, participation in technical legal organizations such as the United Nations Commission on International Trade Law (UNCITRAL), the extent to which other countries of the same legal system have ratified, and countries' participation in the investment arbitration regime (ratification of BITs and the ICSID convention), which employ the same legal "technology"—arbitration. Federal countries are also shown to be less likely to ratify.

Amongst these results, the fact that trade itself does not correlate with ratification is immensely useful to the present study, since it ameliorates the principal endogeneity concern. However, it may be the case that several of the causes of NYC ratification themselves increase trade, creating the illusion that the Convention itself is the cause. To control for this problem, I adopt an instrumental variables approach using a two-stage least-squares model. This method requires the selection of instrumental variables that drive NYC ratification, but that, by themselves, have no effect upon a country's trade. This requirement excludes several of the variables that Hale determines to be associated with NYC ratification: applying to join the WTO, participation in the trade of "reference priced" goods,[36] and judicial independence. Strong theoretical reasons exist to expect that each of these variables will be associated with trade, and so they cannot function as instruments for the effect of NYC ratification on trade.

---

[35] Hale, T. (2013). The Rule of Law in the Globl Economy: Explaining Intergovernmental Backing for Private Commercial Tribunals. *American Political Science Association Annual Meeting*. Chicago.

[36] Rauch, J. E. (1999). "Networks versus Markets in International Trade." *Journal of International Economics* **48**: 7–35.

Fortunately, many of the variables that drive NYC ratification via ideational mechanisms—transnational legal networks—are highly unlikely to act independently on trade. These include membership in UNCITRAL and the number of other countries with the same legal origin that have ratified the NYC. We can also include participation in the investment arbitration regime (i.e., ratification of BITs and ICSID). These latter variables may indeed have an effect upon trade over time. To the extent that they encourage investment (as noted previously, it is uncertain that they in fact do), they may be associated with intra-firm trade and the creation of supply chains that would be reflected in bilateral trade flows. However, because factories and other products of investment take years to begin production, we can be confident that ratification of ICSID or BITs will not drive trade in the year of ratification. These variables thus serve as useful instruments for NYC ratification.

First I estimate a structural equation via OLS that measures the correlation between the identified causes of ratification and NYC membership. This equation has the form:

$$NYC_{ijt} = \beta_1 UNCITRAL_{it} + \beta_2 UNCITRAL_{jt} + \beta_2 ICSID_{it} + \beta_4 ICSID_{jt} + \beta_5 BIT_{it} + \beta_6 BIT_{jt} + \varepsilon_{ijt}.$$

The predicted values from this model are then substituted for NYC membership in the gravity model. The resulting estimation then separates the effect of the NYC on trade from those factors that are thought to cause NYC ratification.

4 Results

The regression results are presented in Table 8.2. Substantive interpretations of the impact of NYC membership on trade are reported in Table 8.3.[37]

The baseline models appear in columns 1 and 2 of Table 8.2. As predicted, membership in the NYC has a substantial positive effect on trade. When only year fixed effects are included, dyads in which one country is a member increase their trade by 8 percent on average, while dyads in which both countries are members see their trade increase by 35 percent. When dyad fixed effects are included as well, the NYC-related benefit climbs to 30 percent for one member and 63 percent for two members. These are substantial increases, significantly higher than Leeson and slightly above Hale. However, while Hale found similar substantive effects between the WTO and the NYC, the present study finds significantly higher effects for the WTO. Using both year

---

[37] From the results, we can calculate the estimated average percentage increase in trade that results from participation in the arbitration regime via the formula $e^\beta - 1$.

Table 8.2. The effect of the NYC and the GATT/WTO on bilateral trade, 1946–2004 (***p<0.01, **p<0.05, *p<0.1. Variable not reported: common country)

Variables	(1)	(2)	(3)	(4)	(5)
	Base	Base	Low judicial indp.	Instrumental	Instrumental w/low Judicial indep.
Both NYC	0.30***	0.49***	0.94***	1.00***	1.08***
	(0.02)	(0.02)	(0.03)	(0.10)	(0.12)
One NYC	0.08***	0.26***	0.30***		
	(0.01)	(0.02)	(0.02)		
Both GATT/WTO	2.05***	1.40***	0.87***	1.79***	1.74***
	(0.02)	(0.02)	(0.03)	(0.02)	(0.03)
One GATT/WTO	0.97***	0.46***	0.34***	0.93***	0.89***
	(0.01)	(0.02)	(0.02)	(0.02)	(0.02)
Log GDP A	1.24***	1.04***	1.06***	1.30***	1.33***
	(0.00)	(0.01)	(0.01)	(0.01)	(0.01)
Log GDP B	1.73***	1.46***	1.51***	1.84***	1.90***
	(0.00)	(0.01)	(0.01)	(0.01)	(0.01)
Log GDP/Pop A	0.71***	0.67***	0.69***	0.84***	0.70***
	(0.01)	(0.01)	(0.01)	(0.01)	(0.01)
Log GDP/Pop B	0.59***	0.58***	0.56***	0.66***	0.49***
	(0.01)	(0.01)	(0.01)	(0.01)	(0.01)
Log distance	−2.07***			−2.30***	−2.34***
	(0.01)			(0.01)	(0.02)
Log area of A	−0.19***			−0.22***	−0.26***
	(0.00)			(0.00)	(0.01)
Log area of B	−0.24***			−0.23***	−0.30***
	(0.00)			(0.00)	(0.01)
Land border	1.15***			1.49***	1.88***
	(0.05)			(0.05)	(0.06)
Landlocked	−0.46***			−0.42***	−0.40***
	(0.01)			(0.01)	(0.02)
Islands	0.23***			0.30***	0.23***
	(0.01)			(0.02)	(0.02)
Same language	0.30***			0.66***	0.60***
	(0.02)			(0.03)	(0.03)
Same religion	0.45***			0.28***	0.11***
	(0.01)			(0.01)	(0.02)
Hostility	−1.46***			−1.59***	−1.73***
	(0.08)			(0.07)	(0.08)
Com. colony	1.11***			1.13***	1.26***
	(0.02)			(0.02)	(0.02)
Colony	2.84***			2.28***	2.71***
	(0.05)			(0.08)	(0.10)
Colonizer	3.44***			3.24***	3.67***
	(0.06)			(0.08)	(0.10)
Cur. colony	−1.09***	−2.04***	1.66***	−0.24	−11.51**
	(0.20)	(0.20)	(0.46)	(1.38)	(5.67)
Cur colonizer	−0.46**	−1.00***	3.15***	−3.91***	−9.46*
	(0.20)	(0.20)	(0.49)	(1.38)	(5.67)
Remote	0.00	0.70***	0.64***	−0.02***	−0.05***
	(0.00)	(0.01)	(0.01)	(0.01)	(0.01)
Alliance	1.11***	2.14***	2.37***	0.80***	1.09***
	(0.02)	(0.03)	(0.04)	(0.03)	(0.03)
Customs Union	1.55***	3.46***	2.96***	1.43***	1.36***
	(0.04)	(0.07)	(0.09)	(0.05)	(0.05)

Table 8.2. (Continued)

Variables	(1)	(2)	(3)	(4)	(5)
	Base	Base	Low judicial indp.	Instrumental	Instrumental w/low Judicial indep.
Pref. trade agreement	1.25***	0.97***	1.11***	1.02***	1.04***
	(0.02)	(0.02)	(0.03)	(0.03)	(0.03)
GSP from A to B	2.82***	1.18***	0.33***	2.74***	2.89***
	(0.02)	(0.02)	(0.03)	(0.03)	(0.03)
GSP from B to A	3.07***	1.44***	0.43***	3.07***	3.28***
	(0.02)	(0.02)	(0.03)	(0.03)	(0.03)
Constant	−3.14***	−20.01***	−20.92***	−3.34***	−2.10***
	(0.09)	(0.14)	(0.17)	(0.13)	(0.15)
Year FE	Yes	Yes	Yes	Yes	Yes
Dyad FE	No	Yes	Yes	No	No
Observations	1,184,525	1,184,525	763,494	718,909	587,548
R-squared	0.51	0.65	0.65	0.51	0.46

Table 8.3. Average increase in trade from participation in the New York Convention

	One in NYC	Both in NYC
Year FE	8%	35%
Year and dyad FE	30%	63%
Low judicial independence; year and dyad FE	35%	156%
Instrumental var. (year FE)	NA	172%
Instrumental var. for low judicial independence dyads (year FE)	NA	194%

and dyad fixed effects, we find that dyads in which one country is a member of the WTO see a 58 percent increase in trade, while having two members increases trade by 306 percent. These results are very close to those found for the WTO in Liu's study.

Column 3 of Table 8.2 looks at the effect on trade of dyads in which one or both members exhibit low scores for judicial independence (below the mean value, 0.47). As expected, the effect of NYC ratification is significantly stronger for these countries, rising to a 35 percent increase for one member and a 156 percent increase for both members. When the opposite half of the sample is considered (i.e., dyads with above average scores of judicial independence for one or both members), the effect of the NYC is diminished; one member increases trade by only 21 percent, while two members increases it by only 34 percent (results not depicted in Table 8.2). This interaction between judicial quality and NYC membership provides evidence for the partial substitutability between domestic and transnational dispute settlement mechanisms, as the "three-level games" framework expects.

Interestingly, looking only at countries with low judicial independence also significantly diminishes the effect of the WTO. This result is consistent with other studies that find that the principal beneficiaries of the GATT/WTO system were the industrialized countries, where judicial independence is, on average, higher.[38]

Columns 4 and 5 of Table 8.2 show the results of the instrumental variable regressions. Strikingly, these suggest that NYC ratification has an even stronger effect on trade, increasing bilateral imports by over 170 percent when both countries are members. For dyads in which at least one member suffers from weak judicial institutions, bilateral trade increases nearly threefold. Measured in this way, the boost to trade from NYC membership is approximately half that of the WTO.

5 Conclusion

This chapter presents robust evidence that delegating judicial authority to private arbitration—measured by ratification of the NYC—has played a substantial role in undergirding global trade in the post-war period. The study has employed a larger and more refined dataset than previous studies, and also corrected for problems of both endogeneity and potential omitted variables. While the effect of NYC ratification is found to be largely consistent with Hale's results and above Leeson's, it does not reach the scale obtained by the WTO.

The results confirm our expectation that the rule of law "matters" for global economic exchange. Moreover, they also support the idea that domestic courts and private arbitration are partially substitutable alternatives for public good provision. When public courts are strong, empowering private arbitration adds relatively little to trade. When courts are weak, policies that support arbitration boost trade significantly.

---

[38] Subramanian, A. and S.-W. Wei (2007). "The WTO Promotes Trade Strongly, but Unevenly." *Journal of International Economics* 72: 151–175.

9

The Contested Legitimacy of Investment Arbitration and the Human Rights Ordeal: The Missing Link

Horatia Muir Watt

1 Introduction

This chapter proceeds from the conviction that the language of human rights—understood here as encompassing collective social and economic needs[1]—is the most disruptive common vocabulary[2] that can be mobilized today, with normative leverage, in order to address at least some of the negative distributional consequences of the current international investment regime.[3] Among these, the most prominent is the imbalance between

---

[1] The language of human rights obviously encompasses a variety of singular versions, distinct either by reason of geographical scope (international, regional, national), degree of institutionalization (with or without specialized courts to enforce them) or "generation" (individual, social, economic, environmental or capability-building). In this context, the reference to human rights will be generic, covering a category of widely accepted fundamental values in comparative constitutional and international law. In the context of investment arbitration, collective property rights and rights to cultural heritage, the right to food and water, indigenous people's rights to self-determination, or environmental values, may all have the potential to open up an exclusively contractual, privatized regime.

[2] The author wishes to express particular thanks to Robert Wai for coining the *disruptive vocabulary* concept in reaction to a first draft of this paper. His own work on migrating human rights norms is considered below (see FN 35).

[3] The reference to the *international investment regime* is designed to cover the whole fabric of multilateral (ICSID, NAFTA) and bilateral investment treaties, with their accompanying arbitration mechanisms (see FN 6). It is true that in certain respects the various existing treaty regimes should be differentiated: for instance, because the NAFTA regime is embedded in a broader context of multilateral trade relations, arbitrators tend to be more willing to look to a wider set of concerns than, say, ICSID arbitrators in a purely bilateral context (although it is of course difficult to generalize in this field). However, this contribution is not about the comparison of various arbitral regimes or an analysis of arbitral case-law. It is about the search for the *missing link* which explains why, to date, investment arbitrators have not been under pressure to embrace human rights arguments systematically.

the advantages accruing to the investor and the lack of correlative obligations or duties on its part toward the host State, whose hands are tied contractually, moreover, on many issues of public regulation. At the same time, the conduct of corporate investors abroad, encouraged and facilitated by the same investment treaties, has not hitherto been subject to any significant degree of regulation in their "home State."[4] The general impression of impotence (or complicity) of private international mechanisms in this respect[5] has recently been reinforced by the refusal of the US Supreme Court to extend jurisdiction for human rights violations by private economic actors, extraterritorially.[6] Given this lack of home State judicial supervision of corporate conduct in the course of (industrial or extractive) activities abroad, this chapter explores the strategic potential of human rights, invoked as a defense to an investor claim (treaty or contract) before the arbitral forum.

Since to a large extent the inequalities frequently denounced within the investment regime are perpetuated through arbitration, which is designed to implement the very regime that contains them, the conundrum addressed here is how to introduce these concerns within the very forum whose design has hitherto served to exclude them.[7] Human rights, complete with a battalion of public and private international legal tools are tested here as a possible step in this direction.[8] The idea is to sound out the extent to which the available tools of the law may be used to reduce or neutralize systemic inequalities within the existing legal framework governing international investment, and, particularly, to give normative teeth to challenges directed to various forms of inequality and exclusion in the context of investment arbitration.

Collision between the two regimes—international investment and human rights—is often cited as a paradigmatic example of the negative effects of

[4] For the purposes of what follows, any reference to the "home State" of the private investor is to be understood as meaning, formally, the State signatory to a bilateral investment treaty, and, economically, the polity which derives commercial and fiscal benefits from the activities of its corporate citizens or domiciliaries abroad, in the country which hosts the investment as co-party to the bilateral investment treaty.

[5] See Horatia Muir Watt, "Private International Law Beyond the Schism," (2011) 2(3) *Transnational Legal Theory* 347–427.

[6] *Kiobel v. Royal Dutch Petroleum Co.*, 133 S.Ct. 1659 (2013).

[7] This is not to say, however, that some arbitrators, particulary in the NAFTA context, are not already sensitive to human rights concerns . In general, however, bilateral investment treaty arbitrators tend to refuse and exclude any general reference to the collective rights of the population of the host State that would be of a nature to rebalance the content of the treaty.

[8] This chapter is no more, therefore, an apology for human rights as a specifically liberal institution, any more than it is, on the other hand, an obstacle to robust critique of the political economy of international investment law and the way in which its arbitration mechanism functions to support it. As Olivier de Schutter has shown in a different context, implementation of a fundamental right to food can go a long way to questioning the political economy of the whole system in which these rights are inevitably embedded and might, if endorsed, carry far reaching redistributive consequences (Olivier De Schutter & Kaitlin Y. Cordes, *Accounting for Hunger. The Right to Food in the Era of Globalisation*, Hart, 2011, especially, O. de Schutter, *International Trade in Agriculture and the Right to Food*, 137, p. 181 *et seq.*).

fragmentation within the international legal order. Moreover, through the conjunction of its largely contractual components and its far-reaching social, economic, and ecological consequences, the international investment field is seen to illustrate the epistemological blurring which appears to be the hall-mark of global law, straddling the liberal divides between national and inter-national law, or public and private spheres. To date, the debate has focused on the real or apparent antinomies between human rights and the investment regime, and proposals for improvements have been made accordingly—either through the resources of interpretation by arbitrators, or more radically through renegotiation of the general content of BITs. This chapter pursues a different perspective. Within a context of proliferating autonomous regimes, it is an attempt to harness the internal economy of each of them in order to create productive mutual irritation between them.

More specifically, it is suggested here that the very existence of the interna-tional investment regime is the missing link which—as a matter of legal argu-ment with normative leverage—is currently needed for a State to be held responsible for the extraterritorial conduct of the private corporate investors from which it derives fiscal revenue (and to which it serves as "home" by providing a corporate charter or a domicile, and access to the benefits of the local market). In turn, and conversely, this argument may be the key by which the arbitral forum could be opened up to a productive challenge of the appli-cable investment regime, in the shadow of the "horizontal effect" of that same home State's human rights obligations. In other words, it is submitted that a private corporate actor, beneficiary of a bilateral investment treaty, which files a claim against the host State under that treaty (or under the con-tract for which it serves as an umbrella), could be held to account for human rights violations[9] before an investment arbitration tribunal without any radi-cal change in the applicable law (such as renegotiation of the investment treaty or the terms of the contract). Much energy has recently been devoted within the international community to remedying the lack of State account-ability for the conduct of its corporate investors abroad through the creation of international public soft law; furthermore, attention has focused upon the issue of enforceability of private corporate codes of conduct. However, nei-ther the use of the international investment regime as the means to discipline private economic actors, nor the path which leads from there to the invest-ment arbitration context, have hitherto been explored.

To go about this exploration, the structure of the chapter is as follows. Part 1 will set out the conundrum of the "human rights ordeal" within the

---

[9] Given that the claimant in investment arbitration is the private investor, this would mean, under a minimalist interpretation, the rejection of the claim, or the moderation of damages due to that investor under the contract or treaty. However, beyond this point, in case of a counter-claim, it is up to the arbitral tribunal to understand its powers as extending, or not, to the award of compensation or restitution as against the investor.

framework of the existing international investment regime. The question is how to bring productive contestation of structural inequalities before the very forum which currently serves to perpetuate them. In an attempt to answer this question, Part 2 will examine various contemporary analyses of the components of global disorder and the processes of transformative legal change in the global arena, which suggest that the most promising path by which to achieve a rebalancing of the investment regime without ungluing the legal and economic system necessary to ensure equitable development, is through the construction of "spaces of contestation"—or, in a different vocabulary, sites of "learning pressure"—outside the investment regime, with a potential trickle-down effect inside it. In light of this idea, Part 3 then analyzes the structural problem from which the investment regime currently suffers: the lack of external human rights justiciability for the acts of corporate investors or their home State explains that any distributional concerns voiced before the arbitrator have hitherto been deprived of any normative thrust. Part 4 suggests that the missing link may lie therefore in the horizontal effect of the human rights commitments of the home State. Such horizontal effects could be such as to induce a correlative liability on the part of the private investors, enforceable in the domestic courts of the home State, which might be opposed by the host State in the course of arbitration. Part 5 locates the final step within the international investment regime itself. In this context, the very existence of an international legal agreement facilitating foreign investment seems to warrant a correlative commitment by the home State signatory to ensure that its private corporate beneficiaries do not violate fundamental human rights at the place of investment.

2 The Conundrum and The Project: Addressing Negative Distributional Consequences of the International Investment Regime in the Contractual Forum

As witnessed by a growing body of literature,[10] the contemporary quasi-worldwide foreign direct investment regime is generating increasing unease. It is well known that this regime, which rests largely on a massive number of

[10] See, for example, a series of excellent studies approaching the intersection between the investment regime and human rights through analysis of arbitration cases: Luke Eric Peterson and Kevin R. Gray, "International Human Rights in Bilateral Investment Treaties and in Investment Treaty Arbitration," *Research paper prepared by the International Institute for Sustainable Development* (IISD) for the Swiss Department of Foreign Affairs, April 2003; Marc Jacobs, "International Investment Agreements and Human Rights," INEF Research Paper Series on Human Rights, Corporate Responsibility And Sustainable Development 03/2010; Ursula Kriebaum, "Privatizing Human Rights. The Interface between International Investment Protection and Human Rights," A. Reinisch and U. Kriebaum (eds.), *The Law of International Relations—Liber Amicorum Hanspeter Neuhold* 165–189. © 2007 Eleven International Publishing, Netherlands.

bilateral treaties (BITs),[11] was born of a widespread distrust of customary public international law, seen as providing too volatile an environment for the foreign investment required for the purposes of development. The first bilateral BIT between Germany and Pakistan was negotiated in 1959, at the very beginning of the post-colonial struggle for a new distribution in the world economy.[12] In such a context, collective social and economic rights were all but unformulated; public awareness of environmental issues very limited; claims of newly independent developing countries' States to control their natural resources as yet unarticulated; the status of indigenous peoples distinct from the sovereign State as yet equally unchartered. That BITs multiplied and prospered along identical lines even after the hotly disputed oil and gas arbitrations of the 1960s, the emerging foundations of a new economic order in the 1970s, and the demise of the Washington consensus in the 1990s, bears witness both to the extent of the influence of the World Bank's lending policy and to the pull of the downward regulatory spiral among developing States in pursuit of private foreign capital.[13] Nevertheless, today, while development economics still posits that the inflow of capital is vital to ensure the needs of populations in terms of access to essential public infrastructures and services, the distribution of rights and obligations within the treaty regime, along with the accompanying arbitration process which upholds it, is progressively stigmatized as imbalanced to the detriment of the host State, in favor of the private foreign investor. This perception may of course have much to do with switching trends in global capital flows and the new awareness of States which were formerly the home to private investors that, under the terms of the BITs, their own regulatory powers in respect of local

---

[11] There are some 2300 bilateral investment treaties (BITs), of which 1700 are in force (UNCTAD, Research Note, Recent developments in international investment agreements, August 30, 2005, UNCTAD/WEB/ITE/IIT/2005/1, at 1). Many are concluded between State parties to ICSID (International Centre for the Settlement of Investment Disputes) established under the Convention on the Settlement of Investment Disputes between States and Nationals of Other States, which now counts over one hundred and forty member States. Similar agreements between States are found in investment chapters of regional or multilateral trade agreements such as the North American Free Trade Agreement NAFTA, whose chapter 11 allows investors to bring a case against a foreign host State if alleging expropriation without compensation, or unfair or discriminatory treatment.

[12] General Assembly resolution 1803 (XVII) 1962 declares that "The right of peoples and nations to permanent sovereignty over their natural wealth and resources must be exercised in the interest of their national development and of the well-being of the people of the State concerned. . . . Violation of the rights of peoples and nations to sovereignty over their natural wealth and resources is contrary to the spirit and principles of the Charter of the United Nations and hinders the development of international cooperation and the maintenance of peace." Then, in 1966, permanent sovereignty over natural resources became a general principle of international law when it was included in common Article 1 of the Covenant on Civil and Political Rights and the Covenant on Economic, Social and Cultural Rights.

[13] See Zachary Elkins, Andrew T. Guzman, and Beth Simmons, *Competing for Capital: The Diffusion of Bilateral Investment Treaties: 1960–2000*, 2004.

consumers or environment are now seriously curtailed in favor of incoming foreign capital.[14]

Contemporary critique of the international investment regime takes several forms. The most overtly political, which has led several host countries to withdraw from the ICSID framework, focuses on the perceived structural bias of the whole regime, famously described by José Alvarez as a special interest human rights regime for investors.[15] Thus, BITs, or their accompanying contractual arrangements between host government and private investor,[16] result in a confiscation of local regulatory sovereignty, in fields as sensitive as taxation, public health, and environment; if public interest is persistently side-lined, it is no doubt because the negotiation of such treaties and the accompanying contractual regime takes place outside the public sphere.[17] Moreover, while foreign capital input is clearly a condition of access to economic growth for the most impoverished countries, the real contribution of foreign direct investment as it is currently designed is called into question, since incoming capital has no countervailing duties, and profits from delocalized production rarely flow back into the local economy. Worse, contracts for the extraction of natural resources such as oil and gas concessions may come with an infernal cycle of indebtedness that makes the host

[14] Muthucumaraswamy Sornarajah, *The International Law on Foreign Investment* (Cambridge University Press, 3rd edn, 2010), emphasizing the contemporary reversal under which Western States, previously exporters of capital and now the largest recipients of foreign investment, are becoming wary of the legal arguments and tools developed within 20th century investment law (see p. 25, citing examples of contestation, in the context of arbitration or multilateral dispute resolution, by Canada and the United States, of facets of foreign investment regimes which they had initially crafted, particularly those which hamper the regulatory power of the host State).

[15] Jose Alvarez, "Critical Theory and the North American Free Trade Agreement's Chapter Eleven" (1997) 28 *University of Miami Inter-American Law Review* 303, p. 308.

[16] BITs are international treaties which create obligations for the State parties (in fact, essentially, for the host, capital-importing, State) under international law. They are inseparable from the development of a doctrine of international State contracts or Host Government Agreements (HGAs), which are concluded directly between private investors and foreign governments. While these are "private" international contracts (domestic public law providing the conditions of State party's consent) and not international treaties, public international law may nevertheless be chosen by the parties as governing law. This blurring of categories tends to work to the advantage of the private party (see H. Muir Watt, "Private International law Beyond the Schism").

[17] This "participation deficit" critique is thus formulated by Marc Jacob (op cit, sub § 2.4.2): "(A) potential concern is the fact that, despite the ultimately far-reaching impact of major international investments (e.g., power plants, water and sewage infrastructure, landfills, mining pits etc.), the BITs providing the basic legal framework for such large-scale projects have traditionally been negotiated and concluded outside the public sphere. This acute participation deficit of concerned sectors of society and NGOs is of course not uncommon when it comes to international treaties. One curt answer to this is that the citizens' consent can be indirectly derived from their respective governments' participation in the treaty-making process. This places a potentially unwarranted degree of faith in national governments' ambitions to promote and protect human rights, which some States will unhesitatingly subordinate to economic development. Another reply furtively questions the wisdom of even having the public participate in all aspects of what is essentially a highly specialised technocratic exercise . . . (I)t is important to note that public awareness and participation, and therefore ultimately democracy and legitimacy, have traditionally been side-lined in erecting the fundamental tenets of the current investment regime."

country easy prey for vulture funds;[18] land-grabbing or various short-sighted policy choices dictated by the interests of international agro-industry may impact upon access to food. Ethical and social concerns highlight repeated abuses by foreign multinational investors, whether in the form of violence, exploitation or discrimination in respect of the local workforce. Environmentalists point in turn to the negative externalities generated locally by intensive industrial activities, in the form of pollution and other durable ecological harm, while local cultural or religious heritage may not come out unscathed.

But a specific set of complaints targets the arbitration mechanism which is consubstantial to the bilateral arrangements. Indeed, the compulsory offer of arbitration by the host State, and the correlative privilege of the private investor to trigger the arbitration process—once touted as the *nec plus ultra* of impartial international dispute resolution—is now often perceived as exemplifying a lack of mutuality, through which is then ensured the intangibility of the contractual *acquis* in favor of foreign capital. In this context, while host State consent, the cornerstone of the entire regime, purports to legitimate any perceived infringement of its sovereignty,[19] challenges to investment arbitration stigmatize a privatized regime which entrusts law-making on highly sensitive issues of public interest to expert panels devoid of any democratic legitimacy. Moreover, the contractual nature of arbitration makes it ill-equipped to consider the effects of any negative externalities generated by investment-linked activities for third parties. Indeed, treaties generally lack any specific procedure whereby communities or individuals whose interests are unaligned with those of the host State may be heard. Beyond these factors of systemic bias specific to the investment context, attention is drawn, furthermore, to the lack of transparency which characterizes the arbitration process in general.[20] Thus, recruitment is seen to depend on old-boy networks, or on a market for complicit arbitrators.

---

[18] Jonathan C. Lippert, "Vulture Funds: The Reason Why Congolese Debt May Force A Revision Of The Foreign Sovereign Immunities Act" (2008) 21 *New York International Law Review* 1.

[19] On the power of consent in this respect, see Shotara Hamamoto, *Requiem for Indirect Expropriation: On the Theoretical and Practical Uselessness of a Contested Concept*, PILAGG e-series (pilagg/blog/sciencespo), 2012. However, when consent is the result of an unequal economic system, the sovereignty of consent is a circular argument.

[20] There are various current attempts to improve the transparency of the arbitration process and enlarge its ambit so as to include the voice of third parties (see Diego P. Fernandez Arroyo, "Private Adjudication Without Precedent?" in D. Fernandez Arroyo and H. Muir Watt (eds.), *Private international Law as Global Governance*, OUP forthcoming, 2014). Case-law might then develop informally, providing better consistency and less suspicion of arbitrariness, while the interests of affected individuals or communities outside the arbitration process may be taken into account by allowing third party interventions, class actions, or amicus briefs supported by NGOs, as shown in other papers in this book (see A. Claire Cutler, A. Stone Sweet). All these paths are promising and have already been thoroughly mapped. But there may be room for other paths of change and further transformation.

Whether such concerns touch upon the substantive content of the investment treaties or the specific dispute resolution mechanism designed to enforce the commitments of the host State, they are frequently couched in human rights language. Indeed, an increasing number of claims before investment arbitrators[21] tend to show that the whole investment regime is now facing what might be termed a "human rights ordeal." This development is to some extent a paradox. At first sight at least, human rights appear to be "part of the problem"[22] of the pro-investor bias of the whole treaty regime. Indeed, while the economic justification for weighting the design of bilateral investment arrangements so as to restrict the regulatory powers of the host State was found in the desirability of fostering foreign direct investment through a stable environment, the robust protection provided to the contract and property rights of the private investor was also generally touted as contributing significantly to the rule of law in the host State. Thus, the investment regime was initially perceived to accommodate a human rights component, in that it was linked to the supposed impotence of the private investor vis-à-vis the unbridled power of the local sovereign. This is why the substantive guarantees provided for incoming capital flows in bilateral investment treaties tellingly comprise a commitment on the part of the host country both to non-discrimination and fair and equitable treatment of the investor, who thereby secures a first-mover advantage in the context of the struggle for capital in which the host is inevitably engaged.

In stark contrast to the initial quest to safeguard investor interests by means of a liberal private law framework of individual property rights, contemporary critics therefore denounce the inherent dissymmetry of such a framework and seek to open the investment regime to collective social and economic rights, variously termed "third generation" or capability-building rights—framed or not under the ambivalent heading of "development" —such as access to food or water, or the need for clean environment or inviolate habitat. A similar evolution can be observed within other specialized international regimes such as the WTO, which is also seen to be weighted against the interests of the poorest local populations and unaccountable to their hunger.[23] Such similarity may be the sign that human rights, understood as encompassing collective social and economic needs, represent the most disruptive common language available

---

[21] For an excellent overview of the cases, see Ursula Kriebaum, "Privatizing Human Rights," p. 167 *et seq.*

[22] David Kennedy, "The international human rights movement: part of the problem?" (2001) 3 *European Human Rights Law Review*, pp. 245–267.

[23] On the possible use of WTO law to provide a legal foundation for the duty of those States which are home to corporate agribusinesses to ensure the protection of access to food by the populations of the third world, see Olivier de Schutter and Kaitlin Cordes, *Accounting for Hunger* (Hart Publishing, 2011).

today, with reasonable consensus within the international community as to its normative leverage, through which to bring to light and challenge the negative distributional consequences of the current international trade and development regimes. This chapter proceeds from this conviction. It attempts to suggest ways by which the available argumentative or doctrinal resources of the law may be strategized—right now and within the existing framework for international investment—in order to reduce its self-perpetuating structural inequalities. Such a project suggests that a good place to start is within the arbitral forum itself.[24]

However modest such a project may seem as a critical undertaking, it may well be the only means, short of massive renegotiation of bilateral agreements, by which any headway is to be achieved in changing the current imbalance in the international investment regime. Moreover, it is no easy task. First, as previously emphasized, the investment arbitration process—in which it is proposed to introduce concerns of social and economic inequality through the vocabulary of human rights—is designed in such a way as to exclude consideration both of content beyond the contractually applicable law and of consequences beyond the bilateral relationship between host State and investor. Second, since beyond the protection of investor property and security, the relevant treaties are precisely devoid of any explicit reference to human rights (whatever the generation), any new challenge to the investment regime from the perspective of collective social and economic needs must inevitably reside, before the arbitrator, on external sources; and, as a matter of law, sources beyond the contractual or conventional framework are currently considered by most investment arbitrators as lying beyond the confines of their jurisdiction.[25] This explains why the human rights ordeal—the current confrontation between the international investment regime and the values embodied in collective social and economic rights—bears potentially wider theoretical implications for the structure and content of the international legal order.

---

[24] Of course, this does not prevent other types of action, such as collective renegotiation of investment treaties with enhanced mutuality of obligation as between private capital and the host State. While such renegotiation of BITs is currently on the agenda of both the US and the EU, and may possibly lead to greater balance of content, one might nevertheless suppose that an initiative by groups of host States might have more leverage.

[25] See the analysis of the cases by Ursula Kriebaum, "Privatizing Human Rights," *op cit*, p. 187. According to this account, most arbitrators state that their competence is limited to the standards provided for in the relevant investment treaty. As an extreme example, the Tribunal in *Biloune and Marine Drive Complex Ltd. v. Ghana Investments Centre and the Government of Ghana, Award on Jurisdiction and Liability,* 27 October 1989, 95 ILR 184 found that it was not even competent to decide on the alleged human rights violations inflicted upon the investor. Kriebaum concludes "A tribunal would be even less competent to decide on human rights violations of persons affected through the privatization of formerly public services who are not parties in the proceedings."

3 Regime-collision as Productive Irritation: Creating External Spaces of Contestation

Absent the reassuring vision of a hierarchical, unitary international legal order built upon customary or universally accepted foundational norms administered by a world court, many attempts have been made to understand what role law has to play and what form it takes beyond, above, or across the sovereign nation-State. The difficulty of such an exercise owes much to the emergence of multiple specialized or regional supranational law-making bodies and courts, which now govern a significant part of world trade and finance; to the economic significance of non-State profit and non-profit actors wielding informal power at a global level; and to the growth of a parallel, semi-private system of investment arbitration with no clearly defined relationship with parallel public interest regimes. While some still place faith in the unity of customary international law, project all-encompassing constitutional orders,[26] or turn to the conflict of laws for the design of a meta-signpost rule,[27] others point more realistically to the fragmentation in multiple colliding expert regimes, of which human rights on the one hand, and world trade and investment on the other, are excellent examples.[28] But, beyond new forms of pragmatism,[29] efforts to conceptualize this global disorder are few and far between.[30]

Potentially, a bilateral investment treaty may well clash violently, in terms of outcomes and values, with a competing human rights regime. One can easily imagine, for example, that in the name of the latter, an indigenous people might claim title to land which, within the framework of the former, has been conceded by the national government to a foreign investor.[31] If ever such concession were to be contested successfully before national courts of the host State, it would immediately be countered by an arbitration claim brought against that State by the private investor whose (more formal) property rights

---

[26] See the various contributions to Jeffrey Dunoff and Joel Trachtman (eds.), *Ruling the World? Constitutionalism, International law and Global Governance* (Cambridge University Press, 2009).

[27] Christian Joerges, "The Idea of a Three-Dimensional Conflicts Law as Constitutional Form" in Joerges and Petersmann (eds.), *Constitutionalism, Multilevel Trade Governance and International Economic Law* (Hart Publishing, 2011) 413.

[28] Martti Koskenniemi, *From Apology to Utopia: The Structure of International Legal Argument*, (Cambridge University Press, 2005), whose point is that fragmented specialization also means depolitization: "What we see now is an international realm where law is everywhere—the law of this or that regime—but no politics at all . . ." p. 359.

[29] Benoit Frydmann, "Approche pragmatique du droit global," in D. Fernandez Arroyo and H. Muir Watt (eds.), *Private international Law as Global Governance* (OUP forthcoming, 2014).

[30] One remarkable exception is Gunter Teubner"s system theory approach as applied to colliding regimes: see FN 44.

[31] This example is illustrated by the "Belize" case, used by Katarina Pistor in "Contesting Property Rights," and discussed below.

under the concession are adversely affected by a court ruling favorable to the native occupants. In such a case, the autonomy of the two regimes makes for a destructive collision. When the human rights regime, administered by the public court system, conflicts with investment arbitration bypassing domestic fora (with the host State trapped here between the hammer and the anvil[32]), the resulting disorder is beyond the sway of the usual tools of coordination between competing norms, such as the quest for an "overlapping consensus," or the search for the greater relevance of one or other regime. Indeed, it is not a mere conflict of laws, to be arbitrated in favor of one or the other by the competent forum. It involves a deadlock in a push for primacy as between autonomous regimes as a whole, complete with their foundational values or biases, their courts or dispute resolution processes, and their modes of enforcement or coercion.

In such cases, the last word belongs to the party with the most extra-judicial leverage. Indeed, the resulting disorder could look much like the landscape emerging in a case such as the notorious Chevron saga,[33] involving a head-on clash between autonomous systems constituted by the courts both of host and home States, and an arbitration panel under the aegis of the Permanent Court of Arbitration at the Hague.[34] Whatever the wrongs

---

[32] As shown below, any compensation for expropriation awarded to the private investor against the host government will be detrimental to the local population, since it is implies using taxes or development aid to make the payment. Indeed, it is doubtful that the terms of any such concession, obtained within a wider context of fierce competition for capital, would be sufficiently favorable to cover the (even equitable) costs.

[33] A judgment in Ecuador in favor of the claims of indigenous forest-dwellers of the Amazon against Shell for ecological damage, has led to a deadlock, involving the wielding of judicial retaliatory weapons such as global anti-suit injunctions, while international arbitrators give orders which purport to bind the Ecuadorian judiciary. The result is that Ecuador has now denounced its participation in ICSID. An arbitrator acting under the aegis of the Permanent Court of Arbitration at the Hague ordered provisional measures to prevent the enforcement of the judgment of Ecuador, the sovereign party, to the extent that its award of damages to indigenous peoples dwelling at the site of the oil and gas extraction interfered with the protection of a private property right guaranteed under the bilateral agreement. See Permanent Court of Arbitration at the Hague, Interim Award of February 9, 2011. On January 25, 2012 the same tribunal asserted its jurisdiction to decide on the company's liability under an investment treaty. Then a global anti-suit injunction was ordered in favour of Chevron, only to be lifted a year later (see District Court, Southern District of New York, Orders of February 6 and April 7, 2011; Federal Court of Appeals for the Second Circuit, Judgment of March 17, 2011). On January 26, 2012 Judge Gerard Lynch of the US Court of Appeals for the Second Circuit said that such an injunction could only be sought "defensively, in response to an attempted enforcement." In the present case, the Ecuadorean plaintiffs "made no effort to enforce their judgment in New York (nor indeed, in any other jurisdiction)." The Ecuadorian judgment was handed down by the Court of Sucumbíos, Lago Agrio, Ecuador, on February 14, 2011. The arbitration under the BIT here was a United Nations Commission on International Trade Law (UNCITRAL) arbitration.

[34] To borrow Katarina Pistor's imagery, the "glue" which held the whole system together until now has dissolved. See Katharina Pistor, "Contesting Property Rights: Towards an Integrated Theory of Institutional and System Change," (2011) *Global Jurist:* Vol. 11: Iss. 2 (Frontiers), Article 6. Available at <http://www.bepress.com/gj/vol11/iss2/art6>.

involved in either a specific case or in the structure of the whole international investment regime, this also means that unless it has leverage to renegotiate its own BITs, the recalcitrant State is cut off from external supplies of capital. Is there, then, no other answer than to accept that deadlock is inevitable in a context of plural systems, each equipped with its own values, and tools? One avenue of reflection may be found by looking at three strands of contemporary scholarship which analyze the forces which work in favor of legal change in a context of global fragmentation. Combined, they suggest that the most promising way by which to help reduce the risk of destructive stalemate while sowing transformative seeds would be—perhaps counter-intuitively—to secure sites of contestation at the interface of the two regimes.

Thus, first, Colin Scott and Robert Wai have called attention to the ways in which private law contestation before domestic courts may operate to effect a "migration" of human rights norms to new sites.[35] The starting point is the conviction that "the current transnational order involves more interaction between and among systems in different legal venues than some systems theories of global networks imagine." They then explore how "governance strategies that would promote the objectives of international human rights norms can be developed through the migration of these norms into legal interpretation and application in venues of transnational private litigation in domestic courts." In this latter context, they seek to show that "human rights law provides a vehicle for the introduction and consideration of alternative policy considerations and value-laden premises . . . that help channel and structure reasoning within law." The two significant insights of this project are, on the one hand that, when wielded in a *different* forum—here, before domestic courts—international human rights norms may help to bring out the *internal conflicts* that have been obscured within the importing— here, the domestic—system. Bringing such internal contradictions to the surface through a change of fora appears, then, to be the condition under which the inter-systemic "migration" of human rights norms takes place. Second, we are urged to consider a "rough" version of transnational law, far from the smooth picture of custom, community, and consensus which tends to characterize narratives of the emergence of the *lex mercatoria*.[36]

---

[35] Colin Scott and Robert Wai, "Regulating Corporate Conduct through the Migration of Human Rights Norms: The Potential Contribution of Transnational Private Litigation," in Colin Scott (ed.), *Torture as Tort: Comparative Perspectives on the Development of Transnational Human Rights Litigation*, (Oxford, Hart Publishing, 2001), p. 287. The following excerpts are from pp. 289ff.

[36] Robert Wai, "The Interlegality of Transnational Private Law" (2008) 71 *Law and Contemporary Problems* p. 107.

This alternative account sees the global legal order as fraught with conflict through which plural competing systems interconnect in the language of the law. They are seen to evolve through mutual interaction, operating through (often hidden) tensions within the importing system. These insights on the links between (private law) contestation and the migration of legal norms lays the groundwork for considering further the complex interdependencies between human agency, institutions, and wider social systems (which may well be wider than the nation-State), on which hinges a second account of legal change.

Second, then, in Katarina Pistor's account,[37] mutual interactions between institutions and systems are depicted through what she describes as a "weaving metaphor":[38] social systems are represented as open, institutions may have interfaces with multiple systems, and interdependencies work both ways.[39] Such interdependencies suppose, however, a common "glue," which takes the form of shared sources of legitimacy. To the extent that the institutional regimes "become exclusive legal orders for particularized interests, they may erode common sources of legitimacy on which a broader legal system rests. Such a system, however, is needed to provide a space for contesting priorities among competing regimes."[40] Applied to the investment regime, which looks much like "an exclusive legal order for particularized interests" in this description, such an analysis requires locating a space in which the regime can be contested and changed in light of human rights. Indeed, when the space opened for institutional contestation is beyond the system (if the system is the nation-State, the opened space may be transnational or supranational), such contestation will in turn impact upon it from the outside, inducing legal change within it. This analysis carries implications of particular significance for imagining the impact wrought upon institutions protected by the investment regime of contestation produced in a

---

[37] See Katharina Pistor, "Contesting Property Rights." This study departs from recent trends in literatures on institutions and institutional change by focusing on the complex *interdependencies* between systems and institutions.

[38] Pistor, p. 10: "The relation between institutional regimes and systems is therefore better captured by a weaving pattern than a pyramid."

[39] In this framework, "a system comprises multiple institutions or institutional regimes, but not necessarily in a hierarchical fashion. Instead, an institutional regime can develop outside a given system and can interface with more than one. It can have rule makers and rule takers different from other institutional regimes, and from those found in the systems they seek to affect" (p. 10). Pistor's point is that the relationship between systems and institutions may be two-way, since institutions may impact in turn upon systems, which are open (and not closed as in accounts which often take place within the nation-State). Like Scott and Wai, she also emphasizes the role of human agency within institutions, in the form of contestation.

[40] Pistor, p. 26.

space external to it.[41] However, at the same time, Pistor's analysis also points to the risk of deadlock, as evidencing the strain put upon the wider system by institutional contestation challenges the system's own legality. In such a case, the survival of the system itself is threatened, with the disappearance of the consensus on its own parameters for balancing between competing institutions.[42]

[41] A first example of contested property rights is used to show how contestation within a transnational institutional regime may endorse the legitimacy of the wider social system with which it interfaces. The example is particularly apposite for our purposes, since it concerns a situation in which there is a clear tension between human rights and the requirements of foreign investment, at least as mediated through the governmental policy of the host State. Thus, the *Belize* case documents the struggle of the Maya people to retain lands which they had occupied historically (albeit without formal title), and from which the Belize government had sought to evict them, in order to provide concessions to foreign oil and gas investors. After appealing in vain to the national authorities, they took their case to the Inter American Court of Human Rights (IACtHR), which recognized their property rights over the land under an "autonomous" definition of property (October 12, 2004, Merits Report No. 40/04, *Maya Indigenous Communities of the Toledo District Belize*). Lack of reaction by the Belize government ultimately led to their title being endorsed by the national Supreme Court, which judged the ruling of the IACtHR to be "persuasive," and integrated the outcome into its own findings on a distinct legal (constitutional) basis. Interestingly, this mode of interdependency is recognizable as an example of "relevance" in systems theory and has long been an essential tool for managing pluralism of legal orders in conflict of laws theory. For the purposes of the proposed framework for analysis of legal change, the availability of a place of contestation for the institutional regime, outside the constitutional system, led in the end to change within. The intermediation of the domestic supreme court ensured the structural change. Thus, "the establishment of dispute resolution mechanisms outside the sovereign's reach was critical—and so was the discovery of these mechanisms by international NGOs, law firms, and other norm entrepreneurs" (Katharina Pistor, "Contesting Property Rights," p. 24).

[42] Thus (p. 12): "As long as institutional regimes endorse a system's common source of legitimacy for determining their relation to other institutional regimes, even when this conflicts with their own preferences, they remain an integral part of that system. If and when this common source of legitimacy is openly challenged, the relation becomes more tenuous; and when they claim that their source of legitimacy is superior to that of legality, frictions occur that may weaken the commonality of legality as a source of legitimacy. Put differently, institutional regimes may weaken the legitimacy of existing systems not only by contesting a particular form of ordering . . ., but by offering alternative sources of legitimacy." To illustrate this point, Katharina Pistor provides a second example, taken this time from the field of NAFTA investment arbitration, which heralds significantly different outcomes from the *Belize* case. It seems to show that while a contractual forum may similarly open a space for external contestation, legal change may not necessarily ensue when there is insufficient interface, and lack of legitimacy consensus, with the wider system. Thus, in the *Metalclad* case (*Metalclad Corporation v. United Mexican States*, Case No. ARB(AF)/97/1 under the auspices of the International Centre for Settlement of Investment Disputes (Additional Facility) of August 30, 2000), a NAFTA tribunal allowed an expropriation claim against the Mexican government when, despite approval given by this government, a municipality blocked a project led by an American company and its Mexican subsidiary to build a hazardous waste landfill. Here, federal distribution of power interfered with the enforcement of the investment agreement. As Katarina Pistor points out (p. 21), "there was no involvement in this case of any domestic court in adjudicating whether the actions of the municipality did indeed amount to a violation of property rights. Since NAFTA gives investors the option to go directly to outside tribunals that have the power to grant them monetary relief against the host State, there is therefore no need to re-litigate the dispute domestically. By the same token, there are no mechanisms by which the normative conclusions of the case are transposed into national law or by which the findings of the tribunal would be contested within the domestic legal system. It is doubtful therefore whether the condemnation of the Mexican government here will actually bring about any significant amendment within the domestic system."

Thus, legal change will depend not only on the design of the contestable space, but also on the remedies available to the tribunal. The lack of structural remedies—indeed, the absence of intermediation of any domestic tribunal—means that outsourcing dispute settlement and establishing a parallel transnational property rights regime may not work to bring change in domestic regimes. More significantly still, "the major reason appears to be that they lack the legitimacy associated with the domestic legal system, which would require contestation within that system." Outsourcing of the dispute "ignores legitimate competing interests within the domestic regime and thereby delegitimizes . . . property rights regime in its member States."[43] For the contestation to sow the seeds of change, it would therefore need to find space both outside *and* within the domestic legal system. Thus the conclusion goes in a similar direction to Robert Wai's account of the way in which contestation couched in the unfamiliar terms of migrating norms serves to make visible internal tensions already present within the host system, albeit hitherto hidden beneath its surface.

Framed in still different terms, Gunther Teubner provides an analytic of "regime collisions" in the global arena which nevertheless leads to a similar conclusion.[44] Thus, clashes between autonomous specialized orders may in certain circumstances induce their own combination and an ensuing refoundation of a new regime. A remarkable example, used to illustrate the deep transformation of a contested regime through collision, is the constitutionalization of corporate codes of conduct.[45] Flagging improved corporate governance, these private codes were initially designed far more to protect their corporate promoter from liability (in an attempt, directed essentially at the green consumer market, to show best efforts in compliance in the field of human rights and environment), rather than to generate legally binding obligations which could be invoked by third parties harmed by transnational corporate activities. However, gaining gradual support from the outside, through parallel—though equally "soft"—human rights norms developed in international fora, the corporate governance mechanism appears to be evolving very gradually into a fully blown new legal order, complete with the teeth of enforceability in domestic courts. Seeking to understand how soft corporate codes brought about real change in the form of improved labor conditions, increased environmental protection, or higher human rights standards,

[43] Pistor, "Contesting Property Rights," p. 22. Here the text refers to NAFTA arbitration, but the observation is of course equally valid in the context of other investment regimes.
[44] A. Fischer-Lescano and G. Teubner, "Regime-Collisions: The Vain Search for Legal Unity in the Fragmentation of Global Law" (2004) 25 *Michigan Journal of International Law* 999.
[45] Gunther Teubner, "Self-Constitutionalizing TNCs? On the Linkage of 'Private' and 'Public' Corporate Codes of Conduct", in Gralf-Peter Calliess (ed.), "Governing Transnational Corporations—Public and Private Perspectives" (2010) *Indiana Journal of Global Legal Studies* 17.

Teubner notes that the interplay of private and public codes has led not only to a "juridification," but also of a "constitutionalization" of their content.[46] Such transformation is explained by the fact that strain put upon society and the environment by globalized markets and corporations (unhampered by regulatory initiatives by the nation-State) through "the negative effects of their own differentiation, specialization and high-performance orientation," has reached a tipping point. "It is only a question of time until the released energies trigger, apart from positive, also such negative effects that emerging social conflicts force a drastic correction."

What matters here, according to Teubner, is "learning pressures, i.e., internal changes induced by external constraints".[47] Evocative of the external and internal spaces of contestation present in Katerina Pistor's analysis, Teubner's hypothesis is that "both elements have to be present in order to enable public and private codes to act in combination: an internal change of cognitive and normative structures and external pressure directed towards it . . ."[48] The tipping point is already apparent in positions taken by domestic courts, which appear to be increasingly ready to make corporate codes containing obligations in sensitive human rights fields "backfire" and provide grounds for— and not a shield from—the liability of their maker.[49] However, clearly, such a transformation, announcing a radical reshaping of the contested regime for corporate liability for human rights violations, could only happen if the various institutional factors needed to create sufficient interface between the colliding regimes were actually present.

Drawing these three strands of scholarship together in the specific context of the international investment arbitration, it seems therefore that the next avenue must be a search for sites where the requisite processes for elaboration and reformulation, in light of human rights, may take place.[50] Once again, this may mean creating spaces for productive contestation of the investment

---

[46] The concept of "constitutionalization" requires some explanation: "Corporate codes fulfil constitutional functions in a twofold sense: They establish constitutive rules for corporate autonomy and—at present increasingly—limitative rules meant to counter their socially harmful tendencies. . . . Corporate codes need to be characterized as constitutions in their own right, if they develop features typical for a constitution—double reflexivity and binary meta-coding" (Gunter Teubner, "Self-Constitutionalizing TNCs?" p. 5).

[47] "Behind the metaphor of "voluntary codes", therefore, lies anything but voluntariness. Transnational corporations enact their codes neither on the basis of their understanding of common good requirements nor due to motives of corporate ethics. They comply only "voluntarily," when massive learning pressures on them are exerted from the outside. The learning process does not proceed within the legal system from code to code via validity transfer of rules, but on a long-winding detour through other social systems and other media of communication." (Gunter Teubner, "Self-Constitutionalizing TNCs?"p. 16.)

[48] Gunter Teubner, "Self-Constitutionalizing TNCs?" p. 14.

[49] For examples in case involving the corporate codes of Nike and Total, see Horatia Muir Watt, "Private international law beyond the Schism," p. 416.

[50] In areas of public law, the lessons drawn from the *Solange* case in terms of "overlapping consensus" are not dissimilar (see J. Cohen and C. Sabel, "Directly-Deliberative Polyarchy" (1997) 3 *European Law Journal* p. 314).

regime. The *"Belize"* case, encountered above, serves as an excellent illustration of the fact that

> the major impetus for change came from institutional regimes outside Belize, specifically from the increasing recognition of (collective) customary land use practices as enforceable property rights. By appealing to law and legality as the source of legitimacy for resolving the dispute, the plaintiffs and their representatives created an opening for the Supreme Court of Belize to follow international and foreign examples (not precedents in any formal sense) and to embrace similar legal arguments, notwithstanding political pressure to the contrary.[51]

This can be taken to mean that in order for the investment regime to integrate transformative values of mutuality of obligations and accountability—ultimately enforceable, moreover, through its own arbitration processes—we need to explore its interfaces with human rights in order to make a legal case for change. Another detour is necessary, therefore, in the quest for the link that is missing to date in international legal doctrine to make this happen. Perhaps more than a detour, however, it is a loop: it takes us back to the investment regime itself, and its significance as the hitherto exclusive legal argument needed to bring external contestation back into the arbitration arena.

4 The Structural Problem: The Lack of External Human Rights Justiciability in Respect of Lack of Supervision by the Home State over its Corporate Investors

Contestation of property rights under the investment regime in terms of third-generation human rights can potentially take place in several different contexts and fora. In some cases, the victims of human rights violations will be indigenous peoples who complain that their property, cultural, or ecological interests were sacrificed by the government to the foreign investor, to whom, for instance, land or the exploitation of natural resources, was conceded. In such a case, the collective right invoked appears to be in direct collision with the content of a contractual or treaty-conferred property right.[52] In other instances, it may be less the content of the contract than the tortious conduct of the investor which is the source of the violation. Indeed, violence, pollution, deforestation, or various other abuses are unlikely to be part of the contractual package.[53] To what extent can investment arbitration make room for these two categories of concerns?

---

[51] Katharina Pistor, *Contesting Property Rights*, p. 17.

[52] This is again well illustrated by the *Belize* case, discussed in FN 41.

[53] These are typically instances for which attempts have been made to use the resources of the Alien Tort Statute in the US. While clearly litigation on the basis of this statute allows for the migration of legal norms (as shown by Scott & Wai, *op cit*), uncertainty as to the direction of the case-law of the US Supreme Court on this point at the time of writing has led us to exclude its specific consideration here.

A tentative response to this last part of the puzzle may be, firstly, that while structural bias might appear to disqualify arbitration as a likely forum for transformative arguments, welcome incremental change may already be taking place through diverse interpretative techniques. To date, however, more radical transformation seems unlikely. Looking, therefore, for spaces of contestation outside the arbitration forum, more significant moves might be expected in regional human rights courts. However, the only one to date to have brushed directly or indirectly with the international investment regime is the Inter-American Court of Human Rights. Its impact is limited, however, because, structurally, its brushes with the investment regime have involved (at least until now) capital-importing States as defendants, and not the reverse (in other words, not home States). The crux of the difficulty, therefore, is to find a forum in which to establish the responsibility of the investor. The most plausible place to look is of course in the domestic courts of its home State. However, given the apparent demise of US jurisdiction under the Alien Tort Statute for this function, through its use of territoriality, the most promising avenue lies with the domestic courts of European home States which, invested with jurisdiction, are bound by enforceable human rights obligations.[54] It is in this context that the international investment regime may possibly serve as the (hitherto missing) link: it may serve to impose the human rights duties of those States which, as home to investors, reap the benefits of bilateral investment treaties. Thereafter, horizontal effect can ensure that such obligations trickle down to the investors themselves, thus entering the scene of investment arbitration.

What then should an arbitrator do if made aware of the violation of a human right not mentioned in the contract, and moreover not part of the sources of contractually applicable law? There are obviously several possible responses.[55] As noted previously, many arbitrators position themselves upon a purely jurisdictional terrain to decline to bring human rights issues into a strictly contractual dispute. More interestingly, others accept to engage in the weighing process that now accompanies collisions of rights in human rights *fora*, with no mandate other than the demands of equity within the applicable law. This approach includes "factoring in" human rights into the calculus of compensation due to the investor under a proportionality test.[56] Still

---

[54] Realistically, in particular, those contained in the European Convention of Human Rights (or ultimately the Charter of the European Union, if the content of the international investment regime binding the Member States as capital importers were to be brought within the ambit of European Union law).

[55] On the following points, see again the overviews of arbitral awards proposed by Ursula Kriebaum, "Privatizing Human Rights," p. 178 *et seq*; Marc Jacobs, "International Investment Agreements and Human Rights," § 2.1.

[56] As A. Stone Sweet emphasizes in his contribution to this volume, the introduction of proportionality reasoning in investment arbitration signals a turn away from the private law model of adjudication.

others use techniques of interpretation to integrate the persuasive authority of human rights case-law in the reading of concepts used by the applicable law, or in the determination of the scope and density of rights to which it might implicitly or explicitly defer.[57] References to judicial rulings and dicta are frequent when defining key categories in investment treaties. While many of these cross-references have served to cement the protection of investor property rights (through the definition of expropriation, for instance), a body of arbitral doctrine more favorable to a rebalancing of the terms of the investment relationship in favor of the host State has been growing incrementally. Thus, for example, under the doctrine of "police powers," a host State may escape any duty to compensate for economic harm that is a consequence of *bona fide* regulation designed to enhance the general welfare (in fields such as public health or safety, taxation, cultural property, and, far more controversially, environmental protection).[58]

Moreover, certain NAFTA decisions are perceived to display sensitivity to the wider context in which investment takes place, highlighting its public dimension.[59] As Katarina Pistor has pointed out, "context" here is typically a proxy for interdependencies between an institutional regime and its systemic environment.[60] It is used to allow a more holistic perspective on investment, which then appears embedded in a larger package of economic and social relations. To this extent, therefore, the multilateral investment treaty may make more room for human rights considerations than BITs. According to Mark Jacobs, its multi-faceted design might help to explain why its investment chapter, and consequently also certain NAFTA arbitrations, do not seek to push investment protection to the maximum, a tendency to which individual BITs are more prone. "Investment protection is increasingly seen not as a privilege for a special group of people but as one component of a State's foreign and economic policy network on matters such as trade, industry, the mobility of persons and capital, development, and the environment."[61] Arbitration may therefore be less of an unlikely forum for change within the investment regime than global trends in awards would tend to show. However, the whole

[57] The willingness to refer to the broader context of international legal fabric is a highly significant opening.

[58] On the unclear borderline between regulatory takings and police power, see Ursula Kriebaum, "Privatizing Human Rights," p. 178 *et seq.*

[59] Marc Jacobs, "International Investment Agreements and Human Rights," § 2.2.1 (citing *Glamis Gold, Ltd v. United States of America (Glamis)*, NAFTA Ch.11 Tribunal, Award, 8 June 2009, paras 5–8) but concluding that there remains "ample uncertainty... While the purpose of regulation is increasingly being factored into arbitral decisions, public welfare is by no means a definite trump card. States managing public affairs with human rights in mind will likely continue to find themselves at the receiving end of expropriation claims."

[60] Katharina Pistor, "Contesting Property Rights," p. 1. "The context metaphor, of course, can also be interpreted as a reference to the broader *social system,* that is, the structures that determine the *collective* reproduction of allocative and authoritative resources in a given system."

[61] Marc Jacobs, "International Investment Agreements and Human Rights," § 6.3

arbitration regime is nevertheless affected by a structural defect which requires that arbitrators decide, as purely contractual disputes, situations which clearly create negative externalities for unrepresented interests (whether local or indeed foreign, in cases of cross-border pollution, for instance). Procedurally, the difficulty is then whether to allow third party interventions or amicus briefs. While a trend seems to be appearing in favor of the former,[62] many arbitrators are nevertheless ill at ease with such interferences, which point to legitimacy conflicts within the whole system. A recent ICSID arbitration rejecting requests for amicus intervention by human rights groups and indigenous communities, in a case asserted to "raise critical questions of international human rights law, which engage both the duty of the Zimbabwean State and the responsibility of the investor company, with regard to the affected indigenous peoples" well illustrates this arbitral caution.[63] The arbitrators felt that the submissions did not address an issue which came within the scope of the dispute. Clearly, and in line with the conclusions outlined above, the impetus for greater consideration of human rights needs to come from outside the regime.

Of the various courts entrusted with human rights adjudication, the only one to date which appears to have dealt directly with the international investment regime, is the Inter-American Court of Human Rights. However, two obvious limits on the Court's action are immediately apparent. First, the judicial process is triggered by claims against the host State, not against the private investor. Moreover, second, since the jurisdiction of the Court obviously covers non-contractual claims against the host State—that is, claims based on the violation of human rights, distinct from claims for the enforcement of the investment regime as between the parties to a State contract or covered by a bilateral treaty—brought against the host State, the typical scenario is one in which *third parties* challenge the negative impact of an investment regime in respect of their own rights or interests. The problem then becomes one of the accountability of the State for the actions of the private contractor.[64] Typically, when the claim is successful, the host/defendant State is judged to have positive obligations to ensure that human rights are exercised.

While the terms of the potential conflicts thus appear to be relatively simple, the human rights claims made in such cases are nevertheless problematic for two reasons. The first is structural, and connected to the liberal Westphalian paradigm, on the basis of which both the investment regime and the

---

[62] Notably, the US Model BIT (2004) provides for a tribunal to have the authority both to accept submissions from non-disputing parties and provide documents to the wider public.

[63] See *Bernhard Von Pezold And Others (Claimants) v. Republic Of Zimbabwe (Respondent)* (ICSID Case No. Arb/10/15).

[64] For a classic instance involving abuses committed by Coca Cola's Guatemalan subsidiary, for which Guatemala was held liable by the InterAmerican Commission: see Case 4425 (*Guatemala*) June 25, 1982 (IACHR 1980–81).

regional human rights regime were designed. Both assume that the interests of affected communities are aligned to those of the State. Thus, in theory, neither type of conflict between the investment regime and the rights of affected local communities should exist. If the violation is alleged to stem from the contract, the theory goes that the interests of such communities were represented in the negotiation process by the territorial sovereign, while the benefit accruing to the State in terms of foreign investment is also their own. Similarly, if the violation is linked to abusive conduct of the investor, the State supposedly has the means to take care of its own and call the investor to account under the terms of the contract or the bilateral treaty with the investor's home State. However, the assumption of alignment of governmental interests and those of local communities is clearly overly optimistic. Indeed, cases where the defendant/host State is condemned for violation of human rights by the Inter-American Court of Human Rights (neglect of property rights, or abusive conduct insufficiently discouraged) clearly signal that the supposed alignment does not exist.

The difficulty, however, is that in such a case, the obligation to provide compensation to the private investor will come out of fiscal revenue. Once again, this makes sense when interests of the host State, party to the contractual investment arrangement, and the affected communities, coincide. When this is not so, those who bear the burden either of governmental shortsightedness in the pursuit of short-term benefits (or corruption of officials), or of the regulatory competition which makes it unavoidable to accept the investment arrangements on the investor's terms, are always the uncompetitive, immobile local workforce or inhabitants. In such a case, the host State will be torn between conflicting loyalties and obligations, of which one may be imposed by the Court and the other by arbitration. It may decide it has no choice but to pull out of one or the other. This is what happened when Ecuador walked out of ICSID in the context of the Chevron saga.[65] Why not, then, look to the investor's home State in order to ensure, at the very least, non-abusive conduct on the part of the private investor in its activities abroad? This is the point of the 2011 "Ruggie Principles," which seek to establish both public and private accountability for human rights abuses abroad. However, for the moment at least, such principles stop short of demonstrating legal teeth:

(I-A-2): States should set out clearly the expectation that all business enterprises domiciled in their territory and/or jurisdiction respect human rights throughout their operations.

---

[65] See FN 31.

Commentary: At present States are not generally required under international human rights law to regulate the extraterritorial activities of businesses domiciled in their territory and/or jurisdiction.[66]

5 The Missing Link: The Horizontal Effect of the Human Rights Commitments of the Home State in its Domestic Courts

European States, with domestic constitutional commitments to human rights as well as extensive obligations under the European Convention of Human Rights (ECHR) (and/or the European Union Charter), have so far not been called to enter the fray, as far as collisions between their human rights commitments and bilateral investment regimes are concerned. The reason for this may be twofold. First, beyond the right to private property, the first-generation individual liberal rights written up in liberal constitutions and the European Convention are less immediately likely to enter into conflict with an investment regime than later-generation rights to development, water, or food, which tend to be confined to international instruments.[67] Second, the status of many of the European States is, or has been traditionally, that of capital-exporter rather than host to foreign investment. As home countries to the private investor, they have not therefore been much concerned by investment arbitration as host States under BITs. Thus, they have not found themselves in circumstances of divided loyalty, as between the investor and the local population, typically generated by regulatory competition for capital. In other words, as yet, no "Belize" type of case has arisen in the European setting.

The asymmetry between the thrust of human rights obligations to which capital exporting and importing States are subject is clearly problematic. It adds to the already one-sided nature of foreign direct investment arrangements. While the host State may be doubly subject to arbitration and regional human rights obligations, the home State appears to be correlatively beyond the pale on both counts. In turn, this puts the private investor in a particularly comfortable position, because, benefiting from a unilateral

[66] In context, this 2nd principle reads after the following: "I. The State duty to protect human rights.—A. Foundational principles.—1. States must protect against human rights abuse *within their territory and/or jurisdiction* by third parties, including business enterprises. This requires taking appropriate steps to prevent, investigate, punish and redress such abuse through effective policies, legislation, regulations and adjudication."

[67] This hurdle may be more apparent than real, however, given the interpretative resources already used in many instances by the Court. Indeed, article 2 (right to life) might provide the legal basis for such rights. Similarly, article 8 (right to respect for private and family life) has been successfully invoked in a broad array of cases involving the environment. Moreover, the Court has developed various techniques (such as so called "pilot cases") by which it can deal with plural applications, or ensure collective effect to its rulings (for instance, on issues such as immigration or discrimination).

235

option to take the disputes to arbitration under the investment treaty, it is also free from the horizontal obligations to which a domestic court—that of its home country—would be bound to give effect under a human rights regime, specifically that of the European Convention. It may therefore be time to think again, and to reconsider the interface, or the potential for interdependency, between human rights and investment on the investor's side. This may not simplify matters, of course, since it is potentially likely to enhance the global disorder in places which now appear to be consensual, or at least uncontested for want of contestants. Nevertheless, it may also be the opportunity to consider the productive impact of contestation, in which legitimacy issues may be fought out in legal terms rather than kept below the surface.

But how, then, might an investment dispute reach a (European) domestic court, home to the corporate investor and subject to human rights obligations?[68] Conceivably, a claim might be brought by the population (as such, or by some of its members) harmed (either by expropriation or by tortious activity) in relation to the activities of a private investor in a foreign capital-importing host State bound by a bilateral investment treaty with the State of the forum. At first glance, redress—or at least, human rights jurisdiction over the claim—would appear to be the very least that should be provided in cases of abusive activity abroad by an individual or corporate citizen of the forum State. But such a claim is likely to encounter unexpected hurdles. The United States are not alone in using the territoriality principle to restrict the scope of jurisdiction and thereby shelter extraterritorial private conduct from human rights liability. Under the case-law of the European Court (which does not appear to differ from international law in general on this point), while positive obligations of the home State would certainly extend to preventing its citizens from causing harm at home, they do not appear to extend extraterritorially, so that claims arising out of tortious acts in foreign lands are not justiciable when not caused by a public official.[69]

As noted previously, the 2011 "Ruggie Principles" confirm the existence of a missing link at this point, where private conduct is concerned. The legal explanation lies in the fact that, on the one hand, State liability for acts committed abroad rests on an agency foundation; such liability is not engaged, therefore, by the conduct of private actors, the State being accountable only

---

[68] One (unlikely) case would arise in the context of a request for enforcement, before the courts of a European Contracting State, of an arbitral award obtained by a private investor against a third, host State. However, this avenue is excluded in ICSID arbitrations, at least when the enforcement State is also a party to ICSID, given the limited grounds on which recognition and enforcement can be refused (under article 52 ICSID).

[69] For an excellent overview and analysis, see Jacco Bomhoff, "The Reach of Rights: The Foreign and the Private in Conflict of Laws, State Action, and Fundamental Rights Cases with Foreign Elements" (2008) 70 *Law and Contemporary Problems* 39.

for the conduct of the public agents which represent it formally in foreign territory. On the other hand, while acts committed by private citizens may generate liability under a theory of positive obligations, these arise only on home ground—that is, within the limits of the defendant State's jurisdiction. A (perhaps not-so-curious?) vestige of territoriality therefore shelters the private actors in their activity abroad. One might say that this immunity of States for the conduct of corporations abroad is provided by the public/private divide. This factor is arguably similar to the principle of territoriality on the basis of which the United States Supreme Court decided the *Kiobel* case.[70] In both contexts, its effect is to inhibit the extraterritorial thrust of any positive obligation of the home State to ensure that its citizens or corporations respect human rights when exercising an economic activity abroad.

The essential thesis here is that the international investment regime provides the means to bridge this gap. A State which has encouraged its own citizens or corporations to take up the opportunities laid out by the bilateral investment agreement is surely accountable, in return, when their actions then lead to abuse. For instance, in a context similar to that of the *Kiobel* case, indigenous river-dwellers who show that the industrial activities of the corporate defendant have despoiled them of their environment or livelihood, might legitimately argue that the defendant's home State, which encouraged it to invest locally with a view to creating a flow of commercial or fiscal revenues, should also have provided correlative control over such activities and ensured that human rights were not violated in the process. If such positive obligation were accepted, then the obligations incumbent upon the home State could also naturally be invoked horizontally. This would mean that the national courts bound by the European Convention would be obliged in turn to give effect to such obligations, in all those relationships between claimant and investor which fell within their jurisdiction, notably by virtue of the domicile of the defendant.[71] In a European context, this could be crucial as a means to set aside the application of the law of the place of the harm to which Regulation Rome II inevitably leads.[72]

---

[70] If territoriality is now to be the guiding principle for the reach of federal legislation including the Alien Tort Statute (despite its jurisdictional nature), it can potentially inhibit corporate responsibility even before the courts of the home state.

[71] Under article 1 ECHR, Contracting States must implement human rights to the benefit of all who are within their jurisdiction. This in turn seems to mean that when a national court has jurisdiction, for a Member State of the European Union, this would refer essentially to jurisidction under Regulation *Brussels I* in civil and commercial matters.

[72] Article 4 of Regulation *Rome II* locks the victims into local law (law of the place of the harm), which may well contain less protective tort standards—indeed that may well be part of the attraction to investors—and furthermore locks the host State into the race to the bottom, by preventing it from raising those standards for fear of losing attractivity for investment. The virtues of human rights law in such a case is that it introduces external standards which are thereby beyond the control of the host State, and cannot be circumvented by relocating corporate activity. Of course, a corporation might always relocate its seat outside the reach of the human rights norms (say, outside the whole of European territory), but that is perhaps a less likely move.

6 The Final Step: The Migration of Home State Commitments to Human Rights into the Investment Regime Through Arbitration

Supposing this line of reasoning in international human rights law to be convincing, the question is now, of course, how could it impact upon the arbitration process itself? The route may appear all the more roundabout that the defendant State in the European human rights context, typically home State to the private investor, is not party to the investment arbitration; the bilateral investment treaty merely opens access to the arbitration process to its corporate investors. Moreover, the arbitrator is clearly not a human rights forum as such; fundamental rights can only be brought into the picture as a defense against a contract or treaty claim. However, while the path is admittedly somewhat sinuous, it must be remembered that the project here is to create a space of contestation outside the investment regime itself in order to induce legal change within it.[73] At this point, and in view of the steps outlined above,[74] a final move is needed to progress from the acceptance of home State human rights duties in home State or regional courts, to the endorsement of such duties by investment arbitrators.

Thus, in the context of an investment arbitration in the course of which a private investor claims to have been subjected to unfair and inequitable treatment (for instance, as in the "*Belize*" case, through a ruling in domestic courts on the primacy of customary property rights over more recent and more formal concession in favor of the investor), there is no reason why the host State, torn between its contractual (or treaty) commitments and its (constitutional) duties to local constituencies,[75] might not oppose the extraterritorial human rights obligations of the private investor (that is, the horizontal effect of the home State's positive obligations) as outlined previously. Even if the relevant bilateral treaty does not make any reference to such obligations, they are inserted (as it were) into the fabric of the applicable law

---

[73] If the move were simple, it would have been made long ago. Here again, the "Ruggie principles" show how both public and private accountability for corporate misconduct abroad are not endowed with hard legal teeth, and are therefore unlikely candidates to generate a swift change if invoked as such in the course of investment arbitration.

[74] By way of reminder of the steps outlined above: the starting point is that the home State is held by its own courts to be under a positive obligation to ensure respect by its corporate investors of human rights in the country where investment has taken place under the aegis of a bilateral treaty. Such rights would encompass the right to life and, potentially, the various guarantees which derive from it. In such a context, it might be convincingly argued that such guarantees include collective access to food and water to the integrity of the environment. Moreover, such duties of the home State have horizontal effect and may be invoked in domestic courts of that State against the private corporate investors which benefit from the bilateral treaty.

[75] Or indeed, these constituencies themselves, in the rare cases where they are allowed a voice within the arbitral process.

from the outside.[76] Arbitrators who currently assert that human rights viola-tion suffered by the population of the host State (not party to the arbitration) are not within their jurisdiction would have little choice but to reconsider this jurisdictional issue in light of the positive obligations of the home State to ensure against corporate misconduct, and the impact of the horizontal effect of such obligations on its corporations.

By virtue of this circuitous route, the mutuality of duties as between host States and private investors, which is lacking in the whole investment regime, could then be at least partially restored, and, moreover, be given teeth before the arbitrator. If BITs were not formally renegotiated so as to reduce imbal-ance or one-sidedness of treaty (or contractual) arrangements and at the very least to impose duties human rights obligations on the part of the investor, they could at least be re-read to this effect by courts outside the arbitral forum, and ultimately, through the processes of collision, contestation, and migra-tion of norms, before the latter. By opening up this external space for legal contestation, this "rougher" account[77] of global legal change—with its own obvious risks and perils[78]—might open the way to a rebalancing of the invest-ment regime. In the end, therefore, there is perhaps no need to look too far for the missing link which would enable human rights to enter the invest-ment context: it lies in the existence of the investment regime itself, which arbitrators still tend to read as excluding those very rights.

---

[76] Of course, another simpler way of saying this is that treaties are to be interpreted in the con-text of wider obligations of international law (I. Venzke and J. von Bernstorff (2012), "Ethos, Eth-ics and Morality in International Relations," in R. Wolfrum (ed.), *Max Planck Encyclopedia of Public International Law*, (Oxford, Oxford University Press)). But this argument, which is convincing *per se*, leaves open the question of the content of international law in this broader context. This is the question the suggested reasoning above tries to address.

[77] The oppositon between *rough* v. *smooth* accounts of private law is developed by Robert Wai, "The Interlegality of Transnational Private Law."

[78] There is no guarantee that contestation itself may not lead to deadlock, when, as Katharina Pistor describes it, shared sources of legitimacy are eroded. Both regional human rights Courts are encountering deep contestation of their own legitimacy. At the time of writing, the Lexisnexis International and Foreign Law Community blog (<http://www.lexisnexis.com/legalnewsroom/ international-law>, 07/26/2012 10:25:00 p.m. EST) posts: "Venezuela Abandons the Inter-American Court of Human Rights." The Court is accused of anti-governmental bias. There has been equally strong opposition in Brazil, when, in April 2011, the Court issued precautionary measures in favour of indigenous communities of the Xingu River and ordered the Brazilian government to halt the construction of the Belo Monte hydroelectric dam project.

Index

Index

Printed and bound by CPI Group (UK) Ltd, Croydon, CR0 4YY